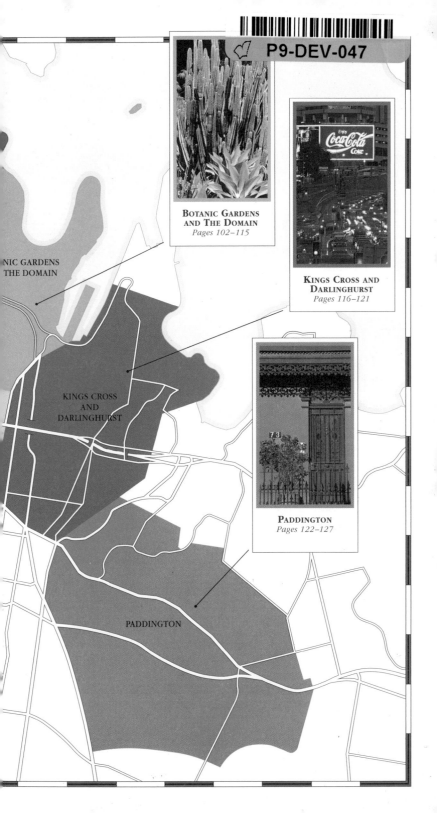

P9-DEV-047

**BOTANIC GARDENS
AND THE DOMAIN**
Pages 102–115

**KINGS CROSS AND
DARLINGHURST**
Pages 116–121

PADDINGTON
Pages 122–127

NIC GARDENS
THE DOMAIN

KINGS CROSS
AND
DARLINGHURST

PADDINGTON

SYDNEY

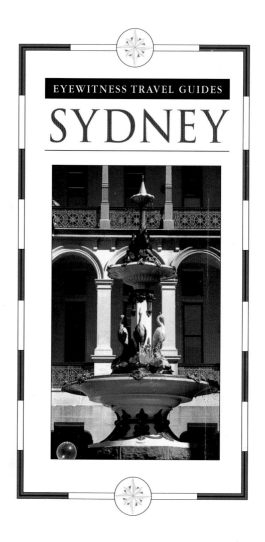

EYEWITNESS TRAVEL GUIDES

SYDNEY

Main Contributors: KEN BRASS & KIRSTY MCKENZIE

DK

LONDON, NEW YORK,
MELBOURNE, MUNICH AND DELHI
www.dk.com

Produced by The Watermark Press, Sydney, Australia
PROJECT EDITOR Siobhán O'Connor
ART EDITOR Claire Edwards
EDITORS Robert Coupe, Leith Hillard, Jane Sheard
DESIGNERS Katie Peacock, Claire Ricketts, Noel Wendtman

Dorling Kindersley Limited
SENIOR EDITOR Fay Franklin
SENIOR ART EDITOR Jane Ewart
SENIOR REVISIONS EDITOR Esther Labi

CONTRIBUTORS
Anna Bruechert, John Dengate, Carrie Hutchinson,
Graham Jahn, Kim Saville, Susan Skelly

PHOTOGRAPHERS
Max Alexander, Simon Blackall, Michael Nicholson,
Rob Reichenfeld, Alan Williams

ILLUSTRATORS
Richard Draper, Stephen Gyapay, Alex Lavroff Associates,
The Overall Picture, Robbie Polley

Reproduced by Colourscan, Singapore
Printed and bound by L. Rex Printing Company Limited, China

First American Edition, 1996
03 04 05 06 07 10 9 8 7 6 5 4 3 2 1

Published in the United States by
DK Publishing, Inc., 375 Hudson Street,
New York, New York 10014

**Reprinted with revisions 1997, 1999, 2000, 2001, 2002
(twice), 2003**

Copyright 2003 © Dorling Kindersley Limited, London
A Penguin Company

ISSN 1542-1554

ISBN 0-7894-9417-5
Floors are referred to throughout in accordance with European usage;
i.e., the "first floor" is one flight up.

**The information in this
DK Eyewitness Travel Guide is checked annually.**
Every effort has been made to ensure that this book is as up-to-
date as possible at the time of going to press. Some details,
however, such as telephone numbers, opening hours, prices,
gallery hanging arrangements and travel information, are liable to
change. The publishers cannot accept responsibility for any
consequences arising from the use of this book, nor for any
material on third party websites, and cannot guarantee that any
website address in this book will be a suitable source of travel
information. We value the views and suggestions of our readers
highly. Please write to: The Publisher, DK Eyewitness Travel
Guides, 80 Strand, London, WC2R 0RL.

A view of the Royal Botanic
Gardens and city skyline

CONTENTS

HOW TO USE THIS GUIDE 6

INTRODUCING SYDNEY

PUTTING SYDNEY ON
THE MAP 10

THE HISTORY OF
SYDNEY 16

SYDNEY AT A
GLANCE 30

SYDNEY THROUGH
THE YEAR 48

SPORTING SYDNEY 52

Tamarama beach and surf club

BEYOND SYDNEY

EXPLORING BEYOND SYDNEY *152*

PITTWATER AND KU-RING-GAI CHASE *154*

HAWKESBURY TOUR *156*

HUNTER VALLEY *158*

BLUE MOUNTAINS *160*

SOUTHERN HIGHLANDS TOUR *162*

RESTAURANTS, CAFÉS AND PUBS *178*

Kangaroo loin fillet served on a bed of wilted greens

SHOPS AND MARKETS *198*

ENTERTAINMENT IN SYDNEY *208*

SURVIVAL GUIDE

PRACTICAL INFORMATION *218*

TRAVEL INFORMATION *228*

SYDNEY STREET FINDER *238*

GENERAL INDEX *250*

ACKNOWLEDGMENTS *263*

TRANSPORT MAP
Inside back cover

THE CITY SHORELINE *56*

SYDNEY AREA BY AREA

THE ROCKS AND CIRCULAR QUAY *62*

CITY CENTRE *78*

DARLING HARBOUR *90*

BOTANIC GARDENS AND THE DOMAIN *102*

KINGS CROSS AND DARLINGHURST *116*

PADDINGTON *122*

Façade of Sydney Town Hall

ROYAL NATIONAL PARK *164*

TRAVELLERS' NEEDS

WHERE TO STAY *168*

Stained-glass window, Queen Victoria Building

FURTHER AFIELD *128*

FOUR GUIDED WALKS *140*

Sydney Opera House

HOW TO USE THIS GUIDE

Strolling at the Royal Easter Show

THIS GUIDE helps you to get the most from your visit to Sydney. It provides both expert recommendations and detailed practical information. *Introducing Sydney* locates the city geographically, sets modern Sydney in its historical and cultural context and describes events through the entire year. *Sydney at a Glance* is an overview of the city's main attractions, including a feature on the city shoreline and Sydney's best beaches. *Sydney Area* *by Area* is the main sightseeing section, covering all the sights, with photographs, maps and drawings. *Further Afield* looks at sights just outside the city centre while *Beyond Sydney* explores other places close to Sydney. Carefully researched tips on hotels, restaurants, pubs and entertainment venues are found in *Travellers' Needs*. The *Survival Guide* contains useful practical advice on everything from the Australian telephone system to public transport.

FINDING YOUR WAY AROUND THE SIGHTSEEING SECTION

The centre of Sydney has been divided into six sightseeing areas. Each area has its own chapter and is colour-coded for easy reference. Every chapter opens with a list of the sights described. All sights are numbered and plotted on an *Area Map*. Detailed information for each sight is presented in numerical order, making it easy to locate within the chapter.

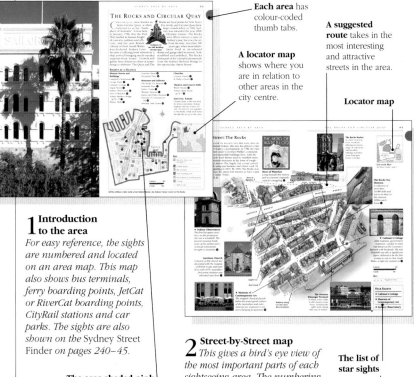

Each area has colour-coded thumb tabs.

A suggested route takes in the most interesting and attractive streets in the area.

A locator map shows where you are in relation to other areas in the city centre.

Locator map

1 Introduction to the area
For easy reference, the sights are numbered and located on an area map. This map also shows bus terminals, ferry boarding points, JetCat or RiverCat boarding points, CityRail stations and car parks. The sights are also shown on the Sydney Street Finder *on pages 240–45.*

The area shaded pink is shown in greater detail on the Street-by-Street map on the following pages.

2 Street-by-Street map
This gives a bird's eye view of the most important parts of each sightseeing area. The numbering of the sights ties in with the area map and the fuller descriptions on the pages that follow.

The list of star sights recommends the places that no visitor should miss.

SYDNEY AREA MAP

THE COLOURED areas shown on this map (see pp14–15) are the six main sightseeing areas – each covered by a full chapter in *Sydney Area by Area* (pp60–149). The six areas are highlighted on other maps throughout the book. In *Sydney at a Glance* (pp30–47), for example, they help locate the top sights, including art galleries and museums and parks and reserves. They are also used to show some of the top restaurants, cafés and pubs (pp184–5) and shopping areas (pp200–201).

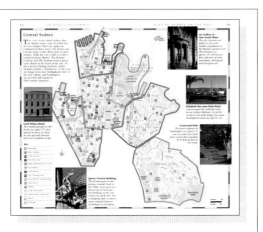

Façades of important buildings are often shown to help you recognize them quickly.

Practical information lists all the information you need to visit every sight, including a map reference to the *Street Finder* (pp240–45).

Numbers refer to each sight's position on the area map and its place in the chapter.

The visitors' checklist provides all the practical information needed to plan your visit.

3 Detailed information on each sight
All the important sights in Sydney are described individually. They are listed in order, following the numbering on the area map. Addresses and practical information are provided. The key to the symbols used in the information block is on the back flap.

Stars indicate the features no visitor should miss.

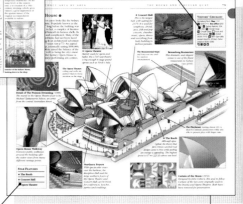

4 Sydney's top sights
Museums and galleries have colour-coded floorplans to help you locate the most interesting exhibits; historic buildings are dissected to reveal their interiors.

INTRODUCING
SYDNEY

PUTTING SYDNEY ON THE MAP 10-15
THE HISTORY OF SYDNEY 16-29
SYDNEY AT A GLANCE 30-47
SYDNEY THROUGH THE YEAR 48-51
SPORTING SYDNEY 52-55
THE CITY SHORELINE 56-59

Putting Sydney on the Map

Sᴛ ɪᴛᴜᴀᴛᴇᴅ ᴏɴ ᴀᴜsᴛʀᴀʟɪᴀ's eastern coastline within the state of New South Wales, Sydney spreads with the rare luxury of space – 3,700 sq km (1,430 sq miles) in all – around what is often described as one of the finest harbours in the world. Greater Sydney is home to over 4 million people and, while it is not the nation's capital, it is Australia's oldest and largest city, as well as its media and financial centre. Sydney is also the main gateway to Australia and it enjoys good air, road and rail links to other major centres.

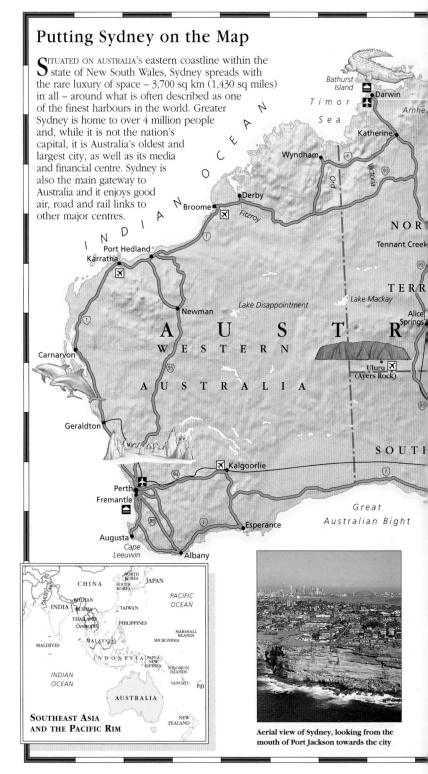

Bathurst
Island
Darwin

Timor
Sea

Arnhe

Katherine

Wyndham

Ord

Victoria

80

Derby

Broome

Fitzroy

NOR

Tennant Creek

Port Hedland

Karratha

95

TERR

Lake Disappointment

Lake Mackay

Newman

Alice
Springs

A U S

T R

W E S T E R N

Carnarvon

95

A U S T R A L I A

Uluru
(Ayers Rock)

Geraldton

95

S O U T H

Kalgoorlie

94

Perth
Fremantle

Great
Australian Bight

95

Augusta
Cape
Leeuwin

Esperance

Albany

CHINA

NORTH
KOREA   JAPAN
SOUTH
KOREA

PACIFIC
OCEAN

BHUTAN
INDIA   BURMA   TAIWAN
THAILAND
CAMBODIA   PHILIPPINES

MALDIVES   MARSHALL
ISLANDS
MALAYSIA   MICRONESIA

INDONESIA   PAPUA
NEW
GUINEA   SOLOMON
ISLANDS

INDIAN
OCEAN   VANUATU   FIJI

AUSTRALIA

**Sᴏᴜᴛʜᴇᴀsᴛ Asɪᴀ
ᴀɴᴅ ᴛʜᴇ Pᴀᴄɪꜰɪᴄ Rɪᴍ**

NEW
ZEALAND

**Aerial view of Sydney, looking from the
mouth of Port Jackson towards the city**

Arafura Sea

Torres *Strait*

Cape York

GREATER SYDNEY AND ENVIRONS

Richmond Windsor

Gulf
Groote *of*
Eylandt *Carpentaria*

Mornington
Island

Penrith Blacktown

Hornsby

Mona
Vale

Western Mwy

See next page

Cooktown

Liverpool

Sydney
Airport

Cairns Camden

Sutherland

Pacific Ocean

Campbelltown

ERN

Townsville

Great Barrier Reef

Flinders

Mount Isa

Mackay

P

ORY

QUEENSLAND

Longreach

Rockhampton

A

ALIA

Blackall

*Fraser
Island*

C

Diamantina

Charleville

I

Lake
Eyre

Toowoomba

Brisbane
Coolangatta

F

Coober
Pedy

AUSTRALIA

Moree

Lake Torrens

Bourke

Coffs Harbour

I

Lake
Gairdner

Darling

NEW

eduna

SOUTH

C

Whyalla

Broken Hill

WALES

Dubbo
Maitland

Newcastle

O

Port
Lincoln

Murray

Mildura

SYDNEY

Adelaide

Wollongong

E

Kangaroo
Island

Wagga Wagga

CANBERRA
AUSTRALIAN
CAPITAL
TERRITORY

A

VICTORIA

N

Melbourne

Geelong

King
Island

Bass Strait

Flinders
Island

Tasman Sea

Launceston

TASMANIA

Hobart

0 kilometres 500

0 miles 250

KEY

☐ Greater Sydney

✈ International airport

✕ Domestic airport

⚓ Passenger ship terminal

━ Freeway or motorway

━ Highway

━ Railway

━ State boundary

Central Sydney and Suburbs

S YDNEY HAS GRADUALLY expanded to fill both sides of the harbour. Parramatta to the west was once a separate settlement, but is now very much a part of the city. To the east are the beaches and seaside suburbs that have come to typify Sydney living. The area as a whole is served by CityRail lines and roads.

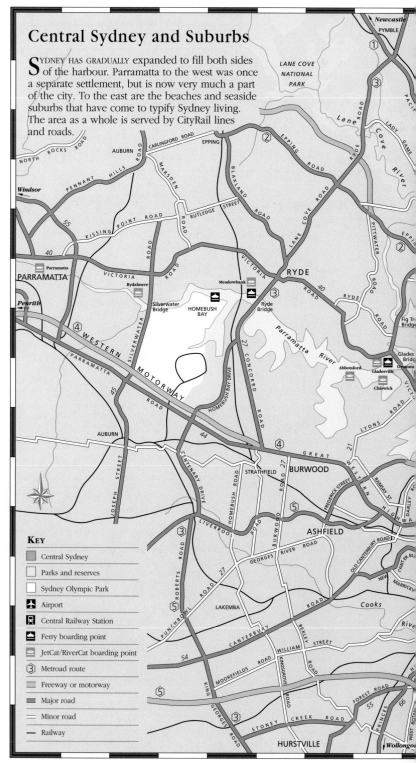

KEY

Central Sydney

Parks and reserves

Sydney Olympic Park

Airport

Central Railway Station

Ferry boarding point

JetCat/RiverCat boarding point

③ Metroad route

Freeway or motorway

Major road

Minor road

Railway

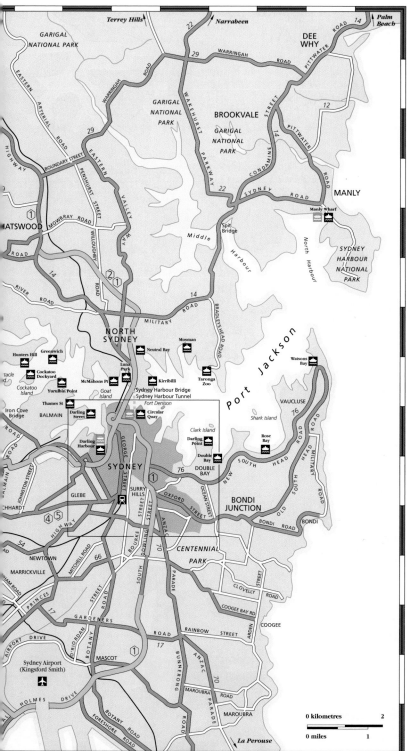

GARIGAL
NATIONAL PARK

Terrey Hills

Narrabeen

22

DEE WHY

WARRINGAH   ROAD

29

GARIGAL
NATIONAL
PARK

BROOKVALE

GARIGAL
NATIONAL
PARK

Palm
Beach

14

ROAD

PITTWATER

12

WAKEHURST PARKWAY

29

BOUNDARY STREET

EASTERN ARTERIAL ROAD

HIGHWAY

WARRINGAH ROAD

EASTERN VALLEY WAY

PENSHURST STREET

WILLOUGHBY ROAD

MOWBRAY ROAD

22

ATSWOOD

14

RIVER ROAD

②①

MILITARY

ROAD

14

SYDNEY   ROAD

CONDAMINE STREET

PITTWATER ROAD

14

MANLY

Spit
Bridge

Middle   Harbour

North Harbour

Manly Wharf

SYDNEY
HARBOUR
NATIONAL
PARK

NORTH
SYDNEY

BRADLEYS HEAD ROAD

Hunters Hill   Greenwich

Cockatoo
Dockyard

tacle

Cockatoo
Island

Yurulbin Point

McMahons Pt

Neutral Bay

Mosman

Luna
Park

Kirribilli

Taronga
Zoo

Port   Jackson

Watsons
Bay

VAUCLUSE

76

Goat
Island

Sydney Harbour Bridge
Sydney Harbour Tunnel

Fort Denison

Iron Cove
Bridge

Thames St

Darling
Street

BALMAIN

Darling
Harbour

Circular
Quay

Clark Island

Shark Island

Darling
Point

Rose
Bay

OLD   SOUTH   HEAD   ROAD

MILITARY ROAD

SYDNEY

①

76

Double
Bay

DOUBLE
BAY

NEW   SOUTH   HEAD   ROAD

BALMAIN

JOHNSTON STREET

GLEBE

GEORGE   STREET

SURRY
HILLS

④⑤

HCHHARDT

HIGHWAY

54

NEWTOWN

MARRICKVILLE

MITCHELL ROAD

66

OXFORD   STREET

BOURKE   STREET

DOWLING   STREET

ANZAC   STREET

BONDI
JUNCTION

BONDI   ROAD

BONDI

OCEAN STREET

CENTENNIAL
PARK

Clovelly

CLOVELLY   ROAD

STREET

PRINCES

17

GARDENERS   ROAD

SOUTH   STREET

DORAN   ROAD

70

COOGEE BAY RD

RAINBOW   STREET

ARDEN   STREET

COOGEE

HAM ROAD

BOTANY   ROAD

17

ANZAC   PARADE

BUNNERONG   ROAD

Sydney Airport
(Kingsford Smith)

MASCOT

①

AIRPORT DRIVE

HOLMES   DRIVE

BOTANY ROAD

FORESHORE   ROAD

MAROUBRA   ROAD

70

MAROUBRA

La Perouse

0 kilometres   2

0 miles   1

Central Sydney

THIS GUIDE DIVIDES inner Sydney into six distinct areas, each of which has its own chapter. Most city sights are contained in these areas. The Rocks and Circular Quay is the oldest part of inner Sydney, while the City Centre is today's central business district. The Botanic Gardens and The Domain form a green oasis almost in the heart of the city. To the west lies Darling Harbour, which includes Sydney's Chinatown. To the east are Kings Cross and Darlinghurst, hub of the café culture, and Paddington, an area that still retains its 19th-century character.

Lord Nelson Hotel
This traditional pub in The Rocks (see pp62–77) first opened its doors in 1834. Its own specially brewed beers are available on tap.

KEY

▨	Major sight
▨	Other building
🚆	CityRail station
Ⓡ	Monorail station
Ⓛ	Sydney Light Rail (S.R.L.) station
▥	Bus terminus
🚌	Coach station
⛴	Ferry boarding point
⛴	JetCat/RiverCat boarding point
🚓	Police station
Ⓟ	Parking
ℹ	Tourist information
✚	Hospital with casualty unit
✝	Church
✡	Synagogue

Queen Victoria Building
This Romanesque former produce market, built in the 1890s, forms part of a fine group of Victorian-era buildings in the City Centre (see pp78–89). Now a shopping mall, it retains many original features, including its roof statues.

Art Gallery of New South Wales
The city's premier art gallery is set in the middle of parkland in the Botanic Gardens and The Domain (see pp102–15). *It houses a fine collection of early Australian, Aboriginal and European art.*

Fort Denison

BOTANIC
GARDENS AND
THE DOMAIN

Farm
Cove

ROYAL
BOTANIC
GARDENS

Art Gallery of
New South
Wales

Elizabeth Bay near Potts Point
A picturesque bay with fine views across Sydney Harbour, it is at the northern end of the Kings Cross and Darlinghurst area (see pp116–21).

Centennial Park
This green expanse in Paddington (see pp122–7) *was once part of a sand dune system that extended from Botany Bay in the south.*

KINGS CROSS
AND
DARLINGHURST

PADDINGTON

MOORE
PARK

Kippax
Lake

SYDNEY
FOOTBALL
STADIUM

SYDNEY
CRICKET
GROUND

ROYAL AGRICULTURAL
SOCIETY SHOWGROUND
(MAIN ARENA)

CENTENNIAL
PARK

0 metres	250
0 yards	250

THE HISTORY OF SYDNEY

Sydney's coat of arms, Sydney Town Hall

THE FIRST inhabitants of Australia were the Aboriginal peoples. Their history began in a time called the Dreaming when the Ancestor Spirits emerged from the earth and gave form to the landscape. Anthropologists believe the Aboriginal peoples arrived from Asia more than 50,000 years ago. Clans lived in the area now known as Sydney, until the Europeans caused violent disruption to this world.

In 1768, Captain James Cook began a search for the fabled "great south land". Travelling in the wake of other European explorers, he was the first to set foot on the east coast of the land the Dutch had named New Holland, and claimed it for King and country. He landed at Botany Bay in 1770, naming the coast New South Wales.

At the suggestion of Sir Joseph Banks, Cook's botanist on the *Endeavour*, a penal colony was established here to relieve Britain's overflowing prisons. The First Fleet of 11 ships reached Botany Bay in 1788, commanded by Captain Arthur Phillip. He felt the land there was swampy and the bay windswept. Just to the north, however, he found "one of the finest harbours in the world," naming it Sydney Cove, after the Home Department's Secretary of State. Here, 1,485 convicts, guards, officers, officials, wives and children landed. This marked the beginning of the rapid devastation of the Aboriginal peoples, as they fell to introduced diseases and battled an undeclared war against the settlers. It is only in recent years that they have been granted full citizenship rights, and their traditions accorded respect.

In stark contrast, the city of Sydney flourished, with the construction of impressive public buildings befitting an emerging maritime power. In 1901, amid a burgeoning nationalism, the federation drew the country's six colonies together and New South Wales became a state of Australia.

In its two centuries of European settlement, Sydney has experienced alternating periods of growth and decline. It has weathered the effects of gold rush and trade booms, depressions and world wars, to establish a distinctive city marked by a vibrant eclecticism. The underlying British culture, married with Aboriginal influences and successive waves of Asian and European migration, has produced today's modern cosmopolitan city.

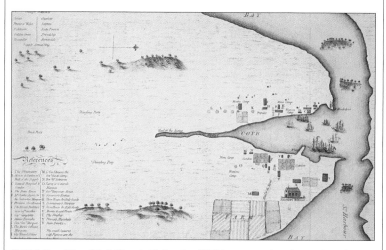

Sketch & Description of the Settlement at Sydney Cove (1788) by transported convict Francis Fowkes

◁ *Desmond, a New South Wales Chief* (about 1825) by Augustus Earle

Sydney's Original Inhabitants

ANTHROPOLOGISTS BELIEVE that Aboriginal peoples reached Sydney Harbour at least 50,000 years ago. One of the clans of coastal Sydney was the Eora. Their campsites were usually close to the shore, particularly in the summer when fish were plentiful. Plant and animal foods supplemented their seafood diet. Artistic expression was a way of life, with their shields decorated with ochre, designs carved on their implements, and their bodies adorned with scars, animal teeth and feathers. Sacred and social ceremonies are still vital today. Oral traditions recount stories of the Dreaming (*see p17*) and describe the Eora's strong attachment to the land.

Hafted stone axe

Aborigines Fishing (*1819*)
Sixty-seven Eora canoes were counted in the harbour on a single day. Spears were used as tools and weapons.

Berowra Waters

This Berowra Waters carving is hard to interpret; experts believe that it may represent a koala.

The name Parramatta means place where eels lie down or sleep, or the head of the river.

Glenbrook Crossing
The Red Hand Caves near Glenbrook in the lower Blue Mountains contain stencils where ochre was blown over outstretched hands.

Glenbrook

Glenbrook Caves ochre hand stencils

Parramatta •

Cabramatta •

Cabramatta means land where the *cobra* grub is found.

Red Ochre and Shell Paint Holder
Ochre was a commonly used material in rock painting. Finely ground, then mixed with water and a binding agent, it would be applied by brush or hand.

ABORIGINAL ROCK ART

There are approximately 5,500 known rock art sites in the Sydney basin alone. Early colonists such as Watkin Tench said that paintings and engravings were on every kind of surface. The history of colonization was also recorded in rock engravings, with depictions of the arrival of ships and fighting.

TIMELINE

43,000–38,000BC Tools found in a gravel pit beside Nepean River are among the oldest firmly dated signs of human occupation in Australia

Diprotodon

20,000 Humans lived in the Blue Mountains despite extreme conditions. Remains found of the largest mammal, *Diprotodon*, date back to this period

11,000 Burial site excavated in Victoria of more than 40 individuals of this period

50,000 BC

20,000 BC

28,000 Funerary rites at Lake Mungo, NSW. Complete skeleton has been found of man buried at this time

23,000 One of the world's earliest known cremations carried out in Western NSW

18,000 People now inhabit the entire continent, from the deserts to the mountains

13,000 Final stages of Ice Age, with small glaciers in the Snowy Mountains

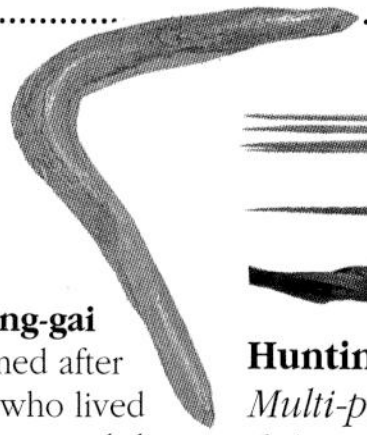

Ku-ring-gai
is named after
clans who lived
in this coastal dis-
trict. It is rich in
rock engravings.

Hunting and Fishing Implements
*Multi-pronged Eora spears were used for
fishing, while canoes were shaped from a
single piece of bark. Boomerangs are still
used today for hunting and music making.*

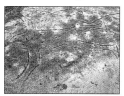

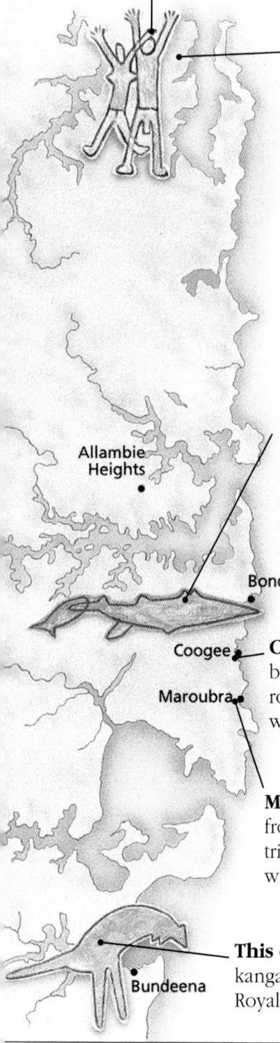

Fish Carving at West Head
*This area in Ku-ring-gai Chase
has 51 figures and is acknowledged as one of the richest sites
in the greater Sydney region.*

**Allambie
Heights**

Bondi is from
boondi, the
sound of water
crashing. This
carving is of a
shark and fish.

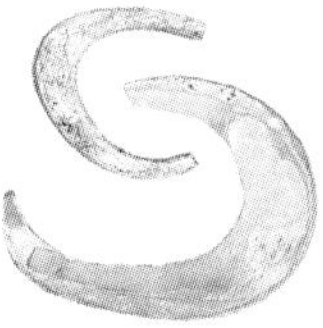

Bondi

Shell Fish-Hooks
*Introduced from the
Torres Strait, these
hooks were ground-
down mollusc shells.*

Coogee — **Coogee** means
bad smell of
rotten seaweed
Maroubra washed ashore.

Maroubra comes either
from the *merooberah*
tribe, or means place
where shells are found.

This carving of a leaping
kangaroo is found in the
Royal National Park.

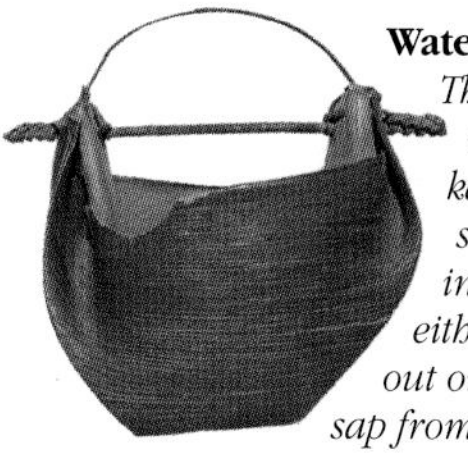

Bundeena

Water Carrier
*These bags were
usually made of
kangaroo skin. The
skin was removed
in one piece and
either turned inside
out or tanned with the
sap from a gum tree.*

8,000 BC The
oldest returning
boomerangs are
in use in South
Australia

5,000 BC Dingo
reaches Australia,
thought to have
been brought by
seafarers

Captain James Cook

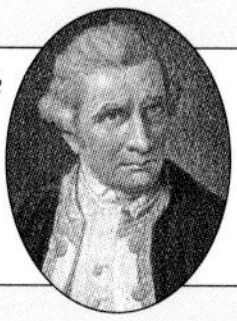

AD 1606 Dutch ship, *Duyfken*, records first
European sighting of the continent. Lands on
the eastern coast of Gulf of Carpentaria

10,000 BC	AD 1

10,000–8,500 BC
Tasmania is separated
from mainland
Australia by rising seas

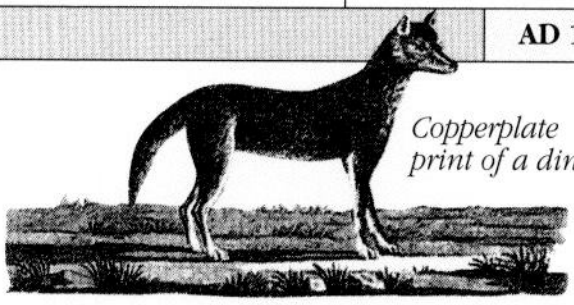

*Copperplate
print of a dingo*

AD 1700 Macassans search
for trepang or sea slugs off
Australia's north coast

AD 1770 James Cook
lands at Botany Bay

The Early Colony

Hat made from cabbage palm

THE COLONY'S BEGINNINGS were rugged and hungry, imbued with a spirit that would give Sydney its unique character. Convicts were put to work establishing roads and constructing buildings out of mud, reeds, unseasoned wood and mortar made from a crushed shell mixture. From these simple beginnings, a town grew. Officers of the New South Wales Corps became farmers, encouraged to work their land alongside convict labour. Because the soldiers paid for work and goods in rum, they soon became known as the Rum Corps, in 1808 overthrowing Governor Bligh (of *Bounty* fame) when he threatened their privileges. By the early 1800s farms were producing crops, with supplies arriving more regularly – as were convicts and settlers with more appropriate skills and trades.

GROWTH OF THE CITY

☐ *Today*   ▨ *1810*

Boat building at the Government dockyard

Pitts Row

First Fleet Ship (*c.1787*)
This painting by Francis Holman shows three angles of the Borrowdale, *one of the fleet's three commercial storeships.*

Government House

Scrimshaw
Engraving bone or shell was a skilful way to pass time during long months spent at sea.

A VIEW OF SYDNEY COVE

This idyllic image, drawn by Edward Dayes and engraved by F Jukes in 1804, shows the Aboriginal peoples living peacefully within the infant colony alongside the flourishing maritime and agricultural industries. In fact, they had been entirely ostracized from the life and prosperity of the town by this time.

TIMELINE

1787 The First Fleet leaves Portsmouth, bound for Botany Bay

1788 First white child born in the colony – and the first man hanged

Barrington, the convict and thespian star of The Revenge

1796 *The Revenge* opens Sydney's first, but short-lived, playhouse, simply named The Theatre

1785   **1790**   **1795**

Bennelong pictured in European finery

1789 The Aboriginal Bennelong is held captive and ordered to act as an intermediary between the whites and blacks

1790 First detachment of the New South Wales Corps arrives in the colony. Fears of starvation are lessened with the arrival of the supply ship *Lady Juliana*

1793 Arrival of the first free settlers

1797 Merino sheep arrive from Cape of Good Hope

The Arrest of Bligh
This shameful, and invented, scene shows the hated Governor William Bligh, in full regalia, hiding under a servant's bed to avoid arrest by the NSW Rum Corps in 1808.

WHERE TO SEE EARLY COLONIAL SYDNEY

The Rocks was the hub of early Sydney. Wharves, warehouses, hotels, rough houses and even rougher characters gave it its colour. Dramatic cuts were made in the rocky point to provide building materials and filling for the construction of Circular Quay, and allow for streets. The houses are gone, except for Cadman's Cottage *(see p68)*, but the irregular, labyrinthine lanes are still rich in the flavour of convict history.

The buildings may look impressive, but most were poorly built with inferior materials.

Male and female convicts housed separately

Waratah *(1803)*
John Lewin, naturalist and engraver, drew delicate and faithful representations of the local flora and fauna.

Barracks housing NSW Rum Corps

Elizabeth Farm *(pp138–9) at Parramatta is the oldest surviving building in Australia. It was built by convicts using lime mortar from the penal colony of Norfolk Island.*

Kangaroo *(1813)*
Naturalists were amazed at Sydney's vast array of strange plant and animal species. The first pictures sent back to England caused a sensation.

Experiment Farm Cottage *an early dwelling (see p139), displays marked convict-made bricks. Masons also marked each brick, as they were paid according to the number laid.*

1799 Explorers Bass and Flinders complete their circumnavigation of Van Diemen's Land (now Tasmania), before returning to Port Jackson

1803 The first issue of the weekly *Sydney Gazette*, Australia's first newspaper, is published

1808 Rum Rebellion brings social upheaval. Estimated population of New South Wales stands at 9,100

1800

1805

1810

1801 Ticket-of-leave system introduced, enabling the convicts to work for wages and to choose their own master

1804 Irish convict uprising at Castle Hill

1802 Aboriginal leader Pemulwy is shot and killed following the killing of four white men by Aboriginal men

Love token

1810 New convict arrivals craft such items as love tokens

The Georgian Era

Merino sheep for export wool

SYDNEY'S EARLY DECADES were times of turbulence and growth. Lachlan Macquarie, governor from 1810 to 1821, was one of the most significant figures. He took over a town-cum-jail and left behind a fully fledged city with a sense of civic pride. Noted for his sympathetic attitude to convicts and freed women and men, he commissioned many fine buildings, including work by convict Francis Greenway (*see p114*). When Macquarie left in 1822, Sydney boasted main roads, regular streets and an organized police system. By the 1830s, trade had expanded and labour and land were plentiful. In 1840, transportation of convicts was abolished. A decade of lively debate followed: on immigration, religion and education.

GROWTH OF THE CITY

☐ *Today*   ▨ *1825*

The domed saloon
is elliptical, and has a cantilevered staircase.

Bedroom

The breakfast room was used for informal dining.

View from the Summit
Blaxland, Lawson and Wentworth were the first Europeans to cross the Blue Mountains in 1813. Augustus Earle's painting shows convicts working on a road into this fertile area.

The Macquaries
Governor Macquarie and his wife Elizabeth arrived in the city with a brief to "improve the morals of the Colonists".

The kitchen was originally in a separate block to avoid the danger of fire.

ELIZABETH BAY HOUSE

This extravagant Regency villa was built from 1835–9 for Colonial Secretary Alexander Macleay (*see p120*). After only six years' occupancy, lavish building and household expenses forced him into bankruptcy.

TIMELINE

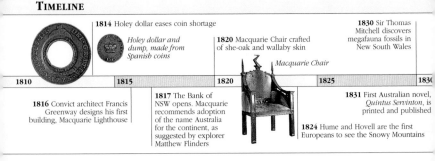

1814 Holey dollar eases coin shortage

Holey dollar and dump, made from Spanish coins

1820 Macquarie Chair crafted of she-oak and wallaby skin

Macquarie Chair

1830 Sir Thomas Mitchell discovers megafauna fossils in New South Wales

| 1810 | 1815 | 1820 | 1825 | 1830 |

1816 Convict architect Francis Greenway designs his first building, Macquarie Lighthouse

1817 The Bank of NSW opens. Macquarie recommends adoption of the name Australia for the continent, as suggested by explorer Matthew Flinders

1824 Hume and Hovell are the first Europeans to see the Snowy Mountains

1831 First Australian novel, *Quintus Servinton*, is printed and published

Lyrebird *(1813)*
As the colony continued to expand, more exotic birds and animals were found. The male of this species has an impressive tail that spreads into the shape of a lyre.

Servants' quarters

Aboriginal Explorer
Bungaree took part in the first circumnavigation of the continent, sailing with Matthew Flinders.

Drawing room

The Classical design was to be complemented by a colonnade, but money ran out.

The dining room was furnished in a florid style out of keeping with the Neo-Classical architecture.

High Fashion, 1838
Stylish ladies would promenade through Hyde Park (see pp86–7) in the very latest London fashions, now available from the recently opened David Jones department store.

WHERE TO SEE GEORGIAN SYDNEY

Governor Macquarie designated the street now bearing his name *(see pp112–15)* as the ceremonial centre of the city. It has an elegant collection of buildings: the Hyde Park Barracks, St James' Church, the Sydney Mint, Parliament House and Sydney Hospital. Other fine examples are the Victoria Barracks *(p127)*, Vaucluse House *(p136)* and Macquarie Lighthouse *(p137)*.

***Old Government House**, the oldest surviving public building in Australia (see p139), was erected in 1799. Additions ordered by Governor Macquarie were completed in 1816.*

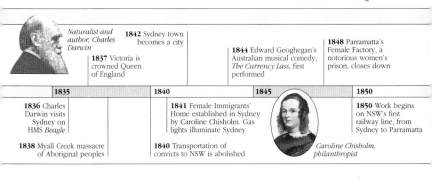

Naturalist and author, Charles Darwin

1842 Sydney town becomes a city

1837 Victoria is crowned Queen of England

1844 Edward Geoghegan's Australian musical comedy, *The Currency Lass*, first performed

1848 Parramatta's Female Factory, a notorious women's prison, closes down

1835	1840	1845	1850

1836 Charles Darwin visits Sydney on HMS *Beagle*

1841 Female Immigrants' Home established in Sydney by Caroline Chisholm. Gas lights illuminate Sydney

1850 Work begins on NSW's first railway line, from Sydney to Parramatta

1838 Myall Creek massacre of Aboriginal peoples

1840 Transportation of convicts to NSW is abolished

Caroline Chisholm, philanthropist

Victorian Sydney

Gold rush memorabilia

I N THE 1850s, gold was discovered in New South Wales and Sydney came alive with gold seekers, big spenders and a new wave of settlers. It was the start of a peaceful period of solid growth. Education became compulsory, an art gallery was opened and the Australian Academy of Arts held its first exhibition. The city skyline became more complex, with spires and "tall" buildings. Terrace houses proliferated. Victorian decorum and social behaviour borrowed from the mother country flourished, with much social visiting and sporting enthusiasm. It was an age of pleasure gardens and regattas, but also a time of unruliness and political agitation. In the 1890s, as the country moved towards Federation, fervent nationalism and an Australian identity began to take shape.

GROWTH OF THE CITY

☐ *Today*　　■ *1881*

The structure was built of hollow pine.

The dome was 30 m (98 ft) in diameter.

Mrs Macquaries Chair *(1855)*
This prime harbour viewing spot (see p106), with the seat carved from rock for the governor's wife, was "the daily resort of all the fashionable people in Sydney".

Boer War
The 1st Australian Horse division was praised for its bushcraft, horsemanship and accurate shooting.

THE GARDEN PALACE
Built in the Botanic Gardens especially for the occasion, in 1879–80, the Garden Palace hosted the first international exhibition held in the southern hemisphere. Twenty nations took part. Sadly, the building and most of its contents were destroyed by fire in 1882.

TIMELINE

1851 The discovery of gold near Bathurst, west of the Blue Mountains, sparks a gold rush

Henry Parkes

1868 The Duke of Edinburgh visits and survives an assassination attempt. The Prince Alfred Hospital is later named in his honour

1872 Henry Parkes elected NSW Premier

1850　　1860　　1870

1867 Henry Lawson born

1857 *Dunbar* wrecked at The Gap with the loss of 121 lives and only one survivor

Henry Lawson, notable poet and author of short stories

1869 Trend in the colony towards the segregation of Aboriginal peoples on reserves and settlements

1870 The last British troops withdraw from the colony

The Waverly
This clipper brig, with its extra sails and tall masts, enabled the fast transport of wool exports and fortune seekers hastening to newly discovered colonial gold fields.

WHERE TO SEE VICTORIAN SYDNEY

Sydney's buildings reflect the spirit of the age. The Queen Victoria Building *(see p82)*, Sydney Town Hall *(p87)* and Martin Place *(p84)* mark grand civic spaces. In stark contrast, the Argyle Terraces and Susannah Place *(p67)* in The Rocks give some idea of the cramped living conditions endured by the working class.

The "Strasburg" Clock
In 1887, Sydney clockmaker Richard Smith began work on this astronomical model now in the Powerhouse Museum (see pp100–101).

St Mary's Cathedral (see p86), built in Gothic Revival style, is thought to be the largest Christian church in the former "Empire", outside Britain.

Some of the exhibits held in the Powerhouse Museum *(see pp100–101)* were rescued from this burning building.

The exhibition attracted over one million people.

Arthur Streeton
In 1891, Streeton and Tom Roberts, both Australian Impressionist painters, set up an artists' camp overlooking Sydney Harbour in Mosman.

Victorian terrace houses, decorated with iron lace, began to fill the streets of Paddington (see pp122–7) and Glebe (p131) from the 1870s onwards.

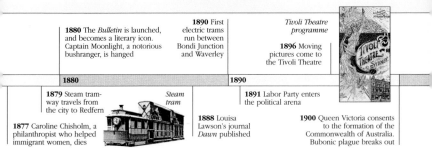

1880 The *Bulletin* is launched, and becomes a literary icon. Captain Moonlight, a notorious bushranger, is hanged

1890 First electric trams run between Bondi Junction and Waverley

Tivoli Theatre programme

1896 Moving pictures come to the Tivoli Theatre

1880

1890

1879 Steam tram-way travels from the city to Redfern

Steam tram

1891 Labor Party enters the political arena

1877 Caroline Chisholm, a philanthropist who helped immigrant women, dies

1888 Louisa Lawson's journal *Dawn* published

1900 Queen Victoria consents to the formation of the Commonwealth of Australia. Bubonic plague breaks out

Sydney Between the Wars

Vegemite spread created in 1923

FEDERATION TOOK PLACE on 1 January 1901 and New South Wales became a state of the Australian nation. In Sydney, new wharves were built, roads widened and slums cleared. The 1920s were colourful and optimistic in "the city of pleasure". The skyline bristled with cranes as modern structures replaced their ornate predecessors. The country was hit hard by the Great Depression in 1931, but economic salvation came in the form of rising wool prices and growth in manufacturing. The opening of the Sydney Harbour Bridge in 1932 was a consolidation of all the changes brought by Federation and urbanization.

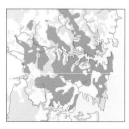

GROWTH OF THE CITY

☐ *Today* ☐ 1945

The poster depicts the youthful vigour of the nation.

Home in the Suburbs
The Federation bungalow became a unique architectural style (see p39). Verandas, gables and chimneys featured amid much red brick.

Surf lifesaver

Bronzed Lifesavers
No surf beach was complete without these icons, forever looking to sea.

"Making Do"
This chair, made in 1910, used packing case timber, cotton reels, fencing wire and the mouldings of picture frames.

SYDNEY CELEBR

MARCH 19ᵗʰ 1932

SYDNEY HARBOUR BRIDGE
After nine years of construction, the largest crowd ever seen in Sydney greeted the bridge's opening. Considered a wonder of engineering at the time, it linked the harbour's north and south shores.

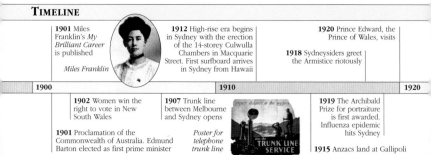

TIMELINE

1901 Miles Franklin's *My Brilliant Career* is published

Miles Franklin

1912 High-rise era begins in Sydney with the erection of the 14-storey Culwulla Chambers in Macquarie Street. First surfboard arrives in Sydney from Hawaii

1920 Prince Edward, the Prince of Wales, visits

1918 Sydneysiders greet the Armistice riotously

1900   1910   1920

1902 Women win the right to vote in New South Wales

1901 Proclamation of the Commonwealth of Australia. Edmund Barton elected as first prime minister

1907 Trunk line between Melbourne and Sydney opens

Poster for telephone trunk line

TRUNK LINE SERVICE

1919 The Archibald Prize for portraiture is first awarded. Influenza epidemic hits Sydney

1915 Anzacs land at Gallipoli

Luna Park

This harbourside amusement park opened in 1935 (see p132). A maniacally grinning face loomed at the entrance way. Millions of Australians recall the terrifying thrill of running the gauntlet through the gaping mouth as children.

One million people crossed the bridge on its opening day.

Donald Bradman
The 1932 English team used "dirty" tactics to outsmart this brilliant cricketer, almost causing a diplomatic rift with Great Britain.

Australian Women's Weekly
This magazine, first published in 1933, becomes a family institution full of homespun wisdom, recipes, stories and handy hints.

WHERE TO SEE EARLY 20TH-CENTURY SYDNEY

The years after Federation yielded stylish and sensible buildings like Central Railway Station, the Commonwealth Bank in Martin Place *(see pp38–9)* and the State Library of New South Wales. The suburbs of Haberfield and Strathfield best exemplify the Federation style of gentrified residential housing.

The Anzac Memorial (1934) is in Hyde Park (see pp86–7). The Art Deco memorial, with its reflecting pool, commemorates all Australians killed in wars.

The wireless became almost a fixture in sitting rooms in the 1930s. This 1935 AWA Radiolette is held at the Powerhouse Museum (see pp100–101).

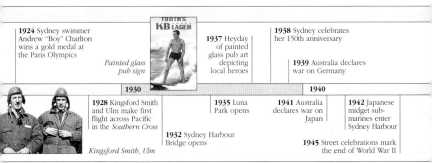

1924 Sydney swimmer Andrew "Boy" Charlton wins a gold medal at the Paris Olympics

Painted glass pub sign

1937 Heyday of painted glass pub art depicting local heroes

1938 Sydney celebrates her 150th anniversary

1939 Australia declares war on Germany

1930

1940

1928 Kingsford Smith and Ulm make first flight across Pacific in the *Southern Cross*

1932 Sydney Harbour Bridge opens

Kingsford Smith, Ulm

1935 Luna Park opens

1941 Australia declares war on Japan

1942 Japanese midget submarines enter Sydney Harbour

1945 Street celebrations mark the end of World War II

Postwar Sydney

1950s Holden sedan

THE POSTWAR baby boom was accompanied by mass immigration and the suburban sprawl. The hippie movement gave youth an extrovert voice that imbued the 1960s with an air of flamboyance. Australian involvement in the Vietnam War led to political unrest in the early 1970s, relieved for one seminal moment by the 1973 opening of the Sydney Opera House *(see pp74–7)*. In the 1980s, vast sums were spent on skyscrapers and glossy redevelopments like Darling Harbour, and on bicentennial celebrations. The city's potential was recognized in 1993 with the announcement that Sydney would host the year 2000 Olympics.

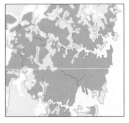

GROWTH OF THE CITY

☐ *Today*   ▨ *1966*

Drag queens pose in their Hollywood-style sequined finery or lampoon public figures of the day.

Sydney to Hobart Yacht Race
Australia's most prestigious and treacherous yacht race runs over 1,167 km (725 miles). Each Boxing Day since 1945, spectators have watched yachts jostle at the starting line.

Elaborate floats and costumes can take a year to make, with prizes given to the best.

Bicentenary
The re-enactment of the First Fleet's journey ended in Sydney Harbour on Australia Day, 1988. A chaotic flotilla greeted the "tall ships".

GAY AND LESBIAN MARDI GRAS

What began as a protest march involving 1,000 people in 1978 is now a multi-million dollar boost for Australian tourism. While the parade lasts for one rude and riotous night only *(see p49)*, the surrounding international festival offers a month of art, sporting and community events.

TIMELINE

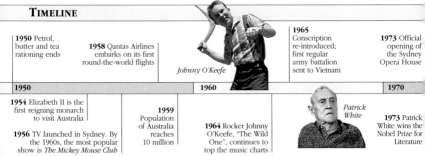

1950 Petrol, butter and tea rationing ends

1958 Qantas Airlines embarks on its first round-the-world flights

Johnny O'Keefe

1965 Conscription re-introduced; first regular army battalion sent to Vietnam

1973 Official opening of the Sydney Opera House

1950	1960	1970

1954 Elizabeth II is the first reigning monarch to visit Australia

1956 TV launched in Sydney. By the 1960s, the most popular show is *The Mickey Mouse Club*

1959 Population of Australia reaches 10 million

1964 Rocker Johnny O'Keefe, "The Wild One", continues to top the music charts

Patrick White

1973 Patrick White wins the Nobel Prize for Literature

Green Bans
In the 1970s, the militant building union placed work bans on developments in the inner city considered destructive to the environment or cultural heritage.

The parade of ornate floats and showy dance troupes stretches for over 2 km (1¼ miles).

MR ETERNITY
Arthur Stace (1885–1967), a reformed alcoholic, was inspired by an evangelist who said that he wanted to "shout eternity through the streets of Sydney". "I felt a powerful call from the Lord to write 'Eternity'." At least 50 times a day, for over 30 years, he chalked this word in perfect copperplate on the footpaths and walls of the city. A plaque in Sydney Square pays tribute to Mr Eternity's endeavours.

Arthur Stace and "Eternity", 1963

Dame Mary Gilmore
This 1957 portrait is by William Dobell, one of the most influential postwar artists. He won the coveted Archibald Prize three times.

Floats are marshalled in Elizabeth Street, before travelling along Oxford and Flinders Streets.

Oz Magazine, 1963–73
This satirical magazine, which had a major international influence, was the mouthpiece of an irreverent generation. It was declared obscene in 1964.

Aboriginal Land Rights
In 1975, the first handover of land was made to Vincent Lingiari, representative of the Gurindji people, by Prime Minister Gough Whitlam.

1977 Kerry Packer launches World Series Cricket

1978 Sydney artist Brett Whiteley wins Archibald Prize, Wynne Prize and Sulman Prize for three different works of art

Façade detail of the Brett Whiteley Studio (see p130)

2000 Sydney plays host to the first Olympic Games of the new millennium

1980

1990

1976 Nude sunbathing allowed on two Sydney beaches

1979 Sydney's Eastern Suburbs Railway opens

1988 Monorail begins operation

1989 Earthquake strikes Newcastle causing extensive damage

1992 Sydney Harbour Tunnel opens

1990 Population of Australia reaches 17 million

SYDNEY AT A GLANCE

THERE ARE MORE THAN 100 places of interest described in the *Area by Area* section of this book. A broad range of sights is covered: from the colonial simplicity of Hyde Park Barracks *(see p114)* to the ornate Victorian terraces of Paddington; from the tranquillity of Centennial Park *(see p127)* to the bustle of the cafés and shops of Oxford Street. To help you make the most of your stay, the following 16 pages are a time-saving guide to the best Sydney has to offer. Museums and galleries, architecture and parks and reserves all have sections of their own. There is also a guide to the diverse cultures that have helped to shape the city into what it is today. Below is a selection of attractions that no visitor should miss.

SYDNEY'S TOP TEN ATTRACTIONS

Sydney Opera House
See pp74–7

The Rocks
See pp62–77

Art Gallery of New South Wales
See pp108–11

Royal Botanic Gardens
See pp104–5

AMP Tower
See p83

Oxford Street and Paddington
See pp116–27

Darling Harbour and Chinatown
See pp90–101

Taronga Zoo
See pp134–5

Harbour ferries
See pp234–5

Sydney's beaches
See pp54–5

◁ **Sydney Harbour Bridge, opened in 1932** *(see pp70–71)*

Sydney's Best: Museums and Galleries

SYDNEY IS WELL ENDOWED with museums and galleries, and, following the current appreciation of social history, much emphasis is placed on the lifestyles of past and present Sydneysiders. Small museums are also a feature of the Sydney scene, with a number of historic houses recalling the colonial days. These are covered in greater depth on pages 34–5. Most of the major collections are housed in architecturally significant buildings – the

Bima figure, Powerhouse Museum

Classical façade of the Art Gallery of NSW makes it a city landmark, while the MCA or Museum of Contemporary Art has given new life to a 1950s Art Deco-style building at Circular Quay.

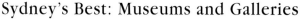

Museum of Sydney
The Edge of the Trees is an interactive installation by the entrance.

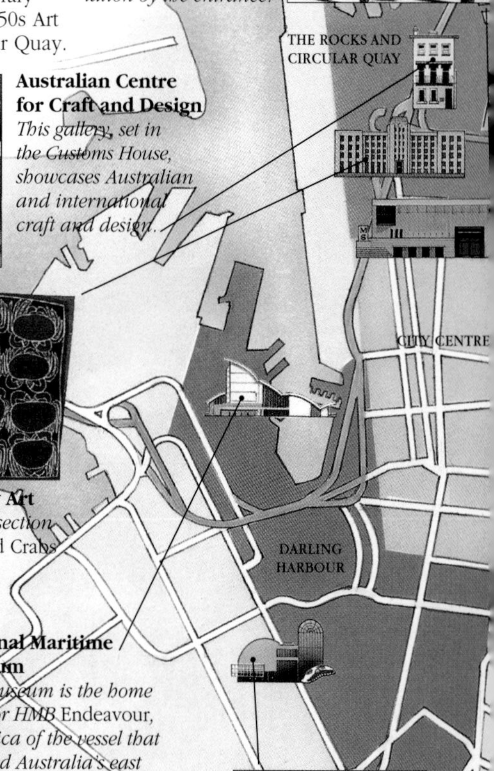

THE ROCKS AND
CIRCULAR QUAY

Australian Centre for Craft and Design
This gallery, set in the Customs House, showcases Australian and international craft and design.

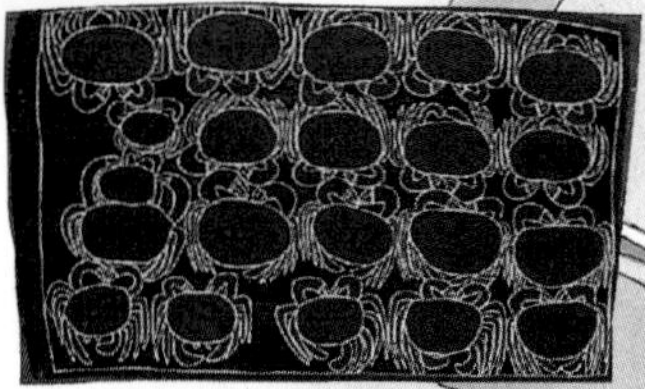

CITY CENTRE

Museum of Contemporary Art
The excellent Aboriginal art section at this museum includes Mud Crabs *by Tony Dhanyula Nyoka.*

DARLING HARBOUR

National Maritime Museum
The museum is the home port for HMB Endeavour, *a replica of the vessel that charted Australia's east coast in 1770, with Captain Cook in command.*

Powerhouse Museum
This museum, set in a former power station, uses both traditional and interactive displays to explore Australian innovations in science and technology.

0 metres   500

0 yards   500

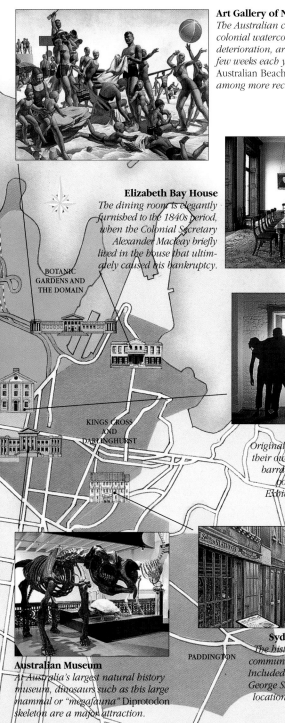

Art Gallery of New South Wales

The Australian collection includes colonial watercolours which, to avoid deterioration, are only shown for a few weeks each year. Charles Meere's Australian Beach Pattern *(1940) is among more recent works.*

Elizabeth Bay House

The dining room is elegantly furnished to the 1840s period, when the Colonial Secretary Alexander Macleay briefly lived in the house that ultimately caused his bankruptcy.

BOTANIC GARDENS AND THE DOMAIN

KINGS CROSS AND DARLINGHURST

Hyde Park Barracks

Originally built by convicts for their own incarceration, these barracks were later home to poor female immigrants. Exhibits recall the daily life of these occupants.

PADDINGTON

Sydney Jewish Museum

The history of the city's Jewish community is documented here. Included is a reconstruction of George Street in 1848, a major location for Jewish businesses.

Australian Museum

At Australia's largest natural history museum, dinosaurs such as this large mammal or "megafauna" Diprotodon skeleton are a major attraction.

Exploring Museums and Galleries

Nautilus scrimshaw, National Maritime Museum

SYDNEY BOASTS a rich variety of museums and galleries that reflects the cultural, artistic and historical heritage of this, the country's oldest city – and of Australia as a whole. The growth of such institutions in recent years parallels a corresponding growth in public interest in all things cultural, a phenomenon that seems at odds with Sydney's predominantly hedonistic image. In fact, Sydney has a long-standing cultural tradition, one that has not always been widely recognized. It may even surprise some people that museums and galleries attract more people than do high-profile football matches.

Detail from *Window of Dreams* at the National Maritime Museum

Collage on one of the internal doors of the Brett Whiteley Studio

VISUAL ARTS

THE TRADITIONALLY conservative curatorial policy of the **Art Gallery of NSW** has been abandoned in recent times, and it now has one of the finest existing collections of modern Australian and Aboriginal art. Thanks to its former policy,

however, it also possesses an outstanding collection of late 19th- and early 20th-century English and Australian works. Thematic temporary exhibitions are also a regular feature.

The far newer **Museum of Contemporary Art** (MCA) is best known for blockbuster exhibitions. Many of these take advantage of its prime harbour site to create a fine sense of spectacle. It also has a considerable permanent collection, and hosts mini film festivals, literary readings and talks.

The **Brett Whiteley Studio** opened even more recently. Housed in the studio of the late artist, it commemorates the life and works of perhaps the most celebrated and controversial Sydney painter of the late 20th century.

The substantial collection of Australian painting and sculpture held by the **SH Ervin Gallery** is supplemented by frequent thematic and other specialized exhibitions.

TECHNOLOGY AND NATURAL HISTORY

THE UNDISPUTED leader in this area is the **Powerhouse**, with traditional and interactive displays covering fields as diverse as space travel, silent films and solar energy. The **National Maritime Museum** has the world's fastest boat, *Spirit of Australia*, as part of its extensive indoor and outdoor displays. The **Motor World Museum and Gallery** has exhibitions of classic vehicles, from vintage cars to contemporary designs.

The **Australian Museum**, in contrast, emphasizes natural history with its displays of the exotic and extinct: from birds, insects and rock samples to giant Australian megafauna.

ABORIGINAL CULTURE

WITH MORE THAN 200 works, both traditional and contemporary, on display, the **Art Gallery of NSW**'s Yiribana Gallery has the best and most

Jabarrgwa Wurrabadalumba's *Dugong Hunt* (1948), Art Gallery of NSW

comprehensive collection of
Aboriginal art in the country.
The **Australian Museum** has
displays ranging from the prehistoric era to the start of European settlement. In its community access space, it also
presents performances that
celebrate Aboriginal culture
and traditions.

The First Australians exhibit
at the **National Maritime
Museum** includes audio and
video material, with traditional
tools made by present-day
Aboriginal communities.

The **Museum of Sydney**
uses images, artifacts and oral
histories to evoke the life of
the Eora, the indigenous
people of the Sydney region,
up to the years of first contact
with the European colonists.

The Georgian-style front bedroom in the cottage at Elizabeth Farm

COLONIAL HISTORY

THE SUPERB interior of
Elizabeth Bay House has
been furnished to show early
colonial life at its most elegant,
but while at first the
house may appear to
celebrate a success
story, the enormous
cost of its construction
brought bankruptcy to
its owner. Also built in
grand style, **Vaucluse
House** celebrates the
life and times of WC
Wentworth, explorer
and politician.

**Experiment Farm
Cottage**, **Hamble-
don Cottage** and
Elizabeth Farm in
and around Parramatta are
testament to the crucial role
of agriculture in the survival
of a colony that was brought
to the brink of starvation. The
former has been restored as a
gentleman's cottage of the
mid-19th century, while the
latter two have been
furnished to the period of
1820–50. Parramatta's **Old
Government House** was
once the vice-regal "inland"
residence when Parramatta had
more people than Sydney. The
colonial furniture on display
predates 1855.

The **Museum of Sydney** is
built on the site of the first
Government House, close to
Sydney Cove. On display are

**Water dip
at Experiment
Farm Cottage**

recently unearthed relics of
that building, some of which
are visible under windows at
the entrance to the museum.
Susannah Place provides an
insight into working-class life
in the 19th century. **Cadman's
Cottage**, also in The Rocks, is
a simple stone dwelling dating
from 1816 and the city's oldest
extant building. Adjacent is the
Sailors' Home, built in 1864
and now The Sydney Visitors
Centre. It also has
permanent exhi-
bitions detailing the
area's architectural,
archaeological and
social heritage. The
important role of gold
in Australia's history
and how it determined
patterns of migration
and expansion are
shown at the **Power-
house Museum**.
Hyde Park Barracks
evokes the often brutal
lives and times of the
convicts who were housed
there in the early 19th century,
while not neglecting its other
place in Australia's history as
an immigration depot.

Side view of the veranda at
Elizabeth Farm, near Parramatta

SPECIALIST MUSEUMS

AUTHOR MAY GIBBS' home on
the harbour, **Nutcote**, has
been refurbished in the style
of the 1930s. The **Justice and
Police Museum** examines a
far less comfortable history,
investigating Australian crime
and punishment, while the
Westpac Museum traces local
financial transactions from first
coins through to credit cards.
Experiences of Jewish migrants
to Australia and the story of the
Holocaust are examined at
the **Sydney Jewish Museum**.

FINDING THE MUSEUMS AND GALLERIES

Art Gallery of NSW *pp108–11*
Australian Museum *pp88–9*
Brett Whiteley Studio *p130*
Cadman's Cottage *p68*
Elizabeth Bay House *p120*
Elizabeth Farm *pp138–9*
Experiment Farm Cottage *p139*
Hambledon Cottage *p139*
Hyde Park Barracks *pp114–15*
Justice and Police Museum *p72*
Motor World Museum and Gallery *p98*
Museum of Contemporary Art *p73*
Museum of Sydney *p85*
National Maritime Museum *pp94–5*
Nutcote *pp132–3*
Old Government House *p139*
Powerhouse Museum *pp100–101*
Sailors' Home *p67*
SH Ervin Gallery, National Trust Centre *p73*
Susannah Place *p67*
Sydney Jewish Museum *p121*
Vaucluse House *p136*
Westpac Museum *p68*

Sydney's Best: Architecture

Fᴏʀ sᴜᴄʜ ᴀ ʏᴏᴜɴɢ ᴄɪᴛʏ, Sydney possesses a remarkable diversity of architectural styles. They range from the simplicity of Francis Greenway's Georgian buildings (see p114) to Jørn Utzon's Expressionist Sydney Opera House (see pp74–7). Practical Colonial structures gave way to elaborate Victorian edifices such as Sydney Town Hall and the same passion for detail is seen on a smaller scale in Paddington's terraces. Later, Federation warehouses and bungalows brought in a particularly Australian style.

Contemporary
Governor Phillip Tower is a modern commercial building incorporating a historical site (see p85)

Colonial Convict
The first structures were very simple yet formal English-style cottages with shingled roofs and no verandas. Cadman's Cottage is a fine representative of this style.

Colonial Georgian
Francis Greenway's courthouse design was ordered to be adapted to suit the purposes of a church. St James Church is the result.

American Revivalism
Shopping arcades connecting streets, such as the Queen Victoria Building, were 1890s vogue.

THE ROCKS
AND
CIRCULAR
QUAY

CITY
CENTRE

Victorian
The Town Hall interior includes Australia's first pressed metal ceiling, installed for fear that the organ would vibrate a plaster one loose.

DARLING
HARBOUR

Contemporary Expressionism
Innovations in sports stadiums and museum architecture, such as the National Maritime Museum, emphasize roof design and the silhouette.

Interwar Architecture
Bruce Dellit's Anzac Memorial in Hyde Park, with sculptures by Raynor Hoff, encapsulates the spirit, form and detail of Art Deco.

| 0 metres | 500 |
| 0 yards | 500 |

Modern Expressionism

One of the world's greatest examples of 20th-century architecture, Jørn Utzon's Sydney Opera House beat 234 entries in a design competition. Work commenced in 1959 and, despite the architect's resignation in 1966, it was opened in 1973.

Early Colonial

The first buildings of character and quality, such as Hyde Park Barracks, were for the government.

BOTANIC GARDENS AND THE DOMAIN

Australian Regency

During the 1830s, the best designed villas were the work of John Verge. Elizabeth Bay House was his masterpiece.

KINGS CROSS AND DARLINGHURST

Colonial Military

Victoria Barracks, designed by engineers, is an impressive example of a well-preserved Georgian military compound.

PADDINGTON

Colonial Grecian

Greek Revival was the major style for public buildings, such as the Darlinghurst Court House, designed by the Colonial Architect in the 1820–50 period.

Victorian Iron Lace

Festooned with a filigree of cast-iron lace in a wide range of prefabricated patterns, Paddington verandas demonstrate 1880s workmanship.

Exploring Sydney's Architecture

Federation era
stained glass

WHILE EUROPEAN SETTLEMENT in Sydney has a relatively short history, architectural styles have rapidly evolved from provincial British buildings and the simplicity of convict structures. From the mid-19th century until the present day, architectural innovations have borrowed from a range of international trends to create vernacular styles more suited to local materials and conditions. The signs of affluence and austerity, from gold rush to depression, are also manifested in bricks and mortar.

Façade of the Colonial Susannah
Place, with corner shop window

COLONIAL ARCHITECTURE

LITTLE REMAINS of the Colonial buildings from 1790–1830. The few structures still standing have a simple robustness and unassuming dignity. They rely more on form, proportion and mass than on detail.

The Rocks area has one of the best collections of early Colonial buildings: **Cadman's Cottage** (1816), the **Argyle Stores** (1826) and **Susannah Place** (1844). The Georgian **Hyde Park Barracks** (1819) and **St James Church** (1820), by Francis Greenway *(see p114)*, as well as the Greek Revival **Darlinghurst Court House** (1835) and **Victoria Barracks** (1841–8) are excellent examples of this period.

AUSTRALIAN REGENCY

JUST AS THE Colonial style was reaching its zenith, the city's increasingly moneyed society abandoned it as undignified and unfashionable. London's residential architecture, exemplified by John Soane under the Prince Regent's patronage, was in favour from the 1830s to the 1850s. Fine examples of this shift towards Regency are John Verge's stylish town houses at **39–41 Lower Fort Street** (1834–6), The Rocks, and the adjoining **Bligh House** built for a wealthy merchant in 1833 in High Colonial style complete with Greek Classical Doric veranda columns.

Regency-style homes often had Grecian, French and Italian details. **Elizabeth Bay House** (1835–8), internally the finest of all John Verge's works, is particularly noted for its cantilevered staircase rising to the arcaded gallery. The cast-iron Ionic-columned **Tusculum Villa** (1831) by the same architect at Potts Point *(see p118)* is unusual in that it is encircled by a double-storeyed veranda, now partially enclosed.

Entrance detail from the Victorian
St Patrick's Seminary in Manly

VICTORIAN

THIS PROSPEROUS ERA featured confident business people and merchants who designed their own premises. Tracts of the city west of York Street and south of Bathurst Street are testimony to these self-assured projects. The cast-iron and glass **Strand Arcade** (1891) by JB Spencer originally included a gas and electricity system, and hydraulic lifts.

Government architect James Barnet's best work includes the "Venetian Renaissance" style **General Post Office**, Martin Place (1864–87), and the extravagant **Lands Department Building** (1877–90) with its four iron staircases and, originally, patent lifts operated by water power. The **Great Synagogue** (1878), **St Mary's Cathedral** (1882), **St Patrick's Seminary** (1885), **Sydney Town Hall** and **Paddington Street** are also of this period.

AMERICAN REVIVALISM

AFTER FEDERATION in 1901, architects looked to styles such as Edwardian, American Romanesque and Beaux Arts from overseas for commercial buildings. The former **National Mutual Building** (1892) by Edward Raht set the change of direction, followed by warehouse buildings in Sussex and Kent Streets. The Romanesque **Queen Victoria Building**

The Australian Regency-style Bligh House in Dawes Point

(1893–98) was a grand council project by George McRae. The Beaux Arts **Commonwealth Savings Bank** (1928) features an elaborate chamber in Neo-Classical style.

INTERWAR ARCHITECTURE

ARCHITECTURE BETWEEN World Wars I and II produced skyscrapers such as the **City Mutual Life Assurance Building** (1936), by Emil Sodersten. This building exhibits German Expressionist influences such as pleated or zigzag windows.

Two important structures are the **ANZAC Memorial** (1929–34) in Hyde Park and **Delfin House** (1938–40), by the Art Deco architect Bruce Dellit. The latter, a skyscraper, features a vaulted ceiling and a granite arch decorated with an allegory of modern life.

MODERN ARCHITECTURE

Modern MLC Centre, Martin Place

FROM THE mid-1950s, modern architecture was introduced to the city through glass-clad curtain-walled office blocks, proportioned like matchboxes on their ends. The contrasting expressed frame approach of **Australia Square** (1961–7) gives structural stability to one of the world's tallest light-weight concrete office towers. This city block was formed by amalgamating 30 properties. Harry Seidler's **MLC Centre** (1975–8) is a 65-storey office tower comprising a reinforced concrete tube structure with column-free floors.

Jørn Utzon's **Sydney Opera House** (1959–73) is widely regarded as one of the architectural wonders of the world.

CONTEMPORARY ARCHITECTURE

DRAMATIC DESIGNS in recent sports and recreation buildings, such as the elliptical **Sydney Football Stadium** (1985–8) by Philip Cox, use advanced steel engineering systems. Beneath the vast roof of the **National Maritime Museum** (1986–9), also by Cox, there is ample space for a wide range of exhibitions.

Detailed masonry has made a return to commercial buildings such as the very highly regarded **Governor Phillip Tower** (1989–94). The dictates of office design do not detract from the historical Museum of Sydney, ingeniously sited on the lower floors.

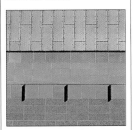

Masonry detail from the contemporary Governor Phillip Tower

FEDERATION ARCHITECTURE

This distinctly urban style of architecture was developed to meet the demands of the prosperous and newly emerging middle classes at the time of Federation in 1901. Particular features are the high-pitched roofs, which form a picturesque composition or architectural tableau, incorporating intricate gables, wide verandas and chimneys. The decorative timber fretwork of the verandas and archways and the leadlight windows reveal the influence of the Art Nouveau period, as do the vibrant red roof tiles. The patriotic references are seen throughout, and Australian flora and fauna are recurring decorative motifs.

"Verona" in The Appian Way, Burwood

WHERE TO FIND THE BUILDINGS

Anzac Memorial *p86*
Argyle Stores *p68*
Australia Square, Cnr George & Bond Sts. **Map** 1 B3.
Bligh House, 43 Lower Fort St, Dawes Point. **Map** 1 B2.
Cadman's Cottage *p68*
City Mutual Life Assurance Building, Cnr Hunter & Bligh Sts. **Map** 1 B4.
Commonwealth Savings Bank of Australia, Martin Place *p84*
Darlinghurst Court House *p121*
Delfin House, 16–18 O'Connell St. **Map** 1 B4.
Elizabeth Bay House *p120*
General Post Office, Martin Place *p84*
Governor Phillip Tower *p85*
Great Synagogue *p86*
Hyde Park Barracks *pp114–15*
Lands Department Building *p84*
39–41 Lower Fort Street, Dawes Point. **Map** 1 A2.
MLC Centre, Martin Place *p84*
National Maritime Museum *pp94–5*
National Mutual Building, 350 George St. **Map** 1 B4.
Paddington Street *p126*
Queen Victoria Building *p82*
St James Church *p115*
St Mary's Cathedral *p86*
St Patrick's Seminary *p147*
Strand Arcade *p84*
Susannah Place *p67*
Sydney Football Stadium, Moore Park. **Map** 5 C4.
Sydney Opera House *pp74–7*
Sydney Town Hall *p87*
Tusculum Villa *p118*
Victoria Barracks *p127*

Sydney's Many Cultures

SYDNEY HAS ONE of the world's most cosmopolitan societies, reflected in the extraordinary variety of restaurants, religions, community centres and cultural activities to be found throughout the city and its environs. Over 235 birthplaces outside Australia were named in the last census. Indeed, the Sydney telephone directory lists interpreting services for 22 languages, including Greek, Italian, Spanish, Chinese, Vietnamese, Turkish, Korean and Arabic, and many of these groups have their own newspapers. While immigrants have settled all over the city, there are still pockets of Sydney that retain a distinctive ethnic flavour.

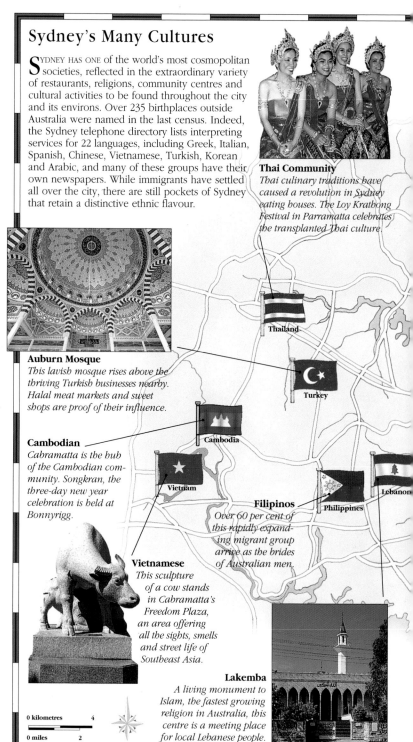

Thai Community
Thai culinary traditions have caused a revolution in Sydney eating houses. The Loy Krathong Festival in Parramatta celebrates the transplanted Thai culture.

Thailand

Auburn Mosque
This lavish mosque rises above the thriving Turkish businesses nearby. Halal meat markets and sweet shops are proof of their influence.

Turkey

Cambodian
Cabramatta is the hub of the Cambodian community. Songkran, the three-day new year celebration is held at Bonnyrigg.

Cambodia

Vietnam

Filipinos
Over 60 per cent of this rapidly expanding migrant group arrive as the brides of Australian men.

Philippines

Lebanon

Vietnamese
This sculpture of a cow stands in Cabramatta's Freedom Plaza, an area offering all the sights, smells and street life of Southeast Asia.

Lakemba
A living monument to Islam, the fastest growing religion in Australia, this centre is a meeting place for local Lebanese people.

0 kilometres   4

0 miles   2

Little Italy
Long home to the Italian community, Leichhardt evokes the flavour of Europe with its bars, cafés, restaurants and a sprawling annual street fair.

Irish Parade
Sydney's first settlers, many of them Irish, made their home in The Rocks. With its proliferation of pubs, it is the focal point for jubilant St Patrick's Day celebrations on 17 March each year.

Jewish Delicatessen
The sizeable Jewish community in the city's eastern suburbs, about half of whom were born in Australia, is well served by kosher supermarkets and butchers' shops.

Ireland

Italy   **China**   **Israel**

Greece

Indigenous Australia

Aboriginal Peoples
Waverley Oval hosts the Survival concert every 26 January, the culmination of a week of cultural exchange.

St Nicholas Church
Marrickville's Greek Orthodox church is the home of worship for the community, mostly based in the southern suburbs.

Chinese New Year
Each year, revellers pack Dixon Street, at the heart of Chinatown, to celebrate with fireworks and Chinese dragons.

Exploring Sydney's Many Cultures

Poster to tempt migrants

IN THE MID-20TH CENTURY, most Australians could trace their ancestry back to the British Isles. The building of postwar Australia, dependent as it was on skilled migrant labour, changed all that. Between 1947 and 1972, there were more than two million arrivals and soon communities of Italians, Greeks, Croatians, Macedonians and Turks had been established. As the country looked to its close neighbours for trade in the 1970s and 1980s, and wars wreaked havoc in Asian countries, priorities changed. Today, more than 8 per cent of New South Wales's population is Asian-born and a large proportion have settled in Sydney.

The Chinese Garden (*see p98*)

The Aboriginal Bangarra Dance Theatre, based in Sydney

ABORIGINAL PEOPLES

SYDNEY CONTAINS the largest urban Aboriginal population in Australia. The largest communities are at La Perouse and Redfern. The richness of the Aboriginal culture in a variety of fields is, however, far more pervasive. Indigenous artwork is now much sought after and there are several specialist Aboriginal art shops in the city (*see pp206–7*). The Yiribana Gallery is a permanent exhibition space at the Art Gallery of New South Wales (*p111*). The Bangarra Dance Theatre (*p213*) and National Aboriginal and Islander Skills Development Association, both based in Sydney, are noted for their innovative blends of traditional and contemporary dance.

In 1988, indigenous peoples in Australia replaced the term "Aborigines" with names from their own languages. "Koori", is now common usage.

THE BRITISH

FOR MORE THAN 150 years, Sydney lifestyle was influenced by Great Britain. From the "mother country" came art, literature, fashion, morals, administration and manners – not to mention breakfast sausages, meat pies, stewed fruit and steamed plum pudding. Many rituals and celebrations have their roots in British tradition, which may explain why a lot of Sydneysiders persist with hot Christmas dinners in the midst of summer, approach cricket with almost religious fervour and take pride in the brewing of many fine local beers.

THE CHINESE

THE FIRST CHINESE arrivals were almost all men who came to seek their fortune when gold was discovered in the 1850s. At the end of the gold rushes, many settled in tight-knit communities with undeservedly dubious reputations. In the cities and towns where they settled, there were many cultural conflicts with the predominantly Anglo-Celtic settlers. Eventually, the Chinese were deterred by taxes and then excluded from settlement after the introduction of the Immigration Restriction Act in 1901. Entry restrictions for non-European migrants were only relaxed in the 1960s.

Many Chinese students were allowed to remain in Australia after the Tiananmen Square massacre in 1989. Today, the

Chinese are the fastest-growing community in Sydney, with most new arrivals from China, Hong Kong and Taiwan. It is not only Chinese Australians who throng to Chinatown. All locals browse, sample the delicacies and treat themselves to lunchtime *yum cha* (*see p180*).

THE GREEKS

SEVEN CONVICTS transported for piracy in 1829, two of whom stayed on, were probably the first Greek arrivals. Although the early pioneers in the 19th century were mainly from islands such as Kythera, many Greeks also arrived from Cyprus and North Africa.

In the 1940s, new migrants began to set up small businesses such as cafés, fish-and-chip shops and greengrocers. The Greek community gradually grew and has maintained its strong networks through the church and social and sporting organizations. Every year, on the Sunday following 6 January, the Greek Orthodox

Dancers in traditional Greek costume at the Opera House

Church celebrates the Feast of the Epiphany with the Blessing of the Waters at Yarra Bay in Sydney's south. The nearby suburb of Sutherland is becoming the city's "Little Athens".

THE IRISH

THE IRISH HAVE HAD a profound impact on politics, literature, music, religion and law in Australia. About one-third of the convicts transported here were Irish, and many more migrated later. In 1831, Cork's Foundling Hospital sent 50 girls, the first government-assisted migrants. The idea was that "in consequence of the very great disproportion of males to females in New South Wales it would be extremely beneficial to . . . have introduced there some females properly educated and of virtuous habits".

While the Irish are much dispersed today, a St Patrick's Day parade runs through the city streets each year (see p50). Many pubs, particularly those in The Rocks, draw boisterous crowds to mark the occasion.

"St Patrick" in St Patrick's Day Parade

THE ITALIANS

ITALIAN IMMIGRATION peaked in the 1950s and 1960s, but the strong Italian community has been established since the gold rushes of the 1850s. The Italians brought with them much-needed industrial labour, as well as cheese-making skills and wine-growing expertise.

Although Italians now live all over Sydney, Leichhardt's Norton Street, with its restaurants, cafés and nightspots, is still the Italian heartland. East Sydney's Stanley Street is the "Little Italy" of the inner city and pasta and cappuccino are as much a part of Sydney life as meat pies and beer.

One of the most important Italian festivals is the Blessing of the Fleet in October (p48). The community also makes its presence felt whenever Italy advances through to the finals of the soccer World Cup.

THE LEBANESE

LEBANESE MIGRANTS first began arriving in the 1840s with the majority being Orthodox Christians or Catholics. It was not until 1976, as a result of Lebanon's civil war, that Muslims began to migrate in large numbers. While early settlers largely comprised shopkeepers living in rural areas, later migrants, being the largest group of Arabic-speaking citizens in the city, established it as the Lebanese centre. In the southwest of Sydney, Punchbowl and Lakemba have a high Lebanese profile. They have places of worship for all Lebanese Australians wishing to maintain their religious and cultural traditions. The city's Arabic-language newspapers are also based there.

THE VIETNAMESE

FROM 1976 TO 1981, 54 boats laden with refugees from war-torn Vietnam reached Darwin in Australia's north. Tens of thousands of "boat people" and other refugees risked rough seas, pirates, starvation and imprisonment to escape.

A number of suburbs have large Vietnamese communities, notably Cabramatta in Sydney's southwest, where they are the most numerous of 109 nationalities. Along with Cambodians, they have made Cabramatta a dynamic commercial centre.

New Zealand Maori dancers taking part in the Te Aroha Festival

THE MELTING POT

AFTER THE CHINESE community, the fastest-growing migrant group in New South Wales is the Filipinos, living predominantly in the western suburbs of Fairfield and Blacktown.

Fairfield also has a booming South American, particularly Chilean, community, as well as a significant group of East Timorese living in exile.

Don Moon, a highly successful Korean businessman, saw huge potential in the run-down suburb of Campsie not far from the city. He encouraged other Korean immigrants to invest in the area, which now has a popular shopping district.

The restaurants and cafés in Randwick show the presence of an Indonesian and Malay community. As a cosmopolitan South Pacific city, Sydney has migrants from Tonga, Western Samoa and Fiji, as well as New Zealanders, including Maoris, dispersed throughout the city.

Pailau Gate at the entrance to Freedom Plaza in Cabramatta

Sydney's Best: Parks and Reserves

Flannel flower

SYDNEY IS ALMOST completely surrounded by national parks and intact bushland. There are also a number of national parks and reserves within Greater Sydney itself. Here, the visitor can gain some idea of how the landscape looked before the arrival of European settlers. The city parks, too, are filled with plant and animal life. The more formal plantings of both native and exotic species are countered by the indigenous birds and animals that have adapted and made the urban environment their home. One of the highlights of a trip to Sydney is the huge variety of birds to be seen, from large birds of prey such as sea eagles and kites, to the shyer species such as wrens and tiny finches.

Garigal National Park
Rainforest and moist gullies provide shelter for superb lyrebirds and sugar gliders.

North Arm Walk
In spring, grevilleas and flannel flowers bloom profusely on this foreshore walk.

Lane Cove National Park
The open eucalypt forest is dotted with grass trees, as well as fine stands of red and blue gums. The rosella, a type of parrot, is common.

Bicentennial Park
Situated at Homebush Bay on the Parramatta River, the park features a mangrove habitat. It attracts many water birds, including pelicans.

Hyde Park
Situated on the edge of the city centre, the park provides a peaceful respite from the hectic streets. The native iris is just one of the plants found in the lush gardens. The sacred ibis, a water bird, is often seen.

Middle Head and Obelisk Bay

Gun emplacements, tunnels and bunkers built in the 1870s to protect Sydney from invasion by sea dot the area. The superb fairy wren lives here and water dragons can at times be seen basking on rocks.

North Head

Coastal heathland, with banksias, tea trees and casuarinas, dominates the cliff tops. On the leeward side, moist forest surrounds tiny harbour beaches.

Grotto Point

Bottlebrushes, grevilleas and flannel flowers line paths winding through the bush to the lighthouse.

Bradleys Head

The headland is a nesting place for the ringtail possum. Noisy flocks of rainbow lorikeets are also often in residence.

South Head

Unique plant species such as the sundew cover this heathland.

Nielsen Park

The kookaburra is easily identified by its call, which sounds like laughter.

The Domain

Palms and Moreton Bay figs are a feature of this former common. The Australian magpie, with its black and white plumage, is a frequent visitor.

Moore Park

Huge Moreton Bay figs provide an urban habitat for the flying fox.

Centennial Park

Open expanses and groves of paperbark and eucalypt trees bring sulphur-crested cockatoos en masse. The brushtail possum is a shy creature that comes out at night.

0 kilometres   4

0 miles   2

Exploring the Parks and Reserves

DESPITE 200 YEARS of European settlement, Sydney's parks and reserves contain a surprising variety of native wildlife. Approximately 2,000 species of native plants, 1,000 cultivated and weed species and 300 bird species have managed to adapt favourably to the changes.

Several quite distinct vegetation types are protected in the bushland around Sydney, and these in turn provide shelter for a wide range of birds and animals. Even the more formal parks such as Hyde Park and the Royal Botanic Gardens are home to many indigenous species, allowing the visitor a glimpse of the city's diverse wildlife.

Colourful and noisy rainbow lorikeets at Manly's Collins Beach

COASTAL HINTERLAND

ONE REASON Sydney has so many heathland parks, such as those found at South Head and North Head, is that the soil along the city's coastline is deficient in almost every known nutrient. What these areas lack in fertility, they make up for in species diversity.

Heathland contains literally hundreds of species of plants, including some unique flora that have adapted to the poor soil. The most surprising ones are the carnivorous plants, which rely on passing insects for their food. The tiny sundew (*Drosera spatulata*), so called because of its sparkling foliage, is the commonest of the carnivorous species. This low-growing plant snares insects on its sticky, reddish leaves, which lie flat on the ground. You will often stumble across them where walking tracks pass through swampy ground, waiting patiently for a victim.

Red bottlebrush (*Callistemon* sp.)

Two other distinctive plants are casuarinas (*Allocasuarina* species) and banksias (*Banksia* species), both of which attract smaller birds such as honeyeaters and blue wrens.

RAINFOREST AND MOIST FOREST

RAINFOREST REMNANTS do exist in a few parts of Sydney, especially in the Royal National Park to the south of the city (*see pp164–5*). Small pockets can also be found in Garigal National Park, Ku-ring-gai Chase (*see pp154–5*) and some gullies running down to Middle Harbour. The superb lyrebird (*Menura novaehollandiae*) is a feature of these forest areas. The sugar glider (*Petaurus breviceps*), a small species of possum, can sometimes be heard calling to its mate during the night.

The deadliest spider in the world, the Sydney funnel-web (*Atrax robustus, see p89*), also lives here, but you are unlikely to see one unless you poke under rocks and logs. A common plant in this habitat is the cabbage tree palm (*Livistona australis*). Its heart was used as a vegetable by the early European settlers.

The soft tree fern (*Dicksonia antarctica*) decorates the gullies and creeks of moist forest. You may see a ringtail possum (*Pseudocheirus peregrinus*) nest at the top of one of these ferns at Bradleys Head. The nest looks rather like a hairy football and is found in hollow trees or ferns and shrubs.

Rainbow lorikeets (*Trichoglossus haematodus*) also inhabit Bradleys Head, as well as Clifton Gardens and Collins Beach. Early in the morning, they shoot through the forest canopy like iridescent bullets.

OPEN EUCALYPT FOREST

SOME OF Sydney's finest smooth-barked apple gums (*Angophora costata*) are in the Lane Cove National Park. These ancient trees, with their gnarled pinkish trunks, lend an almost "lost world" feeling.

Tall and straight blue gums (*Eucalyptus saligna*) stand in the lower reaches of the park, where the soil is better, while the smaller grey-white scribbly gum (*Eucalyptus rossii*), with its distinctive gum veins, lives on higher slopes. If you examine the markings on a scribbly gum closely, you will see they start out thin, gradually become thicker, then take a U-turn and stop. This is the track made by an *ogmograptis* caterpillar the previous year. The grubs that made the track

Coastal heathland lining the cliff tops at Manly's North Head

become small, brownish-grey moths and are commonly seen in eucalypt or gum forests.

Grass trees *(Xanthorrhoea* species), also common in open eucalypt forest, are an ancient plant species with a tall spike that bears white flowers in spring. Lyrebirds, echidnas, currawongs and black snakes are predominant wildlife. The snakes, although beautiful, should be treated with caution.

A smooth-barked apple gum in Lane Cove National Park

WETLANDS

MORE THAN 60 per cent of New South Wales' coastal wetlands have been lost. This makes the remaining areas of wetland especially important. Most of Sydney's wetlands are mangrove swamps, with some of the best-preserved examples at Bicentennial Park and the North Arm Walking Track.

Mangrove swamps are one of the most hostile places for a plant or animal to live. There

A grey mangrove swamp near the Lane Cove National Park

is no fresh water and, unlike soil, the mud has no oxygen whatsoever below the very surface level. Mangroves have developed some fascinating ways around these problems. First, excess salt is excreted from their leaves. Secondly, they get oxygen to the roots by pushing special peg-like roots, called pneumatophores, into the air. At low tide, these can be clearly seen around the base of most mangroves. They allow air to diffuse down into the roots so that they can survive the stifling conditions under the mud. The Sydney rock oyster *(Saccostrea commercialis)*, a popular local delicacy, is found in mangrove areas, particularly around the Hawkesbury and Botany Bay.

CITY PARKS

AN AMAZING number of birds and animals make the city parks their home. Silver gulls *(Larus novaehollandiae)* and sulphur-crested cockatoos *(Cacatua galerita)* are frequent daytime visitors to Hyde Park, Centennial Park, The Domain and the Botanic Gardens.

After dark, brush-tailed possums *(Trichosurus vulpecula)* go in search of food and may be seen scavenging in rubbish bins. Also a night creature, the fruit-eating grey-headed flying fox *(Pteropus poliocephalus)* can be seen swooping through the trees. There is sometimes

The nocturnal grey-headed flying fox, at rest during the daytime

a temporary colony of these marsupials in the Botanic Gardens, where they hang upside down from trees in the park. Most of Sydney's flying foxes come from a large colony in Gordon, in the city's north.

Moore Park and The Domain are good places to spot flying foxes and they also have wonderful specimens of Moreton Bay and other fig species.

While paperbarks *(Melaleuca* species) are a feature of Centennial Park, a range of palms can be seen in the Botanic Gardens. The exquisite superb fairy-wren *(Malurus cyaneus)* can also be seen here, flitting between shrubs, while overhead honeyeaters dart after each other in the tree canopy.

STRANGLER FIGS

The majestic figs in the city parks hide a dark secret. While most of the Moreton Bay figs *(Ficus macrophylla)* you see have been grown by gardeners long past, in the wild these trees have a different approach. They start as a tiny seedling, sprouted from a seed dropped by a bird in the fork of a tree. Over decades, the pencil-thin roots grow downwards. Once they reach the ground, new roots are sent down, forming a lacy network around the trunk of the host tree. They eventually become an iron-hard cage around the host tree's trunk so that it dies and rots away, leaving the fig with a hollow trunk.

The Moreton Bay fig, with its massive spreading canopy

SYDNEY THROUGH THE YEAR

SYDNEY'S TEMPERATE CLIMATE allows for the enjoyment of outdoor activities throughout the year. Seasons in Sydney are the opposite of those in the northern hemisphere. September ushers in the three months of spring; summer stretches from December to February; March, April and May are the autumn months; while the shorter days and falling temperatures of June announce the onset of winter. In reality, however, Sydney seasons often merge

Reveller at the Mardi Gras

into one another with little to mark their changeover. Balmy nights, the sweet, pervasive scent of jasmine blossom and the colourful blooming of shrubs and flowers are typical of spring. Summer caters for sun- and surf-lovers as well as being Sydney's festival season. Autumn, with its warm days and cooler nights, is often perfect for bushwalks and picnics. And the crisp days of winter are ideal for going on historic walks and exploring art galleries and museums.

SPRING

WITH THE WARMER weather, the profusion of spring flowers brings the city's parks and gardens excitingly to life. Food, art and music festivals abound. Footballers finish their seasons with action-packed grand finals, professional and backyard cricketers warm up for their summer competitions and the horse-racing fraternity gets ready to place its bets.

SEPTEMBER

David Jones Spring Flower Show *(first two weeks)*, Elizabeth Street department store. Breathtaking floral artwork fills the ground floor.
Festival of the Winds *(dates vary)*, Bondi Beach *(see p137)*. Multicultural kite-flying festival; music, dance.
Spring Festival *(dates vary)*, in the Royal Botanic Gardens. Among glorious displays of spring blooms, enjoy the minstrels, brass bands, dance displays, sculpture exhibits and food stalls *(see pp104–5)*.

Sacred ibis stilt-dancer at the Royal Botanic Gardens Festival

Traditional costumes at the Blessing of the Fleet, Darling Harbour

Spring Racing Carnival *(Sep–Oct)*. The horse-racing action is shared between Rosehill racecourse and the Royal Randwick racecourse.
Australian Rugby League Grand Final, Stadium Australia, Homebush.
New South Wales Rugby Union Grand Final, Sydney Football Stadium *(see p52)*.
Carnivale *(mid-Sept)*, various venues. Multicultural festival featuring theatre, art, music, dance, films, storytelling, talks and food from a multitude of nations. Runs for three weeks.
Aurora New World Festival *(late Sep–early Oct)*, Darling Harbour *(see pp92–3)*. Fiestas, parades and festivals from all nations, including music, arts, dance, puppets and fireworks.

OCTOBER

Manly International Jazz Festival *(Labour Day weekend)*. World-class jazz at a variety of venues *(see p133)*.

Aurora Blessing of the Fleet *(Labour Day weekend, Sun)*, Darling Harbour *(pp92–3)*. An Italian and Greek tradition: a fleet of gaily decorated fishing boats is officially blessed.
Leura Garden Festival *(early Oct)*, Blue Mountains *(see pp160–61)*. A village fair launches the festival, when magnificent private gardens may be viewed.

NOVEMBER

Melbourne Cup Day *(first Tue)*. The city almost grinds to a halt mid-afternoon to tune in to Australia's most popular horse race. Restaurants and hotels offer special luncheons.
Kings Cross Carnival *(early Nov)*, Darlinghurst Road. Street fair: stalls, bargains and food.
Sydney to the Gong Bicycle Ride *(first Sun)*. From Sydney's Moore Park to Flagstaff Point in Wollongong. Over 10,000 cyclists of all standards line up for this 92-km (57-mile) ride.

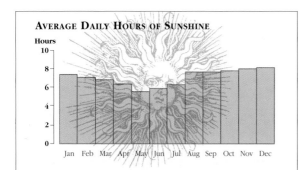

AVERAGE DAILY HOURS OF SUNSHINE

Hours
10 —
8 —
6 —
4 —
2 —
0 —

Jan Feb Mar Apr May Jun Jul Aug Sep Oct Nov Dec

Sunshine Hours

A sunny climate is one of Sydney's main attractions. There are very few days with no sunshine at all, even in the middle of winter. An up-to-date weather forecast is available by telephoning 1196. Coastal weather conditions can be obtained by dialling 11541.

SUMMER

SYDNEY TURNS FESTIVE in the summer months. Christmas pageants and open-air carol singing in The Domain mark the start of the season. Then there is the Sydney Festival, a month of cultural events and other popular entertainment, culminating in Australia Day celebrations on 26 January. Summer, too, brings a feast for sport lovers, with surfing and lifesaving events, yacht races and a host of local and international cricket matches.

"Santa Claus" at the surf: Christmas Day celebrations on Bondi Beach

DECEMBER

Carols in The Domain *(Sat before Christmas)*. Carols by candlelight in the parkland of the city's favourite outdoor gathering spot *(see p107)*.
Christmas at Bondi Beach *(25 Dec)*. Holidaymakers hold their own unofficial party on this famous beach *(see p137)*.
Sydney to Hobart Yacht Race *(26 Dec)*. The harbour teems with small craft as they escort racing yachts out to sea for the start of their journey.
New Year's Eve *(31 Dec)*. Street parties in The Rocks and Circular Quay and fireworks displays on Sydney Harbour.

JANUARY

Opera in the Domain *(throughout Jan)*, The Domain *(see p107)*. A free performance of highlights from productions by Opera Australia.
Cricket Test matches and one-day internationals are held at the Sydney Cricket Ground *(see p52)*.
Symphony under the Stars *(throughout Jan)*, The Domain *(see p107)*. Free concert performed by the Sydney Symphony Orchestra.
Ferrython *(26 Jan)*, Sydney Harbour. Ferries compete fiercely for line honours, as do rigged competitors in the Tall Ships Race held on the same day.
Australia Day Concert *(26 Jan)*. Concerts take place all over the city.
Chinese New Year *(late Jan or early Feb)*. Lion dancing, firecrackers and other New Year festivities take place in Chinatown *(see p99)*, Darling

Chinese New Year lion

Harbour and Cabramatta *(p40)*
Festival of Sydney *(first week–end Jan)*. Fantastic music, theatre, sport and art events.

FEBRUARY

Gay and Lesbian Mardi Gras Festival, various inner-city venues *(see pp28–9)*. A month of events culminating in a flamboyant street parade, mainly on Oxford Street, usually held early March.
Perspecta *(until late Mar, odd-numbered years)*, Art Gallery of NSW *(see pp108–11)*. A prestigious biennial exhibition of the very best contemporary art.
Tropfest *(third Sun)*, Darlinghurst and The Domain. Hugely popular short film festival.
Bondi Beach Cole Classic *(first Sun)*, North Bondi *(see p137)*. A 2-km (1½-mile) race for any swimmer aged from 13 to 70 game enough to enter.
Coogee Surf Carnival *(Sat in early Feb)*, Coogee *(see p55)*.

Australia Day Tall Ships race in Sydney Harbour

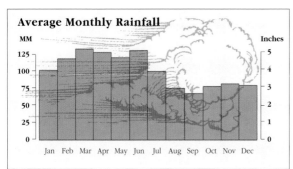

Average Monthly Rainfall

Rainfall
Autumn is Sydney's rainiest season, with March being the wettest month, while spring is the driest time of year. Rainfall, however, can often be unpredictable. Long stretches of sunny weather are common, but so, too, are periods of unrelenting rain.

AUTUMN

AFTER THE HUMIDITY of the summer, autumn brings fresh mornings and cooler days that are tailor-made for outdoor pursuits. There are many sporting and cultural events – some of them colourful and eccentric – to tempt the visitor. For many, the Royal Easter Show is the highlight of the season. Anzac Day (25 April) is a national holiday on which Australians commemorate their war dead.

MARCH

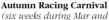

St Patrick's Day Parade *(17 Mar, or closest Sun)*. Hyde Park *(see pp86–7)* to The Domain. Pubs serve green beer on the day.
Kings Cross Bed Race *(Sun in mid-Mar)*, Darlinghurst Road, Potts Point. Fund-raisers push their beds through a challenging but fun 100-m (110-yd) obstacle course.

St Patrick's Day beer

Autumn Racing Carnival *(six weeks during Mar and Apr)*. Top-class races and big prize money, at Rosehill and Royal Randwick racecourses.

EASTER

Sydney Royal Easter Show *(one week before Good Friday)*, Olympic Park. Homebush. Country meets city in 12 days of ring events, livestock and produce judging, wood-chopping competitions, sheepdog trials, arts and crafts displays and sideshow alley attractions.
Darling Harbour Circus and Street Theatre Festival *(Easter school hols)*, Darling Harbour *(see pp92–3)*. Street theatre by magicians, acrobats, mime and other artists.

APRIL

National Trust Heritage Week *(dates vary)*. Celebration of the natural, architectural and

Woodchopping at the Easter Show

cultural heritage of Sydney.
Dragon Boat Races Festival *(early)*, Darling Harbour *(see pp92–3)*. Brilliantly decorated Chinese dragon boats race across Cockle Bay.
Archibald, Wynne and Sulman exhibitions *(until end of May)*, Art Gallery of NSW *(pp108–11)*. Annual exhibition of that year's entries in the portraiture, landscape, genre works and drawing competitions.
Anzac Day *(25 Apr)*. Dawn remembrance service held at the Cenotaph, Martin Place *(see p84)*, with a parade by war veterans along George Street.

MAY

Sydney Writers' Festival *(dates vary)*, State Library of New South Wales *(see p112)*.
Bridge to Bridge Power Boat Classic *(first Sun)*. Race from Brooklyn Bridge to Upper Hawkesbury Power Boat Club, Windsor *(see pp156–7)*.
Sydney Morning Herald Half Marathon *(fourth Sun)*, from Pier One, The Rocks. An open 21-km (13-mile) run.

Traditional decorative dragon boats on Darling Harbour's Cockle Bay

Average Monthly Temperature

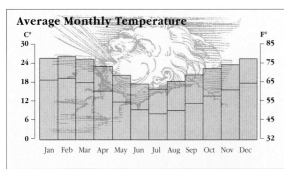

Temperature
This chart gives the average minimum and maximum temperatures for Sydney. Spring and autumn are generally free of extremes, but be prepared for sudden cold snaps in winter and occasional bursts of oppressive humid heat in summer.

WINTER

WINTER IN SYDNEY can be cold enough to require warm jackets; temperatures at night may drop dramatically away from the coast. The days are often clear and sometimes surprisingly mild. Arts are a major feature of winter. There are lots of exhibitions and the Sydney Film Festival, which no film buff will want to miss.

JUNE

A Taste of Manly *(first weekend)*, Manly Beach *(see p133)*. Annual food and wine festival.
Home Computer Show *(fours days over the long weekend)*, Convention and Exhibition Centre, Darling Harbour *(see p98)*. The very latest in personal computer software, hardware and entertainment.
Darling Harbour Jazz Festival *(mid-Jun)*, Darling Harbour *(see pp92–3)*. Constantly changing line-up of jazz, blues, country, gospel and world music bands and performers.
Sydney Film Festival *(two weeks mid-Jun)*, State Theatre *(see p82)*. The latest short and feature films, as well as retrospectives and showcases.
Australian Book Fair *(dates vary)*, Convention Centre, Darling Harbour *(see p98)*. Australian book publishers' trade fair. Open to the public on the weekend, with author appearances, book discussion panels and lots of lively entertainment for children.

Australian soldiers or "Diggers" at an Anzac Day ceremony

The familiar logo of the Film Festival

JULY

Biennale of Sydney *(two months, mid-year)*, various venues. International festival, held in even-numbered years, encompassing many forms of visual art, from painting and installations to photography and performance art.
Yulefest *(throughout winter)*, Blue Mountains *(see pp160–61)*. Hotels, guesthouses and some restaurants celebrate a midwinter "Christmas" with log fires and all the Yuletide trimmings.
Sydney International Boat Show *(late Jul)*, Convention and Exhibition Centre, Darling Harbour *(p98)*.
NAIDOC (National Aboriginal and Torres Strait Islander) Week *(dates vary)*. Week-long celebrations to build awareness and understanding of Aboriginal culture and history.

PUBLIC HOLIDAYS

New Year's Day (1 Jan)
Australia Day (26 Jan)
Good Friday (variable)
Easter Monday (variable)
Anzac Day (25 Apr)
Queen's Birthday (second Mon in Jun)
Bank Holiday (first Mon in Aug: only banks and some financial institutions are closed)
Labour Day (first Mon in Oct)
Christmas Day (25 Dec)
Boxing Day (26 Dec)

AUGUST

City to Surf Race *(second Sun)*. From the city to Bondi Beach *(see p137)*. A 14-km (9-mile) community event that attracts all types, from amateurs to leading marathon runners.
Japan Festival *(dates vary)*, various venues. Ikebana, tea ceremonies, sports and music, with visiting acts of all kinds.

Runners in the City to Surf Race, surging down William Street

SPORTING SYDNEY

THROUGHOUT AUSTRALIA sport is a way of life and Sydney is no exception. On any day you'll see locals on golf courses at dawn, running on the streets keeping fit, or having a quick set of tennis after work. At weekends, during summer and winter, there is no end to the variety of sports you can watch. Thousands gather at the Sydney Football Stadium and Sydney Cricket Ground every weekend while, for those who cannot make it, sport reigns supreme on weekend television.

CRICKET

DURING THE SUMMER months Test cricket and one-day internationals are played at the Sydney Cricket Ground (SCG). Tickets for weekday sessions of the Tests can often be bought at the gate, although it is advisable to book well in advance (through **Ticketek**) for weekend sessions of Test matches and for all the one-day international matches.

Australia versus the All Blacks, SFS

RUGBY LEAGUE AND RUGBY UNION

THE POPULARITY of rugby league knows no bounds in Sydney. This is what people are referring to when they talk about "the footie". There are three major competition levels: local, State of Origin – which matches Queensland against New South Wales – and Tests. The "local" competition fields teams from all over Sydney as well as Newcastle, Canberra, Brisbane, Perth, the Gold Coast and Far North Queensland.

These matches are held all over Sydney, although the Sydney Football Stadium (SFS) is by far the biggest venue. Tickets for State of Origin and

Test matches often sell out as soon as they go on sale. Call Ticketek to check availability.

Rugby union is the second most popular football code. Again, matches at Test level sell out very quickly. For some premium trans-Tasman rivalry, catch a Test match between Australia's "Wallabies" and the New Zealand "All Blacks" at the Sydney Football Stadium. Phone Ticketek for details.

GOLF AND TENNIS

GOLF ENTHUSIASTS need not do without their round of golf. There are many courses throughout Sydney where visitors are welcome at all times. These include **Moore Park**,

St Michael's and **Warringah** golf courses. It is sensible to phone beforehand for a booking, especially at weekends.

Tennis is another favoured sport. Courts available for hire can be found all over Sydney. Many centres also have floodlit courts available for night time. Try **Cooper Park** or **Parkland Sports** Centre.

Playing golf at Moore Park, one of Sydney's public courses

AUSTRALIAN RULES FOOTBALL

ALTHOUGH NOT as popular as in Melbourne, "Aussie Rules" has a strong following in Sydney. The local team, the Sydney Swans, plays its home games at the Sydney Cricket Ground during the season. Check a local paper for details.

Rivalry between the Sydney supporters and their Melbourne counterparts is always strong. Busloads of diehard fans from the south arrive to cheer on their teams. Tickets can usually be bought at the ground on the day of the game.

BASKETBALL

BASKETBALL HAS grown in popularity as both a spectator and recreational sport in recent years. Sydney has male and female teams competing in the National Basketball League. The games, held at the Sydney Superdome at

One-day cricket match between Australia and the West Indies, SCG

Aerial view of the Sydney Football Stadium at Moore Park

Homebush, have much of the pizzazz, colour and excitement of American basketball. Tickets can be purchased from either Ticketek or at the box office at the Superdome.

CYCLING AND INLINE SKATING

SYDNEY BOASTS excellent, safe locations for the whole family to go cycling. One of the most frequented is Centennial Park *(see p127)*. You can hire bicycles and safety helmets from **Centennial Park Cycles**.

Another popular pastime in summer is inline skating. **Bondi Boards & Blades**, near Centennial Park, hires inline skates, helmets and protective gear by the hour. If you're tempted to skate from there to Bondi Beach, remember there are several hills on the way back. **Action Inline** (Parramatta) also hires out skates.

For those who like to keep both feet firmly on the ground, you can watch skateboarders and inline skaters practising their moves at the ramps at Bondi Beach *(see p137)*.

Inline skaters enjoying a summer evening on the city's streets

HORSE RIDING

FOR A LEISURELY RIDE, head to Centennial Park or contact the **Centennial Parklands Equestrian Centre**. They will give you details of the four riding schools that operate in the park. **Samarai Park Riding School** conducts trail rides through Ku-ring-gai Chase National Park *(see pp154-5)*.

Further afield, you can enjoy the magnificent scenery of the Blue Mountains *(see pp160-61)* on horseback. The **Megalong Valley Heritage Farm** has trail rides lasting from one hour to an overnight ride. All levels of experience are catered for.

Horse riding in one of the parks surrounding the city centre

ADVENTURE SPORTS

YOU CAN PARTICIPATE in guided bushwalking, mountain biking, canyoning, potholing, rock climbing and abseiling expeditions in the nearby Blue Mountains National Park. The **Blue Mountains Adventure Company** runs one-day or multi-day courses and trips for all standards of adventurer.

In the centre of Sydney, the **City Crag Climbing Centre** has indoor classes and walls on which you can practise.

Sydney's Beaches

BEING A CITY BUILT AROUND THE WATER, it is no wonder that many of Sydney's recreational activities involve the sand, sea and sun. There are many harbour and surf beaches throughout Sydney, most of them accessible by bus *(see p231)*. Even if you're not a swimmer, the beaches offer a chance to get away from it all for a day or week-end and enjoy the fresh air and relaxed way of life.

SWIMMING

YOU CAN SWIM at either harbour or ocean beaches. Harbour beaches are generally smaller and are sheltered and calm. Popular harbour beaches include Camp Cove, Shark Bay and Balmoral Beach.

One of the most distinctive features of the ocean beaches is the surf lifesavers in their red and yellow caps. Surf life-saving carnivals are held throughout the summer. Call **Surf Life Saving NSW** for a calendar of events.

The beaches can sometimes become polluted, especially after heavy rainfall. The **Beach Watch Info Line** gives updated information about pollution levels at all Sydney beaches and bays.

SURFING

SURFING IS MORE a way of life than a leisure activity for some Sydneysiders. If you're a beginner, try Bondi, Bronte, Palm Beach or Collaroy.

Two of the best surf beaches are Maroubra and Narrabeen. Bear in mind that local surfers know one another well and do not take kindly to "intruders" who drop in on their waves

or leave litter on their beaches. If you'd like to learn, local surf shops should be able to help. To hire a surfboard, try **Bondi Surf Co.** or **Aloha Surf**.

If you'd like to catch some of the action but stay dry, there are plenty of vantage points on the walk from Bondi Beach to Tamarama *(see pp144–5)*.

WINDSURFING AND SAILING

THERE ARE LOCATIONS around Sydney suitable for every level of windsurfer. Boards can be hired from **Balmoral Windsurfing, Sailing and Kayaking School and Hire**. Good spots include Palm Beach, Narrabeen Lakes, La Perouse, Brighton-Le-Sands and Kurnell Point (for beginner and intermediate boarders) and Long Reef Beach, Palm Beach and Collaroy (for the more experienced windsurfer).

One of the best ways to see the harbour is while sailing. A sailing boat, including skipper, can be hired for the afternoon from the **Australian Sailing Academy**. If you'd like to learn how to sail, the **East Sail** sailing club has two-day courses and also hires out sailing boats and motor cruisers to experienced sailors.

Scuba diving at Gordons Bay

SCUBA DIVING

THEERE ARE SOME excellent dive spots around Sydney, especially in winter when the water is clear, if a little cold. More favoured spots are Gordons Bay, Shelly Beach, and Camp Cove.

Pro Dive Coogee offers a complete range of courses, escorted dives, introductory dives for beginners, and hire equipment. **Dive Centre Manly** also runs courses and introductory dives, hires equipment and conducts boat dives seven days a week.

DIRECTORY

Aloha Surf
44 Pittwater Rd, Manly.
☏ 9977 3777.

Australian Sailing Academy
The Spit, Mosman. **☏** 9960 3077.

Balmoral Windsurfing, Sailing and Kayaking School and Hire
Balmoral Sailing Club, Balmoral Beach. **☏** 9960 5344.

Beach Watch Info Line
☏ 1800 036 677.

Bondi Surf Co.
Shop 2, 72–76 Campbell Pde, Bondi Beach. **☏** 9365 0870.

Dive Centre Manly
10 Belgrave St, Manly.
☏ 9977 4355.

East Sail
d'Albora Marinas, New Beach Rd, Rushcutters Bay. **☏** 9327 1166.
w www.eastsail.com.au

Pro Dive Coogee
27 Alfreda St, Coogee.
☏ 9665 6333.

Surf Life Saving NSW
☏ 9984 7188.

Rock baths and surf lifesaving club at Coogee Beach

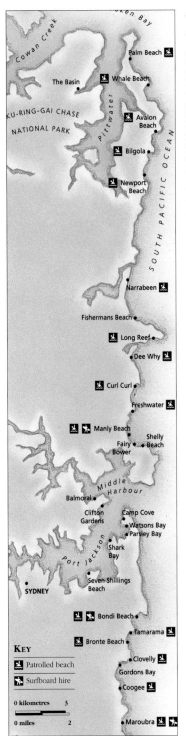

TOP 30 BEACHES

THE BEACHES shown here have been selected for their safe swimming, water sports, facilities available or their picturesque setting.

	SWIMMING POOL	SURFING	WINDSURFING	FISHING	SCUBA DIVING	PICNIC/BARBECUE	RESTAURANT/CAFÉ
Avalon	●	●	●	●		●	
Balmoral	●		●	●		●	
The Basin	●					●	
Bilgola							
Bondi Beach	●	●		●	●	●	●
Bronte	●	●		●	●	●	●
Camp Cove					●		
Clifton Gardens	●		●	●		●	
Clovelly				●	●		
Coogee	●		●	●	●	●	●
Curl Curl	●	●		●			
Dee Why	●	●		●	●	●	
Fairy Bower					●		
Fishermans Beach		●	●	●			
Freshwater	●	●		●	●	●	
Gordons Bay				●	●		
Long Reef		●	●	●	●		
Manly Beach	●	●			●	●	●
Maroubra		●	●	●	●		●
Narrabeen	●	●		●		●	
Newport Beach	●	●	●	●		●	
Obelisk Bay *(naturist)*							
Palm Beach	●	●	●	●		●	
Parsley Bay						●	
Seven Shillings Beach	●					●	
Shark Bay	●					●	●
Shelly Beach					●	●	●
Tamarama		●	●	●	●	●	●
Watsons Bay	●				●		●
Whale Beach	●	●	●	●		●	●

THE TYPES OF WAVES

Cresting waves can be identified by the foam that is created as they break from the top. These waves are ideal for board riding and body surfing.

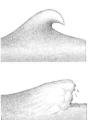

Plunging waves curl into a tube before breaking close to the shore. Fondly known as "dumpers", these waves should only be tackled by experienced surfers.

Surging waves are those that don't appear to break. They often travel all the way into the beach before breaking and can easily sweep a toddler or child off its feet.

KEY

🏊 Patrolled beach

🏄 Surfboard hire

0 kilometres   3

0 miles   2

Garden Island to Farm Cove

Waterlily in the Royal Botanic Gardens

Sydney's vast harbour, also named Port Jackson after a Secretary in the British Admiralty who promptly changed his name, is a drowned river valley which was transformed over millions of years. Its intricate coastal geography of headlands and secluded bays can sometimes confound even life-long residents. This waterway was the lifeblood of the early colony, with the maritime industry a vital source of wealth and supply. The legacies of alternate recessions and booms can be viewed along the shoreline: a representative story in a nation where an estimated 70 per cent of the population cling to the coastal cities, especially along the eastern seaboard.

The city skyline *is a result of random development. The 1960s indiscriminate destruction of architectural history was halted, and towers now stand amid Victorian buildings.*

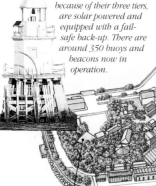

Two harbour beacons, *known as "wedding cakes" because of their three tiers, are solar powered and equipped with a fail-safe back-up. There are around 350 buoys and beacons now in operation.*

The barracks for the naval garrison date from 1888.

Garden Island marks a 1940s construction project with 12 ha (30 acres) reclaimed from the harbour.

Sailing on the harbour *is a pastime not exclusively reserved for the rich and elite. Of the several hundred thousand pleasure boats registered, some are available for hire while others take out groups of inexperienced sailors.*

Mrs Macquaries Chair *is a carved rock seat by Mrs Macquaries Road (see p106). In the early days of the colony, this was the site of a fruit and vegetable garden which was farmed until 1805.*

| 0 metres | 250 |
| 0 yards | 250 |

The Andrew (Boy) Charlton Pool is a favourite bathing spot for inner-city residents, and is named after the Sydneysider who, at the age of 16, won an Olympic gold medal in 1924. It was erected in 1963 on the Domain Baths' site, which had a grandstand for 1,700.

Woolloomooloo Finger Wharf has been developed as a dynamic entertainment and residential complex.

LOCATOR MAP
See Street Finder, map 2

Harry's Café de Wheels, a snack van, has been a Sydney culinary institution for more than 50 years. Photographs of celebrity customers are pinned to the van, attesting to its fame.

The Royal Botanic Gardens display a profusion of both flowering and non-flowering plants. The first trees were planted by the newly arrived European colonists. Some of these plants survive today.

Farm Cove has long been a mooring place for visiting naval vessels. The land opposite, now the Botanic Gardens, has been continuously cultivated for over 200 years.

Sydney Cove to Walsh Bay

Conservatorium of Music

IT IS ESTIMATED that over 70 km (43 miles) of harbour foreshore have been lost as a result of the massive land reclamation projects carried out since the 1840s. That the 13 islands existing when the First Fleet arrived in 1788 have now been reduced to just eight is a startling indication of rapid and profound geographical transformation.

Detail from railing at Circular Quay

Redevelopments around the Circular Quay and Walsh Bay area from the 1980s have opened up the waterfront for public use and enjoyment, acknowledging it as the city's greatest natural asset. Sydney's environmental and architectural aspirations recognize the need to integrate city and harbour.

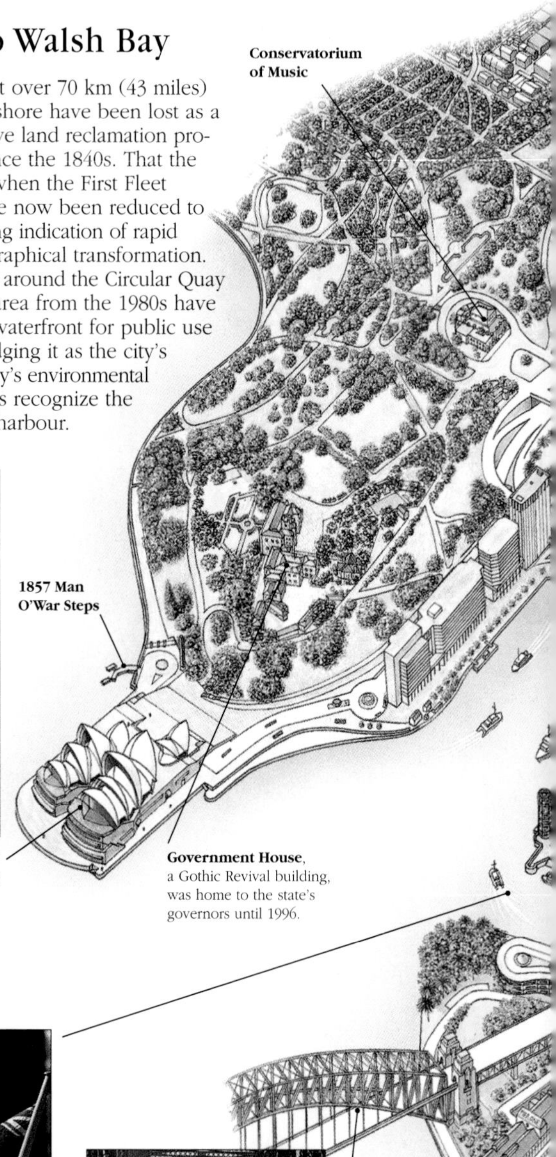

1857 Man O'War Steps

The Sydney Opera House *was designed to take advantage of its spectacular setting. The roofs shine during the day and seem to glow at night. The building can appear as a visionary landscape to the pedestrian onlooker.*

Government House, a Gothic Revival building, was home to the state's governors until 1996.

Harbour cruises *regularly depart from Circular Quay, taking visitors out and about both during the day and in the evening. They are an incomparable way to see the city and its waterways.*

The Sydney Harbour Bridge *was also known as the "Iron Lung" at the time of its construction. During the Great Depression it provided on-site work for approximately 1,400, while many more were employed in the specialist workshops.*

| 0 metres | 250 |
| 0 yards | 250 |

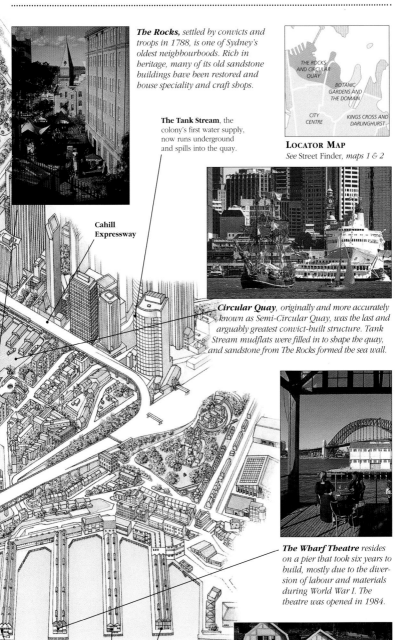

The Rocks, *settled by convicts and troops in 1788, is one of Sydney's oldest neighbourhoods. Rich in heritage, many of its old sandstone buildings have been restored and house speciality and craft shops.*

The Tank Stream, the colony's first water supply, now runs underground and spills into the quay.

LOCATOR MAP
See Street Finder, maps 1 & 2

THE ROCKS AND CIRCULAR QUAY

BOTANIC GARDENS AND THE DOMAIN

CITY CENTRE

KINGS CROSS AND DARLINGHURST

Cahill Expressway

Circular Quay, *originally and more accurately known as Semi-Circular Quay, was the last and arguably greatest convict-built structure. Tank Stream mudflats were filled in to shape the quay, and sandstone from The Rocks formed the sea wall.*

The Wharf Theatre *resides on a pier that took six years to build, mostly due to the diversion of labour and materials during World War I. The theatre was opened in 1984.*

The wharves were completed in 1922.

Imports and exports to and from the city were stored in these wharves until 1977.

The wharves' design *included a rat-proof sea wall around the port. This was an urgent response to the 1900 bubonic plague outbreak, attributed to rats on the wharves.*

SYDNEY AREA BY AREA

THE ROCKS AND CIRCULAR QUAY 62-77
CITY CENTRE 78-89
DARLING HARBOUR 90-101
BOTANIC GARDENS
AND THE DOMAIN 102-115
KINGS CROSS AND DARLINGHURST 116-121
PADDINGTON 122-127
FURTHER AFIELD 128-139
FOUR GUIDED WALKS 140-149

THE ROCKS AND CIRCULAR QUAY

CIRCULAR QUAY, once known as Semi-Circular Quay, is often referred to as the "birthplace of Australia". It was here, in January 1788, that the First Fleet landed its human freight of convicts, soldiers and officials, and the new British colony of New South Wales was declared. Sydney Cove became a rallying point whenever a ship arrived bringing much-needed supplies from "home". Crowds still gather here whenever there is something to celebrate. The Quay and The

Sculpture on the AMP Building, Circular Quay

Rocks are focal points for New Year's Eve revels, and Circular Quay drew huge crowds when, in 1994, Sydney was awarded the year 2000 Olympic Games. The Rocks area offers visitors a taste of Sydney's past, but it is a far cry from the time, less than 100 years ago, when most inhabitants lived in rat-infested slums and gangs ruled its streets. Now scrubbed and polished, The Rocks forms part of the colourful promenade from the Sydney Harbour Bridge to the spectacular Opera House.

SIGHTS AT A GLANCE

Historic Streets and Buildings
Campbell's Storehouses **1**
George Street **2**
Cadman's Cottage **6**
Argyle Stores **8**
Sydney Observatory **10**
Hero of Waterloo **11**
Sydney Harbour Bridge pp70–71 **13**
Writers' Walk **15**

Customs House **17**
Macquarie Place **18**

Museums and Galleries
The Rocks Toy Museum **3**
Susannah Place **4**
Sailors' Home **5**
Westpac Museum **7**
Justice and Police Museum **16**
Museum of Contemporary Art **19**
National Trust Centre **20**

Churches
Garrison Church **9**
St Philip's Church **21**

Theatres and Concert Halls
Wharf Theatre **12**
Sydney Opera House pp74–7 **14**

GETTING THERE
Circular Quay is the best stop for ferries and trains. Sydney Explorer and bus routes 431, 432, 433 and 434 run regularly to The Rocks, while most buses through the city go to the Quay.

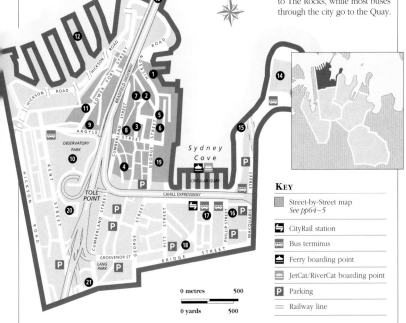

KEY

	Street-by-Street map *See pp64–5*
	CityRail station
	Bus terminus
	Ferry boarding point
	JetCat/RiverCat boarding point
P	Parking
	Railway line

◁ **The brilliant white walls of the Sailors' Home, the Sydney Visitor Centre in The Rocks**

Street-by-Street: The Rocks

Governor Arthur Phillip

N AMED FOR THE RUGGED CLIFFS that were once its dominant feature, this area has played a vital role in Sydney's development. In 1788, the First Fleeters under Governor Phillip's command erected makeshift buildings here, with the convicts' hard labour used to establish more permanent structures in the form of rough-hewn streets. The Argyle Cut, a road carved through solid rock using just hammer and chisel, took 18 years to build, beginning in 1843. By 1900, The Rocks was overrun with disease; the street now known as Suez Canal was once Sewer's Canal. Today, the area is still rich in colonial history and colour.

Hero of Waterloo
Lying beneath this historic pub is a tunnel originally used for smuggling **⓫**

★ **Sydney Observatory**
The first European structure on this prominent site was a windmill. The present museum holds some of the earliest astronomical instruments brought to Australia **⓾**

Garrison Church
Columns in this church are decorated with the insignia of British troops stationed here until 1870. Australia's first prime minister was educated next door **❾**

Argyle Cut

Suez Canal

★ **Museum of Contemporary Art**
The stripped Classical façade belies the avant-garde nature of the Australian and international art displayed in an ever-changing programme **⓳**

Walkway along Circular Quay West foreshore

The Rocks Market is a hive of activity every weekend, offering an eclectic range of craft items and jewellery utilizing Australian icons from gum leaves to koalas.

THE ROCKS AND CIRCULAR QUAY

BOTANIC GARDENS AND THE DOMAIN

CITY CENTRE

LOCATOR MAP
See Street Finder, map 1

The Rocks Toy Museum
A collection of more than 10,000 dolls and toys is on show in this restored 1850s coach house ❸

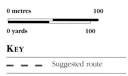

★ **Cadman's Cottage**
John Cadman, government coxswain, resided in what was known as the Coxswain's Barracks with his family. His wife Elizabeth was also a significant figure, believed to be the first woman to vote in New South Wales, a right she insisted on ❻

0 metres   100

0 yards   100

KEY

‒ ‒ ‒   Suggested route

The Overseas Passenger Terminal is where some of the world's luxury cruise liners, including the *QEII*, berth during their stay in Sydney.

STAR SIGHTS

★ **Cadman's Cottage**

★ **Museum of Contemporary Art**

★ **Sydney Observatory**

Campbell's Storehouses ❶

7–27 Circular Quay West, The Rocks.
Map 1 B2. 🚌 *Sydney Explorer, 431, 432, 433, 434.* 📷 🚻

In 1798, the Scottish merchant Robert Campbell sailed into Sydney Cove and soon established himself as a founding father of commerce for the new colony. With trade links already established in Calcutta, his business blossomed. In 1839, Campbell began constructing a private wharf and stores to house the tea, sugar, spirits and cloth he imported from India. Twelve sandstone bays had been built by 1861 and a brick upper storey was added in about 1890. Part of the old sea wall and 11 of the original stores still remain. The area soon took on the name of Campbell's Cove, which it retains to this day.

Today the bond stores contain several harbourside restaurants catering for a range of tastes, from contemporary to Chinese and Italian. It is a delightful area in which to relax with a meal and watch the bustling boats in the harbour go by. The pulleys that were used to raise cargo from the wharf can still be seen on the outside, near the top of the building.

George Street ❷

Map 1 B2. 🚌 *Sydney Explorer, 431, 432, 433, 434.*

Formerly the preserve of wealthy merchants, sailors and the city's working class, George Street today is a popular attraction with visitors to Sydney, who are drawn to its restaurants, art galleries, museums, jewellery stores and craft souvenir shops. For one-stop memento and gift shopping it is ideal, with little of the mass-produced and tacky, but a great deal in the way of modern Australian craft of a very high calibre, with many unique pieces.

One of Sydney's original thoroughfares – some say Australia's first street – it ran from the main water supply, the Tank Stream, to the tiny community in the Rocks, and was known as Spring Street. In 1810 it was renamed in honour of George III. George Street today runs all the way from the Harbour Bridge to the Central Railway Station north of Chinatown.

Many 19th-century buildings remain, such as the 1844 Counting House at No. 43, the Old Police station at No. 127 (1882), and the Russell Hotel at No. 143 (1887).

But it is The Rocks end that most reflects what the early colony must have looked like, characterized by cobbled pavements, narrow side streets, warehouses, bond stores, pubs and shop fronts that reflect the area's early maritime history. Even the Museum of Contemporary Art (*see p73*), constructed during the 1950s, began its life as the Maritime Services Board's administration offices.

In the early 1970s union workers placed "green bans" on the demolition of The Rocks (*see p29*). These streets had been considered slum areas by the government of the day. However many of the buildings in George Street were restored and are now listed by the National Trust. The Rocks remains a vibrant part of the city, with George Street at its hub. A market is held here every weekend, when part of the street is closed off to traffic (*see p203*).

The Rocks Toy Museum ❸

2–6 Kendall Lane, The Rocks.
Map 5 A4. ☎ 9251 9793.
🚌 *Sydney Explorer, 431, 432, 433, 434.* 🕙 *10am–5:30pm daily.*

This museum, in a restored 1850s coach house, is home to a collection of more than 10,000 toys, dating from

Umbrellas shade the terrace restaurants overlooking the waterfront at Campbell's Storehouses

Old-style Australian products at the corner shop, Susannah Place

Sailors' Home ❺

106 George St, The Rocks. **Map** 1 B2.
☎ 9255 1788. 🚌 *Sydney Explorer,
431, 432, 433, 434.* 🕘 *9am–6pm
daily.* ● *25 Dec.* 📷 ♿

BUILT IN 1864 as lodgings for
visiting sailors, the building
now houses The Sydney
Visitors Centre at street level,
with exhibitions on the two
upper levels. The L-shaped
wing that fronts onto George
Street was added in 1926.

At the time it was built, the
Sailors' Home was a welcome
alternative to the many seedy
inns and brothels in the area,
saving sailors from the perils
of "crimping". "Crimps" would
tempt newly arrived men into
lodgings and bars providing
much-sought-after entertainment. While drunk, the sailors
would be sold on to departing
ships, waking miles out at sea
and returning home in debt.

Sailors used the home until
1980, when it was adapted for
use as a puppet theatre. In
1994, it opened as a heritage
centre and a tourist information
and tour-booking facility.

On the second level, a permanent exhibition outlines the
archaeological, architectural
and social heritage of The
Rocks. The third level hosts
temporary exhibitions. On the
same level, at the eastern
end, a re-creation of a 19th-
century sleeping cubicle gives
visitors a good impression of
the spartan nature of the
original accommodation
available to sailors.

the 19th and 20th centuries. It
was assembled by toy lover
Ken Hinds, who continually
adds new finds to the collection. Among the delights on
show over two floors is a
fine assembly of model trains,
including a remarkably
detailed Bing train from the
1920s. On the upper level is a
display of rare
and unusual
Australian dolls,
assembled by the
Doll Collectors
Club of NSW.
There are some
lovely porcelain
dolls, as well as
others made of various
materials, including paper
maché, china and cloth.

**Billy Tea on sale at the
Susannah Place shop**

Susannah Place ❹

58–64 Gloucester St, The Rocks.
Map 1 B2. ☎ 9241 1893. 🚌 *Sydney
Explorer, 431, 432, 433, 434.* 🕘 *Jan:
10am–5pm daily; Feb–Dec: 10am–
5pm Sat & Sun.* ● *Good Fri, 25 Dec.*
♿ 📷 🛍

THIS 1844 TERRACE of four
brick and sandstone houses
has a rare history of continuous
domestic occupancy from the
1840s right through to 1990.
The museum now housed here
examines this working-class
domestic history, evoking the

living conditions of its inhabitants. Rather than re-creating
a single period, the museum
retains the many renovations
made by successive tenants.

Built for Edward and Mary
Riley, who arrived from Ireland
with their niece Susannah in
1838, these solid houses have
basement kitchens and backyard outhouses.
Connections to
piped water and
sewerage had
probably arrived
by the mid-1850s.
The museum sur-
veys the houses'
development over
the years, from wood and coal
to gas and electricity, which
enables the visitor to gauge
the gradual lightening of the
burden of domestic labour.

The terrace, including a corner grocer's shop, escaped the
wholesale demolitions that
occurred after the outbreak of
bubonic plague in 1900, as
well as later clearings of land
to make way for the Sydney
Harbour Bridge and the Cahill
Expressway. In the 1970s, it
was saved once again when
the Builders Labourers' Federation, under the leadership of
activist Jack Mundey, imposed
a conservation "green ban" on
The Rocks *(see p29),* temporar-
ily halting all demolition and
redevelopment work.

**Interior of the Sailors' Home,
looking down to the shop**

Façade of Cadman's Cottage, the oldest extant building in the city

Cadman's Cottage ❻

110 George St, The Rocks. **Map** 1 B2.
🏛 9247 5033. 🚌 431, 432, 433 434.
🕐 9am–5pm daily. ● Good Fri,
25 Dec. 📷

DWARFED BY the adjacent
Sailors' Home, of which it
was once part, this sandstone
cottage serves as the information centre for the Sydney
Harbour National Park and
has information about guided
harbour tours. Built in 1816 as
a barracks for the crews of the
governor's boats, it is Sydney's
oldest surviving dwelling.

The cottage is named after
John Cadman, a convict who
was transported in 1798 for
horse-stealing. By 1813, he was
coxswain of a timber boat and
the following year received a
conditional pardon. In 1821,
he was appointed coxswain of
government craft and granted
a full pardon. Six years later,
he was made boat superinten-
dent and took up residence in
the four-room cottage that
now bears his name.

Cadman married Elizabeth
Mortimer in 1830. She had also
arrived in Sydney as a convict,
sentenced to seven years transportation for the theft of one
hairbrush. The couple, along
with Elizabeth's two daughters,
lived in the cottage until 1846.

When Cadman's Cottage was
built it stood on the foreshore
of Sydney Harbour. At high
tide, the water used to lap just
2.5 m (8 ft) from the door.

Now, as a result of successive
land reclamations such as the
filling-in of Circular Quay in
the 1870s, it is set well back
from the waterfront.

Westpac Museum ❼

6–8 Playfair St, The Rocks.
Map 1 B2. 🏛 9763 5670. 🚌
Sydney Explorer, 431, 432, 433, 434.
🕐 10am–4pm Mon–Thu, 9am–5pm
Fri. ● public hols.

FROM 1817, WHEN the "holey"
dollar was in circulation and
Sydney's first bank opened, to
present-day plastic credit cards,
this museum, located on the
first floor, traces the history
of banking in Australia. It also
covers the Olympic history in
1956 and 2000 as Westpac
was a sponsor of both of
these games. There is a self-
guided tour with interactive
and holographic displays but
this small museum can be
seen in less than an hour.

Bank of New South Wales one pound note from around 1830

Argyle Stores ❽

18–24 Argyle St, The Rocks.
Map 1 B2. 🏛 9251 4800.
🚌 Sydney Explorer, 431, 432,
433, 434. 🕐 10am–6pm daily.
● Good Fri, 25 Dec. 📷 ♿

THE Argyle Stores consists
of a number of warehouses
around a cobbled courtyard.
They have been converted into
a retail complex of mostly
fashion and accessories shops
that retains its period character.

Built between 1826 and the
early 1880s, the stores held
imported goods such as spirits.
All goods forfeited for the
non-payment of duties were
auctioned in the courtyard.
The oldest store was built for
Captain John Piper, but it was
confiscated and sold after his
arrest for embezzlement.

Argyle Centre from the courtyard

Garrison Church ❾

Cnr Argyle and Lower Fort Sts, Millers
Point. **Map** 1 A2. 🏛 9247 1268.
🚌 431, 433. 🕐 9am–6pm daily.
📷 ♿

OFFICIALLY NAMED the Holy
Trinity Church, this was
dubbed the Garrison Church
because it was the colony's
first military church. Officers
and men from various British

regiments, stationed at Dawes Point fort, attended morning prayers here until 1870.

Henry Ginn designed the church and, in 1840, the foundation stone was laid. In 1855, the architect Edmund Blacket was engaged to enlarge the church to accommodate up to 600 people. These extensions, minus the spire that Blacket proposed, were completed in 1878. Regimental plaques hung along interior walls recall the church's military associations.

Other features to look out for are the brilliantly coloured east window and the carved red cedar pulpit. The window was donated by a devout parishioner, Dr James Mitchell, scion of a leading Sydney family. The church also houses a museum displaying early Australian military and historical items.

East window, Garrison Church

Sydney Observatory ⑩

Watson Rd, Observatory Hill, The Rocks. **Map** 1 A2. 📞 *9217 0485.* 🚌 *Sydney Explorer, 343, 431, 432: stop 22.* ⭘ *10am–5pm daily.* **Night viewings** ⭘ *phone for times (bookings essential).* ⬤ *25 Dec.* 📷🚻♿

I N 1982, THIS DOMED building, which had been a centre for astronomical observation and research for almost 125 years, became the city's astronomy museum. It has interactive equipment and games, along with night sky viewings; it is essential to book for these.

The building began life in the 1850s as a time-ball tower. At 1pm daily, the ball on top of the tower dropped to signal the correct time. A cannon was fired simultaneously at Fort Denison. This custom continues today *(see p107).*

In the 1880s, some of the first astronomical photographs of the southern sky were taken here. From 1890–1962, the observatory mapped 750,000 stars as part of an international project that produced an atlas of the entire night sky.

Hero of Waterloo ⑪

81 Lower Fort St, The Rocks. **Map** 1 A2. 📞 *9252 4553.* 🚌 *431, 432, 433, 434.* ⭘ *10am–11pm Mon– Thu, 10am–11:30pm Fri–Sat, 10am– 10pm Sun.* ⬤ *25 Dec.* 📷♿

T HIS PICTURESQUE old inn is especially welcoming in the winter, when its log fires and cosy ambience offer respite from the chill outside. Built in 1844 from sandstone excavated from the Argyle Cut, this was a favourite drinking place for the nearby garrison's soldiers. Unscrupulous sea captains were said to use the hotel to recruit. Patrons who drank themselves into a stupor were pushed into the cellars through a trapdoor. From here they were carried along underground tunnels to the wharves close by and then onto waiting ships.

Wharf Theatre ⑫

Pier 4, Hickson Rd, Walsh Bay. **Map** 1 A1. 📞 *9250 1700.* 🚌 *431, 432, 433, 434.* **Box office** ⭘ *9am–8:30pm Mon–Sat;* 📷 ♿ *phone in advance. See* **Entertainment** *p210.*

T HE THEN RECENTLY formed Sydney Theatre Company took possession of this early 20th-century finger wharf at Walsh Bay in 1984. Pier 4/5 is

The corner façade of the Hero of Waterloo hotel in Millers Point

one of four finger wharves at Walsh Bay, reminders of the time when this was a busy part of the city's maritime industry.

Pier 4/5 fulfilled the Sydney Theatre Company's need for a base large enough to hold theatres, rehearsal rooms and administration offices. The ingenious conversion of the once-derelict heritage building into a modern theatre complex is recognized as an outstanding architectural achievement.

Since then, the main theatre, a small and intimate space, has been a venue for many of the company's productions. It has seen premieres of plays from leading Australian playwrights such as Michael Gow and David Williamson, as well as performances of new works from overseas and plays from the standard repertoire.

At the tip of the wharf, the bar area and Wharf Restaurant *(see p189)* command superb harbour views across to the Harbour Bridge *(see pp70–71).*

The Wharf Theatre, a former finger wharf, jutting on to Walsh Bay

Sydney Harbour Bridge 🔞

Cༀ OMPLETED IN 1932, the construction of the
Sydney Harbour Bridge was an economic
feat, given the depressed times, as well as an
engineering triumph. Prior to this, the only links
between the city centre on the south side of the
harbour and the residential north side were by ferry
or a circuitous 20-km (12½-mile) road route with
five bridge crossings. Known as the "Coathanger",
the single-span arch bridge was manufactured in

**Ceremonial
scissors**

sections and took eight years to build, including
the railway line. Loans for the total cost of
approximately 6.25 million Australian pounds were paid
off in 1988. Intrepid visitors can make the vertiginous
climb to its summit, with spectacular views as reward.

The 1932 Opening
*The ceremony was disrupted
when zealous royalist Francis
de Groot rode forward and
cut the ribbon, in honour, he
claimed, of King and Empire.*

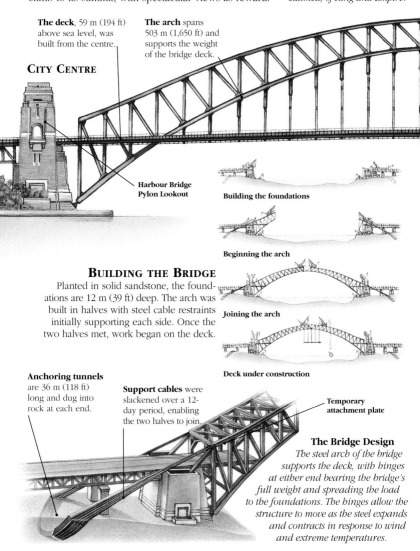

The deck, 59 m (194 ft)
above sea level, was
built from the centre.

The arch spans
503 m (1,650 ft) and
supports the weight
of the bridge deck.

CITY CENTRE

Harbour Bridge
Pylon Lookout

Building the foundations

Beginning the arch

BUILDING THE BRIDGE

Planted in solid sandstone, the foundations are 12 m (39 ft) deep. The arch was
built in halves with steel cable restraints
initially supporting each side. Once the
two halves met, work began on the deck.

Joining the arch

Deck under construction

Anchoring tunnels
are 36 m (118 ft)
long and dug into
rock at each end.

Support cables were
slackened over a 12-
day period, enabling
the two halves to join.

**Temporary
attachment plate**

The Bridge Design
*The steel arch of the bridge
supports the deck, with hinges
at either end bearing the bridge's
full weight and spreading the load
to the foundations. The hinges allow the
structure to move as the steel expands
and contracts in response to wind
and extreme temperatures.*

BridgeClimb
Thousands of people have enjoyed the spectacular bridge-top views after a 3.5-hour guided tour up ladders, catwalks and finally the upper arch of the bridge.

VISITORS' CHECKLIST

Map 1 B1. 9247 3408. all routes to The Rocks. Circular Quay. Circular Quay, Milsons Point. **BridgeClimb** 8274 7777 to book. **Harbour Bridge Pylon Lookout** 10am–5pm daily. 25, 31 Dec.

Over 150,000 vehicles cross the bridge each day, about 15 times as many as in 1932.

Bridge Workers
The bridge was built by 1,400 workers, 16 of whom were killed in accidents during construction.

NORTH SHORE

Maintenance
Painting the bridge has become a metaphor for an endless task. Approximately 30,000 litres (6,593 gal) of paint are required for each coat, enough to cover an area equivalent to 60 soccer pitches.

The vertical hangers support the slanting crossbeams which, in turn, carry the deck.

FATHER OF THE BRIDGE
Chief engineer Dr John Bradfield shakes the hand of the driver of the first train to cross the bridge. Over a 20-year period, Bradfield supervised all aspects of the bridge's design and construction. At the opening ceremony, the highway linking the harbour's south side and northern suburbs was named in his honour.

Paying the Toll
The initial toll of sixpence helped pay off the construction loan. The toll is now used for maintenance and to pay for the 1992 Sydney Harbour Tunnel.

Strolling along a section of the Writers' Walk at Circular Quay

Sydney Opera House **⑭**

See pp74–7.

Writers' Walk **⑮**

Circular Quay. **Map** 1 C2.
🚌 *Circular Quay routes.*

THIS SERIES OF PLAQUES is set in the pavement at regular intervals between East and West Circular Quay. It gives the visitor the chance to ponder the observations of famous Australian writers, both past and present, on their home country, as well as the musings of some noted literary visitors.

Each plaque is dedicated to a particular writer, with a quotation and a brief biographical note. Australian writers include novelists Miles Franklin and Peter Carey, poets Oodgeroo Noonuccal and Judith Wright, humorists Barry Humphries and Clive James, and the influential feminist writer Germaine Greer. Among visiting writers are Charles Darwin, Joseph Conrad and Mark Twain.

Justice and Police Museum **⑯**

Cnr Albert & Phillip sts. **Map** 1 C3.
📞 9252 1144. 🚌 *Circular Quay routes.* ◯ *10am–5pm Sat–Sun (Sat–Thu during Festival of Sydney).* ● *Good Fri, 25 Dec.* 📷 🚻 ♿

THE MUSEUM'S buildings were originally the Water Police Court, designed by Edmund Blacket in 1856; Water Police

Station, designed by Alexander Dawson in 1858; and Police Court designed by James Barnet in 1885. Here the rough-and-tumble underworld of quayside crime, from the petty to the violent, was dealt swift and, at times, harsh justice. The museum exhibits bear vivid testimony to that turbulent period, as they document and re-create legal and criminal history. Late-Victorian legal proceedings can be easily imagined in the fully restored courtroom.

Menacing implements from knuckledusters to bludgeons are displayed as the macabre relics of violent and notorious crimes. Other aspects of policing and justice are highlighted in regularly changing exhibitions. The charge room, remand cell, prison uniforms, prison artifacts and slideshow evoke powerful images of the penal code of the time.

Montage of criminal "mug shots", Justice and Police Museum

Customs House **⑰**

31 Alfred St, Circular Quay. **Map** 1 B3. 📞 9247 2285. 🚌 *Circular Quay routes.* **Gallery** ◯ *10am–5pm Tue-Sun.* 📷 🖥 ♿ ● *25 Dec, Good Fri.*

COLONIAL ARCHITECT James Barnet designed this 1885 sandstone Classical Revival building on the site of an earlier Customs House. It recalls the days when trading ships loaded and unloaded their goods at the quay. Features include columns in polished granite, a sculpted coat of arms and a clock face, added in 1897, bearing a pair of tridents and dolphins. The Australian Centre for Craft and Design (The Object Gallery) is found here, and its shop, The Object Store, sells contemporary glassware by Australian designers. There are also shops, cafés and a performance space. The City Exhibition Space explores Sydney's architecture and its plans for the future.

Detail from Customs House

Macquarie Place **⑱**

Map 1 B3. 🚌 *Circular Quay routes.*

IN 1810, GOVERNOR Lachlan Macquarie created this park on what was once part of the vegetable garden of the first Government House. The sandstone obelisk, designed by convict architect Francis Greenway *(see p114),* was erected in 1818 to mark the starting point for all roads in the colony. The gas lamps recall the fact that this was also the site of Sydney's first street lamp, installed in 1826.

Also in this little triangle of history are the remains of the bow anchor and cannon from HMS *Sirius,* flagship of the First Fleet. There is also a statue of Thomas Mort, a 19th-century industrialist whose vast business interests embraced gold, coal and copper mining, dairy and cotton farming, wool auctioning and ship repair. These days his statue is a marshalling place for the city's somewhat kamikaze bicycle couriers.

Façade of the Museum of Contemporary Art

Museum of Contemporary Art ⑲

Circular Quay West, The Rocks.
Map 1 B2. 🛈 9252 4033. 🚌 Sydney Explorer, 431, 432, 433 434. 🕐 10am–5pm daily. ⬤ 25 Dec. 📷 ⚊ book in advance. ✉

Sydney's substantial collection of contemporary art has grown steadily, but largely out of public view, since 1943. This was the year John Power died, leaving his art collection and a financial bequest to the University of Sydney.

In 1991 the permanent collection, including works by Hockney, Warhol, Lichtenstein and Christo, was transferred to this 1950s mock Art Deco former Maritime Services Board Building at Circular Quay West, which also hosts exhibitions. A two-year renovation project is planned to commence in 2002.

At the front of the building the MCA Café (*see p194*) spills out onto a terrace with superb views across to the Sydney Opera House. The MCA Store sells distinctive gifts by Australian designers.

National Trust Centre ⑳

Observatory Hill, Watson Rd, The Rocks. **Map** 1 A3. 🛈 9258 0123. 🚌 Sydney Explorer, 343, 431, 432, 433, 434. 🕐 11am–5pm Tue–Fri. **Gallery** 🕐 11am–5pm Tue–Fri, noon–5pm Sat & Sun. ⬤ some public hols. ⚊

The buildings that form the headquarters of the conservation organization, the National Trust of Australia, date from 1815, when Macquarie chose the site on Observatory Hill for a military hospital.

Today they house tea rooms, a National Trust shop and the SH Ervin Gallery, containing works by prominent 19th- and 20th-century Australian artists such as Thea Proctor, Margaret Preston and Conrad Martens.

St Philip's Church ㉑

3 York St (enter from Jamison St). **Map** 1 A3. 🛈 9247 1071. 🚌 George St routes. 🕐 11am–2pm Tue–Fri. ⬤ 26 Jan, 25 Apr. 📷 ⚊ 🛈 8am, 10am, 5pm Sun, 1pm Wed.

Despite its elevated site, this Victorian Gothic church seems overshadowed in its modern setting. Yet, when it was first built, the tall square tower with its decorative pinnacles was a local landmark.

Begun in 1848, St Philip's is by Edmund Blacket, dubbed "the Christopher Wren of Australia" for the 58 churches he designed. In 1851, work was disrupted when its stonemasons left for the gold fields, but was completed by 1856.

A peal of bells was donated in 1858, with another added in 1888 to mark Sydney's centenary. These bells still announce the services each Sunday.

The interior and pipe organ of St Philip's Anglican church

***The Founding of Australia** by Algernon Talmage, which hangs in Parliament House (see pp112–13)*

A FLAGPOLE ON THE MUDFLATS

It is easy to miss the modest flagpole in Loftus Street near Customs House. It flies a flag, the Union Jack, on the spot where Australia's first ceremonial flag-raising took place. On 26 January 1788, Captain Arthur Phillip came ashore to hoist the flag and declare the foundation of the colony. A toast to the King was drunk and a musket volley fired. On the same day, the rest of the First Fleet arrived from Botany Bay to join Phillip and his men. (On this date each year, the country marks Australia Day with a national holiday.) In 1788, the flagpole was on the edge of mudflats on Sydney Cove. Today, because of the large amount of land reclaimed to build Circular Quay, it is some distance from the water's edge.

Sydney Opera House ⑭

Advertising poster

NO BUILDING ON EARTH looks like the Sydney Opera House. Popularly known as the "Opera House" long before the building was complete, it is, in fact, a complex of theatres and halls linked beneath its famous shells. Its birth was long and complicated. Many of the construction problems had not been faced before, resulting in an architectural adventure which lasted 17 years *(see p77)*. An appeal fund was set up, eventually raising $900,000, while the Opera House Lottery raised the balance of the $102 million final cost. As well as being the city's most popular tourist attraction, the Sydney Opera House is also one of the world's busiest performing arts centres.

★ **Opera Theatre**
Mainly used for opera and ballet, this 1,547-seat theatre is big enough to stage grand operas such as Verdi's Aida.

The Opera Theatre ceiling and walls are painted black to focus attention on the stage.

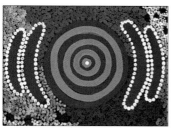

Detail of The Possum Dreaming *(1988)*
The mural in the Opera Theatre foyer is by Michael Tjakamarra Nelson, an artist from the central Australian desert.

Opera House Walkway
Extensive public walkways around the building offer the visitor views from many different vantage points.

STAR FEATURES
★ **The Roofs**
★ **Concert Hall**
★ **Opera Theatre**

Northern Foyers
With spectacular views over the harbour, the Reception Hall and the large northern foyers of the Opera Theatre and Concert Hall can be hired for conferences, lunches, parties and weddings.

★ **Concert Hall**
This is the largest hall, with seating for 2,679. It is used for symphony, choral, jazz, folk and pop concerts, chamber music, opera, dance and everything from body building to fashion parades.

The Monumental Steps and forecourt are used for outdoor entertainment.

Bennelong Restaurant
This dramatic and elegant venue is one of the finest restaurants in Sydney (see p193).

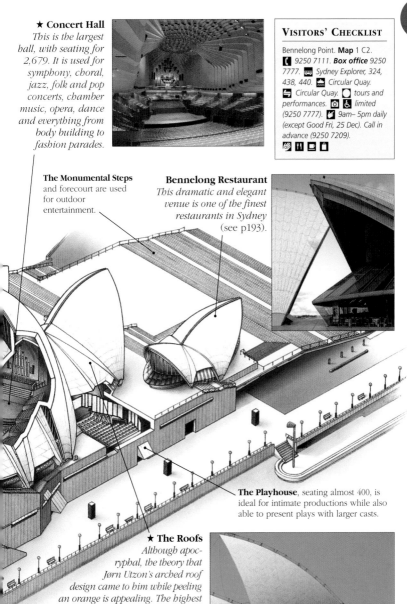

The Playhouse, seating almost 400, is ideal for intimate productions while also able to present plays with larger casts.

★ **The Roofs**
Although apocryphal, the theory that Jørn Utzon's arched roof design came to him while peeling an orange is appealing. The highest point is 67 m (221 ft) above sea level.

Curtain of the Moon *(1972)*
Designed by John Coburn, this and its fellow Curtain of the Sun were originally used in the Drama and Opera Theatres. Both have been removed for preservation.

Exploring Sydney Opera House

THE SYDNEY OPERA HOUSE covers almost 2 ha (4.5acres), and is the fourth building to stand on this prominent site. Underneath the ten spectacular roofs of varying planes and textures lies a complex maze of more than 1,000 rooms of all shapes and sizes. It is constantly evolving: the newest space is The Studio, dedicated to innovative, contemporary performing arts.

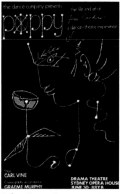

Sydney Dance Company poster

Coppelia **in the Opera Theatre**

OPERA THEATRE

THE RELATIVELY compact size of this venue is a bonus for patrons who savour intimacy. Stage designers continue to demonstrate the opera theatre's great versatility for both opera and dance. The proscenium opening is 12 m (39 ft) wide, and the stage extends back 21 m (69 ft), while the orchestra pit accommodates up to 70–80 musicians. It is rumoured that Box C plays host to a resident ghost.

CONCERT HALL

THE RICH concert acoustics under the vaulted ceiling of this venue are much admired. Sumptuous Australian wood panelling and the 18 acoustic rings above the stage clearly reflect back the sound. The 10,500 pipe Grand Organ was designed and built by Ronald Sharp from 1969–79.

DRAMA THEATRE AND PLAYHOUSE

THE DRAMA THEATRE was not in the original building plan, so jackhammers were brought in to hack it out of the concrete. Its stage is 15 m (160 ft) square, and can be clearly viewed from every seat in the auditorium. Refrigerated aluminium panels in the ceiling control the temperature.

Fine Australian art hangs in the Playhouse foyer, notably Sidney Nolan's eye-catching *Little Shark* (1973) and a fresco by Salvatore Zofrea (1992–3), inspired by the play *Summer of the Seventeenth Doll.*

BACKSTAGE

ARTISTS PERFORMING at the Opera House have the use of five rehearsal studios, 60 dressing rooms and suites and a green room complete with restaurant, bar and lounge.

The scene-changing machinery works on very well-oiled wheels; most crucial in the Opera Theatre where there is regularly a nightly change of performance, with an average of 16 operas being performed in repertoire each year.

John Olsen's *Salute to Five Bells* **(1973) in the Concert Hall foyer**

TIMELINE

1955 International design competition announced

1948 Sir Eugene Goossens lobbies government and Bennelong Point is chosen as opera house site

1957 Utzon's design wins and a lottery is established to finance the building

1963 Building of roof shells begins

Roof in mid-construction

1973 Opera House officially opened by Queen Elizabeth II

1945	1950	1955	1960	1965	1970

1959 Construction begins

Old tram shed at Bennelong Point

1963 Utzon opens Sydney office

1966 Utzon resigns. Australian architects appointed to complete interior design

1967 Concrete roof shells completed

1973 Prokofiev's opera *War and Peace* is the first public performance in Opera House

The Design of the Opera House

Jørn Utzon

IN 1957, JØRN UTZON won the international competition to design the Sydney Opera House. He envisaged a living sculpture that could be viewed from any angle – land, air or sea – with the roofs as a "fifth façade". It was boldly conceived, posing architectural and engineering problems that Utzon's initial compendium of sketches did not begin to solve. When construction began in 1959, the intricate design proved impossible to execute and had to be greatly modified. The project remained so controversial that Utzon resigned in 1966 and an Australian design team completed the building's interior. However, he has since been reappointed as a consultant, to develop a set of guiding principles for any future alterations.

The Red Book, *as submitted for the 1957 design competition, contains Utzon's original concept sketches for the Sydney Opera House.*

Segmented globe

Segments separated

Roof comes into view

Several pieces *cut out of a globe were used in an ingenious manner by architect Jørn Utzon to make up the now familiar shell roof structure.*

UTZON'S OPERA HOUSE MODEL

Shell membrane roof

The northern foyers overlook Sydney Harbour.

Utzon visualized a building that "floated" on water.

The construction materials remain clearly exposed.

Stepped base

Utzon's original interiors and many of his design features now exist only in model form. The architect donated his models and plans to the State Library of NSW (see p112).

The pre-cast roof has its inspiration in nature. The basic idea for the formwork of the roof was taken from the fanlike ribs of a palm. Realizing this deceptively simple idea took Utzon six years of design work.

The roof tiles were not fixed in place individually, but installed in panels to create the smooth and continuous roof surface.

THE ARCHIBALD MEMORIAL FOUNTAIN

CITY CENTRE

Australia's first thoroughfare, George Street, was
originally lined with
clusters of mud and wattle
huts. The gold rushes brought
bustling prosperity, and by the
1880s shops and the architecturally majestic edifices of
banks dominated the area.
The city's first skyscraper – Culwulla
Chambers in Castlereagh Street – was
completed in 1913, but the city council
then imposed a 46-m (150-ft) height
restriction which remained in place
until 1956. Hyde Park, on the edge of
the city centre, was first used as a race-

**Mosaic floor detail,
St Mary's Cathedral**

course, attracting illegal betting
and gambling taverns to Elizabeth Street. The park later
hosted other amusements:
wrestling matches, circuses,
public hangings and, from
1804 onwards, cricket matches
between the army and the
town. Today it provides a
peaceful oasis, while the city's
commercial centre is an area of
glamorous boutiques, department
stores, arcades and malls. Exercise
needs are also catered for: the Cook
& Phillip Park Centre in College Street
is a great pool and gym complex.

SIGHTS AT A GLANCE

**Historic Streets and
Buildings**
Marble Bar **1**
Queen Victoria Building **2**
Strand Arcade **5**
Martin Place **6**
Lands Department Building **7**
Sydney Town Hall **12**

Museums and Galleries
Museum of Sydney **8**
*Australian Museum
pp88–9* **14**

Landmarks
*Sydney Tower
p83* **4**

Cathedrals and Synagogues
St Mary's Cathedral **9**
Great Synagogue **11**
St Andrew's Cathedral **13**

Parks and Gardens
Hyde Park **10**

Theatres
State Theatre **3**

GETTING THERE
Town Hall, Wynyard, Martin
Place, St James and Museum
railway stations serve the area.
There are frequent buses, particularly along Elizabeth and
George Streets. Monorail stops
are at City Centre, Park Plaza
and World Square.

0 metres   500

0 yards   500

KEY

    Street-by-Street map
    See p80–81

    CityRail station

    Monorail station

    Bus terminus

    Parking

◁ **Mythological figures in the Archibald Fountain, Hyde Park**

Street-by-Street: City Centre

Sculpture outside the MLC Centre

ALTHOUGH CLOSELY RIVALLED by Melbourne, this is the business and commercial capital of Australia. Vibrant by day, at night the streets are far less busy when office workers and shoppers have gone home. The comparatively small city centre of this sprawling metropolis seems to be almost jammed into a few city blocks. Because Sydney grew in such a haphazard fashion, with many of today's streets following tracks from the harbour originally made by bullocks, there was no allowance for the expansion of the burgeoning city into what has become a major international centre. A colourful night scene of cafés, restaurants and theatres is emerging, however, as more people return to the city centre to live.

★ **Queen Victoria Building**
Taking up an entire city block, this 1898 former produce market has been lovingly restored and is now a shopping mall ❷

State Theatre
A gem from the era when the movies reigned, this glittering and richly decorated 1929 cinema was once hailed as "the Empire's greatest theatre" ❸

To Sydney Town Hall

The Queen Victoria Statue was found after a worldwide search in 1983 ended in a small Irish village. It had lain forgotten and neglected since being removed from the front of the Irish Parliament in 1947.

Marble Bar
Once a landmark bar in the 1890 Tattersalls hotel, it was dismantled and re-erected in the Sydney Hilton in 1973 ❶

STAR SIGHTS

★ **Queen Victoria Building**

★ **AMP Tower**

★ **Martin Place**

0 metres   100

0 yards   100

KEY

— — — Suggested route

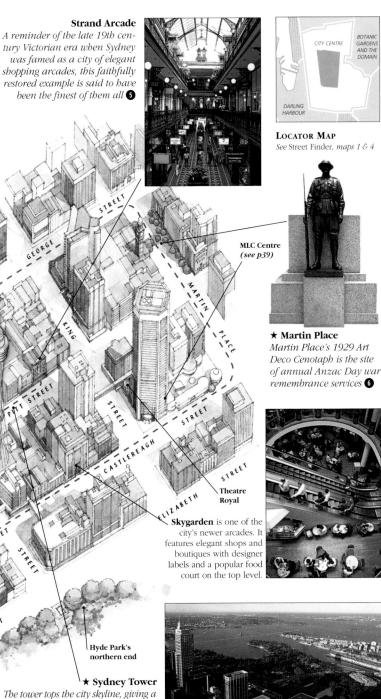

Strand Arcade
A reminder of the late 19th century Victorian era when Sydney was famed as a city of elegant shopping arcades, this faithfully restored example is said to have been the finest of them all **5**

LOCATOR MAP
See Street Finder, maps 1 & 4

MLC Centre
(see p39)

★ **Martin Place**
Martin Place's 1929 Art Deco Cenotaph is the site of annual Anzac Day war remembrance services **6**

Theatre Royal

Skygarden is one of the city's newer arcades. It features elegant shops and boutiques with designer labels and a popular food court on the top level.

Hyde Park's northern end

★ **Sydney Tower**
The tower tops the city skyline, giving a bird's eye view of the whole of Sydney. It rises 305 m (1,000 ft) above the ground and can be seen from as far away as the Blue Mountains **4**

Entrance to the Marble Bar

The Marble Bar ❶

259 Pitt St. **Map** 1 B5. 🔲 9266 2000 🚌 George St routes. ⏲ 3pm–11pm Mon–Wed, 3pm–midnight Thu, 3pm–2am Fri, 5pm–2am Sat. ⬤ public hols. 📷 See **Restaurants, Cafés and Pubs** p197.

T HE MARBLE BAR, originally part of George Adams' Tattersalls Hotel built in 1893, is an inspired link with the Sydney of an earlier era. The bar, whose rich and decadent Italian Renaissance style had made it a local institution, was dismantled before the demolition of the hotel in 1969. Its colonnade entrance, fireplaces and counters were re-erected in the Sydney Hilton basement and reopened in 1973.

During the week, the bar attracts a broad range of city workers for after-work drinks. On Fridays and at weekends if a band is playing, the bar bustles with a younger crowd who come to hear the mostly jazz and rhythm and blues music.

Queen Victoria Building ❷

455 George St. **Map** 1 B5. 🔲 9264 9209. 🚌 George St routes. ⏲ 9am–6pm Mon–Wed, 9am–9pm Thu, 9am–6pm Fri & Sat, 11am–5pm Sun & public hols. 📷 ♿ 🛍 See **Shops and Markets** pp198 and 200.

F RENCH DESIGNER Pierre Cardin called the Queen Victoria Building "the most beautiful shopping centre in the world". Yet this spacious and ornate Romanesque building, better known as the QVB, began life as the Sydney produce market. The dust, flies, grime and shouts as horses struggled with heavy loads on the slippery ramps are now difficult to imagine. Completed to the design of City Architect George McRae in 1898, the dominant features are the central dome, sheathed in copper, as are the 20 smaller domes, and the glass barrel vault roof which lets in a flood of natural light.

The market closed at the end of World War I and the building fell into disrepair. It had various roles during this time, including that of City Library. By the 1950s, after extensive remodelling and neglect, it was threatened with demolition.

Refurbished at a cost of over $75 million, the QVB reopened in 1986 as today's grand shopping gallery, housing over 190 shops and boutiques on four levels. At the Town Hall end a wishing well incorporates a

Roof detail, Queen Victoria Building

stone from Blarney Castle, Ireland and a sculpture of Islay, beloved dog of Queen Victoria. In 1983, a worldwide search began for a statue of the queen herself. One was finally found in the village of Daingean, Republic of Ireland, where it had lain forgotten since its removal from the front of the Irish Parliament in 1947.

Now fully restored, the Queen Victoria Statue stands near the wishing well. Inside the QVB, suspended from the ceiling, is the Royal Clock. Weighing more than 1 tonne and over 5 m (17 ft) tall, the clock was designed by Neil Glasser in 1982. The upper structure features part of Balmoral Castle above a copy of the four dials of Big Ben. At one minute to every hour, a fanfare is played and there follows a parade depicting six scenes from the lives of various kings and queens of England.

State Theatre ❸

49 Market St. **Map** 1 B5. 🔲 9373 6861. **Tours** 9373 6660. 🚌 George St routes. **Box office** ⏲ 9am–5:30pm Mon–Fri. ⬤ Good Fri, 25 Dec. ♿ 🛍 bookings essential. 🌐 www.statetheatre.com.au.

W HEN IT OPENED in 1929, this picture palace was hailed as the finest that local craftsmanship could achieve. The State Theatre is one of the best examples in Australia of the architectural fantasies used to entice people to the movies.

Its Cinema Baroque style is evident right from the Gothic foyer, with its vaulted ceiling, mosaic floor, richly decorated marble columns and statues. Inside the brass and bronze doors, the auditorium, which seats over 2,000 people, is lit by a 20,000-piece chandelier. The Wurlitzer organ (currently under repair) rises from below stage just before performances. Now one of Sydney's premier concert and theatre venues, it is also the main base for the Sydney Film Festival, held in June of each year (see p51).

The ornately decorated Gothic foyer of the State Theatre

Sydney Tower ④

THE HIGHEST OBSERVATION DECK in the Southern Hemisphere, the Sydney Tower, formerly known as the AMP Tower, was conceived as part of the 1970s Centrepoint shopping centre, but was not completed until 1981. Approximately a million people visit the turret each year to appreciate stunning 360-degree views, often stretching for over 85 km (53 miles). A landmark in itself, it can be seen from almost anywhere in the city, and far beyond.

The 30-m (98-ft) spire completes the total 305 m (1,000 ft) of the tower's height.

The water tank holds 162,000 litres (35,500 gallons) and acts as an enormous stabilizer on very windy days.

Level 4: **Observation**

Level 3: **Coffee shop**

Level 2: **Buffet restaurant**

Level 1: **A la carte restaurant**

Observation Level
Views from Level 4 stretch to Pittwater in the north, Botany Bay to the south, westwards to the Blue Mountains, and along the harbour out to the open sea.

The turret's nine levels, with room to hold almost 1,000 people at a time, include two revolving restaurants, a coffee shop and the Observation Level.

The windows comprise three layers. The outer has a gold dust coating. The frame design prevents panes falling outwards.

The 56 cables weigh seven tonnes each. If laid end to end, they would reach from New Zealand to Sydney.

The shaft is designed to withstand wind speeds expected only once in 500 years, as well as unprecedented earthquakes.

The stairs are two separate, fireproofed emergency escape routes. Each year in September or October Sydney's fittest race up the 1,474 stairs.

Construction of Turret
The eight turret levels were erected on the roof of the base building, then hoisted up the shaft using hydraulic jacks.

Double-decker lifts can carry up to 2,000 people per hour. At full speed, a lift takes only 40 seconds to ascend the 76 floors to the Observation Level.

New Year's Eve
Every year, fireworks are set off on top of the tower as part of the official public fireworks displays to mark the New Year.

Strand Arcade ❺

412–414 George St. **Map** 1 B5.
☎ 9232 4199. 🚌 George St routes.
🕐 9am–5:30pm Mon–Wed & Fri,
9am–9pm Thu, 9am–4pm Sat,
11am–4pm Sun. ● most public
hols. 📷 See **Shops and Markets**
pp198–201.

VICTORIAN SYDNEY was a city
of grand shopping arcades.
The Strand, joining George and
Pitt Streets and designed by
English architect John Spencer,
was the finest jewel in the city's
crown. The blaze of publicity
surrounding its opening in
April 1892 was equalled only
by the natural light pouring
through the glass roof and the
artificial glare from the chan-
deliers, each carrying 50 jets
of gas as well as 50 lamps.
    The boutiques and shops in
the galleries make window
shopping a delight in this airy
building which, after a fire in
1976, was restored to its original splendour. Be sure to stop,
as shoppers have done since
opening day, for refreshments
at the Old Sydney Coffee Shop
near the Pitt Street entrance.

**The Pitt Street entrance to the
majestic Strand Arcade**

Martin Place ❻

Map 1 B4. 🚌 George St & Elizabeth
St routes.

RUNNING FROM George Street
across Pitt, Castlereagh and
Elizabeth Streets to Macquarie
Street, this plaza was opened
in 1891 and made a traffic-free
precinct in 1971. It is busiest at
lunchtime when city workers
enjoy their sandwiches while
watching free entertainment,

Interior of National Australia Bank, George Street end of Martin Place

sponsored by the Sydney City
Council, in a performance
space near Castlereagh Street.
    Every Anzac Day, a national
day of war remembrance on
25 April, the focus moves to
the Cenotaph at the George
Street end. Thousands of past
and present servicemen and
women attend a dawn service
and wreath-laying ceremony,
followed by a march-past. The
shrine, with bronze statues of a
soldier and a sailor on a granite
base, by Bertram MacKennal,
was unveiled in 1929.
    On the southern side of the
Cenotaph is the symmetrical
façade of the Renaissance-
style General Post Office,
considered to be the finest
building by James Barnet,
Colonial Architect. Con-
struction of the GPO, as
Sydneysiders call it, took
place between 1866 and
1874, with additions in
Pitt Street between 1881
and 1885. Most contro-
versial were the relief
figures executed by
Tomaso Sani. Although
Barnet declared that
the figures represented
Australians in realistic form,
they were labelled "grotesque".
    A stainless steel sculpture
of upended cubes, the Dobell
Memorial Sculpture stands
above a waterfall which was

**Statue of explorer
Gregory Blaxland**

funded by public subscription
following a donation by artist
Lloyd Rees. The sculpture, a
tribute to the artist William
Dobell (see p29), was created
by Bert Flugelman in 1979.

Lands Department
Building ❼

23 Bridge St. **Map** 1 B3. 🚌 325,
George St routes. 🕐 only 2 weeks in
the year, dates vary. &

DESIGNED BY the Colonial
Architect James Barnet, the
three-storey Classical Revival
    sandstone edifice was built
    between 1877 and 1890.
    As for the GPO building,
    Pyrmont sandstone was
    used for the exterior.
    Decisions about the sub-
    division of much of rural
    eastern Australia were
    made in offices within.
    Statues of explorers and
    legislators who "pro-
    moted settlement" fill
    23 of the façade's 48
    niches; the remainder
    are still empty. The
    luminaries include the
explorers Hovell and Hume,
Sir Thomas Mitchell, Blaxland,
Lawson and Wentworth (see
p136), Ludwig Leichhardt, Bass
and Matthew Flinders and the
botanist Sir Joseph Banks.

Museum of Sydney ➑

Cnr Bridge & Phillip Sts. **Map** 1 B3.
☎ 9251 5988. **🚌** Circular Quay
routes. **◯** 9:30am–5pm daily. **◯**
Good Fri, 25 Dec. **🎫 📷 ♿**

Sɪᴛᴜᴀᴛᴇᴅ ᴀᴛ the base of
Governor Phillip Tower, the
Museum of Sydney is on the
site of the first Government
House, the home, office and
seat of authority for the first
nine governors of NSW from
1788 until its demolition in
1846. The design assimilates
a valuable archaeological site
into a modern office block.
The museum itself traces the
city's turbulent history, from
the 1788 arrival of the British
colonists until the present day.

Indigenous Peoples
The museum sits on Cadigal
land. A new gallery explores
the culture, history, continuity
and place of Sydney's original
Aboriginal inhabitants, and the
"turning point" of colonization/
invasion. Collectors' chests
hold items of daily use such
as flint and ochre, each piece
painstakingly catalogued and
evocatively interpreted.

There are two audio-visual
exhibits which explore the
history of indigenous peoples
from a contemporary

**The Lookout, Level 3, overlooking
the piazza towards Circular Quay**

perspective. In the square at
the front of the complex, the
acclaimed *Edge of the Trees*
sculpture, with its collection
of 29 sandstone, steel and
wooden pillars, symbolizes
the first contact
between the
Aboriginal peoples
and Europeans.
Haunting voices
in the Eora tongue
fill the space.
Inscribed in the
wood are signa-
tures of the First
Fleeters and
names of botanical
species in both the
indigenous language and
Latin. Incisions made in the
pillars are filled with organic
materials such as ash, feathers,
bone, shells and human hair.

**Display from Trade
exhibition on Level 2**

History of Sydney
Outside the museum, a paving
pattern outlines the site of first
Government House. Original
foundations, lost under street
level for many years, can be
seen here through a window.
Inside the entrance a viewing
floor reveals more foundations.
A segment of wall has been
reconstructed using sandstone
excavated during archaeological exploration of the site.

The Colony display on
Level 2 focuses on Sydney
during the critical decade of
the 1840s when convict
transportation ended, the
town officially became a city
and suffered an economic
depression. There is also a set
of scale models of the 11 First
Fleet ships. The Museum
presents stories
of the Fleet's
journey, arrival,
first contacts with
Indigenous
people and the
survival challenges
faced by those
on board.

On Level 3, 20th
century Sydney
is explored with
panoramic images
of the developing city
providing a vivid backdrop.
The Museum of Sydney has a
changing exhibition program
every four months.

Edge of the Trees **sculptural installation by Janet Laurence and Fiona Foley (1995)**

Terrazzo mosaic floor in the crypt of St Mary's Cathedral

sculpted by Bertram MacKennal, also responsible for the Martin Place Cenotaph *(see p84)* and the Shakespeare group outside the State Library *(see p112)*. The crypt's Celtic-inspired terrazzo mosaic floor took 15 years to complete.

St Mary's Cathedral ⑨

Cathedral St. **Map** 1 C5. 9220 0400. Elizabeth St routes. 6:30am–6:30pm Mon–Fri, 8am–7:30pm Sat, 6:30am–7:30pm Sun. with advance notice. noon Sun. www.sydney.catholic.org.au

ALTHOUGH Catholics arrived with the First Fleet, the celebration of Mass was at first prohibited in case the priests provoked civil strife among the colony's large Irish Catholic population. The first priests were appointed in 1820 and services allowed. In 1821, Governor Macquarie laid the foundation stone for St Mary's Chapel on the site of today's cathedral, the first land granted to the Catholic Church in Australia.

The initial section of the Gothic Revival style cathedral was opened in 1882. In 1928, the building was completed, but without the twin southern spires proposed by the architect, William Wardell. By the entrance steps are statues of Australia's first cardinal, Moran, and Archbishop Kelly who laid the stone for the final stage in 1913. They were

Great Synagogue ⑪

187 Elizabeth St, entrance on 166 Castlereagh St. **Map** 1 B5. 9267 2477. 394, 396, 380, 382. for services and tours. noon Tue, Thu, except public & Jewish hols.

THE LONGEST established Jewish Orthodox congregation in Australia, consisting of more than 900 families, assembles in this synagogue, consecrated in 1878.

Candelabra from the Great Synagogue

Although Jews had arrived with the First Fleet, worship did not begin until the 1820s. With its carved entrance columns and magnificent stained-glass windows, the synagogue is perhaps the finest work of Thomas Rowe, the architect of Sydney Hospital *(see p113)*. The panelled ceiling is decorated with hundreds of tiny gold leaf stars.

Hyde Park ⑩

Map 1 B5. Elizabeth St routes.

FENCED AND NAMED after its London equivalent by Governor Macquarie in 1810, Hyde Park marked the outskirts of the township. It was a popular exercise field for garrison troops and later incorporated a racecourse and a cricket pitch. Though much smaller today than the original park, it still provides a peaceful haven in the middle of the bustling city centre.

Anzac Memorial
The 30-m (98-ft) high Art Deco memorial, reflected in the poplar-lined Pool of Remembrance, commemorates those Australians who were killed at war in the service of their country. Opened in 1934, the Anzac Memorial now includes a photographic and military artifact exhibition downstairs.

Sandringham Garden
In spring, the pergola in this sunken garden is a cascade of mauve-flowering wisteria. The garden, a memorial to the English kings George V and George VI, was opened by Queen Elizabeth II in 1954.

Tomb of the Unknown Soldier in the Art Deco Anzac Memorial

Diana, goddess of purity and the chase, Archibald Fountain

Archibald Fountain
This bronze and granite fountain commemorates the French and Australian World War I alliance. It was completed by François Sicard in 1932 and donated by JF Archibald, one of the founders of the *Bulletin*, a popular literary magazine which encouraged the work of Henry Lawson and "Banjo" Paterson, among many others. It was Archibald's bequest that established the Archibald Prize for portraiture *(see p50)*.

The Grand Organ in Sydney Town Hall's Centennial Hall

Sydney Town Hall ⓬

483 George St. **Map** 4 E2.
📞 9265 9333. 🚌 George St routes.
🕐 8:30am–6pm Mon–Fri.
⬤ public hols. ♿ 📠 8223 3815.

THE STEPS of this sandstone building, central to George Street's Victorian architecture, have been a favourite Sydney meeting place since it opened in 1869. Walled burial grounds had originally covered the site.

It is a fine example of high Victorian architecture, even though the plans of the original architect, JH Wilson, proved

beyond the builders' capabilities. A rapid succession of designers was brought in. The vestibule – an elegant salon with intricate plasterwork, lavish stained glass and a crystal chandelier – is the work of Albert Bond. The Bradbridge brothers completed the clock tower in 1884. From 1888–9, other architects were used for the Centennial Hall, with its coffered zinc ceiling and an imposing 19th-century organ with more than 8,500 pipes.

On the façade, you will see numerous carved lion heads. Just to the north of the main entrance, facing George Street, a lion has been carved with one eye shut. This oddity appeared because of the head stonemason's habit of checking the line of the stonework by closing one eye. The sly joke was not found until work was finished.

Some people have concluded that Sydney Town Hall became the city's most elaborate building by accident, as each architect strove to outdo his predecessors. Today, it makes a magnificent venue for concerts, dances and balls.

The Great Bible, St Andrew's Cathedral

St Andrew's Cathedral ⓭

Sydney Square, Cnr George & Bathurst Sts. **Map** 4 E3. 📞 9265 1661. 🚌 George St routes. 🕐 Contact the cathedral for opening hours and tour times. 📷 ♿

WHILE THE FOUNDATION stone for the country's oldest cathedral was laid in 1819, almost 50 years elapsed before the building was consecrated in 1868. The Gothic Revival design is by Edmund Blacket, whose ashes are interred here. Inspired by York Minster in England, the twin towers were completed in 1874. In 1949, the main entrance was moved to the eastern end near George Street.

Inside are memorials to Sydney pioneers, including Thomas Mort (see p72). A 1539 bible and beads collected in the Holy Land are among the religious memorabilia.

The southern wall incorporates stones from London's St Paul's Cathedral, Westminster Abbey and the House of Lords.

Obelisk
This monument was dubbed "Thornton's Scent Bottle" after the mayor of Sydney who had it erected in 1857. The mock-Egyptian edifice is in fact a ventilator for a sewer.

***Emden* Gun**
Standing at the corner of College and Liverpool Streets, this monument commemorates a World War I naval action. HMAS *Sydney* destroyed the German raider *Emden* off the Cocos Islands on 9 November 1914, and 180 crew members were taken prisoner.

City Circle Railway
The park we see today bears very little resemblance to the Hyde Park of old. In fact, the dictates of city railway tunnels have largely created its present landscape. Tunnels were excavated through an open cut that

ran through the park, and after the rail system was opened in 1926 the entire area had to be remodelled and replanted.

Busby's Bore Fountain
This is a reminder of Busby's Bore, the city's first piped water supply opened in 1837.

John Busby, a civil engineer, conceived and supervised the construction of the 4.4-km (2¾-mile) tunnel. It carried water from bores on Lachlan Swamp, now within Centennial Park (see p127), to horse-drawn water carriers on the corner of Elizabeth and Park Streets.

Game in progress on the giant chessboard, near Busby's Bore Fountain

Australian Museum ⑭

Model head of
Tyrannosaurus rex

THE AUSTRALIAN MUSEUM, the nation's leading natural science museum, founded in 1827, was the first museum established and remains the premier showcase of Australian natural history. The main building, an impressive sandstone structure with a marble staircase, faces Hyde Park. Architect Mortimer Lewis was forced to resign his position when building costs began to far exceed the budget. Construction was completed in the 1860s by James Barnet. The collection provides a journey across Australia and the near Pacific, covering prehistory, biology, botany, environment and cultural heritage. Australian Aboriginal traditions are celebrated in a community access space also used for dance and other performances.

Museum Entrance
The façade features massive Corinthian square pillars or piers.

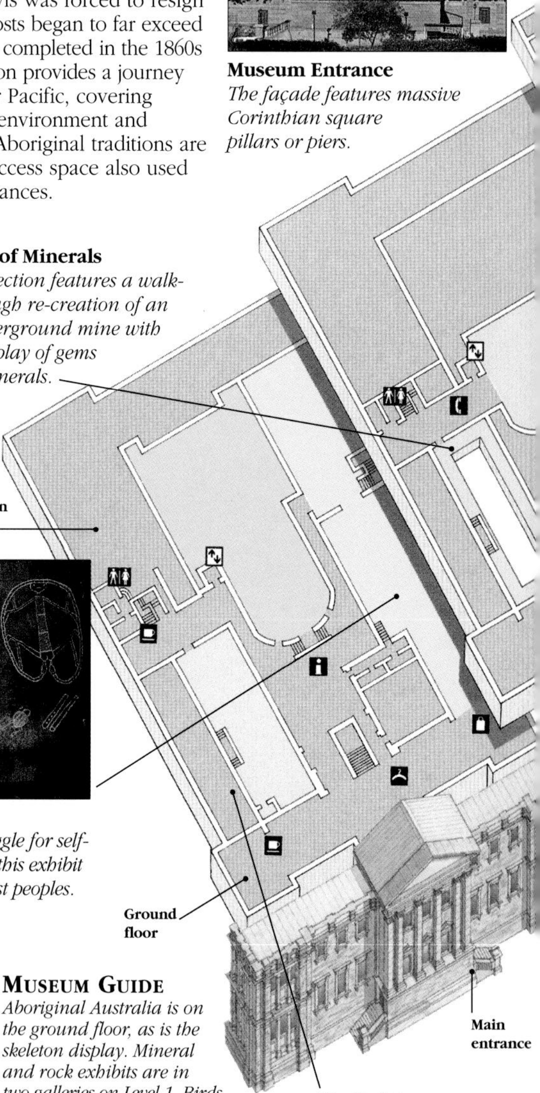

Planet of Minerals
This section features a walk-through re-creation of an underground mine with a display of gems and minerals.

Rhodochrosite   Cuprite

Mesolite with green apophyllite

Education Centre

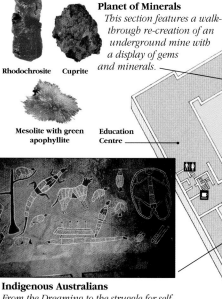

Indigenous Australians
From the Dreaming to the struggle for self-determination and land rights, this exhibit tells the stories of Australia's first peoples.

Ground floor

Main entrance

The Skeletons Gallery, on the ground floor, provides a different perspective on natural history.

STAR EXHIBITS

★ **More than Dinosaurs**

★ **Kids' Island**

★ **Search & Discover**

MUSEUM GUIDE
Aboriginal Australia is on the ground floor, as is the skeleton display. Mineral and rock exhibits are in two galleries on Level 1. Birds and Insects are found on Level 2, along with Human Evolution, Kids' Island, Biodiversity, Search and Discover and More than Dinosaurs.

★ **Search & Discover**
Sydneysiders bring bugs, rocks and bones to this area for identification. The public can also access CD-Roms for research.

VISITORS' CHECKLIST

6 College St. **Map** 4 F3.
 9320 6000. Sydney Explorer, 323, 324, 325, 327, 389. Museum, Town Hall.
 9:30am–5pm daily. 25 Dec.
 www.amonline.net.au

Level 2

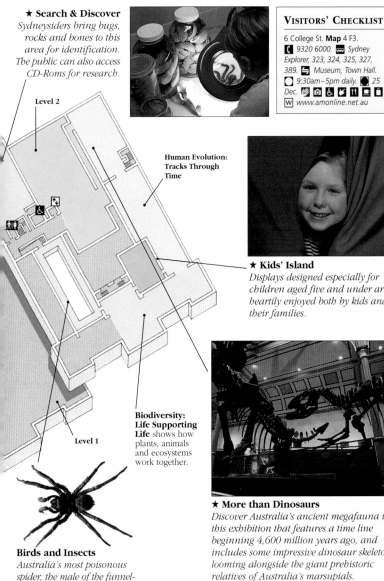

Human Evolution: Tracks Through Time

★ **Kids' Island**
Displays designed especially for children aged five and under are heartily enjoyed both by kids and their families.

Biodiversity: Life Supporting Life shows how plants, animals and ecosystems work together.

Level 1

★ **More than Dinosaurs**
Discover Australia's ancient megafauna in this exhibition that features a time line beginning 4,600 million years ago, and includes some impressive dinosaur skeletons looming alongside the giant prehistoric relatives of Australia's marsupials.

Birds and Insects
Australia's most poisonous spider, the male of the funnel-web species, dwells exclusively in the Greater Sydney region.

KEY TO FLOORPLAN

 Australian Environments
 Kids' Island
 More than Dinosaurs
 Indigenous Australians
 Temporary exhibition space
 Non-exhibition space

"WELCOME STRANGER" GOLD NUGGET

In 1869, the largest gold nugget ever found in Australia was discovered in Victoria. It weighed 71.06 kg (156 lb). The museum holds a cast of the original in a display examining the impact of the gold rush, when the Australian population doubled in ten years.

← 67.5 cm (26½ in) wide →

DARLING HARBOUR

NAMED IN HONOUR of the seventh governor of New South Wales, Ralph Darling, this area was originally called Cockle Bay because of the molluscs early European settlers collected here. Darling Harbour was an unsavoury place in the late 19th century, known for its thieves' dens and bawdy houses. Its docks, backed by a railway yard, were an embarkation point for wool and other exports. The country's industrial age began here in 1815 with the opening of a steam mill. Darling

Horatio Nelson, National Maritime Museum

Harbour continued as, first, a grimy workplace and, later, with the industrial decline of Sydney Harbour, an obsolete and run-down backwater. In the 1980s, it was decided to make this prime city site a focal point of the 1988 Bicentenary. The project was the largest urban redevelopment ever carried out in Australia. Today Darling Harbour is an extension of the city centre with a mixture of fine museums, shopping and open space. It has become a popular and lively area of Sydney.

SIGHTS AT A GLANCE

Historic Districts and Buildings
Pyrmont Bridge ❸
Chinatown ❼

Museums and Galleries
National Maritime Museum pp94–5 ❶
Motor World Museum and Gallery ❹
Powerhouse Museum pp100–101 ❿

Parks and Gardens
Chinese Garden ❻

Entertainment
Sydney Aquarium pp96–7 ❷
Convention and Exhibition Centre ❺

Theatres
Capitol Theatre ❽

Markets
Paddy's Market ❾

GETTING THERE
Harbourside, Convention and Haymarket monorail stations are convenient. Ferries run to Darling Harbour wharf, while the most useful buses are the Sydney Explorer, 456 and 501.

KEY

▨	Street-by-Street map See pp92–3
🚇	CityRail station
🚝	Monorail station
🚋	Sydney Light Rail (SLR)
🚌	Bus terminus
🚍	Coach station
⛴	Ferry boarding point
⛴	JetCat/RiverCat boarding point
P	Parking

PYRMONT BAY PARK

Cockle Bay

SUSSEX STREET
DARLING
PYRMONT STREET
HARRIS STREET
BATHURST ST
HARBOUR STREET
LIVERPOOL ST
SUSSEX STREET
GOULBURN STREET
PIER STREET
HAY STREET
GEORGE STREET
PITT STREET
ELIZABETH STREET
BELMORE PARK
EDDY AVENUE
ULTIMO ROAD
HARRIS STREET
RAILWAY SQUARE
BROADWAY
LEE STREET
REGENT STREET
CHALMERS STREET

0 metres   250
0 yards   250

◁ **View from Harbourside Shopping Centre looking east towards the city**

Street-by-Street: Darling Harbour

Carpentaria lightship, National Maritime Museum

DARLING HARBOUR was New South Wales' bicentennial gift to itself. This imaginative urban redevelopment, in the heart of Sydney, covers a 54-ha (133-acre) site that was once a busy industrial centre and international shipping terminal catering for the developing local wool, grain, timber and coal trades. In 1984 the Darling Harbour Authority was formed to examine the area's commercial options. The resulting complex opened in 1988, complete with the National Maritime Museum and Sydney Aquarium, two of the city's tourist highlights. Free outdoor entertainment, appealing to children in particular, is a regular feature, and there are many shops, waterside cafés and restaurants, as well as several major hotels overlooking the bay.

Harbourside Complex offers restaurants and cafés with superb views over the water to the city skyline. There is also a wide range of speciality shops, selling unusual gifts and other items.

Walkway to Harris Street Motor Museum

Convention and Exhibition Centre
This complex presents an alternating range of trade shows displaying everything from home decorating suggestions to bridal wear **5**

DARLING DRIVE

WESTERN DISTRIBUTOR

WESTERN DISTRIBUTOR

The Tidal Cascades sunken fountain was designed by Robert Woodward, also responsible for the El Alamein Fountain (*see p120*). The double spiral of water and paths replicates the circular shape of the Convention Centre.

IMAX large-screen cinema

Chinese Garden of Friendship

The Chinese Garden of Friendship is a haven of peace and tranquillity in the heart of Sydney. Its landscaping, with winding pathways, waterfalls, lakes and pavilions, offers an insight into the rich culture of China.

STAR SIGHTS

★ **Sydney Aquarium**

★ **National Maritime Museum**

Pyrmont Bridge
The swingspan bridge opens for vessels up to 14 m (46 ft) tall. The monorail track running above the walkway also opens up to allow access for even taller boats ❸

LOCATOR MAP
See Street Finder, *maps 3 & 4*

Swingspan supports for Pyrmont Bridge are sunk 10 m (33 ft) below the harbour floor.

Star City

★ **National Maritime Museum**
The seafaring history of the nation, both before and after European settlement, is recorded in a range of compelling exhibits ❶

The *Vampire* destroyer (1959) is the largest in the vessel fleet moored outside the museum.

Wharf for harbour cruise departures

★ **Sydney Aquarium**
The aquatic life of Sydney Harbour, the open ocean and the Great Barrier Reef is displayed in massive tanks which can be seen from underwater walkways ❷

0 metres	100
0 yards	100

KEY

– – – Suggested route

Cockle Bay Wharf, vibrant and colourful, is an exciting food and entertainment precinct.

National Maritime Museum

1602 Willem Blaeu Celestial Globe

BOUNDED AS IT IS by the sea, Australia's history is inextricably linked to maritime traditions. The museum displays material in a broad range of permanent and temporary thematic exhibits, many with inter-active elements. As well as artifacts relating to the enduring Aboriginal maritime cultures, the exhibits survey the history of European exploratory voy-ages in the Pacific, the arrival of convict ships, successive waves of migration, water sports and recreation, and naval life. Historic vessels on show at the wharf include a flimsy Vietnamese refugee boat, sailing, fishing and pearling boats, a navy patrol boat and a World War II commando raider.

Museum Façade
The billowing steel roof design by Philip Cox suggests both the surging sea and the sails of a ship.

Passengers
The model of the Orcades *reflects the grace of 1950s liners. This display also charts harrowing sea voyages made by migrants and refugees.*

Merana Eora Nora – First People traces the seafaring traditions of Aboriginal peoples and Torres Strait Islanders.

The Tasman Light was used in a Tasmanian lighthouse.

★ **Navigators**
This 1754 engraving of an East Indian sea creature is a European vision of the un-charted, exotic "great south".

The *Sirius* anchor is from a 1790 wreck off Norfolk Island.

Main entrance (sea level)

KEY TO FLOORPLAN

- ☐ Navigators and Merana Eora Nora
- ☐ Passengers
- ☐ Commerce
- ☐ Watermarks
- ☐ Navy
- ☐ Linked by the Sea: USA Gallery
- ☐ Temporary exhibitions
- ☐ Non-exhibition space

The Navy exhibit examines naval life in war and peace, as well as the history of colonial navies.

Linked by the Sea honours enduring links between the US and Australia. American traders stopped off in Aust-ralia on their way to China.

STAR EXHIBITS

- ★ **Navigators and Merana Eora Nora**
- ★ **Watermarks**
- ★ **Vampire**

FEDERATED
SHIP PAINTERS & DOCKERS UNION

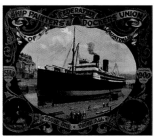

Commerce
This 1903 Painters' and Dockers' Union banner was carried by waterfront workers in marches. It shows the Niagara *entering the dry dock at Cockatoo Island* (see p106).

VISITORS' CHECKLIST

Darling Harbour. **Map** 3 C2. 9298 3777. *Sydney Explorer, 443, 888.* *Pyrmont Bay.* *Town Hall.* *Harbourside.* *9:30am–5pm daily.* *25 Dec.*
www.anmm.gov.au

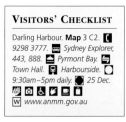

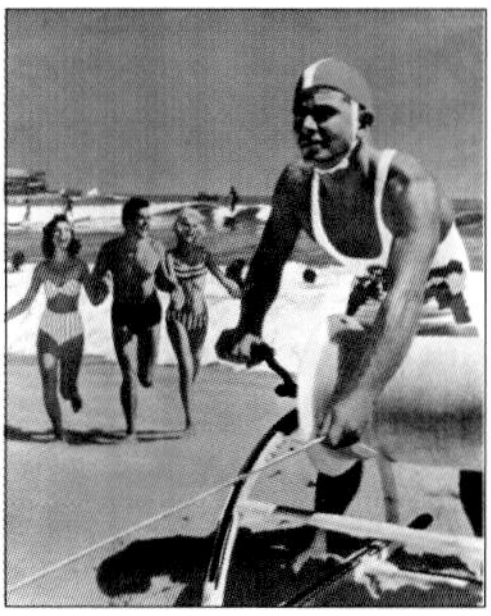

★ Watermarks
This 1960s poster for Bondi beach is part of the museum's Watermarks – adventure, sport and play *exhibition. The displays, including fully-rigged boats and profiles of world champion scullers and swimmers, celebrate Australia's love affair with the water.*

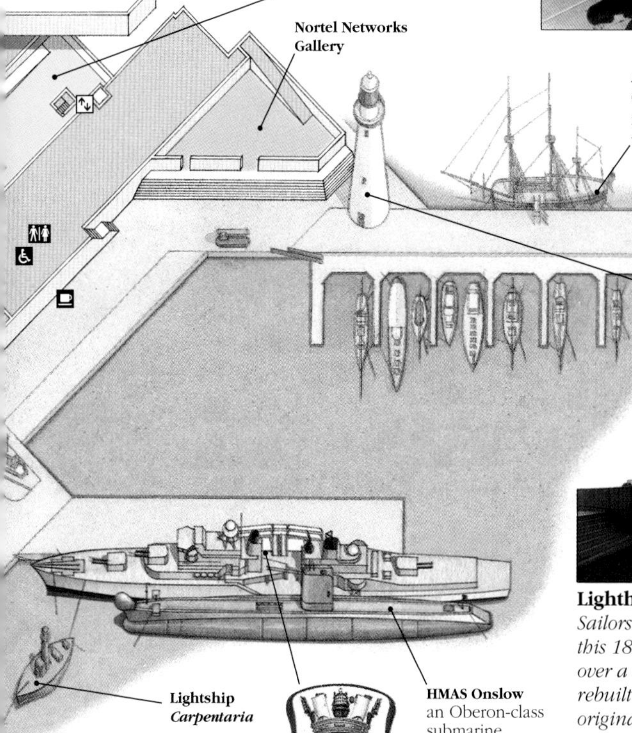

Level 1
Nortel Networks Gallery
Lightship *Carpentaria*
HMAS Onslow an Oberon-class submarine.

A replica of Captain Cook's *Endeavour* moors at this wharf when in Sydney.

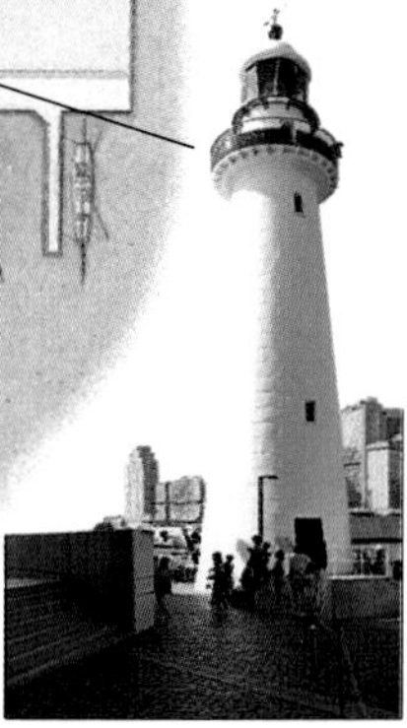

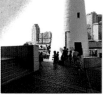

Lighthouse
Sailors were guided by this 1874 lighthouse for over a century. It was rebuilt complete with original kerosene lamp.

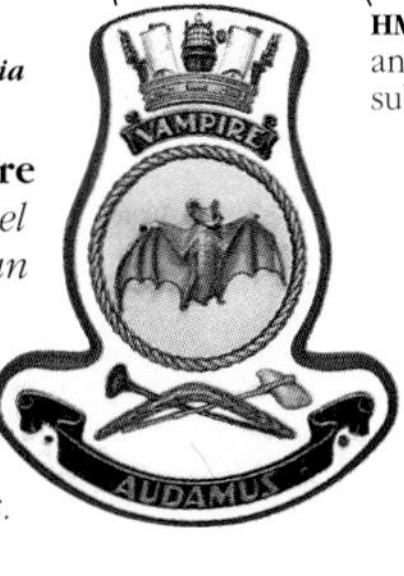

VAMPIRE
AUDAMUS

★ Vampire
The museum's largest vessel is the 1959 Royal Australian Navy destroyer, whose insignia is shown here. Tours of "The Bat" are accompanied by simulated battle action sounds.

MUSEUM GUIDE
The Leisure, Navy and Linked by the Sea: USA Gallery exhibits are located on the main entrance level (sea level). The First Australians, Discovery, Passengers and Commerce sections are found on the first level. There is access to the fleet from both levels.

Sydney Aquarium ❷

SYDNEY AQUARIUM contains the country's most comprehensive collection of Australian aquatic species. Over 11,000 animals from 650 species are held in a series of re-created marine environments. For many visitors, the highlight is a walk "on the ocean floor" through two floating oceanaria with 145 m (480 ft) of acrylic underwater tunnels. These allow close observation of sharks, stingrays and schools of fish. Fur and harbour seals may be viewed above and below water in a special seal sanctuary. None of the displays is harmful to the creatures, and many of the tanks display practical information about marine environmental hazards.

Tropical sea star

Saltwater Crocodiles
The largest and most dangerous species of crocodile, "salties" live in the swamps and estuaries of Australia's north.

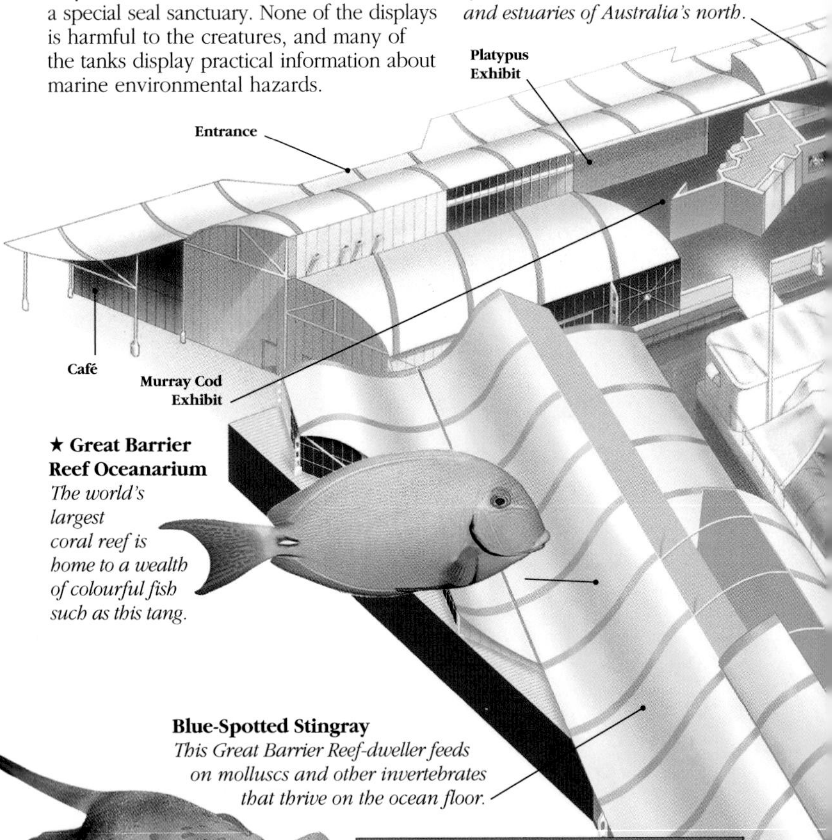

Platypus Exhibit

Entrance

Café

Murray Cod Exhibit

★ Great Barrier Reef Oceanarium
The world's largest coral reef is home to a wealth of colourful fish such as this tang.

Blue-Spotted Stingray
This Great Barrier Reef-dweller feeds on molluscs and other invertebrates that thrive on the ocean floor.

Aquarium Building and Pier
The stark white design of the aquarium is Structuralist (see p39), an architectural style that dominates Darling Harbour.

Touch Pool

This area, resembling a rock pool, gives the visitor a rare chance to touch, with care, marine invertebrates found along the coastline. They include sea urchins, tubeworms, crabs and sea stars.

VISITORS' CHECKLIST

Aquarium Pier, Darling Harbour. **Map** 4 D2. 📞 9262 2300. 🚌 *Sydney Explorer.* ⛴ *Darling Harbour.* 🚆 *Town Hall.* 🅿 *Darling Park.* 🕐 *9am–10pm daily (last adm 9pm).* ♿ 📷 ♿ 🍴 🛍 Ⓦ *www.sydneyaquarium.com*

Mangrove habitat

Southern Ocean Display

Rivers of the Far North

The rivers of northern Australia are affected by the tropical seasons, which provide a changing habitat for some unique animals – for instance the barramundi, which changes sex after 4 years.

"Sails" form a roof over the aquarium.

The underwater walk allows close-up viewing of the seals.

Pontoons surround the floating pool.

Underwater viewing tunnel

Seal Sanctuary

Australian fur seals are carnivorous mammals that live in colonies in the cool waters of the southern Australian coast.

★ **The Open Ocean**
Take a walk through the glass tunnel and become surrounded by large sharks and fish at close range. Giant stingrays are also a feature.

STAR EXHIBITS

★ **Great Barrier Reef Oceanarium**

★ **The Open Ocean**

Pyrmont Bridge ❸

Darling Harbour. **Map** 1 A5.
🚉 *Darling Park, Harbourside.*
📷 ♿ ✏️

The architectural geometry of the Convention and Exhibition Centre

Pᴛʀᴍᴏɴᴛ ʙʀɪᴅɢᴇ opened in 1902. The world's oldest electrically operated swingspan bridge, it was fully functional before Sydney's streets were lit by electricity. It was the second Pyrmont Bridge and provided access to what, at the time, was a busy international shipping terminal with warehouses and wool stores. Electricity for the new bridge came from the Ultimo power station, the building that now houses the city's Powerhouse Museum *(see pp100–101)*.

Percy Allan, the bridge's designer, achieved overseas recognition for his two central steel swingspans and went on to design 583 more bridges in the course of his career. JJ Bradfield, the designer of the Sydney Harbour Bridge *(see pp70–71)*, was also involved in construction of this bridge.

The 369-m (1,200-ft) long Pyrmont Bridge has 14 spans, with only the two central swingspans being made of steel. The remaining spans are made of ironbark, an Australian hardwood timber. The bridge was permanently closed to road traffic in 1981, but reopened to pedestrians when the Darling Harbour complex opened in 1988. A portion of the monorail route travels along the bridge. The central steel swingspans are still driven by their original motor. The bridge is opened regularly to allow boats access to and from Cockle Bay.

Anthony Quinn's 1959 Chevrolet, Harris Street Motor Museum

Motor World Museum and Gallery ❹

320 Harris St, cnr of Allen St, inside Secure Parking Building, Pyrmont. **Map** 3 C3. 📞 *9552 3375.* 🚉 *Convention Centre.* 🕐 *10am–5pm Fri–Sun.* ⬤ *Public hols.* 🎫 📷 💻 🎁 ♿

Cᴇʟᴇʙʀᴀᴛɪɴɢ ᴀ ᴄᴇɴᴛᴜʀʏ of automotive history, the museum has more than 200 classic motor cars, commercial vehicles and motorcycles on display, along with stories of the great car designers. Exhibits include an Edward VII Gardener's Serpollet steam car, the unique Delorean, a Model T BP tanker and actor Anthony Quinn's 1959 Chevrolet. In the midst of the exotic cars are everyday vehicles such as the Morris, Vauxhall and Buick.

Housed in a former 1890s woolstore, the museum also has the country's largest international standard slot car track. Two eight-lane tracks run over 67 m (220 ft), with the "driver" racing against the clock.

Convention and Exhibition Centre ❺

Darling Drive, Darling Harbour. **Map** 3 C3. 📞 *9282 5000.* 🚉 *Convention.* 🕐 *daily (check in advance).* 📷 💻 ♿

Tʜɪs ᴘᴜʀᴘᴏsᴇ-ʙᴜɪʟᴛ facility was completed in 1988. Major international and local conventions are held in the main auditorium. For trade shows and exhibitions, the Exhibition Centre's five halls can be combined to form a column-free area the size of five sports fields. The roof is supported by a system of sail-like masts and rigging, which reflects the maritime history of Darling Harbour. Works of art by such noted Australian artists as Brett Whiteley and John Olsen hang within.

Chinese Garden ❻

Darling Harbour. **Map** 4 D3. 📞 *9281 6863.* 🚉 *Haymarket.* 🕐 *9:30am daily. Closing time varies, so phone in advance.* 🎫 📷 💻 ♿

Kɴᴏᴡɴ ᴀs the Garden of Friendship, the Chinese Garden was built in 1984. It is a tranquil refuge from the city streets. The garden's design was a gift to Sydney from its Chinese sister city of Guangdong. The Dragon Wall is in the lower section beside the lake. It has glazed carvings of two dragons, one representing Guangdong province and the other the state of New South Wales. In the centre of the wall, a carved pearl, symbolizing prosperity, is lifted by the

The view from Pyrmont Bridge looking up towards the city centre

waves. The lake is covered with lotus and water lilies for much of the year and a rock monster guards against evil. On the other side of the lake is the Twin Pavilion. Waratahs (New South Wales's floral symbol) and flowering apricots are carved into its woodwork, and also grow at its base.

A tea house, found at the top of the stairs in the Tea House Courtyard, serves traditional Chinese tea and cakes.

Chinatown ⑦

Dixon St Plaza, Sydney. **Map** 4 D4. 🚇 Haymarket.

ORIGINALLY concentrated around Dixon and Hay Streets, Chinatown is expanding to fill Sydney's Haymarket area, stretching west to Harris Street, south to Broadway and east to Castlereagh Street. It is close to the Sydney Entertainment Centre, where some of the world's best-known rock and pop stars perform and indoor sporting events are held.

For years, Chinatown was a run-down district at the edge of the city's produce markets where many Chinese migrants worked. Today Dixon Street, its main thoroughfare, has been

Chinatown entrance, Dixon Street

spruced up, with street lanterns and archways, and a new wave of Asian migrants fills the now up-market restaurants.

Chinatown is a distinctive area with greengrocers, traditional herbalists and butchers' shops with wind-dried ducks hanging in their windows. Jewellers, clothing shops and confectioners fill the arcades. There are also two Chinese-language cinema complexes.

Capitol Theatre ⑧

13 Campbell St, Haymarket. **Map** 4 E4. 📞 9320 5000. 🚌 George St routes. ⭕ performances only. **Box office** ⭕ 9am–5pm Mon–Fri, 9am–8pm during performances. ♿

IN THE MID-1800s a cattle and corn market was situated here. It became Paddy's Market Bazaar with sideshows and an outdoor theatre, which were

in turn replaced by a circus with a floodable ring. The present building was erected in the 1920s as a luxurious picture palace. In the mid-1990s, the cinema was restored, in keeping with the original theme of a Florentine Garden.

The Capitol reopened as a lyric theatre with productions of *West Side Story* and *Miss Saigon* being staged beneath its Mediterranean-blue ceiling studded with twinkling stars reflecting the southern sky.

The lavishly renovated Capitol Theatre in Chinatown

Paddy's Market ⑨

Cnr Thomas & Hay Sts, Haymarket. **Map** 4 D4. 📞 1300 361 589. 🚇 Haymarket. ⭕ 10am–6pm Thu, 9am–4pm Fri–Sun & public hols. ● 25 Apr, 25 Dec. 📷 ♿ See also **Shops and Markets** p203.

HAYMARKET, in Chinatown, is home to Paddy's Market, Sydney's oldest market. It has been in this area, on a number of sites, since 1869 (with only one five-year absence). The name's origin is uncertain, but is believed to have come from either the Chinese who originally supplied much of its produce, or the Irish, their main customers.

Once the shopping centre for the inner-city poor, Paddy's Market is now an integral part of an ambitious development including residential apartments and the Market City Shopping Centre, with fashion outlet stores, an Asian food court and a cinema complex. However, the familiar clamour and chaotic bargain-hunting atmosphere of the original marketplace remain. Every weekend the market has up to 800 stalls selling everything from fresh produce to chickens, puppies, electrical products and leather goods.

Pavilion in the grounds of the Chinese Garden

Powerhouse Museum ⑩

Woman's skirt, North Laos

THIS FORMER POWER STATION, completed in 1902 to provide power for Sydney's tramway system, was redesigned to cater for the needs of a modern, hands-on museum. Revamped, the Powerhouse opened in 1988. The early collection was held in the Garden Palace hosting the 1879 international exhibition of invention and industry from around the world *(see pp24–5)*. Few exhibits survived the devastating 1882 fire, and today's huge and ever-expanding holdings were gathered after this disaster. The buildings' monumental scale provides an ideal context for the epic sweep of ideas encompassed within: everything from the realm of space and technology to the decorative and domestic arts. The museum emphasizes Australian innovations and achievements celebrating both the extraordinary and the everyday.

Cyberworlds: Computers and Connections
This display explores the past, present and future of computers. Pictured here is a Japanese tin toy robot.

Soviet Organic Satellite Model
Replica spacecraft and a "habitation module", complete with kitchenette and sleeping area, detail the past and future of space exploration.

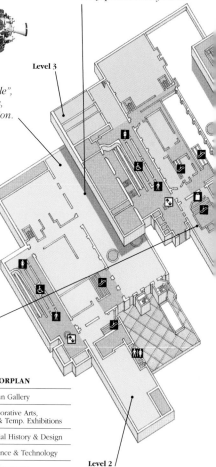

Level 3

Level 2

Bayagul: Contemporary Indigenous Australian Communication
This handtufted rug, designed by Jimmy Pike, is displayed in an exhibit showcasing Aboriginal and Torres Strait Island cultures.

MUSEUM GUIDE

The museum is two buildings: the former powerhouse and the Neville Wran building. There are over 20 exhibitions on four levels, descending from Level 5, the restaurant level. The shop, entrance and main exhibits are on Level 4. Level 3 has thematic exhibits and a Design Gallery. Level 2 has experiments and displays on space, computers and transport.

KEY TO FLOORPLAN

- ☐ Level 5: Asian Gallery
- ☐ Level 4: Decorative Arts, Innovation & Temp. Exhibitions
- ☐ Level 3: Social History & Design
- ☐ Level 2: Science & Technology
- ☐ Non-exhibition space

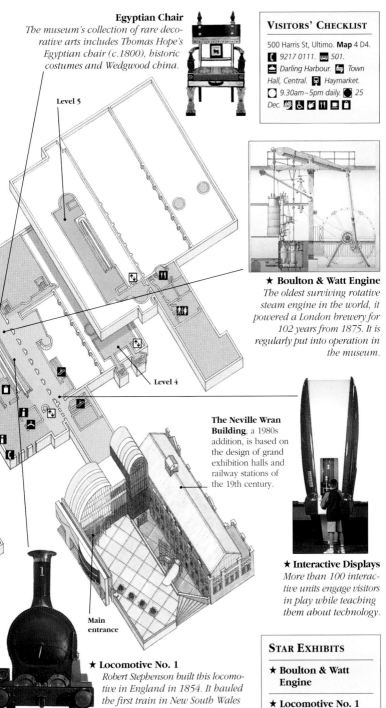

Egyptian Chair
The museum's collection of rare decorative arts includes Thomas Hope's Egyptian chair (c.1800), historic costumes and Wedgwood china.

Level 5

★ **Boulton & Watt Engine**
The oldest surviving rotative steam engine in the world, it powered a London brewery for 102 years from 1875. It is regularly put into operation in the museum.

Level 4

The Neville Wran Building, a 1980s addition, is based on the design of grand exhibition halls and railway stations of the 19th century.

★ **Interactive Displays**
More than 100 interactive units engage visitors in play while teaching them about technology.

Main entrance

★ **Locomotive No. 1**
Robert Stephenson built this locomotive in England in 1854. It hauled the first train in New South Wales in 1855. Using models and voices, the display re-creates a 19th-century day trip for a group of Sydneysiders.

STAR EXHIBITS

★ **Boulton & Watt Engine**

★ **Locomotive No. 1**

★ **Interactive Displays**

BOTANIC GARDENS AND THE DOMAIN

THIS TRANQUIL PART of Sydney can seem a world away from the bustle of the city centre. It is rich in the remnants of Sydney's convict and colonial past: the site of the first farm, and the boulevard-like Macquarie Street where the barracks, hospital, church and mint – bastions of civic power – are among the oldest surviving public buildings in Australia. This street continues to assert its dominance today as the home of the state government of New South Wales. The Domain, an open, grassy space, was originally set aside by the colony's first governor for his private use. Today it is a democratic place with joggers and touch footballers sidestepping picnickers. In January, during the Festival of Sydney, it hosts outdoor concerts with thousands of people enjoying fine music. The Botanic Gardens, which with The Domain was the site of Australia's first park, is a haven where visitors can stroll around and enjoy the extensive collection of native and exotic flora.

Wooden angel, St James Church

SIGHTS AT A GLANCE

Historic Streets and Buildings
Conservatorium of Music ❷
Government House ❸
Woolloomooloo Finger
  Wharf ❻
State Library of NSW ❾
Parliament House ❿
Sydney Hospital ⓫
Sydney Mint ⓬
Hyde Park Barracks ⓭

Museums and Galleries
*Art Gallery of New South
  Wales pp108–11* ❼

Churches
St James Church ⓮

Islands
Fort Denison ❺

Monuments
Mrs Macquaries Chair ❹

Parks and Gardens
*Royal Botanic Gardens
  pp104–5* ❶
The Domain ❽

GETTING THERE
Visit on foot, if possible. St James and Martin Place train stations are close to most of the sights. The 311 bus from Circular Quay runs near the Art Gallery of NSW and past the Woolloomooloo Finger Wharf. The Sydney Explorer also stops at several sights.

0 metres   500
0 yards   500

KEY

◼ Royal Botanic Gardens
  See pp104–5

P Parking

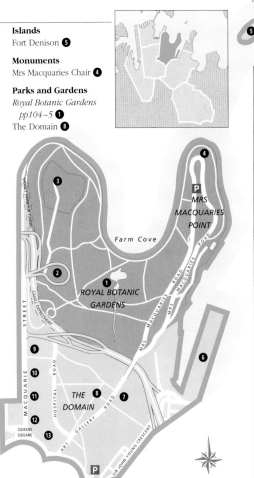

FARM COVE

MRS MACQUARIES POINT

ROYAL BOTANIC GARDENS

THE DOMAIN

QUEENS SQUARE

◁ **Succulents and cacti from the Succulent Garden in the Royal Botanic Gardens**

Royal Botanic Gardens **❶**

Statue in the Botanic Gardens

T HE ROYAL BOTANIC GARDENS, an oasis of 30 ha (74 acres) in the heart of the city, occupy a superb position, wrapped around Farm Cove at the harbour's edge. Established in 1816 as a series of pathways through shrubbery, they are the oldest scientific institution in the country and house an outstanding collection of plants from Australia and overseas. A living museum, the gardens are also the site of the first farm in the fledgling colony. Fountains, statues and monuments are today scattered throughout. Plant specimens collected by Joseph Banks on Captain James Cook's epic voyage along the east coast of Australia in 1770 are displayed in the National Herbarium of New South Wales, an important centre for research on Australian plants.

LOCATOR MAP
See Street Finder, maps 1 & 2

Government House (1897)

★ Palm Grove
Begun in 1862, this cool summer haven is one of the world's finest outdoor collections of palms. There are about 180 species. Borders planted with kaffir lilies make a colourful display in springtime.

★ Herb Garden
Herbs from around the world used for a wide variety of purposes – culinary, medicinal and aromatic – are on display here. A sensory fountain and a sundial modelled on the celestial sphere are also features.

0 metres   200

0 yards   200

★ Sydney Tropical Centre
Two glasshouses contain tropical ecosystems in miniature. Native vegetation is displayed in the Pyramid, while the Arc holds plants not found locally, commonly known as exotics.

Macquarie Wall
In 1810, work began on this 290-m (950-ft) long wall intended to separate the convict domain from the town's "respectable Class of Inhabitants". Only a small section remains standing today.

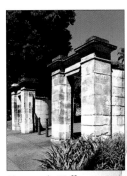

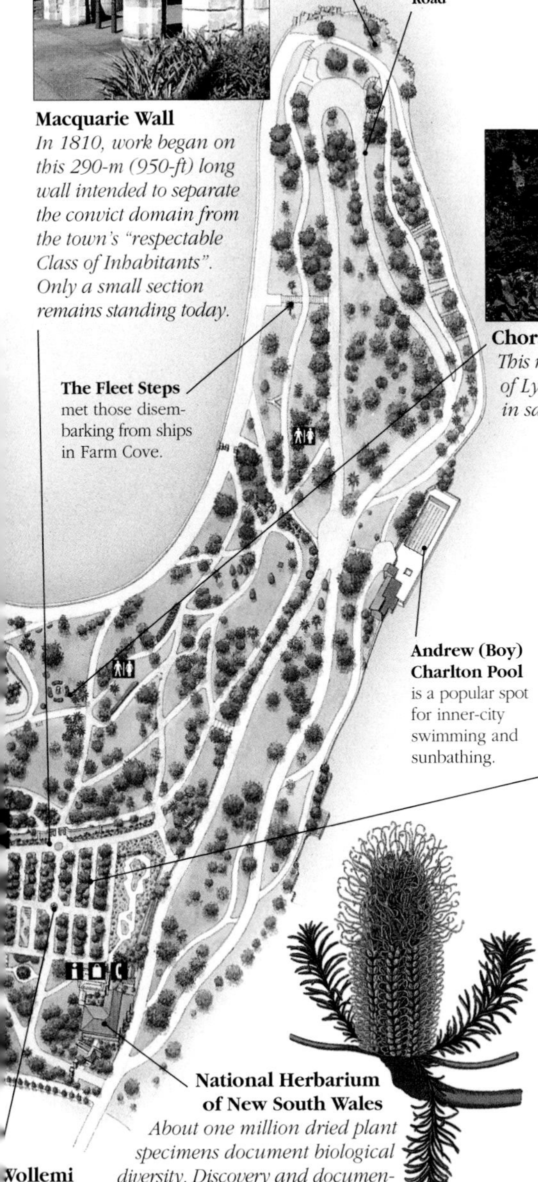

Mrs Macquaries Chair, where the governor's wife liked to sit and watch the harbour, is marked by a carved rock ledge seat.

Mrs Macquaries Road

The Fleet Steps met those disembarking from ships in Farm Cove.

Andrew (Boy) Charlton Pool is a popular spot for inner-city swimming and sunbathing.

National Herbarium of New South Wales
About one million dried plant specimens document biological diversity. Discovery and documentation of new plants aims to slow down extinction rates of species.

Wollemi Pine

Visitors' Checklist

Mrs Macquaries Rd. **Maps** 1 & 2. *9231 8111.* ***Guided tours*** *9231 8125. Sydney Explorer, 438, 440, 441, 470, 888. Circular Quay. Martin Place, St James, Circular Quay. 7am–8pm Nov–Mar, 7am–6:30pm Oct, 7am–6pm Apr & Sep, 7am–5:30pm May & Aug, 7am–5pm Jun & Jul. 10:30am daily (not public hols) 1pm Mon–Fri.* ***Tropical Centre*** *10am–4pm daily.*

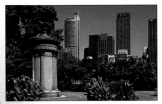

Choragic Monument *(1870)*
This replica of the eponymous statue of Lysicrates in Athens was carved in sandstone by Walter McGill.

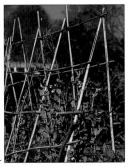

★ Australia's First Farm
It is claimed that some Middle Garden oblong beds follow the direction of the first furrows ploughed in the colony.

Star Sights

- ★ **Sydney Tropical Centre**
- ★ **Australia's First Farm**
- ★ **Palm Grove**
- ★ **Herb Garden**

Conservatorium of Music ❷

Macquarie St. **Map** 1 C3. ☎ 9351
1222. 🚌 Sydney Explorer, Circular
Quay routes. ☐ 9am–5pm Mon–Fri,
9am–4pm Sat (public areas only). ●
public hols, Easter Sat, 24 Dec–2 Jan.
📷 ♿ 🎧 by appointment (phone
9351 1296 for details).

W HEN IT WAS finished in
1821, this striking castellated Colonial Gothic building
was meant to be stables and
servants' quarters for Government House, but construction
of the latter was delayed for
almost 25 years. That stables
should be built in so grand a
style, and at such great cost,
brought forth cries of outrage
and led to bitter arguments
between the architect, Francis
Greenway (see p114), and
Governor Macquarie – and a
decree that all future building
plans be submitted to London.
   Between 1908 and 1915,
"Greenway's folly" underwent
a dramatic transformation. A
concert hall, roofed in grey
slate, was built on the central
courtyard and the building in
its entirety was converted for
the use of the new Sydney
Conservatorium of Music.
   Recently added facilities
include a café which holds
regular lunchtime concerts
during the school term and an
upper level with great harbour
views. "The Con" continues to
be a training ground for
future musicians as well as
being a great place to visit.

THE HISTORY OF COCKATOO ISLAND

**HMS *Orlando* in dry dock at
Cockatoo Island in the 1890s**

Now deserted, the largest of
the 12 Sydney Harbour
islands was used to store
grain from the 1830s. It was
a penal establishment from
the 1840s to 1908, with
prisoners being put to work
constructing dock facilities.
The infamous bushranger
"Captain Thunderbolt" made
his escape from Cockatoo in
1863 by swimming across to
the mainland. From the 1870s
to the 1960s, Cockatoo
Island was a thriving naval
dockyard and shipyard, the
hub of Australian industry.

Government House ❸

Macquarie St. **Map** 1 C2. ☎ 9931
5222. 📠 9931 5200. 🚌 Sydney
Explorer, Circular Quay routes. **House**
☐ 10am–3pm Fri–Sun. ● public hols.
Garden ☐ 10am–4pm daily.
📷 ♿ 🎧

W HAT USED to be the official
residence of the governor
of New South Wales overlooks
the harbour from within the
Royal Botanic Gardens, but the
grandiose, somewhat sombre,
turreted Gothic Revival edifice
seems curiously out of place
in its beautiful park setting.
   It was built of local sandstone and cedar between
1837 and 1845. A fine
collection of 19th- and early
20th-century furnishings and
decoration is housed within.

**Resting on the carved stone seat
of Mrs Macquaries Chair**

Mrs Macquaries Chair ❹

Mrs Macquaries Rd. **Map** 2 E2.
🚌 Sydney Explorer, 888. ♿

T HE SCENIC Mrs Macquaries
Road winds alongside much
of what is now the city's Royal
Botanic Gardens, from Farm
Cove to Woolloomooloo Bay
and back again. The road was
built in 1816 at the instigation
of Elizabeth Macquarie, wife
of the Governor. In the same
year, a stone bench, inscribed
with details of the new road,
was carved into the rock at the
point where Mrs Macquarie
would stop to admire the view
on her daily constitutional.
   Although today the outlook
from this famous landmark is
much changed, it is just as
arresting, taking in the broad
sweep of the harbour and foreshore with all its landmarks.

The Conservatorium of Music at the edge of the Royal Botanic Gardens

Historic Woolloomooloo Finger Wharf redevelopment, including apartments, restaurants and a hotel

Fort Denison ❺

Sydney Harbour. **Map** 2 E1.
📞 *9247 5033.* 🚢 *from Circular Quay.* 🏛️📷💻🛒 *visit is by guided tour only (booking essential).*

FIRST NAMED Rock Island, this prominent, rocky outcrop in Sydney Harbour was very quickly dubbed "Pinchgut". This was probably because of the meagre rations given to convicts who were confined there as punishment. It had a grim history of incarceration in the early years of the colony.

In 1796, con-victed murderer Francis Morgan was hanged on the island in chains. His body was left to rot on the gallows for three years as a grisly warning to the other convicts.

Fort Denison in 1907

Between 1855 and 1857, the Martello tower (the only one in Australia), gun battery and barracks that now occupy the island were built as part of Sydney's defences and the site was renamed after the gover-nor of the time. The gun, still fired at 1pm each day, was an important aid for navigation, allowing mariners to set their ships' chronometers.

Today the island is a popu-lar tourist spot, commanding spectacular views of Sydney Harbour, the Opera House and Kirribilli. To explore Fort Denison, book one of the daily boat tours.

Woolloomooloo Finger Wharf ❻

Cowper Wharf Roadway, Woolloomooloo. **Map** 2 E4.
🚌 *Sydney Explorer, 311.* 📷

THIS IS THE LARGEST of several finger wharves that jut out into the harbour. The wharf, completed in 1914, was one of the points of embarkation for soldiers bound for both world wars. Following World War II, it was a landing place for many of the thousands of immigrants who came to Australia.

The wharf was the subject of public controversy in the late 1980s and early 1990s, when demolition plans were thwart-ed by conservation groups. Since then, this National-Trust-listed maritime site has been redeveloped to include a hotel, lively restaurants and bars, and apartments.

Art Gallery of New South Wales ❼

See pp108–11.

The Domain ❽

Art Gallery Rd. **Map** 1 C4.
🚌 *Sydney Explorer, 888.* 📷♿

PEOPLE WHO SWARM to the January concerts and other Festival of Sydney events in The Domain *(see p49)* are part of a long-standing tradition.

This extensive public space has long been a rallying point for crowds of Sydneysiders whenever emotive issues of public importance have arisen, such as the attempt in 1916 to introduce military conscription or the dismissal of the elected federal government by the then governor-general in 1975.

From the 1890s, part of The Domain was also used as the Sydney version of "Speakers' Corner". Today, you are more likely to see joggers or office workers playing touch foot-ball in their lunch hours, or simply enjoying the shade.

A dramatic view of Sydney Opera House from Mrs Macquaries Chair

Art Gallery of New South Wales ❼

E STABLISHED IN 1874, the art gallery has occupied its present imposing building since 1897. Designed by the Colonial Architect WL Vernon, the gallery doubled in size following 1988 building extensions. Two equestrian bronzes – *The Offerings of Peace* and *The Offerings of War* – greet the visitor on entry. The gallery itself houses some of the finest works of art in Australia. It has sections devoted to Australian, Asian, European, photographic and contemporary and photographic works, along with a strong collection of prints and drawings. The Yiribana Gallery, the largest in the world to exclusively exhibit Aboriginal and Torres Strait Islander art and culture, was opened in 1994.

Cycladic figure (c.2,500 BC)

Lower Level 3

Sofala *(1947)*
Russell Drysdale's visions of Australia show "ghost" towns laid waste by devastating natural forces such as drought.

Sunbaker *(1937)*
Max Dupain's iconic, almost abstract, Australian photograph of hedonism and sun worship uses clean lines, strong light, and geometric form. The image's power lies in its simplicity.

Madonna and Child with Infant St John the Baptist
This oil on wood (c.1541) is the work of Siena Mannerist artist Domenico Beccafumi.

STAR EXHIBITS

- ★ **The Golden Fleece – Shearing at Newstead by Tom Roberts**

- ★ **Pukumani Grave Posts**

GALLERY GUIDE

The collection has five levels. The Upper Level is used only as offices. The Ground Level has European and Australian works. Temporary exhibitions are held on Lower Level 1, 20th-century European prints are on Lower Level 2 and the Yiribana Aboriginal Gallery is on Lower Level 3.

Ground Level

★ **Pukumani Grave Posts** (1958)
Carved by Tiwi people of Melville Island (north of Australia) and now in the Yiribana Gallery, these posts represent qualities of the deceased whose grave they solemnly surrounded.

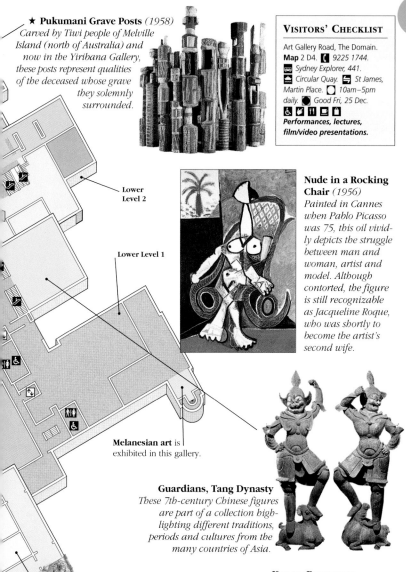

Lower Level 2

Lower Level 1

Nude in a Rocking Chair (1956)
Painted in Cannes when Pablo Picasso was 75, this oil vividly depicts the struggle between man and woman, artist and model. Although contorted, the figure is still recognizable as Jacqueline Roque, who was shortly to become the artist's second wife.

Melanesian art is exhibited in this gallery.

Guardians, Tang Dynasty
These 7th-century Chinese figures are part of a collection highlighting different traditions, periods and cultures from the many countries of Asia.

★ **The Golden Fleece** (1894)
Also known as Shearing at Newstead, *this work by Tom Roberts marks the coming of age of Australian Impressionist art.*

The sandstone entrance was added in 1909.

KEY TO FLOORPLAN

☐ Australian Art
☐ European Art
☐ Asian Art
☐ International
▨ Prints, Drawings and Watercolours
▨ Contemporary Art
▨ Domain Theatre
▨ Aboriginal Art
▨ Temporary exhibition space
▨ Non-exhibition space

Exploring the Art Gallery's Collection

ALTHOUGH LOCAL WORKS had been collected since 1875 the gallery did not seriously begin seeking Australian and non-British art until the 1920s, and not until the 1940s did it begin acquiring Aboriginal and Torres Strait Islander paintings. These contrasting collections are now its great strength. Major temporary exhibitions are also regularly staged, with the annual Archibald, Wynne and Sulman prizes being most controversial and highly entertaining.

Grace Cossington Smith's 1955 *Interior with wardrobe mirror*

AUSTRALIAN ART

AMONG THE MOST important colonial works is John Glover's *Natives on the Ouse River, Van Diemen's Land* (1838), an image of doomed Tasmanian Aborigines.

The old wing holds paintings from the Heidelberg school of Australian Impressionism. Charles Conder's *Departure of the Orient – Circular Quay* (1888) and Tom Roberts's *The Golden Fleece – Shearing at Newstead* (1894) hang alongside fine works by Frederick McCubbin and Arthur Streeton. Rupert Bunny's sensuous *Summer Time* (c.1907) and *A Summer Morning* (c.1908), and

George Lambert's heroic *Across the black soil plains* (1899), impress with their huge size and complex compositions.

Australia was slow to take up Modernism. *Implement blue* (1927) and *Western Australian Gum Blossom* (1928), both by Margaret Preston, are her most assertive of the 1920s. Sidney Nolan's works range from *Boy in Township* (1943) to *Burke* (c.1962), exploiting myths of early Australian history. There are fine holdings of William Dobell and Russell Drysdale, as well as important collections of Arthur Boyd, Fred Williams, Grace Cossington Smith and Brett Whiteley *(see p130)*.

EUROPEAN ART

THE SCOPE OF the scattered European collection ranges from the medieval to the modern. British art from the late 19th to the early 20th centuries forms an outstanding component. Among the Old Masters are some significant Italian works that reflect Caravaggio's influence. There are also several notable works from the Renaissance in Sienese and Florentine styles.

***Study for Self Portrait*, a Francis Bacon painting from 1976**

Hogarth, Turner and Joshua Reynolds are represented, as are Neo-Classical works. *The Visit of the Queen of Sheba to King Solomon* (1884–90) by Edward Poynter has been on display since 1892. Ford Madox Brown's *Chaucer at the Court of Edward III* (1845–51) is the most commanding work in the Pre-Raphaelite collection.

The Impressionists and Post-Impressionists, represented by late-1880s Pissarro and Monet, are housed in the new gallery wing. Bonnard, Kandinsky, Braque and many other well-known European artists are also here. *Old Woman in Ermine* (1946) by Max Beckmann and *Three Bathers* (1913) by Ernst Kirchner are strong examples of German Expressionism. The gallery's first Picasso, *Nude in a Rocking Chair* (1956), was purchased in 1981. Among distinguished sculptures is Henry Moore's *Reclining Figure: Angles* (1980), found resting by the side of the entrance.

Henry Moore's *Reclining Figure: Angles* (1980)

PHOTOGRAPHY

AUSTRALIAN photography from 1975 to today, represented in all its various forms, is a major part of the collection. In recent years, however, the emphasis has been on building up a body of 19th-century Australian work in a range of early mediums. Nearly 3,000

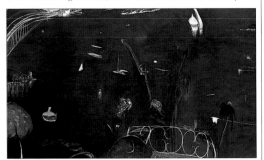

Brett Whiteley's vivid *The Balcony (2)* from 1975

prints constitute this collection with pieces by Charles Kerry, Charles Bayliss and Harold Cazneaux, the latter a major figure of early 20th-century Pictorialism. Such international photographers as Muybridge, Robert Mapplethorpe and Man Ray are also represented here.

ASIAN ART

THIS COLLECTION is one of the finest in Australia. Chinese art is represented by a chronological presentation of works from the pre- Shang dynasty (c.1600–1027 BC) to the 20th century. The Ming porcelains, earthenware funerary pieces *(mingqi)* and the sculptures deserve close attention.

The Japanese painting collection contains fine examples by major artists of the Edo period (1615–1867). The Indian and Southeast Asian holdings consist of lacquer, ceramics and sculptures, with painting displays changing regularly.

PRINTS AND DRAWINGS

AS SO MANY of the works in this collection are fragile, the exhibitions are changed frequently. The collection represents the European tradition from the High Renaissance to the 19th and 20th centuries, with work by Rembrandt, Constable, William Blake and Edvard Munch. A strong bias towards Sydney artists from the past 100 years has resulted in a fine gathering of work by Thea Proctor, Norman and Lionel Lindsay and Lloyd Rees.

Egon Schiele's *Poster for the Vienna Secession* (1918)

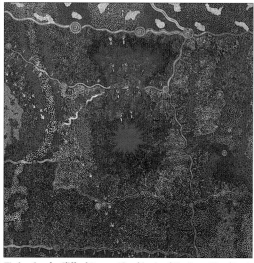

***Warlugulong* by Clifford Possum Tjapaltjarri and Tim Leura Tjapaltjarri**

CONTEMPORARY ART

THE SIGNIFICANCE of the art of our time is reflected in the dynamic collection of recent work by international and Australian artists. The collection highlights the artistic themes that have been central to art practice of the last two decades. Works of Australian artists such as Imants Tillers, Ken Unsworth and Susan Norrie are on display alongside notable international artists of the calibre of Cindy Sherman, Yves Klein, Philip Guston and Anselm Kiefer. The gallery also has a contemporary project space that features temporary experimental installations.

***Fruit Bats* (1991) by Lin Onus**

YIRIBANA GALLERY

DEVOTED TO the exhibition of Aboriginal and Torres Strait Islander artworks bought since the 1940s, traditional bark paintings hang alongside innovative works from both desert and urban areas. The ability of contemporary artists to apply traditional ceremonial body and sand painting styles to new media forms, and the endurance of "Aboriginality",

are repeatedly demonstrated. The significant early purchases are mainly natural pigment paintings on bark and card, often containing a simple, figurative motif of everyday life. Also of interest are two sandstone carvings by Queenslanders Linda Craigie and Nora Nathan, the only women artists in the collection until 1985. Topographical, geographical and cultural mapping of the land is displayed in a number of intricate landscapes.

The qualities and forms of the natural world, and the actions and tracks of Ancestral Beings, are coded within the images. These paintings are maps of Ancestral journeys and events. The bark painting *Three Mimis Dancing* (1964) by Samuel Wagbara examines the habitation of the land by Spirits and the recurrence of the Creation Cycles.

Pukumani Grave Posts Melville Island (1958) is a solemn ceremonial work dealing with death, while the eminent Emily Kame Kngwarreye honours the land from which she comes. The canvases of her intricate dot paintings, created using new tools and technology, appear to move and shimmer, telling stories of the animals and food to be found there.

Mosaic replica of the Tasman Map in the State Library of NSW

State Library of NSW ❾

Macquarie St. **Map** 4 F1.
📞 9273 1414. 🚌 Sydney Explorer, Elizabeth St routes. 🕐 9am–9pm Mon–Fri, 11am–5pm Sat & Sun. ⬤ some public hols. Mitchell Library closed Sun. 🖳 🛈 ♿ ✉

THE STATE LIBRARY is housed in two separate buildings connected by a passageway and a glass bridge. The older building, the Mitchell Library wing (1906), is a majestic sandstone edifice facing the Royal Botanic Gardens. Huge stone columns supporting a vaulted ceiling frame the impressive vestibule. On the vestibule floor is a mosaic replica of an old map illustrating the two voyages made to Australia by Dutch navigator Abel Tasman in the 1640s. The original Tasman Map is held in the Mitchell Library as part of its large collection of historic Australian paintings, books, documents and pictorial records.

The Mitchell wing's vast reading room, with its huge skylight and oak panelling, is just beyond the main vestibule.

The newest section, a contemporary structure facing Macquarie Street, houses the State Reference Library.

Outside the library, also facing Macquarie Street, is a statue of explorer Matthew Flinders. Behind him on the windowsill is a statue of his co-voyager, his faithful cat, Trim.

Parliament House ❿

Macquarie St. **Map** 4 F1.
📞 9230 2111. 🚌 Sydney Explorer, Elizabeth St routes. ✍ book in advance by calling the booking office on 9230 2637. ⬤ most public hols. ♿

THE CENTRAL SECTION of this building, which houses the State Parliament, is part of the original Sydney Hospital built from 1811–16. It has been a seat of government since the 1820s when the newly appointed Legislative Council first held meetings here. The building was extended twice during the 19th century and again during the 1970s and 1980s. The current building contains the chambers for both houses of state parliament, as well as parliamentary offices.

Malby's celestial globe, Parliament House

MACQUARIE STREET

Described in the 1860s as one of the gloomiest streets in Sydney, this could now claim to be the most elegant. Open on the northeastern side to the harbour breezes and the greenery of The Domain, a leisurely walk down this tree-lined street is one of the most pleasurable ways to view the architectural heritage of Sydney.

The Legislative Assembly, the lower house of state parliament, is furnished in the traditional green of the British House of Commons.

The new wing of the library was built in 1988 and connected to the old section by a glass walkway.

The Mitchell Library wing's portico (1906) has Ionic columns.

Parliament House was once the convict-built Rum Hospital's northern wing.

STATE LIBRARY OF NSW *(1906–41)*   **PARLIAMENT HOUSE** *(1811–1*

Parliamentary memorabilia is on view in the Jubilee Room, as are displays showing Parliament House's development and the legislative history of New South Wales.

The corrugated iron building with a cast-iron façade tacked on at the southern end was a pre-fabricated kit from England. It was originally intended as a chapel for the gold fields, but was diverted from this purpose and sent to Sydney. In 1856, this dismantled kit became the chamber for the new Legislative Council. Its packing cases were used to line this chamber; the rough timber is still on view inside.

Stained glass at Sydney Hospital

the Rum Hospital because the builders were paid by being allowed to import rum for resale. Both the north and south wings of the Rum Hospital survive as Parliament House and the Sydney Mint. The central wing, which was in danger of collapsing, was demolished in 1879 and the new hospital, which still functions today, was completed in 1894. The Classical Revival building boasts a Baroque staircase and elegant floral stained-glass windows in its entrance hall.

Florence Nightingale approved the design of the 1868 nurses' wing. In the inner courtyard, there is a brightly coloured Art Deco fountain (1907).

At the front of the hospital sits *Il Porcellino*, a brass boar. It is a copy of a 17th-century fountain in Florence's Mercato Nuovo. Donated in 1968 by an Italian woman whose relatives had worked at the hospital, the statue is an enduring symbol of the close friendship between Italy and Australia.

Like his Florentine counterpart, *Il Porcellino* is supposed to bring good luck to all those who rub his snout. All coins tossed in the shallow pool at his feet for luck and fortune are collected for the hospital.

Sydney Hospital ⓫

Macquarie St. **Map** 1 C4.
📞 9382 7111. 🚌 *Sydney Explorer, Elizabeth St routes.* ⏰ *daily.* 🎫 *for tours.* 📷 ♿ 🏪 *must be booked in advance by telephone.*

THIS IMPOSING COLLECTION of Victorian sandstone buildings stands on the site of what was once the central section of the original convict-built Sydney Hospital – known as

Il Porcellino, **the brass boar in front of Sydney Hospital**

The lamps *hanging over the gateways of Parliament House are reproductions of the 19th-century gas lamps that used to stand here.*

The Little Shop, *a tiny corner store, currently resides in one of two domed former gatehouses.*

The entrance stairs *of Pyrmont sandstone have set the tone for all renovations. The stone, quarried in colonial times, must be matched exactly.*

Corrugated iron and cast-iron façade

Arched sandstone bridges

Arcaded stone verandas with ornate balustrading

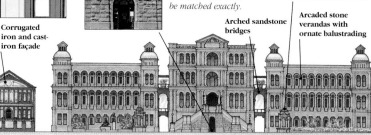

SYDNEY HOSPITAL *(1868–94)*

Sydney Mint ⑫

Macquarie St. **Map** 1 C5.
☐ 9692 8366. ☐ *Sydney Explorer,
Elizabeth St routes.* ● *to the public.*

THE GOLD RUSHES of the mid-
19th century transformed
colonial Australia. The Sydney
Mint opened in the 1816 Rum
Hospital's south wing in 1854
to turn recently discovered
gold into bullion and currency.
It was the first branch of the
Royal Mint to be established
outside London. The Mint
was closed in 1927 as it was
no longer competitive with the
Melbourne and Perth Mints.
The Georgian building went
into its own decline after it was
converted into government
offices. In the 1950s, the front
courtyard was even used as a
car park. In 1982, after restoration, it opened as a branch of
the Powerhouse Museum *(see
pp100–101)*, but the collection
moved to the main museum
in Harris Street.
This building is now under
the auspices of the Historic
Houses Trust of NSW and is
used as a function centre. It is
not open for viewing by the
general public but can, of
course, be viewed from the
outside and there is currently
a small historical display near
the main entrance.

Replica convict hammocks on the
third floor of Hyde Park Barracks

FRANCIS GREENWAY, CONVICT ARCHITECT

**Francis Greenway
(1777–1837)**

Until recently, Australian $10 notes bore
the portrait of the early colonial architect
Francis Greenway, the only currency in
the world to pay tribute to a convicted
forger. Greenway was transported to
Sydney in 1814 to serve 14 years for his
crime. Under the patronage of Governor
Macquarie, who appointed him Civil
Architect in 1816, Greenway designed
more than 40 buildings, of which
only 11 remain today. He received
a full pardon in 1819, but soon fell
out of favour as he persisted in
charging large fees while still on a
government salary. Greenway died
in poverty in 1837.

Hyde Park Barracks ⑬

Queens Square, Macquarie St. **Map**
1 C5. ☐ 9223 8922. ☐ *St James,
Martin Place.* ☐ *9:30am–5pm daily.*
● *Good Fri, 25 Dec.* ⬚ ◘ ☐
level one only. ☐ *book in advance
for group tours.*

DESCRIBED BY Governor
Macquarie as "spacious"
and "well-aired", the beautifully
proportioned barracks are the
work of Francis Greenway and
are considered his masterpiece.
They were completed in 1819

MACQUARIE STREET

Fine examples of Francis Greenway's Georgian
style are within an easy walk of one another at
the Hyde Park end of Macquarie Street. The
brick and sandstone of Hyde Park Barracks, St
James Church and the Old Supreme Court
Building form a harmonious group on the site
the governor envisaged as the city's civic centre.

*Sydney Mint,
like its twin, Parliament
House, has an unusual
double-colonnaded,
two-storeyed veranda.*

*The roof of the Mint
has now been com-
pletely restored to
replicate the original
wooden shingles in
casuarina (she-oak).*

*The stone wall
of Hyde Park Barracks' northwest pavilion still bears the
marks of the convicts' chisels.*

**Hyde Park
Barracks Café**

SYDNEY MINT *(1816)*

by convict labour and designed to house 600 convicts who had previously been forced to find their own lodgings after their day's work. Subsequently, the building housed Irish orphans and then single female immigrants, before becoming courts and legal offices. Refurbished in 1990, it reopened as a museum with exhibits covering the the site and its occupants over the years.

The displays include a room reconstructed as convict quarters of the 1820s, as well as pictures, models and artifacts relating to this period of Australian history. Many of the objects recovered during archaeological digs at the site and now on display had been dragged away by rats to their nests; the scavenging rodents are acknowledged as valuable agents of preservation.

The Greenway Gallery on the first floor holds temporary exhibitions on history, ideas and culture. From the Barracks Café, which incorporates the original confinement cell area, the visitor can enjoy refreshment, gazing out over the now serene courtyard, once the scene of brutal convict floggings.

Detail from the Children's Chapel mural in the St James' Church crypt

St James Church ⑭

173 King St. **Map** 1 B5. 9232 3022. St James, Martin Place. 8:30am–5:30pm daily
Free concerts Wed 1.15pm.

THIS FINE GEORGIAN building, constructed with convict-made bricks, was designed as a courthouse in 1819. The architect, Francis Greenway, was forced to convert it into a church in 1820, when plans to build a grand cathedral on George Street were abandoned.

Greenway unhappy about the change, designed a simple yet elegant church. Consecrated in 1824 by Samuel Marsden, the infamous "flogging parson", it is Sydney's oldest church. Many additions have been carried out, including designs by John Verge in which the pulpit faced towards high-rent pews, while convicts and the military sat behind the preacher where the service would have been inaudible. A Children's Chapel was added in 1930.

Prominent members of early 19th-century society, many of whom died violently, are commemorated in marble tablets. These tell the full and bloody stories of luckless explorers, the governor's wife dashed to her death from her carriage, and shipwreck victims.

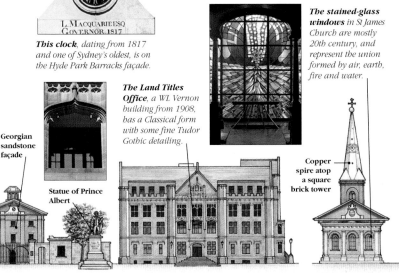

This clock, dating from 1817 and one of Sydney's oldest, is on the Hyde Park Barracks façade.

L. MACQUARIE ESQ GOVERNOR 1817

The stained-glass windows in St James Church are mostly 20th century, and represent the union formed by air, earth, fire and water.

The Land Titles Office, a WL Vernon building from 1908, has a Classical form with some fine Tudor Gothic detailing.

Georgian sandstone façade

Statue of Prince Albert

Copper spire atop a square brick tower

DE PARK BARRACKS (1817–19)   LAND TITLES OFFICE (1908–13)   ST JAMES (1820)

KINGS CROSS AND DARLINGHURST

SITUATED ON the eastern fringe of the city, Kings Cross, known as "The Cross", and Darlinghurst are a couple of Sydney celebrities. Their allure is tarnished – or enhanced, perhaps – by trails of scandal and corruption. Kings Cross, particularly, is still regarded as a hotbed of vice; both areas still bear the taint of 1920s gangland associations. In fact, both are now cosmopolitan areas – among the most densely populated parts of

Façade detail, Del Rio (see p119)

Sydney, famed as much for their street life and thriving café culture as for their unsavoury features. Kings Cross exudes a welcome breath of bohemia, in spite of the sleaze of Darlinghurst Road and the flaunting of its red light district. Darlinghurst comes brilliantly into its own every March, when the flamboyant Gay and Lesbian Mardi Gras parade, supported by huge crowds of spectators, makes its triumphant way along Oxford Street.

SIGHTS AT A GLANCE

Historic Streets and Buildings
Victoria Street **2**
Elizabeth Bay House **3**
Old Gaol, Darlinghurst **6**
Darlinghurst Court House **7**

Museums and Galleries
Sydney Jewish Museum **5**

Parks and Gardens
Beare Park **4**

Monuments
El Alamein Fountain **1**

GETTING THERE
Kings Cross railway station serves the area. Bus number 311 travels through Kings Cross and Darlinghurst, while the 324, 325 and 389 are also useful. Buses 378, 380 and 382 travel along Oxford Street.

0 metres	100
0 yards	100

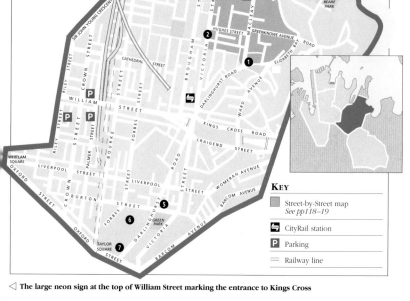

KEY

	Street-by-Street map *See pp118–19*
CityRail station
P	Parking
=	Railway line

◁ **The large neon sign at the top of William Street marking the entrance to Kings Cross**

Street-by-Street: Potts Point

Beare Park fountain detail

THE SUBSTANTIAL VICTORIAN houses filling the streets of this old suburb are excellent examples of the 19th-century concern with architectural harmony. New building projects were designed to enhance rather than contradict the surrounding buildings and general streetscape. Monumental structures and fine details of moulded stuccoed parapets, cornices and friezes, even the spandrels in herringbone pattern, are all integral parts of a grand suburban plan. (This plan included an 1831 order that all houses cost at least £1,000.) Cool and dark verandas extend the street's green canopy of shade, leaving an impression of cool drinks enjoyed on hot summer days in fine Victorian style.

The McElhone Stairs were preceded by a wooden ladder that linked Woolloomooloo Hill, as Kings Cross was known, to the estate far below.

★ **Victoria Street**
In 1972–4, residents of this historic street fought a sometimes violent battle against developers wanting to build high-rise office towers, motels and blocks of flats ❷

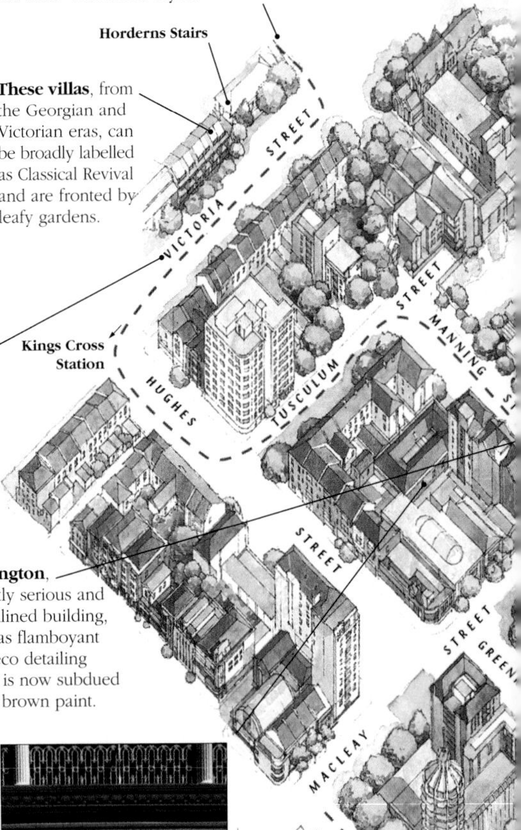

Horderns Stairs

These villas, from the Georgian and Victorian eras, can be broadly labelled as Classical Revival and are fronted by leafy gardens.

Kings Cross Station

Werrington, a mostly serious and streamlined building, also has flamboyant Art Deco detailing which is now subdued under brown paint.

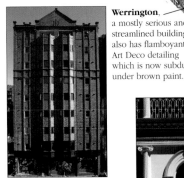

Tusculum Villa was just one of a number of 1830s houses subject to "villa conditions". All had to face Government House, be of a high monetary value and be built within three years.

STAR SIGHTS

★ **Victoria Street**

★ **Elizabeth Bay House**

Challis Avenue is a fine and shady complement to nearby Victoria Street. This Romanesque group of terrace houses has an unusual façade, with arches fronting deep verandas and a grand ground floor colonnade.

LOCATOR MAP
See Street Finder, map 2

Rockwall, a symmetrical and compact Regency villa, was built to the designs of the architect John Verge (see p120) in 1830–7.

Del Rio is a finely detailed high-rise apartment block. It clearly exhibits the Spanish Mission influence that filtered through from California in the first quarter of the 20th century.

Landmark Hotel

★ **Elizabeth Bay House**
A contemporary exclaimed over the beauty of the 1830s garden: "trees from Rio, the West Indies, the East Indies, China . . . the bulbs from the Cape are splendid" ❸

The Arthur McElhone Reserve

Art Deco Birtley Towers

0 metres   50

0 yards   50

KEY

– – – Suggested route

Elizabeth Bay was part of the original land grant to Alexander Macleay (see p120). He created a botanist's paradise with ornamental ponds, quaint grottoes and promenades winding all the way down to the harbour.

El Alamein Fountain, commemorating the World War II battle

El Alamein Fountain ❶

Fitzroy Gardens, Macleay St, Potts Point.
Map 2 E5. 🚌 311.

THIS DANDELION of a fountain in the heart of the Kings Cross district has a reputation for working so spasmodically that passers-by often murmur facetiously, "He loves me, he loves me not." Built in 1961, it commemorates the Australian army's role in the siege of Tobruk, Libya, and the battle of El Alamein in Egypt during World War II. At night, when it is brilliantly lit, the fountain looks surprisingly ethereal.

Victoria Street ❷

Potts Point. **Map** 5 B2. 🚌 311, 324, 325.

AT THE POTTS POINT end, this street of 19th-century terrace houses, interspersed with a few incongruous-looking high-rise blocks, is, by inner-city standards, almost a boulevard. This gracious street was once at the centre of a bitter conservation struggle, one which almost certainly cost a prominent heritage campaigner's life.

In the early 1970s, many residents, backed by the "green bans" *(see p29)* put in place by the Builders' Labourers' Federation of New South Wales, fought to prevent demolition of old buildings for high-rise

development. Juanita Nielsen, publisher of a local newspaper and heiress, vigorously took up the conservation battle. On 4 July 1975, she disappeared without trace. A subsequent inquest into her disappearance returned an open verdict.

As a result of the actions of the union and residents, most of Victoria Street's superb old buildings still stand. Ironically, they are now occupied not by the low-income residents who fought to save them, but by the well-off professionals who eventually displaced them.

Juanita Nielsen

Elizabeth Bay House ❸

7 Onslow Ave, Elizabeth Bay.
Map 2 F5. 📞 9356 3022. 🚌 Sydney Explorer, 311. ⏰ 10am–4:30pm Tue–Sun. ⬤ Good Fri, 25 Dec. ♿ 📷

ELIZABETH BAY HOUSE *(see pp22–3)* contains the finest colonial interior on display in Australia. It is a potent expression of how the 1840s depression cut short the 1830s' prosperous optimism. Designed in the fashionable Greek Revival style by John Verge, it was built for Colonial Secretary Alexander Macleay, from 1835–9. The domed oval saloon with its cantilevered staircase is recognized as Verge's masterpiece. The exterior is less satisfactory, as the intended colonnade and portico were not finished owing to a crisis in Macleay's financial affairs. The present portico dates from

1893. The interior is furnished to reflect Macleay's occupancy from 1839–45, and is based on inventories drawn up in 1845 for the transfer of the house and contents to Macleay's son, William Sharp. He took the house in return for payment of his father's debts, leading to a rift that was never resolved.

Macleay's original 22-hectare (54-acre) land grant was subdivided for flats and villas from the 1880s to 1927. In the 1940s, the house itself was divided into 15 flats. In 1942, the artist Donald Friend, while standing on the balcony of his flat – the former morning room – saw the ferry *Kuttabul* hit by a torpedo from a Japanese midget submarine. The house was restored and opened as a museum in 1977.

The sweeping staircase under the oval dome, Elizabeth Bay House

Beare Park ❹

Ithaca Rd, Elizabeth Bay. **Map** 2 F5. 🚌 311, 350.

ORIGINALLY A PART of the Macleay Estate, Beare Park is now encircled by a jumble of apartment blocks. A refuge from hectic Kings Cross, it is one of only a handful of parks serving a densely populated area. In the shape of a natural amphitheatre, the park puts Elizabeth Bay on glorious view.

The family home of JC Williamson, a famous theatrical entrepreneur who came to Australia from America in the 1870s, formerly stood at the eastern extremity of the park.

Star of David in the lobby of the Sydney Jewish Museum

Sydney Jewish Museum 5

148 Darlinghurst Rd, Darlinghurst. **Map** 5 B2. ☎ *9360 7999.* 🚌 *Sydney Explorer, Bondi & Bay Explorer, 311, 378.* ○ *10am–4pm Mon–Thu, 10am–2pm Fri, 11am–5pm Sun.* ● *Sat, Jewish hols.* 💲 ♿ 👉

SIXTEEN JEWISH convicts were on the First Fleet and many more were to be transported before the end of the convict era. As with other convicts, most would endure and some would thrive, seizing all the opportunities the colony had to offer for those wishing to make something of themselves.

The Sydney Jewish Museum relates stories of Australian Jewry within the context of the Holocaust. The ground floor display explores present-day Jewish traditions and culture within Australia. Ascending the stairs to mezzanine levels 1–6, the visitor passes through chronological and thematic exhibitions which unravel the history of the Holocaust.

From Hitler's rise to power and *Kristallnacht,* through the evacuation of the ghettos and the Final Solution, to the ultimate liberation of the infamous death camps and Nuremberg Trials, the harrowing events are graphically documented. This horrific period is recalled using photographs and relics, some exhumed from mass graves, as well as audiovisual exhibits and oral testimonies.

Holocaust survivors act as guides on each level. Their presence, bearing witness to the recorded events, lends considerable power and moving authenticity to the exhibits throughout the museum.

Old Gaol, Darlinghurst 6

Cnr Burton & Forbes Sts, Darlinghurst. **Map** 5 A2. ☎ *9339 8666.* 🚌 *378, 380, 382* ○ *9am–5pm Mon–Fri.* ● *public hols.* 📷 ♿

ORIGINALLY KNOWN as the Woolloomooloo Stockade and later as Darlinghurst Gaol, this complex is now part of the Sydney Institute of Technology. It was constructed over a 20-year period from 1822.

Surrounded by walls almost 7 m (23 ft) high, the cell blocks radiate from a central roundhouse. The jail is built of stone quarried on the site by convicts which was then chiselled by them into blocks.

No fewer than 67 people were executed here between 1841 and 1908. Perhaps the most notorious hangman was Alexander "The Strangler" Green, after whom Green Park, outside the jail, is thought to have been named. Green lived near the park until public hostility forced him to live in relative safety inside the jail.

Some of Australia's most noted artists, including Frank Hodgkinson, Jon Molvig and William Dobell, trained or taught at the art school which was established here in 1921.

The former Governor's house, Old Gaol, Darlinghurst

Darlinghurst Court House 7

Forbes St, Darlinghurst. **Map** 5 A2. ☎ *9368 2947.* 🚌 *378, 380, 382.* ○ *Feb–Dec: 10am–4pm Mon–Fri.* ● *Jan, public hols.*

ABUTTING THE GRIM old jail, to which it is connected by underground passages, and facing tawdry Taylors Square, this unlikely gem of Greek Revival architecture was begun in 1835 by Colonial Architect Mortimer Lewis. He was only responsible for the central block of the main building with its splendid six-columned Doric portico with fine Greek embellishments. The balancing side wings were not added until the 1880s.

The court house is still used by the state's Supreme Court mainly for criminal cases, and these are open to the public.

Beare Park, a quiet inner-city park with harbour views

PADDINGTON

ADDINGTON IS JUSTLY celebrated for its handsome terraces, but this "village in the city", as it is often dubbed, is also famed for its interesting speciality shops full of oddities and collectables, fine restaurants, small hotels, fashionable art galleries and antique dealers' shops. Paddington boasts a lively street culture, especially on Saturdays when people from far and wide flock to the famous weekly Paddington Bazaar, spilling out into the streets, pubs and cafés of the surrounding area. Stretching from the Victoria Barracks at its western end, along Oxford Street to the green haven of Centennial Park, Paddington slopes away from this bustling central thoroughfare into the narrow lanes and elegant, leafy streets. The suburb has undergone a series of radical transformations. The first Paddington was built in the 1830s as a Georgian weekend retreat for the moneyed class. These gracious homes had a short life, before being knocked down and subdivided. The terraces succeeding them fell into ruin by the 1920s, but are now admired as finely restored Victorian homes with their distinctive wrought-iron "lace" verandas. The glimpses of harbour found in the quiet streets make Paddington one of Sydney's most sought-after residential areas.

Clock tower on Paddington Town Hall

SIGHTS AT A GLANCE

Historic Streets and Buildings
Paddington Street ❶
Fox Studios ❷
Five Ways ❹
Juniper Hall ❺
Paddington Town Hall ❻
Paddington Village ❼
Victoria Barracks ❽

Parks and Gardens
Centennial Park ❾

Markets
Paddington Markets ❸

GETTING THERE
The best way to travel to and around this area is by bus. Buses 378, 380 and 382 run along Oxford Street on their way between the city and beach suburbs, while bus 389 cuts through the back streets.

KEY

Street-by-Street map
See pp124–5

P Parking

0 metres   500
0 yards   500

◁ **The front entrance to a lovingly restored Victorian terrace house in Paddington**

Street-by-Street: Paddington

PADDINGTON BEGAN TO FLOURISH in the 1840s, when the decision was made to build the Victoria Barracks. At the time much of it was "the most wild looking place . . . barren sandhills with patches of scrub, hills and hollows galore". The area began to fill rapidly, as owner builders bought into the area and built short rows of terrace houses, many extremely narrow because of the lack of building regulations. After the Depression, most of Paddington was threatened with demolition, but was saved and restored by the large influx of postwar migrants.

Victorian finial in Union Street

★ Five Ways
This shopping hub was established in the late 19th century on the busy Glenmore roadway trodden out by bullocks ❸

Duxford Street's terrace houses in toning pale shades constitute an ideal of town planning: the Victorians preferred houses in a row to have a pleasingly uniform aspect.

"Gingerbread" houses can be seen in Broughton and Union Streets. With their steeply pitched gables and fretwork bargeboards, they are typical of the rustic Gothic Picturesque architectural style.

The London Tavern opened for business in 1875, making it the suburb's oldest pub. Like many of the pubs and delicatessens in this well-serviced suburb, it stands at the end of a row of terraces.

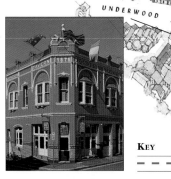

STAR SIGHTS

★ **Paddington Street**

★ **Five Ways**

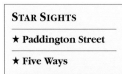

KEY

- - - - -   Suggested route

The Sherman Gallery is housed in a strikingly modern building. It is designed to hold Australian and international contemporary sculpture and paintings. Suitable access gates and a special in-house crane enable the movement of large-scale artworks, including textiles.

Paddington streets are a treasure chest of galleries, bars and restaurants.

LOCATOR MAP
See Street Finder, *maps 5 & 6*

Warwick, built in the 1860s, is a minor castle lying at the end of a row of humble terraces. Its turrets, battlements and assorted decorations, in a style somewhat fancifully described as "King Arthur", even adorn the garages at the rear.

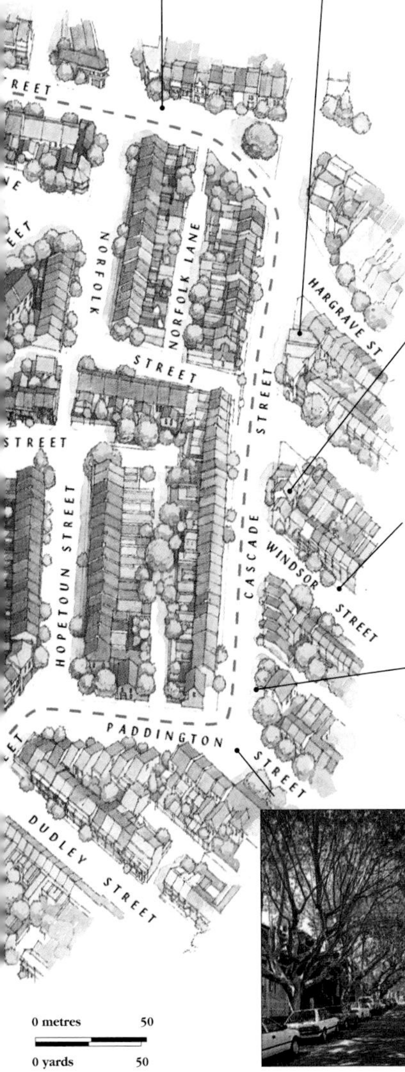

Windsor Street's terrace houses are, in some cases, a mere 4.5 m (15 ft) wide.

Street-making in Paddington's early days was often an expensive and complicated business. A cascade of water was dammed to build Cascade Street.

★ Paddington Street
Under the established plane trees, some of Paddington's finest Victorian terraces exemplify the building boom of 1860–90. Over 30 years, 3,800 houses were built in the suburb ❶

0 metres   50

0 yards   50

Paddington Street terrace house

Paddington Street ❶

Map 6 D3. 🚌 *378, 380, 382.*

WITH ITS HUGE PLANE trees shading the road and fine two-, three- and four-storey terrace houses on each side, Paddington Street is one of the oldest, loveliest, and at the same time most typical of the suburb's streets.

Paddington grew rapidly as a commuter suburb in the late 19th century and most of the terraces were built for renting to the city's artisans. They were cheaply decorated with iron lace (some of which had arrived in ships as ballast), as well as Grecian-style friezes, worked parapets, swagged urns, lions rampant, cornices, pilasters, scrolls and other fancy plastering. By the 1900s, these terraces had become unfashionable but in the 1960s, tastes changed again: the architecture of the terraces became fashionable and Paddington experienced a renaissance.

Paddington Street now has a chic atmosphere where small art galleries operate out of quaint and grand shopfronts.

Fox Studios ❷

Lang Rd, Moore Park. 📞 *9383 4333.* **Map** 5 C5. 🚌 *339, 355.* ◐ *Many retail shops open 10am–10pm.* 🅦 *www.foxstudios.com.au*

THERE IS A VIBRANT atmosphere at Fox Studios, which is located next door to the working studios that

produced some very famous movies, such as *The Matrix* and *Moulin Rouge.*

There are 16 cinema screens where you can watch the latest movies, and at the La Premiere cinema you can enjoy your movie with wine and cheese, sitting on comfortable sofas. There are four live-entertainment venues which regularly feature the latest local and international acts. You can also enjoy a game of miniature golf, bungy trampolining, bowling or seasonal ice-skating, and children will love the three well-designed playgrounds.

There are over fifteen restaurants, cafés and bars offering a range of cuisines, from Modern Australian, Italian and Seafood to Continental and Asian fare.

Every Wednesday you can sample fresh produce at the Farmers Market or try a gourmet delicacy from one of the 40 stallholders at the weekend market. Many of the stalls offer free tastings – from pickled garlic to chilli sauce.

Shops are open until late, and there is a good selection – offering fashion, books and homewares. There is plenty of undercover parking and the Studios are also readily accessible by public transport.

Paddington Markets ❸

395 Oxford St. **Map** 6 D4. 📞 *9331 2923.* 🚌 *378, 380, 382.* ◐ *10am–4pm (5pm daylight saving)* Sat. ● *25 Dec.* 📷 ♿ *See* ***Shops and Markets*** *p203.*

THIS MARKET, which began in 1973, takes place every Saturday, come rain or shine, in the grounds of Paddington Village Uniting Church and its neighbouring school. It is a place to meet and be seen as much as it is to shop. Stallholders come from all over the world, and many young designers, hoping to launch their careers, display their wares. Among the offerings are jewellery, pottery new and secondhand clothing and an array of other arts and crafts.

Whatever you are looking for, you are likely to find it

here, from designer bags and clothes or a tarot reading, to Oriental massages, bonsai trees and handmade soaps.

Five Ways ❹

Cnr Glenmore Rd & Heeley St. **Map** 5 C3. 🚌 *389.*

AT THIS PICTURESQUE junction, a busy shopping hub developed by the tramline that once ran to Bondi Beach. On the five corners stand Victorian and early 20th-century shops, one now a restaurant.

On another corner is the impressive three-storey Royal Hotel *(see p196),* built in 1888. This mixed Victorian and Classical Revival building, has a characteristic intricate cast-iron "lace" screen balcony offering harbour views, is typical of the hotel architecture of the time.

Juniper Hall ❺

250 Oxford St. **Map** 5 C3. 📞 *9258 0123.* 🚌 *378, 380, 382.* ◐ *to public.*

THE EMANCIPIST gin distiller Robert Cooper built this superb example of Colonial Georgian architecture for his third wife, Sarah. He named it after the main ingredient of the gin that made his fortune.

Completed in 1824, it is the oldest building in Paddington still standing. It is probably also the largest and most extravagant. It had to be: he already had 14 children when he declared that Sarah would have the finest house in Sydney.

Juniper Hall was saved from demolition in the mid-1980s and restored in fine style. Now part of the National Trust, it is used as private office space.

Balcony of the Royal Hotel in the heart of Paddington

Paddington Town Hall **6**

Cnr Oxford St & Oatley Rd. **Map** 5 C3.
🚌 378, 380, 382. ⬤ 10am–4pm
Mon–Fri. ⬤ public hols. 📷

THE PADDINGTON Town Hall
was completed in 1891.
An international competition
which, in a spirit of Victorian
self-confidence, was intended
to produce the state's finest
town hall, was won by local
architect JE Kemp. His Classical Revival building, to which
a clock tower was later added,
still dominates the surrounding
area, although it is no longer
a centre of local government.

The building now houses
Chauvel Cinema *(see p210)*,
run by the Australian Film
Institute, Paddington Library,
a radio station, commercial
offices and a large ballroom
that is available for hire.

Paddington Town Hall

Paddington Village **7**

Cnr Gipps & Shadforth Sts. **Map** 5 C3.
🚌 378, 380, 382.

PADDINGTON BEGAN its life
as a working-class suburb.
The community comprised the
carpenters, quarrymen and
stonemasons who supervised
the convict gangs that built
Victoria Barracks in the 1840s.

The artisans and their families occupied a tight huddle of
spartan houses, a few of which
still remain, crowded into the
narrow streets nearby. Like
the barracks, these dwellings
and surrounding shops and
hotels were built mainly of
locally quarried stone.

The lush green expanse of Centennial Park

Victoria Barracks **8**

Oxford St. **Map** 5 B3. 📞 9339 3000.
🚌 378, 380, 382. **Museum** 📞 9339
3330. ⬤ 10am–1pm Thu, 10am–
3pm Sun. ⬤ 25-26 Dec, 1 Jan. 📷
♿ 🎫 **Parade & tour:** 10am Thu.

VICTORIA BARRACKS is the
largest and best-preserved
group of late Georgian architecture in Australia, covering
almost 12 ha (29 acres). It is
widely considered to be one
of the best examples of a
military barracks in the world.

Designed by the Colonial
Engineer, Lieutenant Colonel
George Barney, the barracks
were built between 1841 and
1848 using local sandstone
quarried by mainly convict
labour. Originally intended to
house 800 men, it has been in
continuous military use ever
since, and still operates as a
centre of military planning,
administration and command.

The main block is 225 m
(740 ft) long and has symmetrical two-storey wings with
cast-iron verandas flanking a
central archway. The perimeter
walls, which are designed to

**The archway at the Oxford Street
entrance to Victoria Barracks**

repel surprise attacks, have
foundations 10 m (40 ft) deep
in places. In a former jail
block, a museum traces New
South Wales' military heritage.

Centennial Park **9**

Map 6 E5. 📞 9339 6699. 🚌 Clovelly,
Coogee, Maroubra, Randwick, Bronte,
City, Bondi Beach & Bondi Junction
routes. ⬤ Mar–Apr: 6am–6pm daily,
May–Aug: 6:30am–5:30pm daily,
Sep–Oct: 6am–6pm daily, Nov–Feb
6am–8pm daily. 🎫 on request.

ENTERING THIS 220-ha (544-
acre) park through one of
its sandstone and wrought-iron
gates, the visitor may wonder
how such an extensive and
idyllic place has survived so
close to the centre of the city.

Formerly a common, it was
dedicated "to the enjoyment
of the people of New South
Wales forever" on 26 January
1888, the centenary of the
foundation of the colony. On
1 January 1901, more than
100,000 people gathered here
to witness the Commonwealth
of Australia come into being,
when Australia's first federal
ministry was sworn in by the
first governor-general.

Today picnickers, painters,
runners, and those on horses,
bikes and in-line skates (all of
which can be hired nearby)
use this vast recreation area.

Once the source of Sydney's
water supply, the swamps are
now home to many waterbirds.
Within the park are ornamental ponds, cultivated gardens,
an Avenue of Palms with 400
trees, a sports ground and a
café *(see p194)*.

FURTHER AFIELD

BEYOND THE INNER CITY, numerous places vie for the visitor's attention. Around the harbour foreshores are picturesque suburbs, secluded beaches, scenic outlooks and cultural and historic sights. Taronga Zoo is worth a visit as much for its incomparable setting as for its birds and animals. Manly, stretching between harbour and ocean, is the

Mr and Mrs Luna Park

city's northern playground, while Bondi is its eastern counterpart. In Balmain, Glebe and Surry Hills, the visitor can experience the character of the inner suburbs. Still further afield, out west at Parramatta, there are sights that recall and evoke the first days of European settlement and the colony's initially unsteady steps towards agricultural self-sufficiency.

SIGHTS AT A GLANCE

Historic Districts and Buildings
University of Sydney ❸
Balmain ❻
Kirribilli Point ❽
North Head ⓬
Vaucluse House ⓭
Watsons Bay ⓯
Macquarie Lighthouse ⓰
Captain Cook's Landing Place ⓲
Elizabeth Farm ⓴
Hambledon Cottage ㉑
Experiment Farm Cottage ㉒
Old Government House ㉔

16 km = 10 miles

Parks and Gardens
Nielsen Park ⓮

Museums and Galleries
Brett Whiteley Studio ❶
Nutcote ❾

Entertainment
Luna Park ❼
Taronga Zoo pp134–5 ❿
Sydney Olympic Park ⓳

Beaches
Manly ⓫
Bondi Beach ⓱

Restaurants and Pubs
Surry Hills ❷
Glebe ❹

Markets
Sydney Fish Market ❺

Cemeteries
St John's Cemetery ㉓

KEY

⬜ Main sightseeing areas
⬜ Park or reserve
✈ Airport
③ Metroad route
══ Freeway or motorway
▬ Major road
═ Minor road

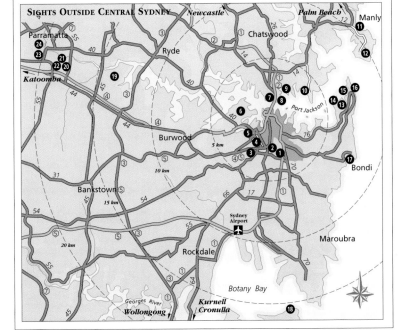

SIGHTS OUTSIDE CENTRAL SYDNEY

◁ **The majestic clock tower rising above the main quadrangle at the University of Sydney**

Brett Whiteley Studio ❶

2 Raper St, Surry Hills. **Map** 5 A4.
🄲 9225 1881. 🚌 343, 372, 393.
🄾 10am–4pm Sat & Sun, or by
appointment on Thu & Fri. ● Easter
Sun, 25 Dec. 🄰 🄵 partial access.

I N JUNE 1992, Brett Whiteley,
enfant terrible of Australian
contemporary art, died unex-
pectedly at the age of 53. An
internationally acclaimed and
prolific artist, he produced
some of the most sumptuous
images of Sydney and its distinctive harbour ever painted.

In 1985, Whiteley bought a
former factory and converted
it into a studio and residence.
The studio is now a public
museum and art gallery. It
features the work of Whiteley
and other artists. Visitors gain
an insight into Whiteley's life
and work through changing
exhibitions and displays of his
effects and memorabilia. The
studio is under the administration of the Art Gallery of New
South Wales *(see pp108–11)*.

Surry Hills ❷

Map 5 A3. 🚌 301, 302, 303, 304,
339, Oxford St routes. See **Shops
and Markets** pp200–201.

T HIS WAS ONCE one of the
more depressed areas of
the inner city. In the 1920s,
Surry Hills was a haunt of the
razor gangs that terrorized
inner-city Sydney. The 1940s
slums were vividly described in
Ruth Park's celebrated novels
Poor Man's Orange and *The*

Shop in Crown Street, Surry Hills

Harp in the South. In the postwar years, the low property
and rental prices attracted a
large number of new migrants
to the already-hectic district.

In recent decades, young
professionals have moved into
the area, lured by the charm
of its Victorian terraces and
closeness to the city. Many
of the suburb's traditional
inhabitants have since
been displaced.

Today Surry Hills
is a curious mixture
of fashion and seedi-
ness. Newly renovated
houses stand alongside
dilapidated dwellings,
while streets of elegant
Victorian terraces abut
modern high-rise flats and
factory warehouses.

For the visitor, the
suburb offers a wide
range of ethnic cuisines, often
at bargain prices. It is famed
for the Lebanese and Turkish
restaurants that cluster near
the intersection of Cleveland
and Elizabeth Streets. You will
also find Indian, Chinese, Thai,

French and numerous Italian
eateries scattered around the
suburb, along with smart and
casual cafés and stylish pubs.

Once the centre of Sydney's
garment trade, it still has factory outlets where clothing,
lingerie and haberdashery can
be purchased at below retail
prices. Alternative fashion and
retro clothing shops are found
at the Oxford Street end of
Crown Street. These boutiques
attract the street-smart crowd.

University of Sydney ❸

Parramatta Rd, Camperdown.
Map 3 B5. 🄲 9351 2222. 🚌 343,
Parramatta Rd & City Rd routes. 🄾
daily. 📷 🄵 🄲 phone 9351 2274
(essential to book one week in advance).

I NAUGURATED IN 1850, this is
Australia's oldest university.
The campus is a sprawling
hotchpotch of buildings
from different eras, of
often dubious architec-
tural merit. However,
the original Victorian
Gothic main building
still stands on its ele-
vated site, dominating
its surroundings. The
work of the Colonial
Architect Edmund
Blacket, it is scrupulously
modelled on the

Statue of Hermes,   architecture of Cam-
Nicholson Museum   bridge and Oxford.

It features intricate stone
tracery, a clock tower with
carved pinnacles, gargoyles
(one, in the quadrangle, represents a crocodile) and a
cloistered main quadrangle.

The gem of the complex,
and probably Blacket's finest
work, is the Great Hall at the
main building's northern end.
This grandly sombre hall, with
its carved cedar ceiling and
stained-glass windows depicting famous philosophers and
scientists, is often used for
public concerts as well as for
university ceremonies.

The Nicholson Museum of
antiquities, the natural history
Macleay Museum and the War
Memorial Art Gallery, which
houses the university's art
collection, are all within the
grounds. They are open to the
public on most weekdays.

Brett Whiteley Studio: former artist's studio, now a museum

Corner view of Badde Manors Café on Glebe Point Road, Glebe

Glebe ❹

Map 3 A4. 🚌 *431, 433. See* **Shops and Markets** *p203.*

T HE WORD "GLEBE" means land assigned to a clergyman as part of his benefice. In 1789, Governor Phillip granted 162 ha (400 acres) to Richard Johnson, the First Fleet chaplain, and his wife Mary. Almost all of the present suburb was once part of that Glebe Estate. Many of its streets wind down to the working harbour and contain terrace houses with Sydney wrought-iron "lace" in varying states of repair.

The once-grand residences of the 19th-century élite were mostly towards the harbour end of Glebe Point Road, with workers' cottages clustered nearer Parramatta Road. It is a mix that survives to this day. Glebe is partly a gentrified member of the café society and partly a humble address, while also being a dormitory suburb for students at the nearby University of Sydney.

It is densely populated and lively, with many restaurants and cafés in all price ranges, traditional and trendy pubs, good bookshops, an art-house cinema and shops selling everything from antique clocks to New Age goods and chattels. Glebe Market is held every Saturday and has stalls ranging from second-hand clothing and silver jewellery to bric-a-brac.

Sydney Fish Market ❺

Cnr Pyrmont Bridge Rd & Bank St, Pyrmont. **Map** 3 B2. 📞 *9660 1611.* 🚌 *501.* 🕐 *7am–4pm daily.* ⬤ *25 Dec.* 📷 ♿ 🎫 *Phone in advance.* 🌐 *www.sydneyfishmarket.com.au See* **Shops and Markets** *pp202–3.*

E VERY WEEKDAY, about 200 seafood retailers and dealers arrive at this cooperative fish market to bid for the previous day's catch. It is sold by Dutch auction, with prices starting high and decreasing, which halves the sale time. The volume and variety of the catch, including fish and seafood makes this the most diverse fish market after Tokyo.

A fair amount of this catch ends up, later in the morning, in the fish market's six large retail outlets which, for the general public, are its main attraction. As well as fresh fish, these retailers sell smoked salmon and roe, sushi, marinated baby octopus and many other ready-to-eat delicacies.

Visitors watch the experts as they tenderize octopus and squid in concrete mixers. As well as fishmongers, there are a number of fresh food shops, several restaurants and a seafood school – cost includes tuition, seafood and wine.

Balmain ❻

🚌 *433, 434, 442. See* **Shops and Markets** *p203 and* **Four Guided Walks** *pp142–3.*

B ALMAIN WAS ONCE one of Sydney's most staunchly working-class areas, with shipyards, a dry dock and repair yards, a coal mine, numerous rough-and-ready pubs and an intimidating criminal element. Its late 19th-century town hall, post office, court house and fire station in Darling Street reflect the civic pride of the suburb in the Victorian era.

In recent years, the many stone and timber cottages of what had become a slum have transformed into a charming, bustling suburb that still retains its village character, with interesting shops, galleries, cafés, restaurants and pubs.

The quietness of the Balmain peninsula, its proximity to the city and its bohemian ambience may explain why many prominent writers – including novelist Kate Grenville and playwright David Williamson – have lived and worked here.

The Saturday market, held at St Andrews Congregational Church in Darling Street, is one of Sydney's best. Antiques, estate jewellery and ingenious art and craft items are on sale.

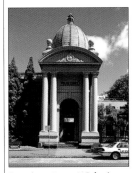

Imposing entrance to Balmain court house on Darling Street

THE COLOURFUL FACES OF LUNA PARK

The gateway to Luna Park is the gaping mouth of a huge laughing face, flanked by two 36-m (129-ft) Art Deco towers. Between 1935 and 1945, four successive canvas, wire and plaster faces fell to the ravages of time. Built in the 1950s, the fifth face was replaced in 1973 with one designed by the Sydney artist Martin Sharp. The seventh, from the 1980s, is now at the Powerhouse Museum *(see pp100–101)*. Today's face is made of polyurethane and painted fibreglass.

The present Luna Park face, crossing the harbour by barge

The Big Dipper at Luna Park

Luna Park ❼

1 Olympic Drive, Milsons Point. ⛴ *Milsons Point.* ◉ ♿

THIS FAMOUS FUN FAIR, built on the site of former Harbour Bridge construction workshops, was modelled on Luna Park at Coney Island, New York. Built in South Australia, Sydney's Luna Park was dismantled and re-erected on its present site in 1935. For the next 43 years it was one of the most conspicuous landmarks on the harbour foreshores. Except during the compulsory blackouts of World War II, its brilliant illuminations were a feature of the city's night scene.

In 1979, seven people were killed in a ghost train fire, a tragedy that led to the park's eventual closure in April 1988. In the early 1990s, Luna Park was refurbished. In 1995, it reopened briefly as a fun fair,

but this has since closed down and Luna Park's future remains uncertain. Redevelopment proposals for the site are currently being considered.

Luna Park retains many of its extravagant features. Las Vegas glitz and 1940s Futurism are just two of the styles decorating one of Sydney's most treasured icons. The old-style fun house Coney Island, Crystal Palace and the gateway face are all protected by heritage listing.

Kirribilli Point ❽

Kirribilli Ave, Kirribilli. ⛴ *Kirribilli North Sydney.*

THE TWO HOUSES occupying this prominent headland, in their delightful garden settings, are typical of the magnificent homes in sprawling grounds that once ringed the harbour. Most have been demolished

now and the land subdivided for apartment living. Kirribilli, meaning "place for fishing", is the most densely populated suburb in Australia.

The larger, more dominant of the two houses is Admiralty House, built as a single-storey residence in 1843. Between 1885 and 1913 it served as the residence of the commanding officer of Britain's Royal Navy Pacific Squadron, which was based in Sydney. Fortifications on the shoreline recall its military history. Now the official Sydney home of Australia's governor-general, it is said that even its shed could be considered the city's best address.

In 1855, the charming Gothic Kirribilli House, with its steep gables and decorative fretwork, was built in the grounds of Admiralty House. Today it is the official Sydney residence of Australia's prime minister.

Nutcote ❾

5 Wallaringa Ave, Neutral Bay. 📞 9953 4453. ⛴ *Kurraba Point, Neutral Bay.* ◯ *11am–3pm Wed–Sun.* ⬤ *some public hols.* ♿ ◉ ✔

ONE OF THE CLASSICS of Australian children's literature, *Snugglepot and Cuddlepie*, was published in 1918. Since then, these two characters – known as the "gumnut" babies along with the cartoon creatures Bib and Bub – have been loved by countless young Australians.

Nutcote was, for 44 years, the home of their creator, illustrator and author May Gibbs. Saved from demolition then

Admiralty House and Kirribilli House, near Sydney Harbour Bridge

Shop façades featuring decorative gables along Manly's Corso

restored and refurbished in the style of the 1930s, it opened in 1994 as an historic house museum. Visitors can view the author's painstakingly kept notebooks and other memorabilia (including the table at which she worked), as well as original editions of her books. There is a garden tea room, with views across the harbour and a shop that sells a range of May Gibbs' souvenirs.

May Gibbs' studio at Nutcote

Taronga Zoo ❿

See pp134–5.

Manly ⓫

🚢 Manly. **Oceanworld** West
Esplanade. 📞 9949 2644. 🕙 10am–
5:30pm daily. ● 25 Dec. 🅿️ 📷
📖 See **Four Guided Walks** pp146–7.

Long after Australia's conversion to the metric system, the slogan "seven miles from Sydney and a thousand miles from care" is still current. It refers to Manly and the 7-mile (11-km) journey from Circular Quay by harbour ferry. If asked to suggest a single excursion to enjoy during your time in the city, most Sydneysiders would nominate a ferry ride to Manly. This narrow stretch of land lying between the harbour and the ocean was named by Governor Phillip, even before the township of Sydney got its name, for the impressive bearing of the Aboriginal men.

As the ferry pulls in to the rejuvenated Manly wharf you will notice on the right many shops, restaurants and bars and on the left, the tranquil harbourside beach known as Manly Cove.

At the far end of Manly Cove is Oceanworld, where visitors can see reptiles, sharks, giant stingrays and other species in an underwater viewing tunnel.

The Corso is a lively pedestrian thoroughfare of souvenir shops and fast food outlets. It leads to Manly's ocean beach, with its promenade lined by towering Norfolk pines. Nearby stands a monument to a local newspaper proprietor who, in 1902, defied bans on daytime bathing and promptly found himself arrested. By the following year, however, Australia's bathing laws were liberalized.

In October each year, Manly plays host to the prestigious Manly Jazz Festival (see p48).

North Head ⓬

📞 9247 5033. 🚢 Manly.
Quarantine Station 🕙 1:10pm
Fri–Mon, Wed. Bookings essential.
Ghost tours Wed, Fri–Sun. Bookings
essential (starting times vary).
● Good Friday, 25 Dec. 🅿️ 📷 ♿
partial access in Quarantine Station.
📖 See **Parks and Reserves** pp44–7.

The majestic cliffs of North Head afford the finest views in Sydney Harbour National Park, providing vistas along the coastline, across to Middle Harbour and towards the city. North Head is also the ideal place for observing the movements of harbour and seagoing craft and especially for seeing off the yachts at the start of the annual Sydney to Hobart race (see p49).

The Quarantine Station nestles just above Spring Cove within the national park. Here, between 1832 and the 1960s, many ships, with their crews and passengers, were quarantined to protect Sydneysiders from the spread of epidemic diseases. More than 500 people died here, leading some people to believe the area is haunted.

Countless migrants spent their first months in Australia in this place of splendid isolation. Many of its internees left poignant messages and poems carved in the sandstone.

First-class quarters at the Quarantine Station, North Head

Taronga Zoo ⓾

Red kangaroo

THIS FAMOUS HARBOURSIDE ZOO is home to almost 2,000 animals, with a special emphasis placed on unique Australian wildlife exhibits. Conspicuous iron bars and fences have been dispensed with, as many of the large enclosures use moats to separate the wandering public from the curious animal onlookers contained in environments closely resembling their natural habitat. The zoo is involved in the breeding of endangered animals, and readily donates or exchanges animals to capitalize on the worldwide "gene pool".

Asiatic Elephant
This relatively large enclosure encourages more natural behaviour as the elephants are freely able to interact.

Australian Birds

Athol Wharf Road

Bradleys Head Road

Lower entrance

Athol Wharf

0 metres　　　　　100

0 yards　　　　　100

The platypus is one of only three species of egg-laying mammals.

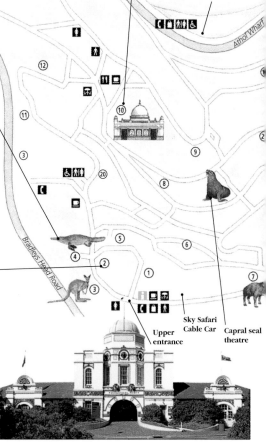

Common Wombat
This ground-dwelling animal is a powerful burrower able to move quickly if disturbed. It feeds on roots and has a pouch for carrying its young.

Bradleys Head Road

Sky Safari Cable Car

Upper entrance

Capral seal theatre

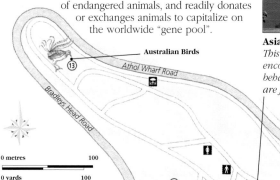

Upper Entrance
This edifice has greeted visitors since the opening in 1916. By 1917, more than half of Sydney's population had paid a visit.

STAR DISPLAYS

★ **Free Flight Bird Show**

★ **Orang-utan Rainforest**

★ **Koala Walkabout**

★ Orang-utan Rainforest
Threatened by widespread destruction of their natural habitat in the Sumatran and Borneo rainforests, these primates are on the world's endangered species list.

Visitors' Checklist

Bradleys Head Rd, Mosman.
☎ *9969 2777.* 🚌 *238, 247, 250.* ⛴ *Taronga Zoo.* 🕘 *9am–5pm daily (last adm 4:30pm).*
📷 ♿ 🍴 🛍
Concerts, talks, performances.

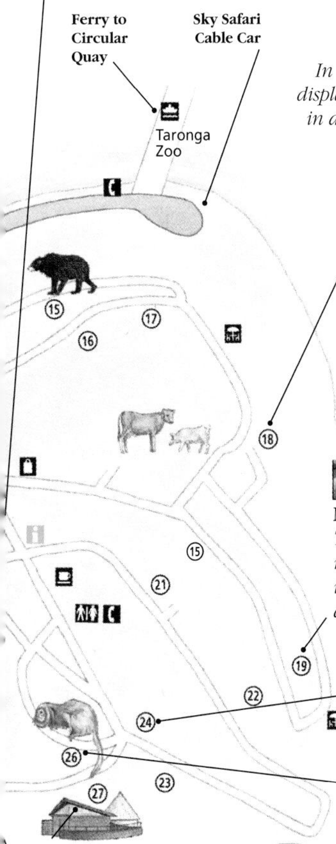
Ferry to Circular Quay
Sky Safari Cable Car
Taronga Zoo
15
17
16
18
15
21
19
22
24
26
27
23

★ Free Flight Bird Show
In this spectacular display, birds fly free in an amphitheatre overlooking the harbour.

Meerkat
This southern African mongoose always forages in groups, with a guard alert for signs of danger.

African Waterhole
Savannah waterholes attract many species. The zoo recreates that environment for giraffes, zebras and pygmi hippopotami.

The golden lion tamarin is the most endangered primate in the world today.

The Serpentaria has amphibians, invertebrates and reptiles.

★ Koala Walkabout
Visitors can see the koalas in their eucalypt habitat at tree level. The spiral ramp allows you to get close to feeding and sleeping animals.

Key to Animal Enclosures

African Waterhole 24
Asian elephant 10
Australian Birds 13
Australian Walkabout 3
Australia's Night Life 5
Bear 15
Chimpanzee Park 23
Creatures of the Wollemi 20
Dingo & Tasmanian devil 7
Echidna & platypus 4
Free Flight Bird Show 18
Golden lion tamarin 26
Gorilla 29
Jungle Cats 12
Koala Walkabout 28
Lion 21
Meerkat 19
Orang-utan Rainforest 25
Otter 16
Penguin 8
Red panda 17
Saltwater crocodile 9
Seals and sea-lions 14
Serpentaria 27
Snow leopard 22
Walk-through Rainforest 6
Wetlands 1
Wombat 2
Yellow-footed rock wallaby 11

Façade of Vaucluse House, with its garden and fountain

Vaucluse House ⓭

Wentworth Rd, Vaucluse.
(9388 7922. ▦ 325. ◯ 10am–4:30pm Tue–Sun. ● Good Fri, 25 Dec. ▨ ▣ �& limited. ▨

Tradition has it that the most riotous party colonial Sydney ever saw took place on the Vaucluse House lawns in 1831. WC Wentworth and 4,000 of his political cronies gathered there to celebrate the recall to England of Governor Ralph Darling, the arch-enemy.

WC Wentworth was a major figure in the colony, being one of the first three Europeans to cross the Blue Mountains *(see pp160–61)*. He was the son of a female convict and a physician forced to "volunteer" his services to the new colony in order to avoid conviction on a highway robbery charge.

The younger Wentworth became an author, barrister and statesman who stood for the Australian-born "currency" lads and lasses against the "sterling" English-born. He lived here with his family from 1829–53, during which time he drafted the Constitution Bill, giving self-government to the state.

Vaucluse House was begun in 1803 by Sir Henry Browne Hayes, a knight of the realm transported for kidnapping a Quaker heiress. Sitting comfortably in 11 ha (27 acres) of parkland, natural bush and cultivated gardens, this Gothic Revival house, with its many idiosyncratic additions, has been compared to a West Indian plantation house. The interior and grounds have been restored to 1840s style and the house contains some furniture that originally belonged to the Wentworth family. A popular tea house is in the grounds.

Greycliffe House, in the tranquil grounds of Nielsen Park

Nielsen Park ⓮

▦ 325. ◯ Sunrise–10pm daily.

Part of the Sydney Harbour National Park, Nielsen Park, with its grassy expanses, sandy beach and netted swimming pool, is the perfect spot for a family picnic. Here visitors can savour the unusual peace that descends on many harbour beaches on an endless sunny day. It is also an ideal vantage point from which to enjoy a spectacular summer sunset or simply to observe the coming and going of ferries and the meandering harbour traffic.

In the midst of this tranquil setting, enhancing its charm, stands Greycliffe House with its decorative gables and ornate chimney stacks. This Victorian Gothic mansion was completed in 1852 for WC Wentworth's daughter and now offers local national park information.

Watsons Bay ⓯

(9391 7100. ⛴ Watsons Bay. See **Four Guided Walks** pp148–9.

As the base for the boats that take the pilots out to arriving ships, this pretty bay has long been a vital part of the working harbour. It is also the home of Doyle's famous waterfront seafood restaurant, long a magnet for Sydneysiders and visitors alike.

Just up the hill and almost opposite the bay on the ocean side is The Gap, a spectacular cliff with tragic associations. Many troubled people have taken a suicidal leap from this rugged cliff on to the wave-lashed rocks below.

It was here that the ill-fated ship *Dunbar* was wrecked in 1857, with the loss of all but one of its 122 passengers and crew. Treacherous conditions had led to miscalculation of the ship's distance from the Heads. All hands were ordered

View over Watsons Bay, looking southwest towards the city

The crescent-shaped Bondi Beach, Sydney's most famous beach, looking towards North Bondi

on deck as The Gap's rock walls loomed. The recovered anchor is now set into the cliff near the shipwreck site.

The 1883 Macquarie Lighthouse overlooking the Pacific Ocean

Macquarie Lighthouse ⑯

🚌 324, 325. 📷 ♿

THIS IS THE SECOND lighthouse on this windswept site that is attributed to the convict architect Francis Greenway *(see p114)*. He supervised the construction of the first tower, which was completed in 1818 and described by Governor Macquarie as a "noble magnificent edifice". The colony's first lighthouse, it replaced the previous system of bonfires lit up along the headland and earned Greenway a conditional pardon. When the sandstone

eventually crumbled away, the present lighthouse was built. Although designed by Colonial Architect James Barnet, it was based on Greenway's original and was illuminated for the first time in 1883.

Bondi Beach ⑰

🚌 380, 382, 389, 321. See **Four Guided Walks** *pp144–5.*

THIS LONG CRESCENT of golden sand, so close to the city, has long been a mecca for the sun and surf set *(see pp54–5)*. Throughout the year, surfing enthusiasts visit from far and wide in search of the perfect wave, and inline skaters hone their skills on the promenade. But the beach life that once defined many Australians has declined in recent times, partly as a result of growing awareness of the dangers of sun exposure *(see p223)*, but also because of a shift in cultural attitudes and preoccupations.

People now seek out Bondi for its trendy seafront cafés and cosmopolitan milieu as much as for the beach. The pavilion, built in 1928 as changing rooms, has been a community centre since the 1970s. It is now a busy venue for festivals, plays, films and craft displays.

BONDI SURF BATHERS' LIFE SAVING CLUB

The founding of the surf lifesaving club at Bondi Beach in 1906 gave impetus to the formation of other local clubs, and ultimately to a global movement. An early club member demonstrated his new lifesaving reel, designed using hair pins and a cotton reel. Now updated, it is standard equipment on beaches worldwide. In 1938, Australia's largest surf rescue was mounted at Bondi, when more than 200 people were washed out to sea by freak waves. Five died, but lifesavers rescued more than 180, establishing their highly dependable reputation.

Bondi surf lifesaving team at the Bondi Surf Carnival, 1937

Captain Cook's Landing Place  ⑱

Captain Cook Drive, Kurnell.
C 9668 9111. 🚌 987. **Toll Gate**
○ 7am–7pm daily. **Discovery
Centre** ○ 11am–3pm Mon–Fri,
10am–4:30pm Sat & Sun. ● 25 Dec.
🅿 📷 ♿

Pampas grass and banana plants in the garden at Elizabeth Farm

Aᴸᴛʜᴏᴜɢʜ ᴅɪꜰꜰɪᴄᴜʟᴛ to get to, visitors will find this place worth the effort. It is, after all, one of Australia's most important European historic sites. Here James Cook, botanists Daniel Solander and Joseph Banks and the crew of HMS *Endeavour* landed on 29 April 1770. Aboriginal peoples waving spears at the invaders were shot at. One, hit in the legs, returned with a shield to defend himself from attack.

Nowadays people can cast a fishing line from the rock where the Europeans stepped ashore. Nearby are the site of

Cook's Obelisk, overlooking Botany Bay, Captain Cook's Landing Place

a well where, Cook recorded, a shore party "found fresh water sufficient to water the ship" and a monument which marks the first recorded European burial in Australia.

There are also monuments to Solander, Banks and Cook, but it is the peaceful ambience that is most impressive. Now part of Botany Bay National Park, Captain Cook's Landing Place has lovely walks, some accessible to wheelchairs, where visitors may roam and observe the flora which led to the naming of Botany Bay.

The Discovery Centre in the park focuses on a number of themes: the bay's wetlands

and the importance of their conservation; an interesting exhibition detailing Cook's exploration of the area; and an introduction to Aboriginal customs and culture.

Sydney Olympic Park ⑲

Homebush Bay. **C** 9714 7958. 🚆
Olympic Park. Visitors Centre (1 Herb
Elliott Ave). ○ 9am–5pm daily.
● Good Fri, 25 Dec, 26 Dec, 1 Jan.
🅿 ♿ ▢ 🏛 Ⓦ www.
sydneyolympicpark.nsw.gov.au

Oɴᴄᴇ ʜᴏꜱᴛ ᴛᴏ the 27th Summer Olympic Games and Paralympic Games, Sydney Olympic Park is situated at Homebush Bay, 14 km (8.5 miles) west of the city centre.

To enjoy the park, visitors can follow a self-guided walk or buy a ticket for a guided tour to access venues such as the Showground and the SuperDome. For nature lovers, there is a tour of the five wetlands of the Bicentennial Park as well as Breakfast with the Birds – breakfast is served after a morning of bird watching. All tickets for tours can be bought at the Visitor's Centre.

Other facilities at the park include the Aquatic Centre, with a kids waterpark, and the Tennis Centre, where you can play in the footsteps of such greats as Lleyton Hewitt. There are picnic areas and cafés throughout the park and on the fourth Sunday of every month you can sample fresh produce and gourmet food at the Boulevarde Market.

Elizabeth Farm ⑳

70 Alice St, Rosehill. **C** 9635 9488.
🚆 Parramatta. 🚆 Parramatta or
Granville. ○ 10am–5pm daily. ●
Good Fri, 25 Dec. 🅿 📷 ♿ ▢ 🍴

Tʜᴇ ᴅɪꜱᴄᴏᴠᴇʀʏ of fertile land at Parramatta, and the harvesting of its first successful grain crop in 1790, helped save the fledgling colony from starvation and led to the rapid development of the area.

This zone was the location of several of Australia's first colonial land grants. In 1793, John Macarthur, who became a wealthy farmer and sheep breeder, was granted 40 ha (100 acres) of land at Parramatta. He named the property after his wife and this was to be Elizabeth's home for the rest of her life. Macarthur was often absent from the farm as the centre of his wool operations had moved to Camden.

Part of the house, a simple stone cottage built in 1793, still remains and it is the oldest European building in Australia. As it was added to over the

John Macarthur, 1766–1834

next 50 years, it developed into a substantial home with many features of a typical Australian homestead. Simply furnished to the period of 1820–50, with reproductions of paintings and other possessions, the house is now a museum that strongly evokes the original inhabitants' life and times.

The kitchen, Hambledon Cottage

Hambledon Cottage 21

63 Hassall St, Parramatta.
📞 9635 6924. 🚉 Parramatta.
🕐 11am–4pm Wed, Thu, Sat, Sun & public hols. 🅿 ♿ 📷

THIS DELIGHTFUL cottage, with its walls of rendered and painted sandstock, was built in 1824 as the retirement home for Penelope Lucas, governess to the Macarthur daughters. It is set in a park containing trees brought to Australia in 1817 by John Macarthur.

Visitors can wander through rooms that have been restored to the period 1820–50. An 1830 Broadwood piano is one of the furniture exhibits. The kitchen has walls of convict-made bricks. It contains such original appliances and utensils as a handmill for grinding wheat and a bread oven.

Experiment Farm Cottage 22

9 Ruse St, Parramatta. 📞 9635 5655.
🚉 Harris Park. 🕐 10:30am–3:30pm Tue–Fri, 11am–3:30pm Sun & public hols. ⚫ Good Fri, 18–31 Dec. 📷 ♿ 📷 (Groups must book in advance).

WHEN HIS SENTENCE expired in 1789, convict farmer James Ruse was given 0.6 ha (1½ acres) of land at Parramatta on which to start a farm, along with a hut, grain for sowing, vital farming tools, two sows and six hens. He successfully planted and harvested a substantial wheat crop with his wife Elizabeth's help. She was the first female convict to be emancipated in New South Wales. In 1791, they were rewarded with a grant of 12 ha (30 acres), the colony's first land grant. Arthur Phillip, governor of the day, called it Experiment Farm.

**Medicine chest (c.1810),
Experiment Farm**

In 1793, Ruse sold this farm to surgeon John Harris for £40. The date of the cottage is not certain, but it is believed to be early 1830s. The woodwork is Australian red cedar and the cottage is furnished according to an 1838 inventory.

St John's Cemetery 23

O'Connell St, Parramatta. 📞 9635 5904. 🚉 Parramatta. 📷 ♿

THIS WALLED cemetery – the oldest European cemetery in Australia – houses the graves of many convicts and settlers who arrived on the First Fleet in 1788. The oldest grave that can be identified is the flat sandstone slab simply inscribed, "H.E. Dodd 1791". Henry Edward Dodd, known to be Governor Phillip's butler, was the tenth person buried in the cemetery, but the location of the other nine graves is unknown. The first recorded burial was of a child on 31 January 1790. One prominent grave is that of churchman Samuel Marsden, who earned the title of the "flogging parson" during his time as magistrate general because of his harsh judgments. The merchant Robert Campbell (see p66) and the father of explorer William Charles Wentworth (see p136), D'Arcy Wentworth, are also buried here.

Old Government House 24

Parramatta Park (entry by Macquarie St gates), Parramatta. 📞 9635 8149. 🚉 Parramatta. 🕐 10am–4pm Mon–Fri, 11am–4pm Sat, Sun & most public hols. ⚫ Good Fri, two weeks before Christmas, 25 Dec. 📷 ♿ limited. 📷

THE CENTRAL BLOCK of Old Government House is the oldest intact public building in Australia. This elegant brick structure, plastered to resemble stone, was built by Governor Hunter in 1799 on the site of a cottage constructed in 1790 for Governor Phillip. Wings to the side and rear were added between 1812 and 1818. The Doric porch, added in 1816, has been attributed to Francis Greenway (see p114).

Australia's finest collection of early 19th-century furniture is now housed inside. A structure on the site has been identified as an early worker's cottage.

The drawing room of Old Government House, Parramatta

FOUR GUIDED WALKS

SYDNEY'S TEMPERATE CLIMATE and natural beauty make it an ideal city for walking. The following walks have been chosen for their distinct character; they all capture a view of the essential Sydney. You can follow the paths that trace the headlands and inlets around Watsons Bay; enjoy

Mural on a Manly surf shop

an invigorating clifftop walk at Bondi; catch glimpses of the original landscape in Manly's unspoilt bushland; or explore the narrow streets of historic Balmain. Three of the walks incorporate ocean or harbourside beaches, so be prepared in warmer weather by packing a swimsuit, towel

and hat and wearing a reliable sunscreen. Please remember when in Sydney's national parks and bushland that all the indigenous flora and fauna is protected. The best sign of appreciation is to leave the bush as you found it. The *Tips for Walkers* provide practical information about each walk, listing accessibility by bus, train or ferry and estimated distance of the walk, along with scenic rest areas, picnic spots, cafés and restaurants en route. Tourism NSW's Information Line *(see p218)* can supply details of the many accompanied walking tours available throughout Sydney.

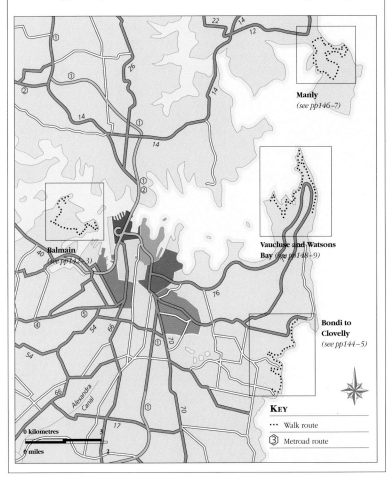

Manly
(see pp146–7)

Vaucluse and Watsons Bay *(see pp148–9)*

Balmain
(see pp142–3)

Bondi to Clovelly
(see pp144–5)

KEY

••• Walk route

③ Metroad route

0 kilometres   3

0 miles   2

◁ **A lookout rising high above the treacherous waters of the Pacific Ocean at The Gap** *(see p148)*

A Two-Hour Walk Around Balmain

HISTORIC BALMAIN VILLAGE was named after William Balmain, a ship's surgeon on the First Fleet. In 1800, he was granted rights to 223 ha (550 acres) of the peninsula, which he later sold for a paltry 5 shillings in a dubious business transaction. From the mid-1800s, much of the land was subdivided for housing to support the then flourishing mining and maritime industries. Today, grand colonial and Victorian buildings stand side by side with tiny workers' cottages, adding variety to every street.

The Waterman's Cottage ③

East Balmain

Begin from the Darling Street Wharf ①. By the 1840s, when the ferry service began, shipyards dotted these foreshores. The sandstone building at No. 10 Darling Street ②, once the Dolphin Hotel then the Shipwright's Arms, was a watering hole for sailors and ferrymen. On the opposite corner is The Waterman's Cottage (1841) ③, home to Henry McKenzie, whose boat ferried residents to and from Sydney Town.

Turn left into Weston Street and walk through the Illoura Reserve for views of the city and Darling Harbour. Leave the park via William and Johnston Streets, stopping in the latter to view Onkaparinga ④, the colonial residence at No. 12. When building started in 1860, mussel shells from Aboriginal feasts stood in mounds upon the harbour foreshore beyond.

Turn left onto Darling Street then right into Duke Street. Gilchrist Place then leads down to Mort Bay Reserve ⑤. Ship's propellers stand as monuments to the area's working past. A path leads up to The Avenue's timber workers' cottages.

Back on Darling Street, turn left down Killeen Street. Take the path across Ewenton Park to Ewenton ⑥ (c.1854). Past the park, Hampton Villa ⑦ at 12B Grafton Street was home to state premier Henry Parkes.

Turn right into Ewenton Street and then left into Wallace Street, with its variety of early Australian architecture. The rough stone home at No. 1 is called the Railway Station as its narrow frontage makes it resemble one. The charming Clontarf ⑧ is at No. 4, while Maitland House ⑨ has a symmetry worth a second glance. Return to Darling Street.

YALUMBA
BALMAIN LIQUOR

Colourful shopfront on Darling Street, Balmain

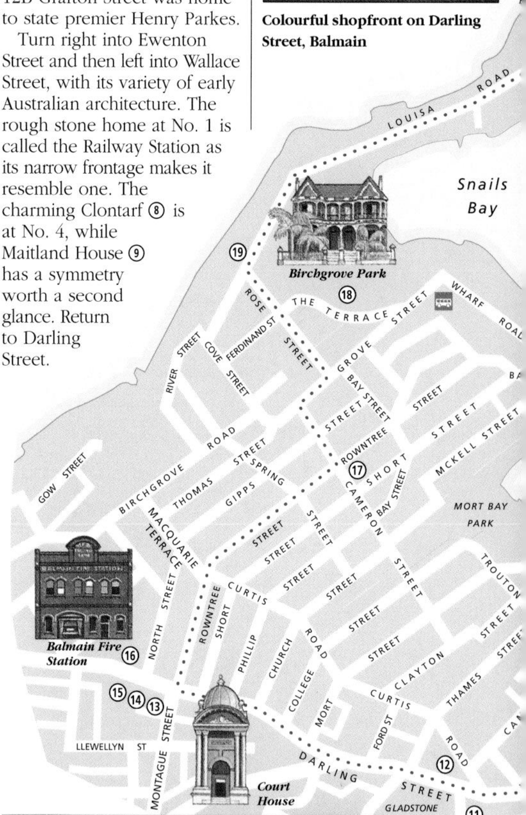
LOUISA ROAD
Snails Bay
Birchgrove Park
⑱
⑲
THE TERRACE
ROSE STREET
FERDINAND ST
COVE STREET
RIVER STREET
GROVE STREET
BAY STREET
WHARF ROAD
ROWNTREE STREET
⑰
SHORT STREET
BAY STREET
MCKELL STREET
CAMERON STREET
MORT BAY PARK
GOW STREET
BIRCHGROVE ROAD
THOMAS STREET
SPRING STREET
GIPPS STREET
MACQUARIE TERRACE
NORTH STREET
ROWNTREE SHORT
CURTIS ROAD
PHILLIP
CHURCH
COLLEGE
MORT
Balmain Fire Station
⑯
⑮ ⑭ ⑬
LLEWELLYN ST
MONTAGUE STREET
Court House
DARLING STREET
CLAYTON
CURTIS
FORD ST
THAMES
TROUTON
ROAD
⑫
⑪
GLADSTONE PARK
The London Hotel

The domestic grandeur of Louisa Road

Historic Links

Sydney's oldest extant lock-up, The Watch House (1854) ⑩ at No. 179 Darling Street, has been restored, but a ghostly female form remains. Further along, enjoy a drink at The London Hotel (1870) ⑪, where the balcony stools are made of old-fashioned tractor seats.

After the roundabout, visit St Andrew's Church ⑫ before losing yourself to the bookshops, cafés and delicatessens of Balmain. Every Saturday, Balmain Market fills the churchyard *(see p203)*.

At the shops' far end, the Victorian Post Office (1887) ⑬ and neighbouring Court House ⑭ reflect 1880s Sydney's prosperity. The Town Hall ⑮ dome was removed during World War II for fear of air raids. Across the street is the Fire Station ⑯ (1894). Set on the crest of a hill, its horse-drawn vehicles always travelled downhill on their outward journey.

Distant views of the city and Sydney Harbour Bridge from Snails Bay

Balmain to Birchgrove

Retrace your steps to Rowntree Street. Turn left and wander down to Birchgrove (about 10 minutes' walk). From Birchgrove shops ⑰, take Cameron Street left and Grove Street right, to Birchgrove Park ⑱ and Snails Bay. Walk down Rose Street to Louisa Road. Two of the most notable homes are Nos. 12 and 14, Keba (1878) and Vidette (1876) ⑲, where deep verandas and iron-lace balconies hint at colonial opulence. A poem in praise of the nearby park is inscribed on a plaque at Keba's entrance. Amid Vidette's formal greenery, a deep well is still fed by a natural spring.

Balmain War Memorial

There is a wealth of interest in the homes that follow: a tiny porch, Victorian entrance tiles, ornate iron lace – plus occasional glimpses of water frontage and private moorings. At the road's end, the reserve at Yurulbin Point ⑳ marks the mouth of Parramatta River. A fishing nook on its eastern corner is a perfect vantage point for taking in the city skyline and passing harbour traffic.

Shops nestled in the quiet Birchgrove village ⑰

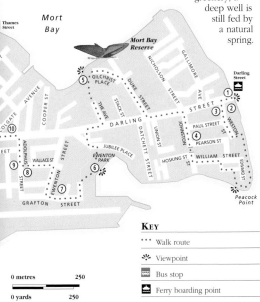

TIPS FOR WALKERS

Starting point: Darling Street Wharf.

Length: 5.5 km (3½ miles).

Getting there: Ferries regularly leave Circular Quay for Darling Street Wharf. The 442 bus from the Queen Victoria Building stops in Darling Street. There is a 15-minute ferry ride at hourly intervals from Birchgrove (pick up a schedule at Circular Quay). Alternatively, take Bus 441 from Grove Street (Snails Bay) back to the city (weekdays only).

Stopping-off points: Darling Street, in particular, has many good delicatessens, pâtisseries, restaurants and cafés. Places to picnic include Mort Bay Reserve, Gladstone Park, Birchgrove Park and Yurulbin Point.

KEY

∴∴∴ Walk route

☆ Viewpoint

🚌 Bus stop

⛴ Ferry boarding point

0 metres   250

0 yards   250

A Two-Hour Walk from Bondi Beach to Clovelly

THIS INVIGORATING OCEANSIDE and clifftop walk explores the beautiful shoreline and surfing beaches of eastern Sydney. The local colour along this scenic trail is at its most vibrant at weekends, when people flock to the cafés and beaches. The Victorian cemetery at the walk's end bears witness to Sydney's multicultural heritage.

Pool at North Bondi Beach

A Seaside Community

Walk north along Campbell Parade ①, passing a colourful array of hotels, beachwear shops and lively cafés that give the street a raffish atmosphere. The stylish Gelato Bar at No. 140 makes an indulgent pit-stop. Keep walking until the Hotel Bondi ②, the parade's most significant building and easily spotted by its pretty clock tower. Opened as a first-class hotel in 1920, it initially stood quite alone by what was then a bush-fringed beach. Turn right, crossing the road in front of the hotel, and walk down to Queen Elizabeth Drive leaving the traffic and noise of Campbell Parade behind as you reach Sydney's most famous beach, Bondi.

Bondi's popularity dates back to the 1880s. Although daylight bathing was banned at the time, the beach was considered a fashionable place to stroll. Bondi trams came into use shortly after and, by the time bathing restrictions were lifted in 1902, the red and white trams were filled with beach-goers. Just ahead you will see Bondi Pavilion ③. Built in 1928 to replace a modest timber building, it was designed on a grand scale and originally housed a ballroom, gymnasium, restaurant, café, Turkish baths and open-air theatre. Although decidedly less glamorous today, the complex is still a thriving local community centre hosting cultural events. Photographs inside recall the romance of Bondi Beach in earlier times.

Statue of lifesaver near Bondi Pavilion

Next to the Pavilion is the home of arguably Australia's oldest surf life saving club, the Bondi Surf Bathers ④ *(see p137)*. Follow the sweep of the beach to its southern end.

Climb a flight of steps to continue on Notts Avenue, above Bondi Baths ⑤ and alongside the Bondi Icebergs clubhouse. Prospective members must swim every Sunday, regardless of weather, 50 weeks of the year for four years to join.

> ### TIPS FOR WALKERS
>
> ***Starting point:*** *Campbell Parade, southern end.*
> ***Length:*** *4 km (2½ miles).*
> ***Getting there:*** *Take the train to Bondi Junction, then Bus 380 to Bondi Beach. Bus 339 runs from Clovelly Beach to Circular Quay. Waverley Cemetery is open from 8am to dusk every day.*
> ***Stopping-off points:*** *Public toilets, showers and food and refreshments are available at Bondi, Tamarama and Bronte Beaches. Take-away cuisine can be bought along Bondi's Campbell Parade as the walk begins. Tamarama's beach café serves refreshing drinks. In warm weather, make the most of four of Sydney's best beaches by packing your swimming gear.*

Tamarama Surf Life Saving Club, at the beach's northern end

Bronte's swimming baths

Bondi to Bronte

Veer left off Notts Avenue as the path drops down and skirts sharp rock formations, the result of years of erosion. Take the steep steps to Mackenzies Point lookout ⑥ on the headland. The magnificent view stretches for 180 degrees from Ben Buckler in the north to Malabar in the distant south.

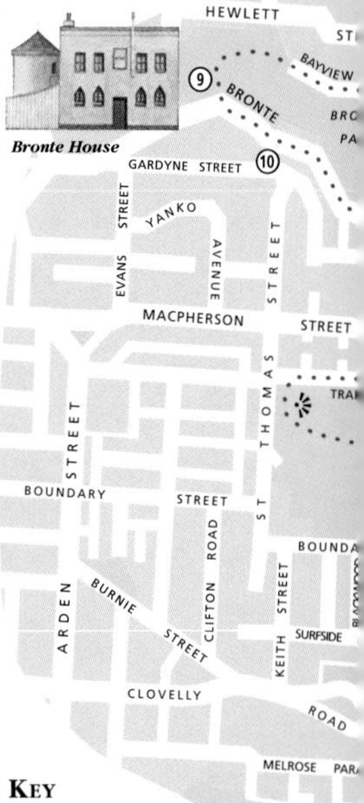

KEY

- ... Walk route
- Viewpoint
- Bus stop
- [P] Parking

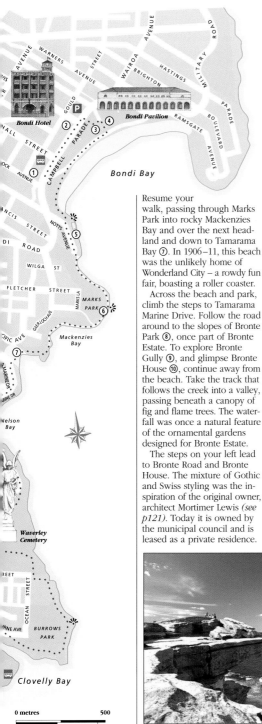

Bondi Hotel ②

P

Bondi Pavilion ④ ③

Bondi Bay

Nelson Bay

Waverley Cemetery

Clovelly Bay

0 metres   500

0 yards   500

Bronte to Waverley
Continue down Bronte Road
towards the southern end of
Bronte Beach. After passing
Bronte's cafés, walk through
the car park and follow the
road uphill, through a cutaway
originally dug for trams. As the
road winds through the cutting
and veers right, take the steps
through Calga Reserve. Walk
down Trafalgar Street to the
Waverley Cemetery ⑪.

In grand displays of Edwardian and Victorian monumental
masonry, English, Italian and
Irish residents have been laid
to rest. Among notable Australians buried here are writers
Henry Lawson and Dorothea
Mackellar; Fanny Durack, the

Irish Memorial, Waverley Cemetery

first woman to win an Olympic
gold medal (in 1912), and do
the Australian crawl swimming
stroke; and aeronautical pioneer Lawrence Hargrave.

The Irish Memorial honours
the 1798 Irish Rebellion and
its leader Michael Dwyer, who
was transported to Australia
for his part in the uprising.

Leave the cemetery at the
southern end. Walk through
Burrows Park, hugging the
coast, to Eastbourne Avenue,
which leads to the walk's end
at Clovelly Beach ⑫.

Resume your
walk, passing through Marks
Park into rocky Mackenzies
Bay and over the next headland and down to Tamarama
Bay ⑦. In 1906–11, this beach
was the unlikely home of
Wonderland City – a rowdy fun
fair, boasting a roller coaster.

Across the beach and park,
climb the steps to Tamarama
Marine Drive. Follow the road
around to the slopes of Bronte
Park ⑧, once part of Bronte
Estate. To explore Bronte
Gully ⑨, and glimpse Bronte
House ⑩, continue away from
the beach. Take the track that
follows the creek into a valley,
passing beneath a canopy of
fig and flame trees. The waterfall was once a natural feature
of the ornamental gardens
designed for Bronte Estate.

The steps on your left lead
to Bronte Road and Bronte
House. The mixture of Gothic
and Swiss styling was the inspiration of the original owner,
architect Mortimer Lewis (see
p121). Today it is owned by
the municipal council and is
leased as a private residence.

Lookout at Mackenzies Point, a popular spot for watching surfers ⑥

A Three-Hour Walk Around Manly

THIS WALK TAKES IN THE holiday atmosphere of downtown Manly and its splendid surf beach, before passing along quieter shorelines and clifftop streets, and through unspoilt bushland replete with native flora and fauna. It features marvellous views, the commanding architecture of Manly's most significant building, St Patrick's Seminary, and the charm of Collins Beach and Fairy Bower.

Brass band plays in The Corso

From Harbour to Ocean

Start at Manly Wharf ①. This suburb was little more than a cosy fishing village until 1852, when entrepreneur Henry Gilbert Smith's vision of a resort similar to fashionable Brighton in his native England started to take shape. The ferry service began in 1855, operating from the same spot in use today.

Leaving Manly Cove, cross The Esplanade and walk down The Corso, a pedestrian mall. At the end of The Corso, to the left, stands the New Brighton Hotel ② in striking Egyptian Classical Revival Style. In 1926, it replaced the original New Brighton, built in 1880 as the resort's first attraction.

Head towards the rolling surf and sweeping sands of Manly Beach ③ then continue south along the promenade. From the 1950s-style Surf Pavilion, follow Marine Parade walkway around to Cabbage Tree Bay. The pretty area around the rock pool was named Fairy Bower ④ for the delicate wildflowers and maidenhair ferns that once grew on the hillside. Beyond the rock pool, continue on the pathway around to Shelly Beach ⑤, a secluded scuba diving and snorkelling spot, which is also ideal for child swimmers. The 1920s beach kiosk has now been stylishly restored and converted into the smart Le Kiosk restaurant.

Detail on the New Brighton Hotel

Shelly Beach to St Patrick's Seminary

Across the park, take the steps to your left to Shelly Beach Headland. A path further left loops around the headland. Viewing platforms ⑥ overlook the vast South Pacific Ocean.

Take the carpark exit into Bower Street. Follow the road as it rounds high above Fairy Bower, passing by homes of diverse architectural styles, from Spanish Mission to Neo-Georgian. Turn left into College Street, then right into Reddall Street, and left again

Houses rising above Fairy Bower

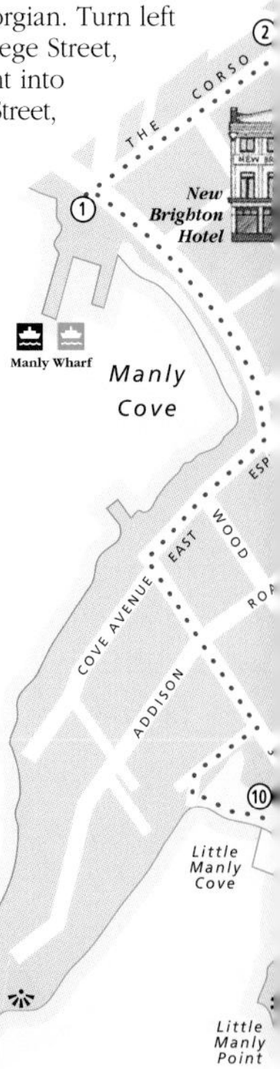

> **TIPS FOR WALKERS**
>
> ***Starting point:*** *Manly Wharf*
> ***Length:*** *7.5 km (4½ miles).*
> ***Getting there:*** *Regular ferry and JetCat services depart from Wharf 2 at Circular Quay.*
> ***Stopping-off points:*** *The wide range of fresh food counters at Manly Pier make it an ideal place to stock up on picnic fare. Restaurants and cafés line The Corso and Manly Beach Promenade. Le Kiosk at Shelly Beach offers the choice of a smart restaurant, barbecue or snack bar. In warm weather, come prepared with a swimsuit, hat, towel and sunscreen.*

The clear waters of sheltered Shelly Beach ⑤

into Addison Road. Opposite the Victorian buildings at Nos. 97–99 and 95, a lane into Fairy Bower Road leads to views of the old St Patrick's Seminary ⑦. Both Romanesque and Neo-Gothic architecture are in evidence in this 1885 Catholic seminary, built only after much deliberation by the essentially Protestant government.

Leave Fairy Bower Road by Vivian Street to turn left into Darley Road and arrive at the seminary. On the opposite side of the road, the Archbishop's House is partially hidden by Norfolk Island pines. Known as the Cardinal's Palace for its lavish interiors, it is, sadly, not open to the public.

The grand Victorian architecture of St Patrick's Seminary ⑦

North Head Reserve
At the top of Darley Road, turn right beneath the Parkhill Sandstone Arch ⑧ into North Head

Reserve. Follow the right-hand fork (leading to the Institute of Police Management) onto Collins Beach Road down through bushland alive with bird calls and native lizards. Paperbarks, smooth-barked apple trees and banksias are some of the native flora growing in abundance.

At the road's end, follow the track to your right across two footbridges, then down steps to Collins Beach ⑨. A stone cairn between the second foot-bridge and the beach marks where Governor Arthur Phillip was speared by the Aboriginal Wil-ee-ma-rin after a misunderstanding. The quiet waterfall and dense bushland make it possible to imagine this beach in pre-colonial days.

Leave to the right of the beach via a rough hillside track onto a concrete pathway, then out into Stuart Street.

Back to the Present
For memorable harbour views, follow the direction of Stuart Street through Little Manly Point Reserve, passing by the baths of Little Manly Cove ⑩. If you are reluctant to end this charming walk, turn left and proceed to the end of Addison Road. Manly Point Peace Park offers a quiet place to take in a panorama of the distant city.

Return down Addison Road, making your way back to the wharf via Stuart Street and the East Esplanade. With its boat sheds and bleached timber yacht clubs, the East Esplanade Park has a nautical amosphere and is a relaxing place to meander. Continue past the attractions of the amusement pier to Manly Wharf, which was your starting point.

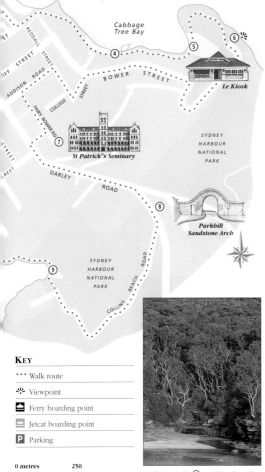

KEY

••• Walk route

Viewpoint

Ferry boarding point

Jetcat boarding point

P Parking

0 metres 250

0 yards 250

Collins Beach ⑨ on the edge of Sydney Harbour National Park

A Three-Hour Walk in Watsons Bay and Vaucluse

TRACING THE PERIMETERS of spectacular South Head, this walk touches on the area's colonial connections and takes in a variety of ocean and harbourside terrain, from headlands with sweeping views and crashing waves, to secluded coves, white sandy beaches and the streets of one of Sydney's most desirable neighbourhoods.

Signal Station ② at Dunbar Head

Macquarie Lighthouse to Camp Cove

The start of this walk is majestic Macquarie Lighthouse (1883) ①. A copy of the country's first lighthouse built in 1818 *(see p137)*, it stands on the same site.

Take the walk northwards, passing by the Signal Station ② following Old South Head Road. Before the station was built in 1848, a flag was hoisted to warn the colony of ships entering the harbour.

Continue along the footpath, where a plaque marks the location of Australia's worst maritime disaster. It was here that the migrant ship *Dunbar* crashed onto the rocks in a gale in 1857 *(see pp136–7)*. The only survivor was hauled to safety up the treacherous cleft in the cliff face known as Jacob's Ladder ③. From here, follow the descending path, arriving at the turbulent seas and jutting stony ledges of The Gap ④. The *Dunbar*'s anchor is here set into concrete, while salvaged personal effects are displayed at the National Maritime Museum *(see pp94–5)*.

Taking the steps down from The Gap, bear right into the entrance of Sydney Harbour National Park. This single-lane roadway leads through natural bushland into HMAS *Watson* Military Reserve. Follow the road up to visit the Naval Memorial Chapel ⑤. A large clear window inside the chapel offers spectacular views of North Head and the Pacific Ocean. Resume your walk by taking the road out of the reserve, and then turn right into Cliff Street. Passing a row of weatherboard cottages on your left, follow the street to its end and onto Camp Cove Beach ⑥. It was here in 1788 that Captain Arthur Phillip first stepped ashore after leaving Botany Bay to explore the coastline.

Bust, Macquarie Lighthouse ①

Camp Cove to Watsons Bay

Take the wooden steps at the northern end of the cove to make the 40-minute return walk to South

Nudist Lady Bay Beach

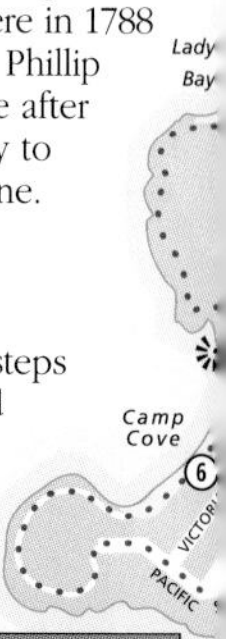
Lady Bay
Camp Cove
6
VICTORIA
PACIFIC

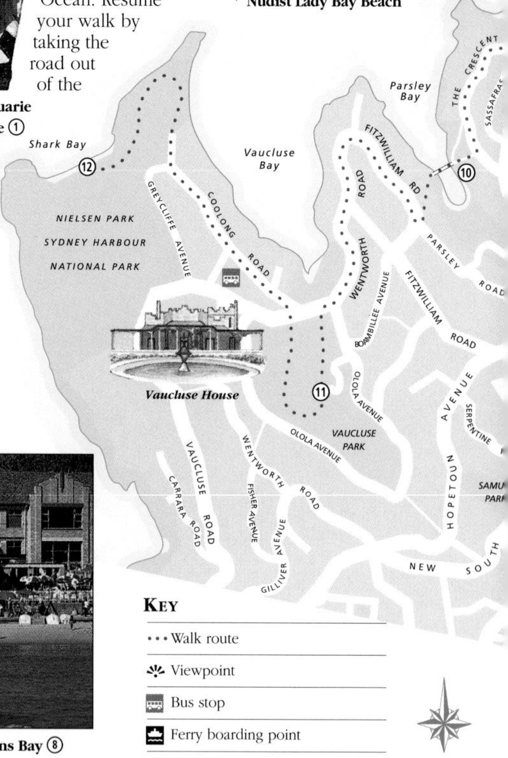
Shark Bay
12
NIELSEN PARK
SYDNEY HARBOUR
NATIONAL PARK
GREYCLIFFE AVENUE
COOLONG ROAD
Vaucluse Bay
Vaucluse House
11
WENTWORTH ROAD
FITZWILLIAM RD
Parsley Bay
THE CRESCENT
SASSAFRAS
10
PARSLEY ROAD
BOAMBILLEE AVENUE
FITZWILLIAM ROAD
OLOLA AVENUE
VAUCLUSE PARK
AVENUE
SERPENTINE
VAUCLUSE ROAD
CARRARA ROAD
WENTWORTH ROAD
FISHER AVENUE
GILLIVER AVENUE
HOPETOUN
NEW SOUTH
KEY
Walk route
Viewpoint
Bus stop
Ferry boarding point

Doyle's well-known restaurant at Watsons Bay ⑧

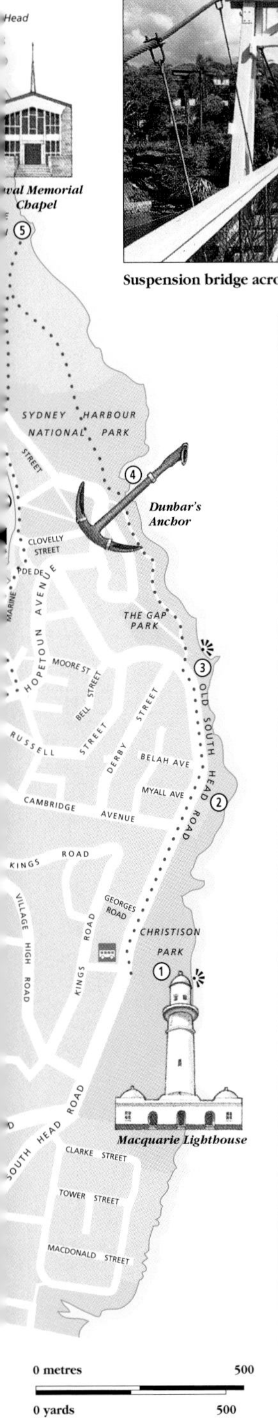
Head
val Memorial
Chapel
SYDNEY HARBOUR
NATIONAL PARK
STREET
Dunbar's
Anchor
CLOVELLY
STREET
THE GAP
PARK
MOORE ST
HOPETOUN AVENUE
BELL
STREET
RUSSELL
STREET
DERBY
STREET
BELAH AVE
MYALL AVE
OLD SOUTH HEAD ROAD
CAMBRIDGE
AVENUE
KINGS
ROAD
GEORGES
ROAD
CHRISTISON
PARK
VILLAGE HIGH ROAD
ROAD
KINGS
Macquarie Lighthouse
SOUTH HEAD ROAD
CLARKE STREET
TOWER STREET
MACDONALD STREET
0 metres
500
0 yards
500

Suspension bridge across Parsley Bay ⑩

Head. Above the steps are signs of colonial defences: a firing wall with rifle slots; a cannon lying further along. After passing Lady Bay Beach, you will reach Hornby Lighthouse ⑦, which marks the harbour's entrance. Retrace your steps to Camp Cove Beach. Climb the western-end stairs to Laings Point, a defence post in World War II. A net stretching across the harbour mouth was anchored here to prevent enemy ships entering.

Follow Pacific Street to Cove Street, then along to Marine Parade and Wharf Beach in Watsons Bay ⑧ *(see pp136–7)*. Named after Robert Watson of the First Fleet's *Sirius*, this was once first port of call for ships entering the harbour. Nearby, Doyle's restaurant offers seafood with a view. Follow the parade past the baths and tea rooms. Pilot boats ⑨ moored close by guide cruise and container ships into the harbour.

Watsons Bay to Vaucluse

Continue to secluded Gibsons Beach, taking the footpath left through native shrubbery, then right onto Hopetoun Avenue. Turn into The Crescent, tracing the curve of this exclusive street around to Parsley Bay Reserve. A short descent opens onto a suspension bridge hung across the waters of tranquil Parsley Bay ⑩. Crossing the bridge, follow the pathway between two houses to arrive on Fitzwilliam Road. Continue right along Fitzwilliam Road, turning left into Wentworth Road to reach the extravagant Vaucluse House ⑪, surrounded by exotic gardens *(see p136)*.

To finish your walk, make your way along Coolong Road to Nielsen Park *(see p136)* and Shark Bay ⑫. Protected from its namesake by a netted enclosure, the natural setting and safe waters of this beach make it a favourite for picnics.

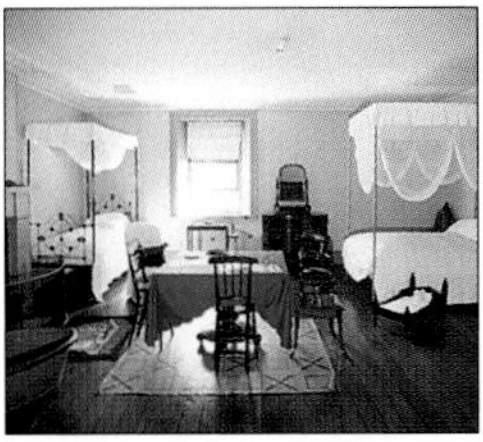

Children's bedroom, one of the exhibits at Vaucluse House ⑪

Dramatic rock cleft known as Jacob's Ladder ③ near The Gap

Tips for Walkers

Starting point: *Macquarie Lighthouse.*
Length: *8 km (5 miles).*
Getting there: *Take Bus 324 from Circular Quay, or Bus 387 from Bondi Junction. Return by Bus 325 from Nielsen Park.*
Stopping-off points: *There are public toilets and showers at Camp Cove, Watsons Bay, Parsley Bay and Nielsen Park. Food and refreshments are available throughout the walk at Watsons Bay, Parsley Bay, Vaucluse and Nielsen Park. The tea rooms at Vaucluse House offer views of the gardens, and the café at Nielsen Park sells homemade fare in generous portions. The walk covers several harbour beaches where you can swim safely. In warm weather, bring a swimsuit, towel, hat and sunscreen, and allow time for swimming, sunbathing and picnicking.*

BEYOND SYDNEY

EXPLORING BEYOND SYDNEY 152–153
PITTWATER AND KU-RING-GAI CHASE 154–155
HAWKESBURY TOUR 156–157
HUNTER VALLEY 158–159
BLUE MOUNTAINS 160–161
SOUTHERN HIGHLANDS TOUR 162–163
ROYAL NATIONAL PARK 164–165

Exploring Beyond Sydney

To the east, Sydney is bounded by the Pacific Ocean; to the west, by the Great Dividing Range. To the north and south, within easy distance of the city, are superb beaches and stretches of coastal scenery, while inland, you will encounter waterfalls, deep valleys and fascinating flora and wildlife. On the Hawkesbury River, to the north and west of the city, are settlements of historical as well as scenic interest while, further north, the Hunter River meanders through sloping vineyards. The excursions on pages 154–65 offer the visitor the chance to sample the rich variety of Sydney landscapes from the exhilarating to the tranquil.

Heritage Farm on the Hawkesbury River

Façade of Rothbury Estate in the Hunter Valley

SIGHTS AT A GLANCE

Blue Mountains **4**
Hawkesbury Tour **2**
Hunter Valley **3**
Pittwater and Ku-ring-gai Chase National Park **1**
Royal National Park **6**
Southern Highlands Tour **5**

GETTING AROUND

All the areas covered in these excursions can be easily reached by road from Sydney. Freeways and motorways take travellers part of the way to the Southern Highlands, Blue Mountains and Hunter Valley, while the other areas are accessible on sealed, well-signposted major roads. A number of tour operators offer guided one-day, or longer, tours to the Blue Mountains, Hunter Valley, Southern Highlands and South Coast, and parts of the Hawkesbury region. CityRail has regular train services to the Blue Mountains, Royal National Park and to parts of the area covered by the Southern Highlands Tour. Ferries offer access to some parts of the Hawkesbury River.

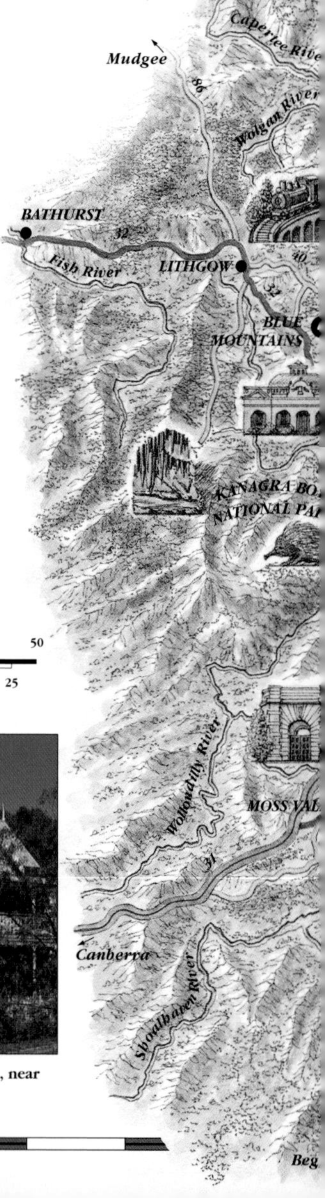

0 kilometres   50
0 miles   25

Mudgee

Cape Hee River

Wolgan River

BATHURST
Orange, Dubbo
Fish River
LITHGOW

BLUE MOUNTAINS

KANAGRA BO...
NATIONAL PA...

Wollondilly River
MOSS VAL...

Canberra

Shoalhaven River

Grand old house in Kiama, near the Southern Highlands

Beg

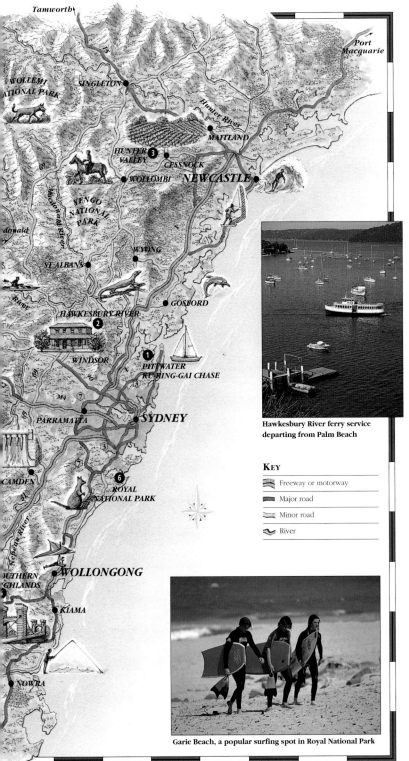

Tamworth
Port Macquarie
WOLLEMI NATIONAL PARK
SINGLETON
Hunter River
MAITLAND
HUNTER VALLEY ❸
CESSNOCK
WOLLOMBI
NEWCASTLE
YENGO NATIONAL PARK
donald
Macdonald River
WYONG
ST ALBANS
GOSFORD
HAWKESBURY RIVER ❷
WINDSOR
PITTWATER ❶
KU-RING-GAI CHASE
M4
PARRAMATTA
SYDNEY
CAMDEN
❻ ROYAL NATIONAL PARK
Nepean River
SOUTHERN HIGHLANDS
WOLLONGONG
KIAMA
NOWRA

Hawkesbury River ferry service departing from Palm Beach

KEY

〰	Freeway or motorway
▬	Major road
〰	Minor road
〰	River

Garie Beach, a popular surfing spot in Royal National Park

Pittwater and Ku-ring-gai Chase ❶

PITTWATER AND THE ADJACENT Ku-ring-gai Chase National Park lie on Sydney's northernmost outskirts. They are bounded to the north by Broken Bay, at the mouth of the Hawkesbury River *(see pp156–7)*. Sparkling waterways and golden beaches are set against the unspoiled backdrop of the national park.

Barrenjoey Lighthouse Picnicking, bushwalking, surfing, boating, sailing and windsurfing are popular pastimes with visitors. The Hawkesbury River system curls around an ancient sandstone landscape rich in Aboriginal rock art, and flora and fauna.

Coal and Candle Creek
The pretty inlet is typical of eroded valleys formed during the last Ice Age. Water melted from the ice caps flooded the valleys to form the bays and creeks of Broken Bay.

Akuna Bay
The isolated marina, general store and café serve the Hawkesbury River boating fraternity.

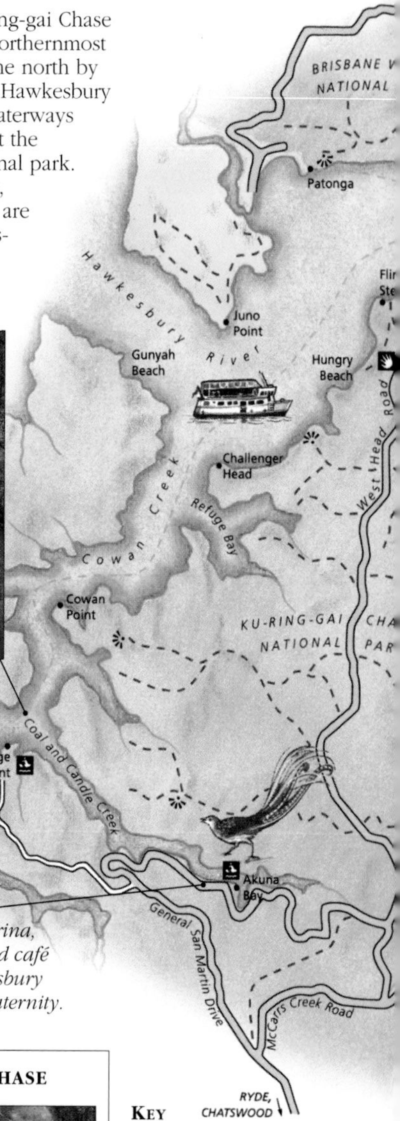

ABORIGINAL ART IN KU-RING-GAI CHASE

Ku-ring-gai Chase has literally hundreds of Aboriginal rock art sites, providing an insight into one of the world's oldest cultures. The most common are rock engravings, generally made in groups with as many as 100 individual figures. They include whales up to 8 m (26 ft) long, fish, sharks, wallabies, echidnas and Ancestral Spirits such as Daramulan, who created the land, its people and animals.

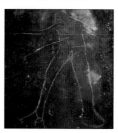

Aboriginal rock art near the Basin, Ku-ring-gai Chase

KEY

- ▬ Major road
- ▬ Secondary road
- — Minor road
- ☐ National Park
- - - - Ferry route
- - - - Walk route
- ⚓ Boat hire
- 🖎 Aboriginal rock art
- ❋ Viewpoint

(Map labels: BRISBANE WATER NATIONAL PARK, Patonga, Hawkesbury River, Juno Point, Gunyah Beach, Hungry Beach, Challenger Head, Refuge Bay, West Head Road, Cowan Creek, Cowan Point, KU-RING-GAI CHASE NATIONAL PARK, Cottage Point, Coal and Candle Creek, Smiths Creek, Akuna Bay, General San Martin Drive, McCarrs Creek Road, RYDE, CHATSWOOD)

Palm Beach Wharf
Palm Beach, a haven for sea birds such as pelicans, is popular with sun-seekers. It is also the base for the boats that visit and deliver supplies to the isolated communities on Pittwater and the Hawkesbury.

Pittwater
This graceful finger of water separates Palm Beach from Ku-ring-gai Chase. Pittwater boasts secluded beaches, picnic areas and several hamlets that can only be reached by water.

Whale Beach
Spectacular houses seem to hug the cliffs overlooking this fine surf beach. The Palm Beach Peninsula's beaches are often less congested than those closer to the city.

0 kilometres 2

0 miles 1

TIPS FOR TRAVELLERS

Distance from Sydney: About 30 km (19 miles).

Duration of journey: About 45 minutes to Mona Vale Beach.

Getting there: Take Military Rd on the city's North Shore and cross the Spit Bridge. Follow Pittwater Rd to Mona Vale Beach.

When to go: The Christmas holiday period is the peak season and beaches can be crowded. Ku-ring-gai Chase offers everything from shoreline to bushwalks and can be enjoyed year round.

Where to stay and eat: Contact the visitors' information centre for full details of facilities.

Tourist information: Bobbin Head Visitors' Centre. 📞 9472 8949. ⏱ 10am–4pm daily (seasonal). 🌐 www.npws.nsw.gov.au

---

Bilgola Beach
A small community of residents backs this patrolled surf beach set against a pretty rainforested valley. Wooden steps lead down from the ridge above through coastal heathland.

Hawkesbury Tour [2]

Australia's longest eastward-flowing river, the Hawkesbury–Nepean, forms Sydney's northern and western boundaries. It was at first thought to be two separate rivers until further exploration revealed that they were in fact one. The section known as the Hawkesbury runs from the Colo River Valley to Broken Bay in the north *(see pp154–5)*.

Settled in 1794, by 1799 the Hawkesbury Valley's small farms produced three-quarters of the colony's grain. Its riverscape is little changed since then and much of the area remains a quiet backwater. It is an area rich in relics of the early colonial period, including towns and villages established during the Macquarie era of 1810–19 *(see p22)*. It is also a place of great scenic grandeur, with magnificent vistas of one of Australia's most beautiful rivers.

Tizzana Winery [5]
A touch of Tuscany on the banks of the Hawkesbury, this sandstone winery was built in 1887 by Dr Thomas Fiaschi. It is open to visitors on Saturdays and public holidays.

Ebenezer Uniting Church [4]
Built in 1809, the church and its 1817 schoolhouse have been superbly restored. The tree under which services were first held still stands.

Portland Reach [6]
On the river, pleasure craft have replaced the grain barges of the past, but the area's farming community survives.

Colo River Drive [3]
This pretty route travels along the Putty Road to Colo, then follows the river to Lower Portland.

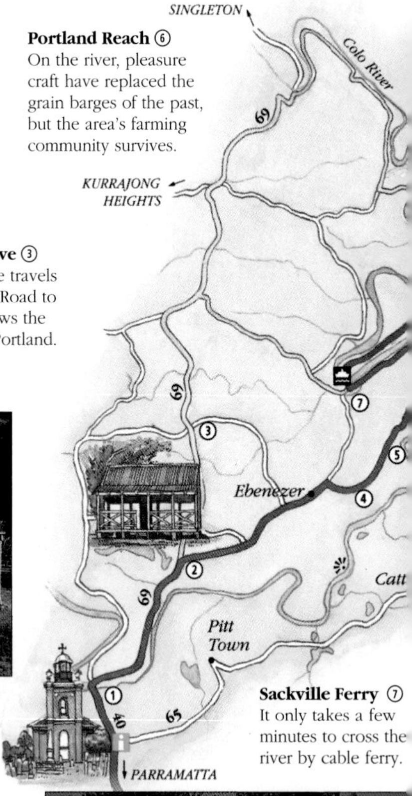
SINGLETON
Colo River
69
KURRAJONG HEIGHTS
69
3
7
5
Ebenezer
4
2
69
Catt
Pitt Town
1
40
65
PARRAMATTA

Hawkesbury Heritage Farm [2]
This collection of original pioneer buildings re-creates an early colonial village. At the centre is Rose Cottage (1811), built of ironbark slabs with she-oak shingle roofing.

Sackville Ferry [7]
It only takes a few minutes to cross the river by cable ferry.

Windsor [1]
Built in 1815, the Macquarie Arms Hotel is just one of Windsor's fine early colonial buildings. Many others, including several by architect Francis Greenway *(see p114)*, remain from the town laid out in 1810.

Settlers Arms Inn ⑩

Once an overnight stop for stage coaches to the Hunter Valley *(see pp158–9)*, this atmospheric 1836 hotel is in the largely unchanged village of St Albans.

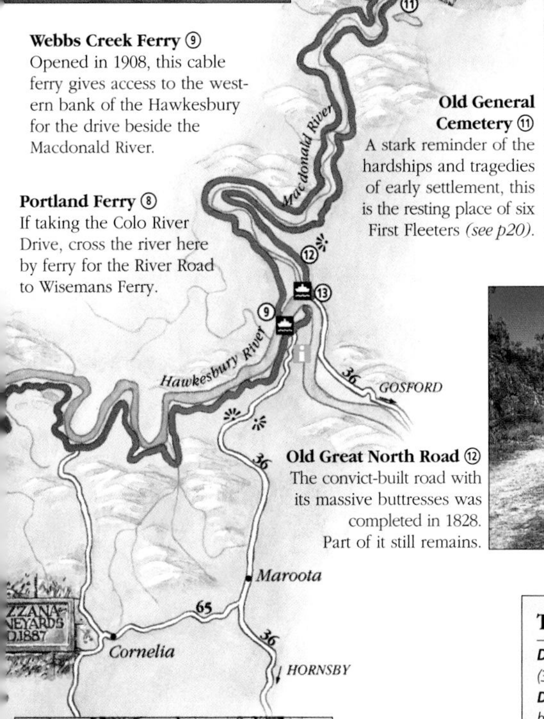

Webbs Creek Ferry ⑨

Opened in 1908, this cable ferry gives access to the western bank of the Hawkesbury for the drive beside the Macdonald River.

Portland Ferry ⑧

If taking the Colo River Drive, cross the river here by ferry for the River Road to Wisemans Ferry.

Old General Cemetery ⑪

A stark reminder of the hardships and tragedies of early settlement, this is the resting place of six First Fleeters *(see p20)*.

Old Great North Road ⑫

The convict-built road with its massive buttresses was completed in 1828. Part of it still remains.

Macdonald River

Hawkesbury River

36 GOSFORD

■ Maroota

65

Cornelia

36

HORNSBY

Wisemans Ferry ⑬

This small village on a bend in the Hawkesbury River is where ex-convict Solomon Wiseman started his ferry service, Australia's oldest, in 1827.

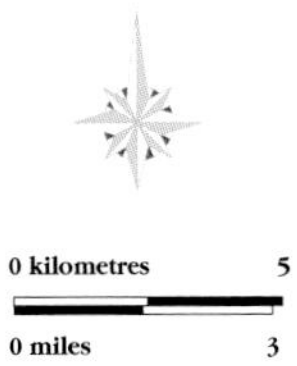

Tips for Drivers

Distance from Sydney: 55 km (35 miles) to Windsor.
Duration of tour: About 3½ hours, excluding stops.
Getting there and back: Follow M4 to James Ruse Drive (53) just before Parramatta, then Windsor Rd (40). To return from Wisemans Ferry, take the Old Northern Rd (36) to Middle Dural, then Galston Rd to Hornsby. From here, follow Pacific Hwy south.
When to go: Peak season is from December to February. The river, national parks and small towns can be enjoyed year round.
Where to stay and eat: Cafés, restaurants and accommodation can be found at Windsor and Wisemans Ferry. The Settlers Arms Inn at St Albans has a few rooms, and a bar and restaurant.
Tourist information: There is a visitors' centre at Hawkesbury Museum, Thompson Square, Windsor. ☏ 4577 2310.

Key

▬	Tour route
═	Scenic route
═	Other road
⛴	Cable ferry
🛈	Tourist information
✳	Viewpoint

0 kilometres 5

0 miles 3

...

Hunter Valley ❸

Cheese made by local producer

SOME OF THE EARLIEST vineyards to be planted in Australia were on the fertile flats of the Hunter River in the 1830s, developing a thriving industry in fortified wine. Since the 1970s, it has evolved into a premium wine district (*see pp182–3*). With some 90 wineries the area is a popular weekend trip from Sydney. Hot air ballooning, golf, horse riding and events of the Harvest Festival (March to May) supplement vineyard visits. The Jazz in the Vines festival takes place in October. Many wineries open daily but it best to phone ahead and check.

Brokenwood
Under the ownership of Ben Riggs, this medium-sized winery has produced some of the region's finest Shiraz from the Graveyard vineyard, as well as an excellent Semillon.

Lindemans
In 1842, Dr Henry John Lindeman resigned his naval commission to establish a vineyard in the Hunter Valley. His company has been a major producer in the Australian wine industry ever since.

PERSONALITIES OF THE HUNTER VALLEY

The wine industry seems to attract or create larger-than-life characters. Among the current living legends is Len Evans, writer, wine judge, *bon vivant* and founder of the ambitious Rothbury Estate and Evans Family Wines (his new venture is Tower Estate). His contemporaries include Max Lake, a Sydney surgeon who started Lake's Folly as a weekend winery, and the late Murray Tyrrell, patriarch of a wine-making family that produced its first Hunter vintage in 1864 and proudly retains its independence.

Len Evans checking grape vines

Rothbury Estate
Founded by Len Evans, this winery is dedicated to wine excellence and education. Dinners and concerts held in the winery's cask hall are popular events.

Pepper's Convent
A restored 1909 convent is now an elegantly appointed guesthouse, with the Pepper Tree vineyard and winery and Robert's Restaurant only a short walk away.

Lake's Folly
Australian growers stopped planting Cabernet Sauvignon vines in the 19th century. But in the 1960s, former owner Max Lake reintroduced the variety.

Golden Grape Estate
A popular coach stop, the winery has a vine gallery showing grape varieties found around the world. There is also a museum which features early wine-making equipment.

TIPS FOR TRAVELLERS

Distance from Sydney: 160 km (100 miles).
Duration of journey: About 2 hours from the centre of Sydney.
Getting there and back: Take the Sydney–Newcastle F3 freeway north of Sydney and follow the signs to Cessnock. Another route is through the picturesque Wollombi Valley. Allow about 3 hours as there are unsealed roads.
When to go: Year round. Vintage is Jan – Mar.
Where to stay and eat: There is a wide variety of motels, guest-houses, self-catering cottages and cabins, cafés and restaurants.
Visitor information: Hunter Valley Wine Country Tourism, Turner Park, Aberdare Rd, Cessnock. 4990 4477.
www.winecountry.com.au
Further afield: The Upper Hunter vineyards are about 40 minutes by car northwest of Pokolbin.

KEY

=	Main road
=	Unsealed road
🏰	Winery
ℹ	Tourist information
🔆	Viewpoint

0 kilometres 2

0 miles 1

Blue Mountains ❹

OR A QUARTER OF A CENTURY after European settlement, the Blue Mountains prevented the colony's westward expansion. In 1813, an expedition led by the explorers Gregory Blaxland, William Lawson and William Charles Wentworth found a way across. The magnificent scenery, characterized by rugged cliffs and rock formations, ravines and waterfalls, is best appreciated on the bushwalks that wind along cliff tops and through valleys. The restaurants, cafés and antique shops will tempt the less energetic. The mountains are named for the perennial blue haze, caused by light striking eucalyptus oil particles in the air.

Zig Zag Railway
A steam train travels through cuttings and tunnels, and over three impressive viaducts built from 1866–9.

Grose Valley from Govetts Leap
Considered by many to be the most imposing view in the Blue Mountains, a great panorama with a series of ridges stretches into the far distance.

The Grose River flows between the two roads crossing the mountains.

Victoria Falls

Mount York

JENOLAN CAVES

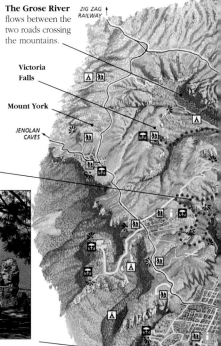

ZIG ZAG RAILWAY

Three Sisters
This giant rock for-mation near Echo Point takes its name from an Aboriginal legend. The story tells of three sisters turned to stone by their witch-doctor father to keep them safe from an evil bunyip or monster.

JENOLAN CAVES

About 55 km (34 miles) south-west of Mount Victoria is a magical series of spectacular underground limestone caves with icy blue rivers and fleecy limestone formations. They are surrounded by an extensive wildlife reserve. People have been making the trek here since the caves were discov-ered in 1838, staying originally in the Grand Arch cave and later in the Edwardian splen-dour of Jenolan Caves House, which still operates today.

The vividly coloured Pool of Cerberus at Jenolan Caves

KEY

▬▬	Major road
	Other road
• • •	Suggested walk
🚶🚶	Starting points for other walks
Ⓐ	Campsite
⛩	Picnic area
ℹ	Tourist information
🔭	Viewpoint

Mount Wilson
A picturesque village with cultivated gardens and exotic trees, it has been called a "little corner of the northern hemisphere". Some gardens are open to the public in spring and autumn.

The Cathedral of Ferns is a remnant of the temperate rainforest that once covered this area.

Mount Tomah Botanic Gardens
This superbly landscaped garden, specializing in cool-climate plants, has sweeping views over the Grose Valley.

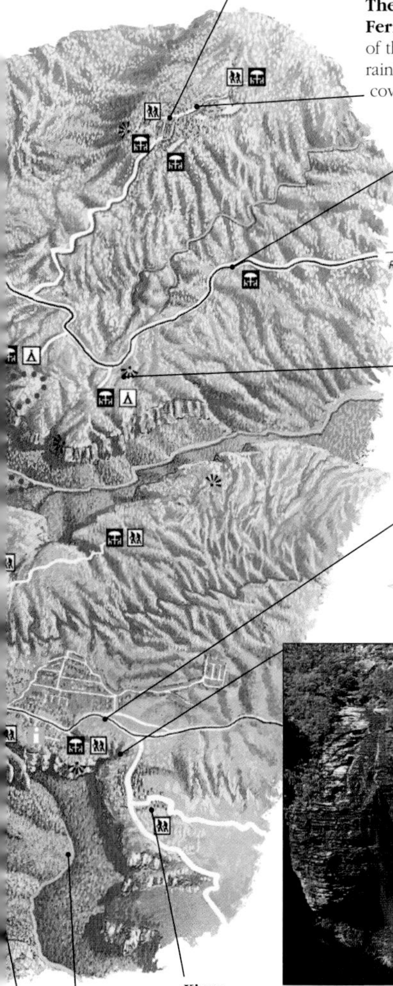

RICHMOND

Mount Banks

Yester Grange
The beautifully restored Victorian country house at Wentworth Falls has tea rooms and a restaurant, as well as a collection of antiques and crafts.

Kings Tableland

Jamison Valley

Leura village is classified by the National Trust. Nearby are Leura Cascades, floodlit at night and one of the prettiest sights in the mountains.

Wentworth Falls
An impressive double water-fall is the starting point for the National Pass track, a challenging four-hour return walk to the next valley.

0 kilometres   5

0 miles   3

TIPS FOR TRAVELLERS

Distance from Sydney: About 105 km (65 miles).
Duration of journey: About 90 minutes to Wentworth Falls.
Getting there and back: Follow Metroad route 4 and the Great Western Highway. Return by Bells Line of Road to Windsor. State Rail has regular services to the area. An Explorer Bus runs from Katoomba train station at 9:30am on weekends and public holidays.
When to go: Year round. Always be prepared for the cold, especially when hiking, as the weather can change rapidly in all seasons.
Where to stay and eat: Contact the visitor information centre.
Tourist information: Blue Mountains Visitors' Information Centre, Echo Point, Katoomba.
📞 1300 653 408. W www.bluemountainstourism.org.au

Southern Highlands Tour ❺

Common wombat

THIS EASILY ACCESSIBLE area to the south of Sydney is often said to be more typical of Great Britain, particularly Scotland, than Australia. It is actually a delightful combination of both: Australian high country and coastal hinterland with many European qualities. It is a land of abrupt hills and valleys, waterfalls and fast-running streams; of quaint villages, cosy restaurants and cafés, antique shops and elegant places to stay. The tour takes in spectacular Seven Mile Beach and the pretty town of Berry before heading to Kangaroo Valley, sleepy Bundanoon and the antique shops of Berrima and Bowral. An exhilarating adjunct to the tour is nearby Minnamurra Falls with its boardwalk through rainforest.

Bowral ⑧
This highlands town holds a famous spring tulip festival every year and is home to cricket's Bradman Museum.

Berrima ⑦
By-passed by the railway in the 19th century, the only Georgian village in the highlands remains one of the most picturesque.

WOMBEYAN CAVES
31
8
7
Moss Vale
48
Sutton Forest
79
31
GOULBURN
Bundanoon Creek
6
Tallowa Dam
MORTON NATIONAL PARK

Bundanoon ⑥
Romantic guesthouses and a glow-worm cave make this town a popular weekend destination.

Fitzroy Falls ⑤
Part of Morton National Park, the falls plunge 80 m (262 ft) into the subtropical rainforest below. The falls lookout has access for the disabled and walking trails with stunning views.

0 kilometres 10

0 miles 5

KEY

- Tour route
- Scenic route (alternative)
- Other roads
- Tourist information
- Viewpoint

Kangaroo Valley ④
Hampden Bridge, a castellated suspension bridge, crosses the Kangaroo River at this small village. The river is an idyllic place for canoeing.

BERRIMA GAOL

Completed in 1839 by convict labour, this Georgian sandstone jail is featured in Rolf Boldrewood's classic 1888 bushranging novel, *Robbery Under Arms*. The fictitious character Captain Starlight, who escapes from Berrima, describes it as "the largest, most severe, the most dreaded of all prisons in New South Wales".

Kiama ①
The historic town began life in the 1820s as a port for shipping cedar. Its blowhole can spurt water as high as 60 m (200 ft).

Seven Mile Beach ②
Part of a national park and best seen from Gerroa's Black Head, the beach is flanked by dunes and hardy coastal vegetation, including forest and swamp. It is a great fishing, swimming and picnicking spot.

TIPS FOR DRIVERS

Distance from Sydney: *120 km (75 miles).*
Duration of tour: *About 3½ hours, excluding stops.*
Getting there and back: *Take Metroad route 1, then follow the F3 freeway and Princes Hwy (1) to Kiama. Return via the F5 freeway (31) from Mittagong, then Metroad route 5 into the city.*
When to go: *Year round. The beaches are best in summer, the gardens in spring and autumn. History buffs, antique-lovers and country-style aficionados will enjoy many of these little towns.*
Where to stay and eat: *Eating places, hotels and guesthouses are found all over the South Coast and Southern Highlands.*
Tourist information: *Kiama Visitors Centre, Blowhole Point, Kiama.* 4232 3322. *Southern Highlands Visitors Information Centre, 62–70 Hume Hwy, Mittagong.* 4871 2888.

Berry ③
This town, surrounded by lush dairy country, is well known for its main street lined with shady trees, antique and craft shops, tea rooms and historic buildings. The Berry Museum, built in 1886, is in a former bank.

Royal National Park ❻

DESIGNATED AS A NATIONAL PARK in 1879, the "Royal" is the oldest national park in Australia. It covers 16,000 ha (37,100 acres) of landscape typical of the Sydney Basin sandstone. To the east, waves from the Pacific Ocean have undercut the sandstone and produced majestic coastal cliffs broken occasionally by small creeks and some spectacular beaches. Streams flowing north and east have incised deep river valleys. Heath vegetation on the plateaus merges with woodlands on the upper slopes. The park is ideal for bushwalking, picnicking, camping, swimming and birdwatching.

Waratah

Hacking River
Boating, fishing and canoe-ing are common water sports.

Audley
A popular picnic area since the Edwardian era, it has a pavili-on that was built in 1901. Look out for the 1920s dance hall also in the park.

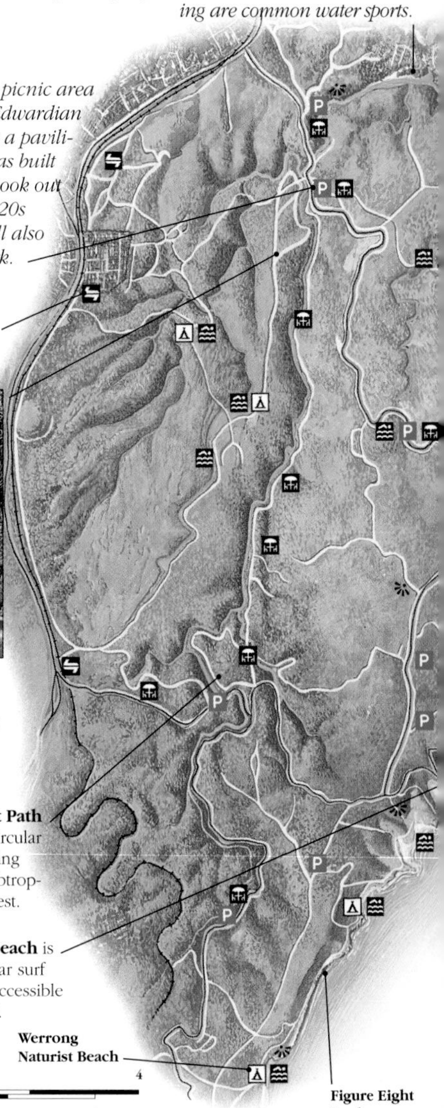

Heathcote

Lady Carrington Drive
Named after a governor's wife and now closed to vehicles, the road is crossed by 15 creeks and is delightful to walk or cycle. It also leads to the track to Palona Cave.

The Forest Path follows a circular route, passing through subtrop-ical rainforest.

Garie Beach is a popular surf beach accessible by road.

Werrong Naturist Beach

Figure Eight Pool

KEY

▬	Main road
	Walking track
🚉	CityRail station
🚢	Ferry boarding point
🏞	Picnic area
⛺	Campsite
🏊	Swimming
🅿	Parking
🔭	Viewpoint

0 kilometres   4

0 miles   2

Bundeena
Enclosed by national park on three sides, the small settlement at the mouth of the Hacking River may be reached by ferry from Cronulla or by road through the national park.

Cronulla

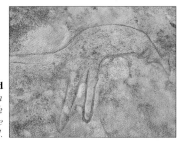

Jibbon Head
Guided tours of the Jibbon Head Aboriginal rock engravings site may be arranged.

Jibbon Lagoon

Deer Pool
One of many fresh-water pools in the park, this sheltered spot is on the track from Bundeena Drive to Marley and Little Marley.

Little Marley Beach

Wattamolla Lagoon
This pretty picnic spot has a lagoon with a waterfall at its edge and a protected ocean beach.

Curracurrang
This rock formation is about halfway along the two-day Coast Walk. Sea eagles and terns nest in caves at the base of this rocky cove which also has a secluded swimming hole and waterfall.

TIPS FOR TRAVELLERS

Distance from Sydney: *34 km (21 miles).*
Duration of journey: *About 1 hour from the centre of Sydney.*
Getting there: *Follow Metroad route 1 south to Sutherland, then follow the signs to Heathcote and Wollongong. The turn-off to Farnell Avenue and the park entrance is shortly after Sutherland and well signposted.*
When to go: *Year round, but conditions for walking in summer can be hot so allow for this. If bushwalking, carry fresh water at all times and check on the fire danger at the Visitors' Centre before setting off.*
Where to stay and eat: *There are kiosks at Audley, Garie Beach and Wattamolla, but it is best to bring your own food. Camping information can be obtained at the Visitors' Centre.*
Tourist information: *Royal National Park Visitors' Centre, Farnell Ave, Audley.* 9542 0648. www.npws.nsw.gov.au

TRAVELLERS' NEEDS

WHERE TO STAY 168-177

RESTAURANTS, CAFÉS AND PUBS 178-197

SHOPS AND MARKETS 198-207

ENTERTAINMENT IN SYDNEY 208-215

WHERE TO STAY

W ITH AUSTRALIA'S recent emergence as a major tourist destination, the urgent need for more high-quality and good-value accommodation became apparent. Previously, most Sydney hotels and guesthouses had been regarded as expensive and of varying standard. There has since been an enormous improvement in both quality and value, and there are excellent choices for visitors ranging from five-star luxury to the homeliness of a small, unpretentious hotel. In addition to hotels, Sydney has self-catering apartments, homestay accommodation and budget and backpacker hostels for those travelling on a budget. Information on these alternatives is given below. From a survey of various types of accommodation in different areas and varying price brackets, we have selected those offering good value for money. Detailed descriptions of each hotel can be found on pages 172–7. At the end of each hotel review is a list of symbols indicating the full range of facilities on offer.

Observatory Hotel doorman (p172)

A view of the rooftop pool at the Hilton Sydney Hotel *(see p173)*

WHERE TO LOOK

M OST OF the expensive hotels are in or near the city centre, but it is possible to find accommodation within most price ranges throughout Sydney. The city centre has the advantage of having many of the larger theatres, galleries and shops at hand, as well as easy transport access to more distant sights and attractions.

Cheaper accommodation can be found in the vibrant Kings Cross district. Choices here range from backpacker hostels to the small "boutique" hotels where the emphasis is on quality and personal service.

In The Rocks area, with its beautifully restored colonial buildings, you can choose from bed and breakfast in a traditional Sydney pub or the opulence of a five-star luxury hotel with good views of the Sydney Opera House.

The hotels around Darling Harbour and Chinatown offer good value for shoppers and are also within easy reach of the city centre. Paddington has smaller hotels and self-catering apartments, while to the east are the up-market hotels of Double Bay. On the other side of Sydney Harbour Bridge, the leafy North Shore provides a more relaxed look at Sydney, and you can travel to and from the city centre by ferry.

The popular beachside suburbs of Bondi and Manly are a little way out of the centre of Sydney, but some visitors may like the opportunity to be close to superb beaches and yet still be reasonably near to the city.

You should also remember that in Australia a hotel can be a pub or a place to drink *(see pp196–7).* Pubs do not always provide accommodation.

HOW TO BOOK

I T IS ADVISABLE to book well in advance, especially for the Christmas school holidays in December and January, the Gay and Lesbian Mardi Gras Festival in February and Mardi Gras Parade in early March, the Easter holidays and July and September school holidays.

Bookings can be made by letter, phone, fax, e-mail or through your local international travel agent. A credit card number or bank cheque in Australian dollars is usually required to secure your booking. Check cancellation requirements and reconfirm before you arrive in Sydney.

The **Sydney Visitors Centre** books certain hotels and will send a brochure pack. **Australian Accommodation Services** does not charge for bookings. If you belong to a motoring association, ask your travel agent to check which **NRMA-**(National Roads and Motorists' Association-) affiliated hotels offer a discount. **Countrylink** agencies at major railway stations offer a comprehensive service and AFTA travel agencies will book most hotels. Some travel

The indoor pool at the Observatory Hotel in The Rocks *(see p172)*

The curvilinear shape of the Four Points Sheraton *(see p174)*

agencies specialize in specific areas. Tourist information centres can also offer valuable advice about where to stay in Sydney.

DISCOUNT RATES

WITH FEWER visitors staying in Sydney from April to October (except during the school holiday periods), some of the more expensive hotels may be willing to negotiate a better rate. This is particularly so if they think you will look elsewhere for accommodation. It is always worth asking for the corporate rate at which hotels give discounts for group or company bookings. Most hotels give these without question.

At the weekend there are fewer business clients around, so this is the time when prices are frequently cheaper in the top hotels. Money can also be saved by booking for a week at a time. Asking for a room without a harbour or ocean view is another good way of reducing the costs.

The **Travellers Information Service** in the city can often arrange up to 50 per cent off regular hotel accommodation rates (this does not normally apply to budget hotels) to those who book in person on the day a room is required.

HIDDEN EXTRAS

BREAKFAST is usually charged on top of the room rate in the more expensive hotels. It is best to avoid consuming any of the contents of the mini-bar until you have checked the price. Alcohol is usually much more expensive here than in shops. Also, be wary of the telephone charges. There will almost certainly be a considerable mark-up on any calls you make from your room. In general, tipping is not widespread, but it is expected in the more expensive hotels. You should make a note of the check-out time when you arrive, or negotiate a late check-out, as a surcharge may be incurred if you stay late.

Stained glass at Simpsons hotel *(see p176)*

SPECIAL OFFERS

HOTELS OFTEN cooperate with airlines, rail services, bus companies, theatres and entertainment promoters to provide package deals that include discounted accommodation. Booking agencies will have brochures with details of these seasonal offers, or ask the hotel for information on any special deals.

"Special occasion" packages (such as for anniversaries or honeymoons) are available at the top end of the market.

DISABLED TRAVELLERS

THE INFORMATION regarding wheelchair access that is given on pages 174–7 relies very much on each hotel's own assessment of its facilities.

The **Australian Quadraplegic Association (AQA)** supplies a booklet *Accessing Sydney* for people who have mobility problems. It is available from the AQA's Mascot office or by post. You can also visit their website (www.aqa.com.au) for more information.

TRAVELLING WITH CHILDREN

IT IS WORTH inquiring about special rates and facilities or deals that allow children to stay in their parents' room for no extra cost. For hotels that cater for children, look for the "children welcome" symbol in the hotel listings on pages 172–7.

SELF-CATERING FLATS

ACCOMMODATION including full kitchen and laundry facilities offers the traveller greater independence. Such self-catering apartments are the latest accommodation trend in Australia. In addition to comfort, they also provide good value because the living space is larger than standard hotel rooms and the prices are competitive: although rates can vary, they are generally on a par with the major chain hotels.

The choice ranges from one- to three-bedroom luxury apartments in the inner city to basic flats at the beach. Some apartments cater for business travellers, complete with fax and other communications amenities. They are also ideal for families, especially those with young children, who appreciate not only the greater amount of space but also the flexibility provided by self-catering.

All the "apartment" hotels in the listings on pages 172–7 offer self-catering facilities. In addition, Sydney has several agencies that can help visitors to arrange self-catering accommodation *(see p170)*.

A luxurious room at the Regents Court hotel in Potts Point *(see p176)*

PRIVATE HOMES

EUROPEAN-STYLE bed-and-breakfast accommodation in a private home can be an ideal way to experience a city. It is fast becoming a popular alternative to more impersonal hotel rooms for many people who choose to visit Sydney.

People from all walks of life offer rooms in a wide variety of house styles and locations. Agencies such as **Bed and** Breakfast Sydneyside and the **Homestay Network** make every effort to match the host and guest if possible, so ring to discuss any preferences before making a reservation.

BUDGET ACCOMMODATION

AS A FAVOURED destination for many young travellers, Sydney has a large number of hostels that cater specifically for their needs. Despite fierce competition, standards vary widely. At their best, hostels offer excellent value.

While it is necessary to book in advance at some hostels, others do not take bookings and beds are on a first come, first served basis. Apartments,

---

DIRECTORY

DISCOUNT AGENCIES

Travellers Information Service
Sydney Coach Terminal, Eddy Ave, Sydney NSW 2000. **Map** 4 E5.
☏ 9281 9366.
FAX 9281 0123.

USEFUL BOOKING ADDRESSES

Countrylink
Central Railway Station
Map 4 E5. ☏ 132232.

Australian Accommodation Services
☏ 9974 4884.
FAX 9974 1692.

Sydney Visitors Centre
106 George St, The Rocks NSW 2000. **Map** 1 A4.
☏ 9255 1788.

DISABLED ASSISTANCE

AQA
I Jennifer St, Little Bay, NSW 2036. ☏ 9661 8855.
Postal Address
South Sydney Corporate Park, Letterbox 40, 184 Bourke St, Alexandria NSW 2015.
W www.aqa.com.au

Ideas Incorporated
PO Box 786, Tumut NSW 2720. ☏ 6947 3377.
FAX 6947 3723.
W www.ideas.org.au

SELF-CATERING AGENCIES

Pacific International Suites
Sydney and Parramatta.
☏ 1800 682 009.

Medina
359 Crown St, Surry Hills NSW 2010. **Map** 5 A3.
☏ 9360 6666.
FAX 9361 5965.
Also at 15 other locations.

Suites on Sussex
132–136 Sussex St, Sydney NSW 2000. **Map** 1 A4.
☏ 9290 9200.
FAX 9262 3032.

HOMESTAY AGENCIES

Bed and Breakfast Sydneyside
PO Box 555, Turramurra NSW 2074.
☏ 9449 4430.

Homestay Network
5 Locksley St, Killara NSW 2071.
☏ 9498 4400.
FAX 9498 8324.

HOSTELS

Alishan Guesthouse
100 Glebe Point Rd, Glebe NSW 2037. **Map** 3 A5.
☏ 9566 4048.

Forbes Terrace
153 Forbes St, Woolloomooloo NSW 2011.
Map 5 B1.
☏ 9358 4327.

Sydney Centre YHA
Cnr Pitt St & Rawson Pl, Sydney NSW 2000.
☏ 9281 9111.

World Youth Hostel
477 Kent St, Sydney.
☏ 9261 1551.

Lamrock Hostel
7 Lamrock Ave, Bondi Beach NSW 2026.
☏ 9365 0221.

University of Sydney
Arundel House
☏ 9660 4881.
International House
☏ 9950 9800.
St John's College
☏ 9394 5200.
Sancta Sophia
☏ 9577 2100.
Wesley College
☏ 9565 3333.
Women's College
☏ 9517 5000.

Wattle House Travellers' Accommodation
44 Hereford St, Glebe NSW 2037. ☏ 9552 4997.

YHA
422 Kent St, Sydney NSW 2000. **Map** 4 D3.
☏ 9261 1111.
FAX 9261 1969.

GAY AND LESBIAN ACCOMMODATION

IGLTA
PO Box 2497, Rozelle NSW 2039. **Map** 4 F3.
☏ 9818 6669.

Breakout Tours
96 Crystal St, Petersham NSW 2049.
☏ 9360 3616.

Destination Downunder
Level 10, 130 Elizabeth St, Sydney, NSW 2000.
☏ 9268 2188.

CAMPING

Blue Mountains National Park
☏ 4787 8877.

Ku-ring-gai Chase National Park
☏ 9457 9322.

Royal National Park
☏ 9542 0648.

Interior of boutique hotel Medusa, Darlinghurst *(see p176)*

rooms and dormitories are all available, but dormitories are often mixed sex; check before arriving. The backpacker scene changes quickly, so ask other travellers for the latest developments. Potts Point and Glebe have the largest concentration of cheap accommodation.

Halls of Residence

Student rooms, with shared bathroom facilities, are available at the University of Sydney over the summer break from December to February. The university is conveniently close to the city and to public transport, and the moderate price includes breakfast.

Gay and Lesbian Accommodation

Lesbian and gay visitors are welcome in all of Sydney's hotels. In fact, quite a number of them cater primarily, if not exclusively, for same-sex couples. Many of the small hotels in the inner city areas of Darlinghurst, Paddington, Newtown and Surry Hills are geared specifically towards gay and lesbian visitors, although most of them also welcome heterosexual guests.

The **IGLTA** (International Gay and Lesbian Travel Association) produces a free accommodation guide. There is a small charge for postage and handling if you are inquiring from overseas.

Travel agencies such as **Destination Downunder** and **Breakout Tours** specialize in holidays and accommodation for gay and lesbian travellers.

Camping

Although not an option in the city itself, camping is available in several national parks close to Sydney. This can be a cheap and idyllic way of enjoying the natural beauty and wildlife of the bushland.

The **Royal National Park** *(see pp164–5)* has a campsite with facilities at Bonnie Vale. Advance booking is required all year round. Free bush or "walk-in" camping is allowed in several other places, but first ring the park to obtain the necessary camping permit.

At The Basin in **Ku-ring-gai Chase National Park** *(see pp154–5)*, bookings should be made and all fees paid before your stay or on arrival. There are toilets, cold showers, barbecue facilities and a phone.

There are basic campsites near Glenbrook, Woodford, Blackheath and Wentworth Falls in the **Blue Mountains National Park** *(see pp160–61)*. You will need to book if you want to camp at the Euroka Clearing near Glenbrook, but this is not necessary for the other sites. Bush camping is also permitted in the park, but there are some restrictions. Contact the national park for more details before you visit.

Manly Pacific Parkroyal *(see p177)*, overlooking Manly's ocean beach

Using the Listings

Hotel listings can be found on pages 172–7. Each hotel is listed according to area of the city and alphabetically within price category.

The symbols summarize the facilities available at each of them.

🛁 all/number of rooms with bath and/or shower

[1] single-rate rooms available

👪 rooms for more than two people available

👶 children welcome (eg babysitting service, cots etc)

[TV] television in all rooms

❄ air conditioning in all rooms

👁 rooms with good views

🏊 hotel swimming pool or beach

♿ wheelchair access

↕ lift

[P] hotel parking available

🌳 garden or grounds

🍴 restaurant

💳 credit cards accepted

Price categories for a double room (not per person), including continental breakfast and service (prices are given in Australian dollars):

$ under $120
$$ $120–$200
$$$ $200–$280
$$$$ $280–$380
$$$$$ over $380

Choosing a Hotel

T HE HOTELS in this guide have been selected across a wide price range for their good value, excellent facilities and locations. The chart lists the hotels by area of the city, starting with The Rocks and Circular Quay, and all entries appear alphabetically within each area. Full restaurant listings can be found on pages 184–93.

	NUMBER OF ROOMS	GYM FACILITIES	BUSINESS FACILITIES	CLOSE TO SHOPS/RESTAURANTS

THE ROCKS AND CIRCULAR QUAY

ANA HOTEL SYDNEY W www.anahotel.com $$$$
176 Cumberland St The Rocks NSW 2000. **Map** 1 A3. (9250 6000. FAX 9250 6250.
Clever use of marble and glass give this hotel a light and airy feel. The rooms are spacious and all enjoy harbour views. Lush grounds and good views from the Horizon cocktail bar. ⊞ ⊞ ⊞ ⊞ ⊞ ⊞ ⊞ ⊞ ⊞ ⊞ ⊞ ⊞

| 573 | | ▪ | ● |

LORD NELSON BREWERY HOTEL W www.lordnelson.com.au $$
19 Kent St, The Rocks, NSW, 2000. **Map** 1 A2. (9251 4044. FAX 9251 1532.
The top floor of this celebrated pub, famous for its home brews, offers cosy bedrooms with stone walls and rustic furnishings. A mix of ensuites and shared bathrooms is available. Breakfast is served in the restaurant. ⊞ ⊞

| 10 | | | ● |

MERCANTILE HOTEL $
25 George St, The Rocks, Sydney, 2000. **Map** 1 B2. (9247 4306. FAX 9247 7047.
This is one of Sydney's older pub hotels and boasts spacious rooms containing period fittings, marble fireplaces and jacuzzis. ⊞ ⊞ ⊞ ⊞ ⊞

| 15 | | | ● |

OLD SYDNEY HOLIDAY INN W www.holiday-inn.com $$$
55 George St, The Rocks, NSW 2000. **Map** 1 B2. (9252 0524. FAX 9251 2093.
This hotel is big enough to offer all the facilities of a grand establishment, yet small enough to offer personal attention. Great location within the historic Rocks area and close to Circular Quay and the Opera House. ⊞ ⊞ ⊞ ⊞ ⊞ ⊞ ⊞ ⊞ ⊞ ⊞ ⊞

| 175 | | ▪ | ● |

THE OBSERVATORY HOTEL W www.observatoryhotel.com.au $$$$$
89-113 Kent St Millers Point NSW 2000. **Map** 1 A2. (9256 2222. FAX 9256 2233.
This smart boutique hotel is tastefully furnished with original antiques, fine tapestries and paintings. All rooms have marble bathrooms. ⊞ ⊞ ⊞ ⊞ ⊞ ⊞ ⊞ ⊞ ⊞ ⊞ ⊞

| 99 | | ▪ | ● |

PARK HYATT SYDNEY W www.sydney.hyatt.com $$$$$
7 Hickson Road, The Rocks, NSW 2000. **Map** 1 B1. (9241 1234. FAX 9256 1555.
A quiet, opulent and splendidly furnished hotel. Guest rooms are well equipped and include a 24-hour butler service. ⊞ ⊞ ⊞ ⊞ ⊞ ⊞ ⊞ ⊞ ⊞ ⊞ ⊞

| 158 | | ▪ | ● |

QUAY GRAND $$$$$
61-69 Macquarie St, Sydney, NSW, 2000. **Map** 1 C3. (9256 4000. FAX 9256 4040.
This modern, five-star hotel is close to the Opera House and has large suites with city and harbour or garden views. Other features include spa baths, kitchen and laundry facilities, televisions and stereos. ⊞ ⊞ ⊞ ⊞ ⊞ ⊞ ⊞ ⊞ ⊞

| 70 | | ▪ | ● |

RUSSELL W www.therussell.com.au $$
143a George St, The Rocks NSW 2000. **Map** 1 B2. (9241 3543. FAX 9252 1652.
Housed in a 19th century building, this hotel has an intimate feel. The interior is decorated with country-style antiques and fresh flowers while the rooftop garden is the perfect spot for a quiet drink. ⊞ ⊞ ⊞ ⊞ ⊞ ⊞

| 29 | | | ● |

THE REGENT SYDNEY $$$$
199 George St, Sydney NSW 2000. **Map** 1B3. (9238 0000. FAX 9251 2851.
This hotel boasts a superb location with wonderful views of the harbour and city. Facilities include a health club and two, first-class restaurants. ⊞ ⊞
⊞ ⊞ ⊞ ⊞ ⊞ ⊞ ⊞ ⊞ ⊞ ⊞

| 594 | | ▪ | ● |

RENAISSANCE SYDNEY W www.renaissancehotels.com $$$$
30 Pitt St Sydney NSW 2000. **Map** 1 B3. (9259 7000. FAX 9251 1122.
A smart but down to earth hotel with rooms offering all the features of a five-star establishment. Rooms are large. ⊞ ⊞ ⊞ ⊞ ⊞ ⊞ ⊞ ⊞ ⊞ ⊞ ⊞

| 579 | ● | ▪ | ● |

THE SEBEL PIER ONE SYDNEY $$$
11 Hickson Rd, Walsh Bay, NSW, 2000. **Map** 1 A2. (8298 9999. FAX 8298 9777.
This is Sydney's first over-the-water hotel, built on a 1912 finger wharff. It is situated beside the Harbour Bridge and the hotel's luxurious rooms combine contemporary design with heritage-styles. ⊞ ⊞ ⊞ ⊞

| 161 | ● | | ● |

<table>
<tr><td colspan="2">

Price categories for a double room (not per person), including continental breakfast and service (prices in Australian dollars):
$ under $120
$$ $120–$200
$$$ $200–$280
$$$$ $280–$380
$$$$$ over $380

</td>
<td colspan="4">

GYM FACILITIES
Fully equipped gymnasiums and saunas available on the premises for guest use

BUSINESS FACILITIES
Indicates the provision of conference rooms, desks, fax and computer service for guests.

CLOSE TO SHOPS/RESTAURANTS
Within a 5-minute walk of a good centre for shops and/or restaurants.

</td></tr>
</table>

	NUMBER OF ROOMS	GYM FACILITIES	BUSINESS FACILITIES	CLOSE TO SHOPS/RESTAURANTS
STAFFORD QUEST APARTMENTS W www.staffordapartments.com.au $$$ 75 Harrington St, The Rocks NSW 2000. **Map** 1 B2. (9251 6711. FAX 9251 3458. This hotel consists of a central property and seven charmingly restored 1870 terrace houses nearby. All apartments have well-equipped kitchens and there is a heated spa for guests.	61	●	▩	●

CITY CENTRE

	NUMBER OF ROOMS	GYM FACILITIES	BUSINESS FACILITIES	CLOSE TO SHOPS/RESTAURANTS
AVILLION HOTEL W www.avillion.com.au $$$ Corner Pitt and Liverpool Sts, Sydney, NSW, 2000. **Map** 4 E3. (8268 1888. FAX 9283 5899. Close to Darling Harbour, this hotel offers comfortable, reasonably-priced rooms with original artworks on the walls. There is live jazz in the restaurant on Friday nights.	445	●	▩	●
ALL SEASONS PREMIER MENZIES HOTEL W www.allseasons.com.au $$$ 14 Carrington St, Sydney, NSW, 2000. **Map** 1 A4. (9299 1000 FAX 9290 3819. This elegant, award-winning, four-star hotel offers many relaxing facilities such as an indoor Roman bath, three saunas and a spa.	446		▩	●
BLACKET HOTEL W www.blackethotel.com.au $$$ 70 King Street, Sydney, NSW, 2000. **Map** 1 A4. (9279 3030. FAX 9279 3020. Opened in June 2001, the Blacket is housed in the refurbished 1850s ANZ Bank site designed by 19th century architect Edmond Samuel Blacket. There are five two-storey lofts featuring large bedrooms, kitchenettes and spa baths.	42			●
CAPITOL SQUARE HOTEL W www.bestwestern.com $$ Corner Campbell and George Streets, Sydney, NSW, 2000. **Map** 4 E4. (9211 8633. FAX 9211 8733. This heritage-listed hotel in the China Town district has easy access to the tram and monorail service. The rooms are comfortable and reasonably priced, making this boutique hotel an affordable option.	94		▩	●
CASTLEREAGH INN W www.castlereaghinn.com.au $$ 169-171 Castlereagh St, Sydney, NSW, 2000. **Map** 1 B5. (9284 1000 FAX 92841 9999. The grand dining room, with its crystal chandeliers, is a special feature of this old-fashioned hotel. Morning paper and continental breakfast are included in the affordable price.	82			●
THE CORUS HOTEL SYDNEY $$ 7 York St, Sydney, NSW, 2000. **Map** 1 A4. (9274 1222. FAX 9274 1274. Previously known as the Sydney Vista Hotel, the Corus is conveniently located next to Wynyard Station in the CBD. Rooms have e-mail service and there are good city views from the roof terrace.	268		▩	●
CENTRAL PARK HOTEL W www.centralpark.com.au $$$ 185 Castlereagh St, Sydney, NSW, 2000. **Map** 1 B4. (9283 5000. FAX 9283 2710. This new boutique hotel has double-story loft apartments for up to six people and is located above a popular bar and restaurant. The smaller rooms have cable TV, CD players and large granite bathrooms including spa baths.	35	●	▩	●
ESTABLISHMENT HOTEL $$$$ 5 Bridge Lane, Sydney, NSW, 2000. **Map** 1 B3. (9240 3100. FAX 9240 3101. This is an intimate, private, luxury hotel. Each room is well appointed with original features and there are two, dual-level penthouse suites.	33	●	▩	●
THE GRACE HOTEL W www.gracehotel.com.au $$$$ 77 York St, Sydney, NSW 2000. **Map** 1 A4. (9272 6888. FAX 9299 8189. This centrally-located hotel has been renovated in art-deco style. Rooms are well-equipped and there is a beauty salon and wine bar.	382	●	▩	●
HYDE PARK PLAZA SUITES $$$ 38 College St, Sydney, NSW, 2000. **Map** 4 F3. (9331 6933. FAX 9331 6022. Well located opposite the southern end of Hyde Park, this hotel offers a wide variety of comfortably furnished self-contained suites.	174			●

Price categories for a double room (not per person), including continental breakfast and service (prices in Australian dollars):
- $ under $120
- $$ $120–$200
- $$$ $200–$280
- $$$$ $280–$380
- $$$$$ over $380

GYM FACILITIES
Fully equipped gymnasiums and saunas available on the premises for guest use

BUSINESS FACILITIES
Indicates the provision of conference rooms, desks, fax and computer service for guests.

CLOSE TO SHOPS/RESTAURANTS
Within a 5-minute walk of a good centre for shops and/or restaurants.

	NUMBER OF ROOMS	GYM FACILITIES	BUSINESS FACILITIES	CLOSE TO SHOPS/RESTAURANTS
HILTON SYDNEY [W] www.hilton.com $$$$ 259 Pitt St, Sydney, NSW, 2000. **Map** 1 B5. 9266 2000. FAX 9265 6065. This grande dame of five-star hotels offers the usual high standard of service and facilities including the ornately-decorated, historic Marble Bar. There are artworks in the lobby and, occasionally, small exhibitions.	585		■	●
RADISSON PLAZA HOTEL [W] www.radisson.com $$$ 27 O'Connell St, Sydney, NSW, 2000. 8214 0000. FAX 8214 1000. Located in the heart of Sydney, adjacent to Australia Square, the Radisson is situated within a heritage-listed sandstone building dating back to 1927. Rooms are suitably luxurious and sophisticated.	363	●	■	●
SYDNEY MARRIOTT [W] www.marriott.com $$$ 36 College St, Sydney, NSW, 2000. **Map** 4 F3. 9361 8400. FAX 9361 8599. This elegant hotel, overlooking Hyde Park, offers tastefully decorated rooms with good facilities including microwave ovens.	241		■	●
SHERATON ON THE PARK [W] www.sheraton.com $$$$ 161 Elizabeth St, Sydney, NSW, 2000. **Map** 1 B5. 9286 6000. FAX 9286 6686. Another creative newcomer in the city, there has been no expense spared on the interior design and furnishings of this hotel. Centrally placed with Hyde Park just across the road.	557		■	●
WALDORF APARTMENT HOTEL [W] www.waldorf.com.au $$$ 57 Liverpool St, Sydney, NSW, 2000. **Map** 4 E3. 9261 5355. FAX 9261 3753. Everything is included in these spacious one and two bedroom apartments. Balconies overlook the city.	48			●
THE WESTIN HOTEL [W] www.westin.com $$$$ 1 Martin Place, Sydney, NSW, 2000. 8223 1111. FAX 8223 1222. This hotel is an integral part of the redevelopment of the historic Sydney General Post Office. Its spacious guest rooms are decorated in a contemporary style. The hotel also features a deluxe health club.	417	●	■	●
THE YORK [W] www.theyorkapartments.com.au $$$$ 5 York St, Sydney, NSW, 2000. **Map** 1 A3. 9210 5000. FAX 9290 1487. There is an understated elegance throughout this well-located hotel. All of its apartments are individually designed and have generous balconies, modern kitchens and large bathrooms.	130		■	●
DARLING HARBOUR				
AARONS'S [W] www.aaronshotel.citysearch.com.au $$ 37 Ultimo Rd, Haymarket, NSW, 2000. **Map** 4 D4. 9281 5555. FAX 9281 2666. This hotel offers modern, clean, en suite rooms in the heart of the tourist district. Airport buses stop in front of the hotel.	94			●
CARLTON CREST [W] www.carltonhotels.com.au $$ 169-179 Thomas St, Haymarket, NSW, 2000. **Map** 4 D5. 9281 6888. FAX 9281 6688. Part of this hotel is made up of the original 1902 Infants' Hospital building. All rooms and suites are large. Excellent guest facilities include a rooftop pool, barbecue area and putting green.	251		■	●
HOLIDAY INN DARLING HARBOUR [W] www.holidayinndarlingharbour.com.au $$ 68 Harbour St, Darling Harbour, NSW, 2000. **Map** 4 D3. 9281 0400. FAX 9281 1212. This heritage-listed hotel, close to the CBD is an excellent choice for busy travellers. A-la-carte and casual dining plus breakfast buffet.	304		■	●
FOUR POINTS BY SHERATON [W] www.fourpoints.com $$$ 161 Sussex St, Sydney, NSW, 2000. **Map** 4 D2. 9290 4000. FAX 9299 3340. Modern design marries well with several restored 19th-century maritime buildings. All rooms are beautifully appointed, some with views over Darling Harbour. An old pub is now the hotel's bar.	643		■	●

NOVOTEL CENTURY W www.novotel.com.au $$$ 224
17 Little Pier St, Sydney, NSW, 2000. **Map 4 D4.** 8217 4000. **FAX** 8217 4400.
Overlooking Darling Harbour, this elegant new hotel is a short distance from
Chinatown and Cockle Bay.

NOVOTEL SYDNEY ON DARLING HARBOUR W www.novotel.com.au $$$ 527
100 Murray St, Pyrmont, NSW, 2009. **Map 3 C2.** 9934 0000. **FAX** 9934 0099.
This modern superstructure towers above Darling Harbour. The rooms are good four-
star quality and have views across the city.

PARKROYAL AT DARLING HARBOUR W www.sixcontinentshotels.com.au $$$ 349
150 Day, St, Darling Harbour, NSW, 2000. **Map 4 D3.** 9261 1188. **FAX** 9261 8766.
A funnel-like atrium rises skyward through the centre of the lobby of this stylish
hotel. Guest rooms are well-equipped and look out over the city skyline and
Darling Harbour.

STAR CITY W www.starcity.com.au $$$ 480
80 Pyrmont St, Sydney, Pyrmont, NSW, 2009. **Map 3 B1.** 9777 9000. **FAX** 9657 8345.
Situated above Sydney's glitzy casino, this hotel offers a range of accommodation
from suites with 24-hour butler service to standard rooms with all the usual
comforts. Facilities are open 24 hours a day.

BOTANIC GARDENS AND THE DOMAIN

HOTEL INTER-CONTINENTAL SYDNEY W www.sydney.interconti.com $$$$ 503
117 Macquarie St, Sydney, 2000. **Map 1 C3.** 9253 9000. **FAX** 9240 1240.
Part of the old 1851 Treasury Building now forms the foyer and lower storeys of
this hotel. The facilities are good and rooms well-equipped rooms. Small music
ensembles frequently perform in the lobby.

MARINERS COURT HOTEL W www.marinerscourt.com $ 40
44-50 McElhone St, Sydney, NSW, 2011. **Map 2 E5.** 9358 3888. **FAX** 9357 4670.
This boutique hotel is situated in a quiet location, close to the city. Standard,
reasonably-priced rooms and a café-style restaurant.

SIR STAMFORD CIRCULAR QUAY W www.stamford.com.au $$$$ 105
93 Macquarie St, Sydney, 2000. **Map 1 C3.** 9252 4600. **FAX** 9252 4286.
There is a refined but relaxed air in this intimate hotel. Features include 18th- and
19th -century antiques and open fireplaces. There are fine views from the rooftop
pool. Room rates include breakfast.

KINGS CROSS AND DARLINGHURST

CRESCENT ON BAYSWATER W www.crescenthotel.citysearch.com.au $$$ 67
33 Bayswater Rd, Kings Cross, NSW, 2011. **Map 5 C1.** 9357 7266. **FAX** 9357 7418.
This modern hotel, with wrought iron balconies, boasts an excellent restaurant.
Rooms are self-contained with kitchenettes.

EURO-ASIA REX HOTEL W www.rexhotel.com.au $$ 255
50-58 Macleay St, Potts Point, NSW, 2011. **Map 2 E5.** 9332 3866. **FAX** 9383 7777.
This is a relatively new hotel with spacious rooms and harbour views. Executive
rooms come with a mini-boardroom.

HOTEL ALTAMONT W www.altamont.com.au $ 14
207 Darlinghurst Road, Darlinghurst, NSW, 2010. **Map 5A2.** 9360 6000. **FAX** 9360 7096.
Formerly a Georgian mansion, this hotel boasts a rooftop terrace and comfortable
rooms with king size beds and leather furniture.

KIRKETON HOTEL W www.kirketon.com.au $$$ 40
229 Darlinghurst Rd, Darlinghurst. **Map 5 A2.** 9332 2011. **FAX** 9332 2499.
This fashionable boutique hotel promises accommodation with imagination and an
upbeat Sydney style. The restaurant, Salt, ranks as one of the city's best, and the
hotel bar, Fix, is one of the most exclusive.

LÓTEL W www.lotel.com.au $$$ 16
114 Darlinghurst Rd, Darlinghurst, NSW, 2010. **Map 5 A2.** 9360 6868. **FAX** 9331 4536.
A stylish boutique hotel located in the café district. The décor is French provincial
with painted furniture, fireplaces and art pieces.

MACLEAY SERVICED APARTMENTS W www.themacleay.com $$ 126
28 Macleay St, Potts Point, NSW, 2011. **Map 2 E5.** 93577755. **FAX** 93577233.
These apartments are minutes away from the CBD, Circular Quay and the city's busy
tourist spots and many overlook the Harbour Bridge and the Sydney Opera House.
Cook or have breakfast and dinner delivered to your room.

					NUMBER OF ROOMS	**GYM FACILITIES**	**BUSINESS FACILITIES**	**CLOSE TO SHOPS/RESTAURANTS**

Price categories for a double room (not per person), including continental breakfast and service (prices in Australian dollars):
$ under $120
$$ $120–$200
$$$ $200–$280
$$$$ $280–$380
$$$$$ over $380

GYM FACILITIES
Fully equipped gymnasiums and saunas available on the premises for guest use

BUSINESS FACILITIES
Indicates the provision of conference rooms, desks, fax and computer service for guests.

CLOSE TO SHOPS/RESTAURANTS
Within a 5-minute walk of a good centre for shops and/or restaurants.

MORGAN'S w www.morganshotel.com.au $$ 26
304 Victoria St, Darlinghurst, NSW, 2010. **Map 2 E5.** (9360 7955. FAX 9360 9217.
This boutique, Art-Deco hotel is set in a leafy location in the café district. A Japanese stone garden, courtyard and fountain add to the hotel's charm. It also has its own wine bar and upmarket restaurant.

MEDUSA w www.medusa.com.au $$$$ 18
267 Darlinghurst Rd, Darlinghurst, NSW, 2010. **Map 5 B1.** (9331 1000. FAX 9380 6901.
Interior designer Scott Weston has turned an old Victorian row-house into a miracle of minimalism, with inspiration from Caravaggio's Medusa. It is situated in the heart of Sydney's café society and offers well-equipped rooms.

REGENTS COURT w www.regentscourt.com.au $$$ 31
18 Springfield Ave, Potts Point, NSW, 2011. **Map 2 E5.** (9358 1533. FAX 9358 1833.
An innovative design team has created one of Sydney's more stylish and individual small hotels. The serviced apartments are spacious and well-equipped. A collection of 20th-century designer furniture is used throughout the hotel with smart results.

SIMPSONS OF POTTS POINT w www.simpsonspottspoint.com.au $$$ 14
8 Challis Ave, Potts Point, NSW, 2011. **Map 2 E4.** (9356 2199. FAX 9356 4476.
Built in 1892 as a family residence, this hotel has been exquisitely restored and boasts elegantly designed rooms, grand hallways and splendid stained-glass windows. Rooms offer every comfort.

VICTORIA COURT w www.victoriacourt.com.au $$ 22
122 Victoria St, Potts Point, NSW, 2011. **Map 2 E5.** (9357 3200. FAX 9357 7606.
This is an historic boutique hotel, centrally located on a quiet leafy street. The building dates back to 1881 and features include marble fireplaces and four poster beds. Some rooms have balconies.

WOOLLOOMOOLOO WATERS APARTMENT HOTEL $ 87
88 Dowling St, Potts Point. **Map 2 D5.** (8356 1500. FAX 9356 4839.
This hotel was once a warehouse and offers spacious, well-appointed rooms. Situated just 15 minutes from the CBD.

W SYDNEY w www.whotels.com $$$$$ 140
6 Cowper Wharf Rd, Woolloomooloo. **Map 2 D5.** (9331 9000. FAX 9331 9031.
This stylish hotel is located on the historic finger wharf on Sydney Harbour. It is housed in a renovated historic building and all rooms, including 36 loft rooms, are equipped with cutting-edge business technology, 27-inch television screens and luxurious Aveda bath products.

PADDINGTON AND WOOLLAHRA

GRAND NATIONAL $ 20
161 Underwood St, Paddington, NSW, 2021. **Map 6 D4.** (9363 3096. FAX 9363 3542.
Once just another of the back-street Paddington pubs, this renovated 100-year-old building boasts a stylish dining room and a cocktail bar that is popular with the trend-setting locals. Good value accommodation with shared bathrooms.

HUGHENDEN BOUTIQUE HOTEL w www.hughendenhotel.com.au $$ 35
14 Queen St, Woollahra, NSW, 2025. **Map 6 E4.** (9363 4863. FAX 9362 0398.
This rambling old building, once a 19th century family home is restored to its original grandeur with beautifully carved staircases and marble fireplaces. Rooms are comfortably furnished and the restaurant is very good.

SULLIVANS HOTEL w www.sullivans.com.au $$ 64
21 Oxford St, Paddington, NSW, 2021. **Map 5 B3.** (9361 0211. FAX 9360 3735.
An uninspiring exterior belies the attractive minimalist interior of this family-owned hotel. Rooms are comfortable with good facilities. There is a central courtyard with pool and bicycles are available for guests to ride.

FURTHER AFIELD

ALISHAN INTERNATIONAL GUESTHOUSE W www.alishan.com.au $ — 19
100 Glebe Point Rd, Glebe, NSW, 2037. **Map 3 A4.** 9566 4048. FAX 9525 4686.
A renovated Victorian mansion offering basic accommodation which includes dorms, doubles with ensuites and family rooms.

CARRINGTON HOTEL $$ — 63
15-47 Katoomba St, Katoomba, NSW, 2780. 4782 1111. FAX 4782 1421.
This hotel, a favourite with honeymooners during the 1920s and 1930s, offers old-world charm in the heart of Katoomba, home of the Three Sisters. Today it is a popular weekend retreat.

CRANBROOK INTERNATIONAL $$ — 46
601 New South Head Road, Rose Bay, NSW, 2029. 9327 7770. FAX 9327 8361.
Located about 20 minutes by bus or ferry from the city, Rose Bay enjoys great views of Sydney Harbour. The hotel offers a mixture of well-equipped, standard and deluxe rooms.

HARBOURSIDE APARTMENTS W www.harbourside-apartments.com.au $$$ — 82
2a Henry Lawson Ave, McMahons Point, NSW, 2060. 9963 4300. FAX 9922 7998.
Most of the executive and family-serviced apartments in this 16-storey building offer some of the best views in Sydney. All apartments are comfortably furnished and have good kitchen facilities.

LILIANFELS BLUE MOUNTAINS W www.lilianfels.com.au $$$$ — 86
Lilianfels Avenue, Katoomba. NSW, 2780. 4780 1200. FAX 4780 1300.
Overlooking the Jamison Valley and a short walk from the Three Sisters in the Blue Mountains, this hotel is listed among the Small Luxury Hotels of the World. It boasts a cosy lounge, open fires and a library.

MANLY PACIFIC PARKROYAL $$$ — 170
55 North Steyne, Manly, NSW, 2095. 9977 7666. FAX 9977 7822.
Situated on Manly's ocean beach, this hotel has unbeatable views of sand and surf. All rooms are light and spacious with balconies.

MEDINA EXECUTIVE APARTMENTS W www.medinaapartments.com.au $$$$ — 47
400 Glenmore Rd, Paddington, NSW, 2021. **Map 6 D2.** 9361 9000. FAX 9332 3484.
Set in landscaped gardens, these two and three-bedroom apartments offer all the conveniences of home, combined with hotel-style services.

PERIWINKLE MANLY COVE W www.periwinklemanlycove.com.au $$ — 18
18-19 East Esplanade, Manly, NSW, 2095. 9977 4668. FAX 9977 6308.
Stylish rooms with high ceilings, wrought-iron verandas, and a leafy courtyard are features of this pretty, family-run guesthouse. There are private outdoor areas where guests can enjoy the tranquility of Manly Cove.

RAVESI'S ON BONDI BEACH W www.ravesis.com.au $$ — 16
Cnr Campbell Parade and Hall St, Bondi Beach, NSW, 2026. 9365 4422. FAX 9365 1481.
Smart and trendy, this small hotel epitomizes the relaxed style of beach life at Bondi. Rooms are furnished in cane and some suites have balconies overlooking the Beach. The restaurant is regarded as one of the best in the area.

RUSHCUTTERS HARBOURSIDE SYDNEY W www.rushcutters.com $$$$ — 260
100 Bayswater Rd, Rushcutters Bay, NSW, 2011. 8353 8988. FAX 8353 8999.
This stylish hotel overlooks beautiful Rushcutters Bay, home of the Cruising Yacht Club. The rooms are light and spacious and the hotel provides a free shuttle service to the city.

SAVOY DOUBLE BAY W www.savoyhotel.com.au $$ — 39
41-45 Knox St, Double Bay, NSW, 2028. 9326 1411. FAX 9327 8464.
This small hotel in the up-market Double Bay, offers excellent value. Rooms are basic and rates include breakfast.

SIR STAMFORD DOUBLE BAY W www.stamford.com.au $$$ — 73
22 Knox St, Double Bay, NSW, 2028. 9363 0100. FAX 9327 3110.
This sumptuously furnished hotel boasts boldly designed rooms with canopied beds, or else New York loft-style rooms complete with mezzanine bedrooms. Room rates include breakfast.

SIR STAMFORD PLAZA W www.stamford.com.au $$$$ — 140
33 Cross St, Double Bay, NSW, 2028. 9362 4455. FAX 9362 4744.
This is a sophisticated hotel offering classically decorated rooms and suites. The central courtyard is in the style of a Mediterranean villa garden, while the rooftop heated pool has fabulous views.

RESTAURANTS, CAFÉS AND PUBS

SYDNEYSIDERS are justifiably proud of their dining scene. Australia's largest city has been populated by successive waves of migrants, all of whom have added something of their home countries to the communal table. These influences have spilled over into contemporary cuisine, which is often called "Modern Australian". This term covers just about any ethnic style the chef may fancy, loosely based on French cuisine. The result is that, in terms of ethnic diversity, Sydney is able

Fresh seafood, Chinese style

to offer many dining options. For a summary of key features and prices of restaurants included in this guide, turn to *Choosing a Restaurant* on pages 184–5. There is a more detailed description of each restaurant in the listings on pages 186–93. Casual eating places, where you can often enjoy food that is as good as at a restaurant but cheaper, are featured on pages 194–7; here you will also find mention of pubs that have recommended bistros and dining areas.

WHERE TO EAT

CIRCULAR QUAY, The Rocks, Darlinghurst, Potts Point and Paddington are the areas where you will find the widest choice of places to eat. Just outside the city centre, and not covered in depth in these listings, are the inner-city "eat streets" of Glebe Point Road, Glebe *(see p131)*, and King Street, Newtown.

On the lower North Shore is Military Road, which extends from Neutral Bay to Mosman. It would be difficult to walk along any of these streets and not find a café or restaurant to suit your taste and budget.

All of the major hotels have at least one restaurant and a few such as Kable's in the Regent Sydney *(see p172)*, serve some of the finest food that Sydney has to offer. Signature restaurants that are recommended in the grander

hotels include Raphael at the Renaissance Sydney, Unkai *(see p191)*, a splendid Japanese dining room in the ANA Hotel and the very Venetian Galileo in the Observatory Hotel *(see p172)*. They aim at the well-heeled diner, but nonetheless offer a high standard of dining for people who want the best and are prepared to pay for it.

HOW MUCH TO PAY

COMPARED WITH other major world capitals, dining out in Sydney is relatively inexpensive. The cost of a three-course meal in an average restaurant is probably 25 per cent lower than its equivalent in, say, New York or London. The cost is further reduced if you choose a BYO restaurant where you can avoid paying the marked-up price of restaurant wine by taking your own alcohol.

Restrained Art Deco style at the tastefully restored Banc *(see p186)*

OPENING TIMES

MOST RESTAURANTS serve lunch from noon to 3pm and dinner from 6pm to about 11pm, though last orders are often at 10:30pm. Cheap and cheerful ethnic kitchens may close earlier, around 9:30pm, but this largely depends on demand. Many restaurants close on some, if not all, public holidays *(see p51)*. This is particularly true of Christmas Day, Boxing Day and Good Friday.

RESERVATIONS

BOOKING IS recommended in most places – earlier in the day is usually adequate. If, you want to be sure of a table for Friday or Saturday in a spot that is currently fashionable, however, you may need to make a reservation at least a week in advance. The more casual brasseries and bistros

The popular Fez Café in Victoria Street, Darlinghurst *(see p193)*

are the exceptions. Many are open all through the day and, as they aren't the sort of place where people linger over their meal, they do not take bookings. You may have to wait a few minutes for a table if you arrive at a busy time.

LICENSING LAWS

SYDNEY RESTAURANTS must be licensed to sell food, but when a place is described as licensed, this usually refers to its licence to sell alcohol. BYO (bring your own) restaurants are not licensed to sell liquor and you will need to buy it beforehand if you want to drink alcohol with your meal. A small amount will probably be charged for "corkage".

BYO restaurants not only reduce the cost of dining out, but also allow wine buffs to choose exactly the wines they wish to drink with their meal. At up-market establishments such as Claude's *(see p192)*, it is a good idea to inquire about the day's menu, so you can choose your wine accordingly.

Relaxing in a café at the top end of Oxford Street, Paddington

DRESS CODES

DRESS STANDARDS in Sydney restaurants are really quite relaxed, even in the more up-market establishments. Most restaurants will draw the line, however, at patrons in beach-wear and flip flops.

Neat and tidy is the general rule. Smart casual dress is the safest option when considering

Surf watching from the balcony at Ravesi's on Bondi Beach *(see p189)*

what to wear. Jackets and ties are a rare sight unless the wearer has come straight from the office or is conducting a business meeting over a meal.

TAX AND TIPPING

IN AUSTRALIA, a GST tax is sometimes added to your bill. Some places include it in its prices but will indicate this on the menu. While tipping is not compulsory, 10 to 15 per cent of the total bill is customary as a reward for good service. You can leave a cash tip after you have paid or add it to the total if paying your bill by credit card.

EATING WITH CHILDREN

MOST RESTAURANTS accept children who can sit still throughout a meal, although you may feel more comfortable in either Chinese restaurants or the cheap pasta eateries in East Sydney, where children are always welcome.

Hamburger chains such as McDonald's and Hungry Jacks have branches throughout the city. For families wanting to dine rather than snack, chains such as Pizza Hut and the Black Stump steakhouses offer special menus for children as well as alcohol for the adults.

The Hard Rock Café *(see p194)* in Darlinghurst has enough of a buzz to drown out any noise young children may make and the menu and upbeat atmosphere are popular with older kids. Perhaps the best spots to dine out with

children are those where they can play safely outside after they have eaten. The Bathers Pavilion *(see p186)* is right on Balmoral Beach *(see pp54–5)*, a sheltered harbour beach which has a netted swimming pool, while Centennial Park Café *(see p194)* is within supervisory range of grassy lawns and a children's playground.

USING THE LISTINGS

Key to symbols in the listings on pp186–93.

🍴 fixed-price menu
🍷 bring your own bottle
🧒 children's portions
♿ wheelchair access
▤ air conditioning
🪑 tables outside
🏖 tables with good views
🚭 non-smoking section
🍾 good wine list
★ highly recommended

Credit cards:
AE American Express
BC Bankcard
DC Diners Club
MC MasterCard/Access
V Visa
JCB Japanese Credit Bureau

Price categories (in Australian dollars) for a three-course evening meal for one person including cover charge and service (but not wine):

$ under $25
$$ $25–35
$$$ $35–50
$$$$ $50–70
$$$$$ Over $70

What to Eat in Sydney

Meat pie with tomato sauce

S YDNEYSIDERS take for granted the quality and variety of produce on offer. The pie with sauce has been pushed aside as restaurateurs seek out regional specialities. From New South Wales, you may sample Sydney rock oysters, honey from Mudgee, mushrooms from Orange, lamb from Illabo and the Southern Highlands' gourmet potatoes. From other states, try the olive oil of South Australia, salmon farmed in Tasmania, soft fruit and dairy produce from Victoria, reef fish and exotic fruit from Queensland and Western Australian farmhouse cheeses.

Eucalypt Honey
Imported bees seem to love the eucalypts. Leatherwood, light in colour, has the strongest flavour.

Potato Wedges
Coated with a spicy seasoning then fried in a two-step process, these chunky variations on the humble chip are usually served with sour cream and chilli sauce.

Yum Cha
Literally "drinking tea", this Chinese feast includes dim sum, or steamed dumplings stuffed with meat, fish or vegetables.

Focaccia
This Italian-inspired sandwich has gourmet antipasto, salad and meat slices between toasted slabs of crusty flat bread.

Lebanese Mezes
Expect an array of appetizers including pulse and vegetable dips, marinated and grilled vegetables and filled pastries.

Crab

Balmain bug

Rock oysters

Seafood Platter
Coming from comparatively clean waters, Australian seafood is both abundant and of extremely high quality.

Scallops

Lobster

King prawns

Mussels

Mixed Leaf Salad
Garden-fresh salad features on most menus. It is served here with feta cheese and grilled vegetables.

Char-grilled Kangaroo Fillet
A relatively recent addition to butchers' shelves, low-fat kangaroo fillet is usually served rare.

Thai Green Curry
Chicken is the favourite variety, but a tasty vegetarian version is also commonly served.

Kebabs

Chicken wings

Baby octopus

Seared Beef Fillet
Australian beef, here wrapped in paperbark, is usually served with the season's vegetables.

Barbecue
Char-grilled meat, poultry and fresh seafood such as baby octopus are served by themselves or in combination, usually accompanied by bread and green salad.

Freshwater Crayfish
Also known as "yabbies", this main dish is usually served simply on a bed of greens with a dipping sauce such as aïoli.

Blue-eyed Cod
Although known as cod, it is in fact trevalla, a deep sea fish of meaty texture and mild flavour. It is often served in thick steaks.

Lamb Loin Fillet
Thick slices of tender seared lamb served on a salad of rocket and fresh snow peas are ideal Sydney summer eating.

Baked Ricotta Cake
Indigenous Australian ingredients such as rosella buds may appear in contemporary desserts.

Pavlova
This meringue dessert is topped with fresh cream and summer fruit such as passionfruit.

Mixed Berry Ice Cream
Homemade ice creams, such as raspberry or honey, are often served with seasonal fruit.

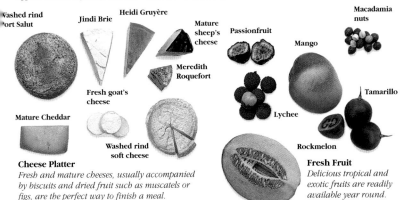

Washed rind Port Salut

Jindi Brie

Heidi Gruyère

Mature sheep's cheese

Passionfruit

Mango

Macadamia nuts

Meredith Roquefort

Fresh goat's cheese

Tamarillo

Mature Cheddar

Lychee

Washed rind soft cheese

Rockmelon

Cheese Platter
Fresh and mature cheeses, usually accompanied by biscuits and dried fruit such as muscatels or figs, are the perfect way to finish a meal.

Fresh Fruit
Delicious tropical and exotic fruits are readily available year round.

What to Drink in Sydney

Semillon Chardonnay

Australia has one of the world's finest cuisines and part of its enjoyment is the marriage of the country's wine with great food. Australians have a very relaxed attitude to food and wine mixes, so red wine with fish and a cold, dry Riesling as an aperitif can easily be the order of the day. Also, many of the restuarants in the wine regions offer exclusive brands, or offer rare wines so these are worth seeking out. Australians also enjoy some of the best good-value wine in the world *(see pp32–3)*. It is estimated that there are 10,000 different Australian wines on the market at any one time. Australians do love their beer, and it remains a popular drink, with a wide range of choices available. While the health-conscious can choose from a variety of bottled waters and select-your-own, freshly-squeezed fruit juices. Imported wines, beers and spirits are also readily available.

SPARKLING WINE

Domaine Chandon in the Yarra Valley produces high-quality sparkling wines

Australia is justly famous for its sparkling wines, from Yalumba's Angas Brut to Seppelts Salinger. Most recently, Tasmania has showed considerable promise in producing some high quality sparkling wines, particularly Pirie from Pipers Brook. However, the real hidden gems are the sparkling red wines – the best are made using the French *Méthode Champenois*, matured over a number of years and helped by a small drop of vintage port. The best producers of red sparkling wines are Rockford and Seppelts. These sparkling wines are available throughout Sydney from "bottle shops", which sell alcohol.

Angus Brut premium

WHITE WINE

Rhine Riesling

Botrytis Semillon

The revolution in wine making in the 1970s firmly established dry wines made from international grape varieties on the Australian table. Chardonnay, Sauvignon Blanc, and more recently Viognier and Pinot Gris are all popular. However, in recent years there has also been a renaissance and growing appreciation for Riesling, Marsanne and Semillon, which age very gracefully. Australia's other great wines are their fortified and desert wines. Australian winemakers use *botrytis cinera*, or noble rot, to make luscious dessert wines such as Muscats and Tokays.

Some of the vines in Australia are the oldest in the world.

GRAPE TYPE	STATE	BEST REGIONS	BEST PRODUCERS
Chardonnay	VIC	Geelong, Beechworth	Bannockburn, Giaconda, Stoniers
	NSW	Hunter Valley	Lakes Folly, Rosemount, Tyrrell's
	WA	Margaret River	Leeuwin Estate, Pierro, Cullen
	SA	Barossa Valley, Eden Valley	Penfolds, Mountadam
Semillon	NSW	Hunter Valley	Brokenwood, McWilliams, Tyrrell
	SA	Barossa Valley	Peter Lehmann, Willows, Penfolds
	WA	Margaret River	Moss Wood, Voyager, Evans & Tate
Riesling	SA	Clare Valley and Adelaide Hills	Grosset, Pikes, Petaluma, Mitchells
	SA	Barossa Valley	Richmond Grove, Leo Buring, Yalumba
	TAS	Tasmania	Piper's Brook
Marsanne	VIC	Goulburn Valley	Chateau Tahbilk, Mitchelton

Vineyards of Leeuwin Estate, Margaret River

RED WINE

A USTRALIA'S BENCHMARK red is Grange Hermitage, the creation of the late vintner Max Schubert in the 1950s and 1960s. Due to his work, Shiraz has established itself as Australia's premium red variety. However, there is also plenty of diversity with the acknowledged quality of Cabernet Sauvignon produced in the Coonawarra. Recently, there has also been a re-appraisal of traditional "old vine" Grenache and Mourvedre varieties in the Barossa Valley and McLaren Vale.

Shiraz   **Pinot Noir**

GRAPE TYPE	BEST REGIONS	BEST PRODUCERS
Shiraz	Hunter Valley (NSW)	Brokenwood, Lindmans, Tyrrells
	Great Western, Sunbury (VIC)	Bests, Seppelts, Craiglee
	Barossa Valley (SA)	Henschke, Penfolds, Rockford, Torbreck
	McLaren Vale (SA)	Hardys, Coriole, Chapel Hill
	Margaret River, Great Southern(WA)	Cape Mentelle, Plantagenet
Cabernet Sauvignon	Margaret River (WA)	Cape Mentelle, Cullen, Moss Wood
	Coonawarra (SA)	Wynns, Lindemans, Bowen Estate
	Barossa, Adelaide Hills (SA)	Penfolds, Henschke, Petaluma
	Yarra Valley, Great Western (VIC)	Yarra Yering, Yerinberg, Bests
Merlot	Yarra Valley, Great Western (VIC)	Bests, Yara Yering
	Adelaide Hills, Clare Valley (SA)	Petaluma, Pikes
Pinot Noir	Yarra Valley (VIC)	Coldstream Hills, Tarrawarra
	Gippsland, Geelong (VIC)	Bass Philip, Bannockburn, Shadowfax

BEER

M OST AUSTRALIAN BEER is vat fermented, or lager, and consumed chilled. Full-strength beer has an alcohol content of about 4.8 per cent, mid-strength beers have around 3.5 per cent while "light" beers have less than 3 per cent. Traditionally heat sterilized, cold filtration is now popular. Fans of real ale should seek out one of the city's pub breweries. Beer is ordered by glass size and brand: a schooner is a 426 ml (15 fl oz) glass and a middy is 284 ml (10 fl oz).

Tooheys Red Bitter   **Cascade Premium Lager**

Middy   **Schooner**

FRUIT JUICES

W ITH THE FABULOUS fresh fruit at their disposal year round, cafés concoct an astonishing array of fruit-based non-alcoholic drinks. They include frappés of fruit pulp and juice blended with crushed ice; smoothies of fruit blended with milk or yoghurt; and pure juices, extracted from everything from carrots to watermelons.

Pear and kiwi frappé   **Banana smoothie**   **Strawberry juice**

COFFEE

S YDNEY'S PASSION for coffee means that short black, macchiato, caffe latte, cappuccino and flat white (with milk) are now available at every neighbourhood café.

Flat white coffee   **Caffe latte**

OTHER DRINKS

T AP WATER in Sydney is fresh and clean, but local and imported bottled water is fashionable. The cola generation has graduated to alcoholic soft drinks and soda drinks. One brand, Two Dogs alcoholic lemonade, was born when a glut of lemons flooded the fruit market.

Alcoholic soda

Choosing a Restaurant

THE RESTAURANTS in this guide have been selected across a wide price range for their good value, facilities and location. This chart, arranged by area and price category, highlights some of the factors which may influence your choice. Full listings, arranged according to cuisine, are on pages 186–193. Café and pub information is on pages 194–7.

	Price	PAGE NUMBER	FIXED-PRICE MENU	GOOD VIEWS	TABLES OUTSIDE	GOOD WINE LIST	SEAFOOD SPECIALITIES	BYO	CHILDREN'S FACILITIES	NON-SMOKING SECTION
THE ROCKS AND CIRCULAR QUAY										
MCA Café *(Mediterranean)*	$$$	193		■	●					■
The Wharf Restaurant *(Bistros and Brasseries)*	$$$	189		■	●		●		●	■
Harbour Kitchen and Bar *(Contemporary)*	$$$$	187		■		■				
Sailors Thai *(Asian)*	$$$$	191			●	■	●			
Aqua Luna *(Italian)*	$$$$$	191								
Bel Mondo *(Italian)*	$$$$$	191		■	●	■				■
Cadmus *(Middle Eastern)*	$$$$$	193	●		■	■				
Guillaume at Bennelong *(French)* ★	$$$$$	193		■		■				
Rockpool *(Seafood)* ★	$$$$$	189				■				
Quay *(Contemporary)*	$$$$$	187		■	●	■				
Unkai *(Japanese)* ★	$$$$$	191	●				●		●	■
CITY CENTRE										
BBQ King *(Chinese)*	$$	189							■	■
Bodhi in the Park *(Asian)*	$$	190			●					■
Casa Asturiana *(Mediterranean)*	$$$	193								
ECQ *(Bistros and Brasseries)*	$$$	188		■			●		●	■
Malaya *(Asian)*	$$$	190		■			●			■
Sushi-E *(Asian)*	$$$	191								
Bistro CBD *(Italian)*	$$$$	192				■				
Certo Ristorante *(Italian)*	$$$$	191				■				
Criterion *(Mediterranean)*	$$$$	193			●	■				
Edna's Table *(Contemporary)* ★	$$$$	186		■	●		●		●	■
Prime *(Contemporary)* ★	$$$$	187				■				
The Summit *(Contemporary)*	$$$$	188		■		■				
Banc *(Contemporary)* ★	$$$$$	186				■	●			■
Beppi's *(Italian)*	$$$$$	191				■				
Celsius *(Contemporary)*	$$$$$	186				■				■
Forty One *(Contemporary)* ★	$$$$$	187	●		●	■			●	■
Restaurant VII *(Asian)*	$$$$$	191	●			■				■
DARLING HARBOUR										
Golden Century *(Chinese)*	$$	190								■
Golden Harbour *(Chinese)*	$$	190	●							■
Marigold *(Chinese)*	$$	190								■
Regal *(Chinese)*	$$	190	●						●	■
Silver Spring *(Chinese)*	$$$	190								■
Coast *(Contemporary)*	$$$$	186		■	●	■				■
Jordon's International Seafood Restaurant *(Seafood)*	$$$$	189		■	●		●		●	■
Kamogawa *(Asian)*	$$$$	190	●							■
BOTANIC GARDENS AND THE DOMAIN										
Botanic Gardens Restaurant *(Contemporary)* ★	$$$$	186		■	●				●	
KINGS CROSS AND DARLINGHURST										
No Names *(Italian)*	$	192							■	■
Fu-Manchu *(Chinese)*	$$	189						■	●	■
Fez Café *(Middle Eastern)*	$$$	193			●					■
Fishface *(Seafood)*	$$$	188					●	■		■

Price categories for a three-course evening meal for one person including cover charge and service (but not wine):
$ under A$25
$$ A$25–$35
$$$ A$35–$50
$$$$ A$50–$70
$$$$$ Over A$70

★ Means highly recommended.

FIXED-PRICE MENU
A menu of two to three courses for a set price which includes coffee but excludes wine and other drinks.

BYO
Bring your own alcohol. A small charge is often made for corkage.

LATE OPENING
Orders will still be accepted at or after 11pm.

		Page Number	Fixed-Price Menu	Good Views	Tables Outside	Good Wine List	Seafood Specialities	BYO	Children's Facilities	Non-Smoking Section
Macleay Street Bistro (Bistros and Brasseries)	$$$	189		●					▦	▦
Oh! Calcutta! (Asian)	$$$	191							▦	▦
Xo (Asian)	$$$	191								
Bayswater Brasserie (Bistros and Brasseries) ★	$$$$	188		●	▦				●	▦
Otto (Contemporary)	$$$$	187		▦	●					▦
Ristorante Riva (Italian)	$$$$	192								
Eleni's (Mediterranean)	$$$$$	193						●	▦	
Mezzaluna (Italian) ★	$$$$$	192		▦	●	▦		●		
Salt (Contemporary)	$$$$$	188				▦				
Tetsuya's (Contemporary) ★	$$$$$	188	●			▦				▦
PADDINGTON AND WOOLLAHRA										
Bistro Lulu (Bistros and Brasseries)	$$$	188		●					▦	
Buzo (Mediterranean)	$$$	193				▦				
Bistro Moncur (French)	$$$$	192		●		●			●	▦
Pruniers (Contemporary)	$$$$	187		●	▦					
Buon Ricordo (Italian)	$$$$$	191				▦				
Claude's (French) ★	$$$$$	192	●			▦			▦	
Lucio's (Italian)	$$$$$	192				▦	●			▦
FURTHER AFIELD										
Billy Kwong (Chinese)	$$	189							▦	
Mohr Fish (Seafood)	$$	189	●				●	▦		
Uchi Lounge (Asian)	$	191							▦	
Alhambra (Mediterranean)	$$$	193		▦	●	▦				
Armstrong's Manly (Bistros and Brasseries)	$$$	188		▦	●				●	▦
Barnaby's Riverside (Contemporary)	$$$	186	●	▦	●		●		●	▦
Doyles on the Beach (Seafood)	$$$	189			●		●			
Frattini (Italian)	$$$	192	●				●	▦	▦	
Sean's Panaroma (Contemporary)	$$$	187			●					
Aqua Dining (Contemporary)	$$$$	186		▦		▦				
The Bathers Pavilion (Contemporary) ★	$$$$	186		▦		▦	●		●	▦
The Boathouse on Blackwattle Bay (Seafood)	$$$$	189		▦			●	▦		
Catalina Rose Bay (Contemporary)	$$$$	186		▦	●		●			
Courtney's Brasserie (Bistros and Brasseries)	$$$$	188			●				●	
Darling Mills (Contemporary)	$$$$	186			●	●				
Elio (Italian)	$$$$	192			●					▦
Grappa (Italian)	$$$$	192			●				▦	
Le Kiosk (Contemporary)	$$$$	187		▦	●		●			▦
Longrain (Asian) ★	$$$$	190					●		●	▦
MC Garage (Contemporary)	$$$$	187				▦				
The Pier (Seafood)	$$$$	189		▦		▦	●			
Ravesi's on Bondi Beach (Bistros and Brasseries)	$$$$	189	●	▦	●		●			
Sorriso (Italian)	$$$$	192			●				▦	
Tabou (French)	$$$$	193				▦				
Watermark (Contemporary)	$$$$	188		●	▦		●			
Ying's (Chinese)	$$$$	190					●		▦	
La Grillade (French)	$$$$$	193			●	▦				
Hugo's (Contemporary)	$$$$$	187		▦	●					▦
Marque (French)	$$$$$	193				▦				

Types of Restaurant

THESE RESTAURANTS have been selected across the wide range of cuisines available in the city. All have been recommended for their good value or exceptional food. Entries are arranged according to type of cuisine and listed alphabetically within each of the categories. For a chart listing restaurants according to area see pages 184–5.

	CREDIT CARDS	VEGETARIAN SPECIALTIES	BAR AREA	LATE OPENING

CONTEMPORARY

AQUA DINING $$$$
Cnr Paul and North Cliff Streets, Milsons Point. 99649998.
This restaurant affords fine views over the harbour. The menu makes the most of local produce and includes dishes such as Yamba prawn tartlet, smoked chicken and mango salad and cauliflower and truffle pannacotta.

Credit Cards: AE BC DC MC V — Late Opening

BARNABY'S RIVERSIDE $$$
66 Phillip St, Parramatta. 96333777.
This colonial cottage overlooking the Parramatta River is a great setting for sampling European- and Asian-influenced cuisine. Try the mixed grill of fresh Australian seafood or the prime beef rib with bearnaise sauce.

Credit Cards: AE BC DC MC V — Vegetarian Specialties

BOTANIC GARDENS RESTAURANT $$$$
Royal Botanic Gardens, Mrs Macquaries Rd. Map 2D4. 92412419.
At this lunchtime venue the influence is French with an emphasis on seafood. Popular dishes include white sausage with lentils and whiting fillets with pea puree and deep fried sage. Sit on the balcony overlooking the gardens.

Credit Cards: AE BC DC MC V — Vegetarian Specialties

BANC $$$$$
53 Martin Place. Map 1B4. 92335300
Located on the ground floor of a former bank, the grand setting of this Art Deco-style restaurant makes for a fine dining experience. The French-influenced menu at boasts quality fresh produce - game, seafood, duck and truffles. Dishes include carpaccio of cooked pig's trotter and fillet of beef rossini. ● Sun, Mon.

Credit Cards: AE BC DC MC V — Vegetarian Specialties

THE BATHERS' PAVILION $$$$
4 The Esplanade, Balmoral. 99695050
Signature dishes at the Pavilion include seared white scallops with oxtail ravioli. The restaurant overlooks the white sands of Balmoral Beach and its accompanying café serves late breakfasts and brunch.

Credit Cards: AE BC DC MC V — Vegetarian Specialties, Bar Area, Late Opening

---

CATALINA ROSE BAY $$$$
1 Sunderland Ave, Lyne Park, Rose Bay. 93710555.
Amongst chef Angel Fernandez's deliciously creative takes on modern Australian dining are snapper fillet with potato and garlic purée, the best local oysters and a celebrated sashimi selection.

Credit Cards: AE BC DC MC V — Bar Area, Late Opening

CELSIUS $$$$$
Radisson Plaza Hotel, 27 O'Connell St, Sydney. Map 4 E1. 82140496.
The menu here consists of simple, modern Australian cuisine using local produce. Chef Peter Doyle's dishes include the crisp-skin john dory fillet with white scallops and Jacqueline sauce, and rib-eye of lamb with summer beans ragoût. ● Sun.

Credit Cards: AE BC DC MC V — Vegetarian Specialties

COAST $$$$
The Roof Terrace, Cockle Bay, Darling Park, 201 Sussex St Sydney. Map 4 D2. 92676700.
From safe options such as the fish and chips and the grilled ocean fish to the crab, prawn, clam and fish stew with romesco sauce, Coast is sure to accommodate a range of tastes. Relaxed atmosphere with great views.

Credit Cards: AE BC DC MC V — Vegetarian Specialties, Late Opening

---

DARLING MILLS $$$$
134 Glebe Point Rd, Glebe, Map 3 A4. 96605666.
This restaurant is set in a spacious sandstone building which has been renovated using recycled church sandstone to gothic effect. It has a rooftop greenhouse that provides the freshest possible produce. Try the grilled duck breast, crab and cauliflower cappucino or the pepper-crusted veal fillet.

Credit Cards: AE BC DC MC V — Vegetarian Specialties, Bar Area, Late Opening

---

EDNA'S TABLE $$$$
204 Clarence St, Sydney. Map 1B4. 92673933.
Tastes of the outback are combined with European-style food at this Australian native cuisine restaurant. Try the grilled kangaroo fillet with beetroot or the grilled emu fillet, braised fennel and nashi. ● Sun.

Credit Cards: AE BC DC MC V — Vegetarian Specialties, Late Opening

Price categories for a three-course evening meal for one person inlcuding cover charge and service (but not wine):
$ under A$25
$$ A$25–$35
$$$ A$35–$50
$$$$ A$50–$70
$$$$$ A over $70

CREDIT CARDS
Indicates which credit cards are accepted: *AE* American Express; *BC* Bankcard; *DC* Diners Club; *MC* Master Card/Access; *V* Visa; *JCB* Japanese Credit Bureau.

VEGETARIAN SPECIALITIES
Vegetarian selections are available on the menu.

BAR AREA
The restaurant has a separate bar area.

LATE OPENING
Orders will still be accepted at or after 11pm.

	CREDIT CARDS	VEGETARIAN SPECIALITIES	BAR AREA	LATE OPENING
FORTY ONE $$$$$ Level 42 Chifley Tower, 2 Chifley Square. Map 1B4. 92212500. This old Sydney favourite offers impressive views of the city and harbour. Chef Dietmar Sawyere's blend of European and Asian flavours are a winning combination. Specialties include wild hare with braised Belgian endive and charteuse jus and oriental duck consommé. ● Sun. 👌📠🍷📖 ★ 🍴 ▣	AE BC DC MC V	●	▦	
HARBOUR KITCHEN AND BAR $$$$ Park Hyatt Hotel. 7 Hickson Rd, The Rocks. Map 1B1. 9256 1661. The dishes here are simple but impressive and include spit-roasted duck breast and wood-roasted veal in a citrus burnt butter. For dessert try the Valrhona chocolate cake with espresso ice-cream. Bookings are essential. 👌📠🍷▣	AE BC DC MC V		▦	
HUGO'S $$$$$ 70 Campbell Parade, Bondi Beach. 93000900. Favourite dishes from chef Peter Evans include the steamed barramundi with lime and coconut sauce and crisp-skinned trout with goats cheese ravioli. Good views over the golden sands of Bondi Beach. 📠📠▣	AE BC DC MC V		▦	●
LE KIOSK $$$$ 1 Marine Parade, Shelly Beach, Manly. 99774122. Set in a subtropical garden at secluded Shelly Beach, this charming sandstone cottage offers one of the best al fresco dining spots in Sydney. The menu comprises fresh, seasonal seafood as well as popular dishes such as the snapper with pipis in an almond and saffron broth. 👌📠🍷📠▣	AE BC DC MC V	●		
MG GARAGE $$$$$ 490 Crown Street, Surry Hills. Map 5 A4. 93839383. The Greek-influenced cuisine here is served with all the slickness of the convertibles parked in the restaurant. Chef Janni Kyritsis's vine leaves break with tradition by enclosing quail and pig trotter sausage. Pomegranate-glazed pigeon is served with dried fig and radish salad. ● Sun (café open). 👌📠🍷	AE BC DC MC V	●	▦	●
OTTO $$$$ The Wharf, 6 Cowper Wharf Rd. Woolloomooloo. Map 2 D5. 93687488. This trendy restaurant in the Finger Wharf complex at Woolloomooloo Bay (see p107), boasts a stylish interior and alto-trattoria food that is full of flavour. Popular dishes include Bistecca di Vitello alla Fiorentina. The indoor bar offers one of the smartest waterside drinking spots. 👌📠🍷📖📠▣	AE BC DC MC V	●	▦	
PRIME $$$$ Lower Ground Floor, GPO. 1 Martin Place Sydney. Map 1 B4. 92297777. Chef Darrell Felstead offers a great selection of beef steaks in a classy restaurant setting. Try some of the favourite dishes which include the venison with chartreuse jus and served with baby beetroot. ● Sun. 👌📠🍷 ★	AE BC DC MC V			
PRUNIERS $$$$$ 65 Ocean St, Woollahra. Map 6 F4. 93631974. Pruniers offers an elegant dining experience in lush garden surroundings. Sample the delicious bistecca fiorentina, which is an aged T-bone steak marinated in olive oil and grilled and served with prosciutto and radicchio shreds. ● Sun. 👌📠🍷📠	AE BC DC MC V		▦	
QUAY $$$$$ Overseas Passenger terminal, Circular Quay West, The Rocks. Map 1 B2. 92515600. This restaurant boasts a top harbourside location and quality produce. Chef Peter Gilmore's modern Australian dishes include crisp pressed duck with garlic purée salsify, baby silverbeet and jus. The deserts are some of the best in town, especially the "five textures of Valrohna" chocolate cake. 👌📠🍷📠▣	AE BC DC MC V		▦	
SEAN'S PANAROMA $$$$ 270 Campbell Parade, Bondi Beach. 93654924. This down to earth restaurant serves up dishes such as eggplant stuffed with mozzerella and anchovies, and a white chocolate and rosemary nougat. 👌📠📠📠	BC MC V	●		

For key to symbols see back flap

Price categories for a three-course evening meal for one person inlcuding cover charge and service (but not wine):
$ under A$25
$$ A$25–$35
$$$ A$35–$50
$$$$ A$50–$70
$$$$$ Aover $70

Credit Cards
Indicates which credit cards are accepted: *AE* American Express; *BC* Bankcard; *DC* Diners Club; *MC* Master Card/Access; *V* Visa; *JCB* Japanese Credit Bureau.

Vegetarian Specialities
Vegetarian selections are available on the menu.

Bar Area
The restaurant has a separate bar area.

Late Opening
Orders will still be accepted at or after 11pm.

The Summit $$$$
Level 47, Australia Square, 264 George St, Sydney. **Map** 1 B3. ☎ *92479777.*
With its spectacular views of the city and great bar, this revolving restaurant in Harry Seidler's Australia Square building is an old favourite. Food is contemporary and includes grilled snapper fillet with cauliflower mash and truffle oil. ♿ 🚭 🍷 ☼

Credit Cards	Vegetarian Specialities	Bar Area	Late Opening
AE BC DC MC V		■	

Salt $$$$$
229 Darlinghurst Road, Darlinghurst. **Map** 5 B1. ☎ *93322566.*
Chefs Luke Mangan and Mark Holmes combine sweet flavours with savoury to produce such dishes as pan fried barramundi with crab, corn and dates in a basil broth. Other specialties on offer in this modern setting include tempura of quail with soy wasabi. Bookings are necessary. 🚭 🍷

Credit Cards	Vegetarian Specialities	Bar Area	Late Opening
AE BC DC MC V	●	■	●

Tetsuya's $$$$$
529 Kent St, Sydney. **Map** 1 A2. ☎ *92672900.*
With its calm interior and chef Tetsuya Wakuda's unparalled Franco-Japanese food, this is arguably Sydney's best restaurant. There is a changing set menu of eight courses at lunch and 12 dishes at dinner or specials like confit of Tasmanian ocean trout with unpasteurised ocean trout roe. Book ahead. ● *Sun.* ♿ 🚭 🍷 ☰ ★ 🍴 ✎

Credit Cards	Vegetarian Specialities	Bar Area	Late Opening
AE BC DC MC V		■	●

Watermark $$$$
2A The Esplanade, Balmoral Beach. ☎ *9968 3433.*
With a terrace overlooking the beach, this is a popular spot for brunch or lunch. The entrées have a strong Asian influence and main course specialties include the Asian antipasto, san choy bau, smoked oysters, veal shank parcel and wok-fried baby snapper and seared kingfish carpaccio. ♿ 🚭 🍷 ★ ☂

Credit Cards	Vegetarian Specialities	Bar Area	Late Opening
AE BC DC MC V		■	

Bistros and Brasseries

Armstrong's Manly $$$
Manly Wharf, Manly. ☎ *99763835.*
Harbour views, a relaxed atmosphere and superb seafood make this a quintessential Sydney dining experience. Enjoy fish and chips, they are second to none, burgers or a cup of coffee and a slice of cake. ♿ 🚭 🚸 ☂ ☼

Credit Cards	Vegetarian Specialities	Bar Area	Late Opening
AE BC DC MC V	●		

Bistro Lulu $$$$
257 Oxford St, Paddington. **Map** 5 C3. ☎ *93806888.*
Located in the heart of the Paddington shopping strip this charming French-influenced neo-bistro serves specialities including rabbit rillettes, sirloin steak and roasted mahi-mahi. ♿ 🚭 🍷 ☰ ☂

Credit Cards	Vegetarian Specialities	Bar Area	Late Opening
AE BC DC MC V	●	■	●

Bayswater Brasserie $$$$
32 Bayswater Rd, Potts Point. **Map** 5 B1. ☎ *93572177.*
This veteran of Kings Cross is famous for its freshly shucked oysters and friendly service. The modern Australian menu changes with the availability of the best produce. Superb, freshly made bread, pastries and ice-cream. ● *Sun.* 🚭 🍷 ★ ☂

Credit Cards	Vegetarian Specialities	Bar Area	Late Opening
AE BC MC V	●	■	●

Courtney's Brasserie $$$$
2 Horwood Pl, Parramatta. ☎ *96353288.*
This building first opened its doors in 1830 as a soldiers' mess. Try the Mandalong lamb with a herb crust and cabernet sauce, the fresh john dory fillets in a champagne butter and the home-made ice cream. ● *Sun.* 🚭 🚸 ☰ ☂

Credit Cards	Vegetarian Specialities	Bar Area	Late Opening
AE BC DC MC V			

ECQ $$$
Quay Grand Hotel, 61 Macquarie St, East Circular Quay. ☎ *9256 4044.*
There are fine views over the harbour from this swish bar that offers a lighter dining experience. Fish and chips, Caesar salads and other Mediterranean fare is on offer along with French champagne and oysters. ♿ 🚭 🚸 ☰ ☼

Credit Cards	Vegetarian Specialities	Bar Area	Late Opening
AE BC DC MC V	●	■	●

Fishface $$$
132 Darlinghurst Rd, Darlinghurst. **Map** 5 B1. ☎ *9332 4803.*
The signature fish and chips, as well as the whole steamed or deep-fried snapper is always fresh and cooked to perfection at this bistro. ● *Sun, Mon.* ♿ 🚭 ☂ ✎

Credit Cards	Vegetarian Specialities	Bar Area	Late Opening
BC MC V			●

MACLEAY STREET BISTRO
73a Macleay St, Potts Point. **Map** 2 E5. ☎ 93584891.
Frequently nominated as Sydney's best BYO, the bistro's French-style menu offers good steak tartare and fillet mignon and the bag-roasted tarragon spatchcock. Relaxed and popular so get there early on Fridays and at weekends.

$$$
AE BC DC MC V

THE WHARF RESTAURANT
Pier 4, Hickson Rd, Walsh Bay. **Map** 1 A1. ☎ 92501761.
This restaurant is home to the Sydney Theatre Company and has good views over the harbour. The simple fare includes pasta, risotto and seafood and chef Aaron Ross' scallop sausage and scotch fillet with eggplant and peppers. ● Sun.

$$$
AE DC MC V

RAVESI'S ON BONDI BEACH
Cnr Campbell Parade and Hall St, Bondi Beach. ☎ 93654422.
Sit on the balcony to catch the sea breeze and enjoy fish and chips with house tartare or grilled atlantic salmon with miso pesto and coriander on a noodle salad. The brunch is served on Sundays.

$$$
AE BC DC MC V

SEAFOOD

THE BOATHOUSE ON BLACKWATTLE BAY
End of Ferry Road, Glebe. **Map** 1 B3. ☎ 95189011.
For city views and fresh oysters visit The Boathouse. French-influenced seafood dishes include snapper pie, oysters, snails and yabbie tails and flounder with plum prawns, orange and pine nuts. ● Mon.

$$$$
AE BC DC MC V

DOYLES ON THE BEACH
11 Marine Parade, Watson's Bay. ☎ 93372007.
Five generations on, the Doyles are still serving great fish and chips. Other popular choices include the salt-and-pepper squid and chargrilled, salmon fillets.

$$$
BC DC MC V

JORDON'S INTERNATIONAL SEAFOOD RESTAURANT
197 Harbourside, Darling Harbour. **Map** 3 C2. ☎ 92813711.
This restaurant overlooks Darling Harbour and offers quality fresh seafood. Sushi, sashimi, char-grilled baby octopus, deep-fried snapper and salmon are available, as is a deluxe platter for two, a hot and cold selection of the market's best.

$$$
AE BC DC MC V JCB

MOHR FISH
202 Devonshire Street, Surry Hills. ☎ 93181326.
Regulars are happy to wait in the pub across the road for one of the four tables at this superior seafood café. Fresh ocean trout accompanied with crisp bok choy, fish of the day in beer batter, john dory with mango salsa and barramundi with avocado salsa are on offer.

$$$
AE BC DC MC V JCB

THE PIER
594 New South Head Road, Rose Bay. ☎ 9327 4187.
Overlooking Rose Bay, this award-winning restaurant offers quality seafood. Popular dishes include salmon pastrami and ocean trout served with nuggets of crisped pig's trotter in a sweet tea-coloured sauce. ★

$$$$
AE BC DC MC V

ROCKPOOL
107 George Street, The Rocks. **Map** 1 B3. ☎ 92521888.
The emphasis here is on modern Australian-, French- and Asian- influenced seafood dishes, such as the blue-swimmer crab omelette. Chef Neil Perry's Chinese roast pigeon with eggplant stuffed with prawns is mouth-watering. ● Sun. ★

$$$$
AE BC DC MC V

CHINESE

BBQ KING
18-20 Goulburn St, Sydney. ☎ 92672433.
Great value and one of Sydney's best loved Chinese restaurants. Try the signature Peking duck, fried squid tossed in chilli salt and braised garlic prawns.

$$
AE BC DC MC V

BILLY KWONG
3/355 Crown St, Surry Hills. **Map** 5A3. ☎ 93323300.
Chef Kylie Kwong serves up modern takes on Chinese food. Popular dishes include crisp skinned duck, silken tofu and vegetable sticky rice parcels with caramelised pork. Small and noisy but well worth a visit.

$$$
AE BC MC V

FU-MANCHU
249 Victoria St, Darlinghurst. ☎ 93609424.
Patrons sit on red vinyl stools along communal tables to enjoy the Chinese and Malaysian fare here. On the menu is crispy tofu, chilli salt cuttlefish and aromatic chicken, salmon wontons and zingy fresh sambal seafood.

$$
BC MC V

<table>
<tr><td colspan="5">

Price categories for a three-course evening meal for one including cover charge and service (but not wine):
$ under A$25
$$ A$25–$35
$$$ A$35–$50
$$$$ A$50–$70
$$$$$ Aover $70

CREDIT CARDS
Indicates which credit cards are accepted: *AE* American Express; *BC* Bankcard; *DC* Diners Club; *MC* Master Card/Access; *V* Visa; *JCB* Japanese Credit Bureau.

VEGETARIAN SPECIALITIES
Vegetarian selections are available on the menu.

BAR AREA
The restaurant has a separate bar area.

LATE OPENING
Orders will still be accepted at or after 11pm.

</td></tr>
</table>

	CREDIT CARDS	VEGETARIAN SPECIALITIES	BAR AREA	LATE OPENING
GOLDEN CENTURY $$ 393-399 Sussex St. **Map 4 E4.** 92123901. Customers at this excellent Cantonese restaurant select their dinner from the tank of live scallops, pippis, prawns, lobster, abalone, King Island crab, parrot fish, coral trout, perch and barramundi. Meals are served until 4am. 🚫🚬📋 ★	AE BC DC MC V JCB	●		●
GOLDEN HARBOUR $$ 31-33 Dixon St. **Map 4 D3.** 92125987. This is a popular destination for yum cha, particularly the dumplings filled with snow-pea leaves. In the evenings, the Cantonese menu emphasizes seafood from the tanks with specials such as squid in spicy salt and curried mud crab. 🚬📋🍴	AE BC DC MC V JCB	●		
MARIGOLD $$ 683 George Street. **Map 4 D3.** 92646744. Something of an inovator when it opened in the early 1980s with its daily yum cha and seafood taken live from tanks, Marigold continues to experiment with unusual ingredients such as crocodile meat (served with chilli). 🚬📋	AE BC DC MC V JCB	●		
REGAL $$ 347 Sussex St. **Map 4 E3.** 92618988. Glittering chandeliers, private rooms and waiters pushing dim sum-laden trolleys are reminiscent of the yum cha places of Hong Kong. Cantonese seafood is popular as well as plenty of hearty roast suckling pig, steamed fish chosen and caught from the tank and great peking duck. 🚫🚬👶📋🍴	AE BC DC MC V JCB	●		●
SILVER SPRING $$$ Level 1 Sydney Central, 477 Pitt St (Cnr Hay St), Haymarket. **Map 4 E4.** 92112232. On an average Saturday or Sunday morning yum cha will be served to 1500 people in this multi-roomed restaurant. The scene is more sedate at night, with Cantonese specialities such as barbecued suckling pig. 🚫🚬📋 ★	AE BC DC MC V JCB	●		●
YING'S $$$$ 270 Pacific Highway, Crows Nest. 99669182. Crisp, fresh flavours and perfect preparation make this one of Sydney's best Chinese restaurants. chilli crab, pipis in Chiu Char broth and great yum cha are among favourite menu choices. 🚫🚬🚫	AE BC DC MC V	●		●

OTHER ASIAN

	CREDIT CARDS	VEGETARIAN SPECIALITIES	BAR AREA	LATE OPENING
BODHI IN THE PARK $$ Lower level Cook and Phillip Park, College St, Sydney. **Map 4 F2.** 93602523. This Asian vegetarian restaurant serves good yum cha along with a variety of dishes including shiitake mushrooms and steamed vegetables. 🚫🍽		●		
KAMOGAWA $$$$ 1st floor, 177 Sussex St. **Map 1 A5.** 92995533. This is an elegant establishment with ten private tatami rooms, where patrons sit on the floor. Kaiseki menus range from eight to 10 courses and the lobster and awabi (abalone) sashimi are popular choices from the main dining room's extensive à la carte menu. 🚬📋🍴	AE BC DC MC V JCB	●	■	●
LONGRAIN $$$$ 85 Commonwealth Street, Surry Hills. **Map 4 F5.** 92802888. Voted best restaurant by the Sydney Morning Herald 2002 Good Food Guide, Longrain is set in a converted warehouse. Patrons sit at long tables to enjoy chef Martin Boetz's egg-net, pork hock in chilli vinegar, deep fried barramundi with with sweet chilli sauce. ● Sun. 🚫🚬👶📋 ★	AE BC DC MC V	●	■	●
MALAYA $$$ 39 Lime St, King Street Wharf. **Map 4 D1.** 9279 1170. Set in slick premises overlooking the water, Malaya offers old favourites such as laksas, sambal and rendang. The beef rendang and spiced fish wrapped in banana leaves are recommended. 🚫🚬🍧	AE BC DC MC V			

OH! CALCUTTA! $$$
251 Victoria St, Darlinghurst. **Map** 5 B2. ☎ *93603650.*
This multi-award winning restaurant offers one of Sydney's best Indian dining experiences. The menu spans the subcontinent from Pakistan and Afghanistan to Sri Lanka and India. Afghani mantu (steamed dumplings) filled with ground lamb, and Duck curry with potato and leek are popular choices. ● *Sun.* 🚭 ▤ ↗
AE BC MC V | ● | | ●

RESTAURANT VII $$$$$
7 Bridge St, Sydney. **Map** 1 B3. ☎ *92527777*
The cusine here is a mixture of Japanese and French. Dishes include ocean perch with buckwheat noodles and étuvée (braised) lobster with wakame sauce. ● *Sun.* ♿ 🚭 🍷 🍴
AE BC DC MC V | | ■ |

SUSHI-E $$$
Establishment Hotel, 252 George St, Sydney. **Map** 1 B3. ☎ *92403040.*
Chef Shaun Presland presents a great selection of Japanese dishes and some of the best-tasting sushi in town. Try the flame-seared salmon belly sushi, the beef tataki, fish teriyaki and the sashimi of snapper. ● *Sun and Mon.* ♿ 🚭
AE BC DC MC V | | | ●

SAILOR'S THAI $$$$
106 George St, The Rocks. **Map** 1 B2. ☎ *92512466.*
This restuarant is located in a Sailor's Home and has a canteen noodle bar upstairs serving low-cost meals. Recommended at the restaurant downstairs are the crispy fish and green papaya salad, and braised beef ribs spiked with chilli. ● *Sun.* 🚭 ⛱
AE BC DC MC V | | ■ |

UCHI LOUNGE $$
15 Brisbane St, Surry Hills. **Map** 4 F4. ☎ *92613524.*
This Japanese restaurant is inexpensive and very good. The dishes are inventive and include deep-fried pieces of chicken wrapped in seaweed, chargrilled seared tuna and beef with wasabi mash. ● *Sun.* 🚭 ↗
AE BC MC V | | | ●

UNKAI $$$$$
Level 36, ANA Hotel, 176 Cumberland St. **Map** 4 E3. ☎ *92506123.*
This restaurant offers good views of the harbour and excellent food. The kaiseki, or chef's selection, is a good choice and includes courses of soup, sashimi, a variety of grilled, steamed or fried dishes and desserts. The sushi bar is among the best in Sydney. ♿ 🚭 🚸 ▤ 🍴 ☀
AE BC DC MC V | ● | |

XO $$$
155 Victoria St, Potts Point. ☎ *9331 8881.*
The menu here presents a variety of interesting Asian flavours. Dishes include caramelised pork belly and pipis in XO sauce. ● *Sun and Mon.*
AE BC DC MC V | | ■ | ●

ITALIAN

AQUA LUNA $$$$$
Shop 18, Opera Quays, East Circular Quay. **Map** 1 C2. ☎ *92510311.*
Chef Darren Simpson from the UK prepares good Italian fare to a mostly theatre crowd. Dishes include risotto of organic rabbit with borlotti beans and rosemary. ♿
AE BC DC MC V | ● | ■ | ●

BUON RICORDO $$$$$
108 Boundary St. Paddington. ☎ *93606729.*
Voted best Italian restaurant by the Sydney Morning Herald 2003 Good Food Guide. Dishes include fettuccine with fried egg and a hint of truffles, risotto with porcini mushrooms and nettles, and baked snapper with artichoke purée. ● *Sun.* 🍷 🚭
AE BC DC MC V | | | ●

BEL MONDO $$$$$
Level 3, 18-24 Argyle St. The Rocks. **Map** 1 B2. ☎ *92413700.*
With a fine menu and views across Circular Quay to the Opera House, Bel Mondo provides one of the best dining experiences in the city. Chef Stefano Manfredi serves northern Italian cuisine prepared using quality local produce. Wines by the glass and antipasti are served at the Antibar. ♿ 🚭 🍷 ▤ ★ ⛱ ☀
AE BC DC MC V | ● | ■ | ●

BEPPI'S $$$$$
Cnr Stanley and Yurong Streets, East Sydney. **Map** 4 F3. ☎ *93604558.*
Owner Beppi Polese is known as the man who will go to extraordinary lengths to give his patrons the best. The food is outstanding as is the vintage wine list offering Australian reds dating back to 1952. ● *Sun.* ♿ 🚭 🍷 ▤
AE BC MC V JCB | ● | | ●

BISTRO CBD $$$$
52 York Street, Sydney. **Map** 1 A4. ☎ *8297 7010.*
Chef John Evans' European cuisine includes duck confit with green beans and onion marmalade, and roasted salmon with fresh horseradish and baby beets. ● *Sat and Sun.* ♿ 🚭 🍷
AE BC MC V | ● | ■ |

Price categories for a three-course evening meal for one inlcuding cover charge and service (but not wine):
$ under A$25
$$ A$25–$35
$$$ A$35–$50
$$$$ A$50–$70
$$$$$ A over $70

CREDIT CARDS
Indicates which credit cards are accepted: *AE* American Express; *BC* Bankcard; *DC* Diners Club; *MC* Master Card/Access; *V* Visa; *JCB* Japanese Credit Bureau.

VEGETARIAN SPECIALITIES
Vegetarian selections are available on the menu.

BAR AREA
The restaurant has a separate bar area.

LATE OPENING
Orders will still be accepted at or after 11pm.

Restaurant	Price	Credit Cards	Vegetarian Specialities	Bar Area	Late Opening
CERTO RISTORANTE Basement, 151 Macquarie Street. **Map 1 C4.** 92411344 Japanese chef, Ritsuko Yumikake trained in Florence and serves classic Italian dishes including lobster tail with mixed seafood and porcini mushroom risotto served in a hollowed out piece of parmesan cheese. ● *Sun.*	$$$$	AE BC DC MC V			
ELIO 159 Norton St, Leichhardt. 95609129. In this stylish restaurant, Chef Robyn Touchard offers a wonderful tumble of zucchini flowers with moist blue-eye cod on lemon risotto. Pasta is made daily on the premises. Reservations are essential.	$$$$	AE BC DC MC V	●	■	
FRATTINI 122 Marion St Leichhardt. 92692997. This trattoria exudes the casual ambience of a traditional Italian eatery. The spinach and ricotta cheese dumplings in gorgonzola sauce are popular, as are neonata (fritters of New Zealand whitebait) and asparagus with Parmesan. Try the mascarpone-filled crepes with liquer-poached strawberries. Book in advance.	$$$	AE BC DC MC V	●		
GRAPPA Shop 1, 267-277 Norton St, Leichhardt. 95606090. W *www.grappa.com.au* Wood-fired pizza with contemporary toppings and specialties like the snapper in rock salt crust are on offer at this atmospheric restaurant.	$$$$	AE BC DC MC V	●	■	
LUCIO'S 47 Windsor St, Paddington. **Map 6 D3.** 93805996. Several varieties of ravioli and grilled Tasmanian salmon are constants on the up-market northern Italian menu here. Crowd pleasers include veal medallions wrapped in pancetta, taglioni with blue swimmer crab, and marinated octopus, baby asparagus and zucchini flowers. ● *Sun.*	$$$$$	AE BC DC MC V			●
MEZZALUNA 123 Victoria Street, Potts Point. **Map 2 E5.** 93571988. This restaurant offers the finest of northern-Italian cuisine as well as excellent wines and wonderful views of the city skyline from the covered terrace. ★	$$$$	AE BC DC MC V	●	■	●
NO NAMES 1st floor, 81 Stanley St, Darlinghurst. **Map 5 A1.** 93604711. This spaghetti canteen offers some of the best value food in town. Choices include spaghetti bolognese or napoletana, grills and gelati. Free bread and cordial.	$		●		
RISTORANTE RIVA 379 Liverpool St, Darlinghurst. **Map 5 B2.** 93805318. Among the offerings in this cosy northern Italian style restaurant are fresh pasta, twice-cooked roast duck, risottos and a selection of game. ● *Sun.*	$$$$	AE BC MC V	●		
SORRISO Level 1, 70 Norton Street, Leichhardt. 95729915. This is one of the more sophisticated restaurants in Sydney's Italian district. Chef Lucas Kitchen's rag pasta with chicken liver and caramelised onions is recommended, as is the antipasti and desserts.	$$$$	AE BC MC V	●		●

FRENCH

Restaurant	Price	Credit Cards	Vegetarian Specialities	Bar Area	Late Opening
BISTRO MONCUR Woollahra Hotel, 116 Queen Street Woollahra. **Map 6 E4.** 93632519. Take a seat at the Woollahra Bar and wait for your turn to enjoy the tripes Lyonnaise, classic Provençal fish soup and entrecote café de Paris.	$$$$	AE BC DC MC V	●	■	
CLAUDE'S 10 Oxford St. Woollahra. **Map 6 D4.** 93312325. This elegant restaurant offers a three- or eight-course tasting menu that changes regularly, but examples include roast aylesbury duck, Lakes Folly cabernet sauce with ox fillet, and rosewater trifle with truffles. ● *Sun and Mon.* ★	$$$$$	AE BC DC MC V			●

LA GRILLADE $$$$$ AE
118 Alexander St, Crows Nest. ⓒ 94393707.   BC
This restaurant is set in an old school with wood fittings. Whether your   DC
choice is an eye fillet steak tartare with truffle mayonnaise, huge hearty steaks or   MC
duck, chef Crosby Max promises excellence. ● *Sun.* 🚗 ⓟ ⓗ   V

GUILLAUME AT BENNELONG $$$$$ AE   ● ■ ●
Sydney Opera House, Bennelong Point. **Map 1 C2.** ⓒ 92411999.   BC
Chef Guillaume Brahimi's exquisite menu includes chargrilled, grain-fed beef   DC
tender loin with merlot sauce, basil-infused rare tuna with mustard seed vinaigrette,   MC
and vanilla panacotta with poached strawberries. 🚗 ⓟ ☰ ★ ⓗ   V
                                                                  JCB

MARQUE $$$$$ AE   ■
355 Crown St, Surry Hills. **Map 5 A3.** ⓒ 93322225.   BC
Chef Mark Best combines classic French cooking with Australian produce for a   DC
finely crafted contemporary result. Try the beetroot tart with fresh horseradish   MC
sauce or the rounds of venison in a velvety white-pepper sauce. ● *Sun.* ⓚ 🚗 ⓟ   V

TABOU $$$$ AE   ● ■ ●
527 Crown St, Surry Hills. ⓒ 93195682.   BC
Modelled on a French bistro, Tabou is full of charm. Try the steak frites,   DC
barramundi with chestnuts and mushrooms or the cassoulet of sweetbreads and   MC
snails There is also a good selection of affordable French wines. ⓟ   V

MEDITERRANEAN AND MIDDLE EASTERN

ALHAMBRA $$$ AE   ●
Shop 1, 54 West Esplanade, Manly. ⓒ 99762975.   BC
Both snacks and full meals are offered at this pleasant restaurant. Tapas choices in-   DC
clude octopus and sardines and Paella typically features as a main dish. Recommended   MC
dishes include the lamb tagine and the bastilla – spiced chicken in pastry. ⓚ ⓗ 🔾   V

BUZO $$$ AE   ● ■ ●
152 Jersey Rd, Woollahra. **Map 6 E4.** ⓒ 93281600.   BC
Chef Daryll Taylor's Mediterranean/Italian menu includes Sicillian roast leg of lamb   DC
and a lasagna made with porcini mushrooms, parma ham, truffle oil and moist   MC
cipollata onions. Desserts include a terrific tiramisu. ● *Sun and Mon.* ⓚ 🚗 ⓟ   V

CASA ASTURIANA $$$ AE   ● ■
77 Liverpool St. **Map 4 E3.** ⓒ 92641010.   BC
Well-known northern favourites such as paella and stuffed sardine fillets, as well as   DC
tapas, are served in this former warehouse which boasts a traditional Castilian   MC
ground floor. Wash it all down with Sangria, Asturian cider or Tio Pepe. ⓚ 🚗 ☰   V

CRITERION $$$$ AE   ●
Shop 802, Lobby Level, MLC Centre, Martin Place. **Map 1 B4.** ⓒ 92331234.   BC
This restaurant offers Mediterranean-influenced cuisine as well as Modern Australian   DC
dishes. The house special is the meze platter of yoghurt balls, marinated vegetables   MC
and pastries. The chargrilled seafood mezza is recommended. ● *Sun.* ⓚ 🚗 ⓟ ☰ ⓗ   V

CADMUS $$$$$ AE   ● ■ ●
Level 10, Opera Quays, 3 Macquarie St, East Circular Quay. **Map 1 C2.** ⓒ 92526800.   BC
There are views of the Opera House and Botanic Gardens from this restaurant   DC
which offers Lebanese food with a French influence. Try the muscovy duck with   MC
caramalised pear or the chicken wrapped in vine leaves. ⓚ ⓟ ☰ 🍴 ⓗ   V

ELENI'S $$$$$ AE   ●   ●
185a Bourke St, East Sydney. **Map 5 A1.** ⓒ 93315306.   BC
Chef Peter Conistis offers modern variations on traditional Greek dishes.   DC
These include rabbit and black olive filo pie, moussaka of eggplant, and seared sea   MC
scallops with taramasalata. ● *Sun.* ⓚ 🚗 🔾   V

FEZ CAFÉ $$$ AE   ●
247 Victoria St, Darlinghurst. **Map 5 B1.** ⓒ 93609581.   BC
Sip coffee on the cushioned window seats and breakfast on couscous and compote   MC
of spiced, dried fruit with nuts and yoghurt. The Turkish cuisine includes a meze   V
platter of dips and pickled vegetables. Moroccan dishes include tagines with
pawns, mussels and blue swimmer crab broth. 🚗 ⓗ

MCA CAFÉ $$$ AE   ●
Museum of Contemporary Art, 140 George St, The Rocks. **Map 1 B2.** ⓒ 92414253.   BC
Wild mushroom risotto, bream fillet with sun-dried tomato paste as well as the ever   DC
popular fish and chips are among the menu selections on offer here. Outdoor seats   MC
have great views over the busy harbour. ⓚ 🚗 ⓗ ⓗ   V

Light Meals and Snacks

Sydney's casual eating scene is extremely competitive and wherever you choose to take a break you will probably enjoy good-value food that approaches the high standards set by more formal establishments. The eateries listed here all have a staunch local following and are particularly recommended for those hungry travellers whose time and budget are limited.

Cafés

Food columnists frequently note the mercurial nature of Sydney's dining scene, by chronicling the multitude of establishments that open and close each year. With cafés, this situation is magnified and, as a result of this competition, the standards are quite high.

Most places serve breakfast in either the eggs-and-bacon or croissant-and-pastry guises, and then move into the day with a menu offering burgers, cheese melts, *focaccia* and salads, pasta and risotto. The night owls can enjoy cakes and desserts, and choose from espresso coffee, *caffe latte* and *cappuccino*, or from a range of teas, juices, milk shakes, fruit *frappés* and smoothies.

Coffee and Tea

Darlinghurst is the caffeine kingdom of Sydney and **Bar Coluzzi**, with its boxing pictures on the walls, is its capital. Media heavies, lawyers and taxi drivers throng here both for the company and the coffee. Across the road at the **Tropicana Coffee Lounge**, the clientele is more likely to be involved in the theatre or the film industry. **Café Hernandez**, open 24 hours, is famous for its Spanish short black, tortillas, cakes and supplies of coffee beans.

Enjoy tea and scones at the **Gumnut Café**, housed in an old, crooked cottage. Sit by the fire if it's cold, or in the pretty courtyard in the summer. **Café Dendu**, in the city centre, is for those who know their coffee, and so too is the nearby **Ccino's** café in the MLC Centre and the **Paradiso Brolga Terrace** in Darling Park, close to Chinatown. For night owls, **City Extra** is open 24 hours.

For something more than a cup of coffee try **Jones The Grocer** in Paddington. Sip and shop for a range of foods, from Iranian candy floss to handmade pasta. Drinks are served at a communal table supplied with daily newspapers.

Snacks and Light Meals

Should you want to start the day in a sun-drenched spot, **Bill's** is a favourite place. You can breakfast on ricotta hot cakes with honeycomb butter or lunch on a delicious steak sandwich. There is a similar mood at **La Passion du Fruit** in Surry Hills, which has a big following for its fruit *frappés*, fresh salads and the hot olive bread pockets filled with any selection from the *antipasto* table. Just a few blocks away, on Crown Street, **Prasit Thai** offers imaginative and aromatic Thai fare from a tiny shopfront that is easy to miss.

Set amid the bustle of Circular Quay, the trattoria-style **Rossini Restaurant** serves reasonably priced Italian standards such as crancini, scallopine and pasta. The service is brisk and cheery, and the venue is popular with city workers and visitors alike.

Shoppers in Paddington usually fit in a lunch at one of the cafés – but on Saturdays there may be queues as this is when the Paddington Bazaar is held *(see p126)*. The **Hot Gossip Deli** has a handy delicatessen adjacent, where you can buy healthy fare to take away. **Sloane's Café** is a real home away from home, with lots to keep vegetarians happy and a small courtyard at the back. For a quick snack before seeing a movie at the Academy Twin, try the nearby **Fat Duck**. In Darlinghurst,

you will find **Betty's Soup Kitchen** which serves a wide range of soups and delicious desserts. At **Una's Coffee Lounge**, the regular clientele are often joined by homesick Germans longing for *schnitzel*, soup and *spaëtzle* (noodles). The **Hard Rock Café** remains true to its international formula, but weekend queues suggest that the demand for burgers and T shirts has not lessened. **Le Petit Crème** is an oasis of *brioche* and *croque madame* .

In Potts Point, check out the jazz photos while enjoying Modern Australian fare at **Roy's Famous**. Some Sunday nights, there's live jazz.

Over in Bondi, **Paris Cake Shop** is the quintessential Parisian patisserie.

Galleries and Gardens

These days, most of the city's galleries, museums and larger parks have good cafés or restaurants – the following are a cut above the average.

Take in the passing parade of joggers, horse riders and cyclists as you tuck into pasta, risotto, salad or a roasted tuna steak with African spices at the **Centennial Park Café and Restaurant**. Wine is available by the bottle or the glass. At the **Concourse Café** in the forecourt of the Opera House, stylish Modern Australian fare is on the menu. Directly across Circular Quay, the **MCA Café** is run by the same team as at the up-market Rockpool restaurant *(see p189)*. The menu here is also strongly Mediterranean.

The food is often influenced by visiting exhibitions at the **Art Gallery Brasserie** and this café is worth a visit even if you do not have time to see the collections. The **Hyde Park Barracks Café** has seating in the courtyard of this convict-built Georgian barracks and the cuisine takes full advantage of the freshest ingredients in Modern Australian style. Alternatively, you can enjoy sandwiches, soups and cream teas in the palm-studded surrounds of **Vaucluse House Tea Rooms**, in the garden of the former home of statesman and explorer, WC Wentworth.

TAKEAWAY FOOD

THE FILLED baguettes practically march out the door of the city's **Deli on Market**. There is also good coffee and a selection of their own cakes, chutneys, cheeses and vinaigrettes to take away. For a far more down-to-earth dining experience, you can drop in to **Harry's Café de Wheels** in Woolloomooloo, to sample an Aussie meat pie and sauce

from the stand-up bar at this caravan diner. This Sydney institution has been satisfying the late-night food cravings of both locals and visitors for decades, and is particularly popular with the sailors from the adjacent naval dockyard. An entirely different sort of treat can be found at the **Maya Indian Sweets Centre** in Surry Hills, where a particularly luscious array of desserts and cakes is available – there are a few tables for tea if you are desperate to eat.

At the opposite end of the spectrum are the food courts in the basements or ground floors of major city buildings.

These serve the city's office workers at lunchtime with a grand assortment of foods to take away or eat at tables nearby. Australia Square, the MLC Centre, Chifley Tower, the Mid City Centre and the American Express Tower all have food courts with shops offering everything from Asian noodles and Mexican nachos to pizza and sushi.

Most of Sydney's markets (*see p203*) have food stalls where a large mixed plate of Indian, Mexican or Asian food will cost only a few dollars. Paddington Bazaar has good, cheap vegetarian food in the hall at the back of the market.

DIRECTORY

THE ROCKS AND CIRCULAR QUAY

City Extra
Circular Quay. Map 1 B3.
[9241 1422.

Concourse Café
Sydney Opera House.
Map 1 C2. [9250 7300 or 9250 7111.

Gumnut Café
28 Harrington St,
Map 1 B3.
[9247 9591.

MCA Café
Museum of Contemporary Art, Circular Quay West.
Map 1 B2.
[9241 4253.

Rossini Restaurant
Opposite Wharf 5,
Circular Quay. Map 1 B3.
[9247 8026.

CITY CENTRE

Ccino's
Level 6 MLC Centre,
Martin Place. Map 1 B4.
[9221 4032.

Deli on Market
30–32 Market St.
Map 4 E2. [9262 6906.

Café Dendu
106 Bathurst St. Map 4 E3.
[9267 2480.

DARLING HARBOUR

Paradiso Brolga Terrace
Darling Park, 201 Sussex St.
Map 4 D2. [9283 1906.

BOTANIC GARDENS AND THE DOMAIN

Art Gallery Brasserie
Art Gallery Rd, The Domain.
Map 2 D4. [9225 1819.

Hyde Park Barracks Café
Queens Square,
Macquarie St. Map 1 C5.
[9223 1155.

KINGS CROSS AND DARLINGHURST

Bar Coluzzi
322 Victoria St,
Darlinghurst. Map 5 B1.
[9380 5420.

Betty's Soup Kitchen
84 Oxford St,
Darlinghurst. Map 5 A2.
[9360 9698.

Bill's
433 Liverpool St,
Darlinghurst. Map 5 B2.
[9360 9631.

Café Hernandez
60 Kings Cross Rd,
Potts Point. Map 5 C1.
[9331 2343.

Hard Rock Café
121–129 Crown St,
Darlinghurst. Map 5 A1.
[9331 1116.

Harry's Café de Wheels
Cowper Wharf Rd,
Woolloomooloo.
Map 2 E5. [9357 3074.

Roy's Famous
176 Victoria St, Potts Point.
Map 5 B1. [9357 3579.

Tropicana Coffee Lounge
227b Victoria St,
Darlinghurst. Map 5 B1.
[9360 9809.

Una's Coffee Lounge
340 Victoria St,
Darlinghurst. Map 5 B1.
[9360 6885.

PADDINGTON

Centennial Park Café and Restaurant
Cnr Grand & Parkes Drives, Centennial Park.
Map 6 E5.
[9380 6922.

Fat Duck
1 Oxford St, Paddington.
Map 5 B3.
[9380 9838.

Hot Gossip Deli
436 Oxford St, Paddington.
Map 6 D4.
[9380 5305.

Jones The Grocer
Moncur St, off Queen St.
Map 5 E4. [9362 1222.

Sloane's Café
312 Oxford St, Paddington.
Map 5 C3.
[9331 6717.

FURTHER AFIELD

Fuel Bistro
488 Crown St, Surry Hills.
Map 6 A3. [9383 9388.

La Passion du Fruit
633 Bourke St, Surry Hills.
Map 5 B3.
[9690 1894.

Maya Indian Sweets Centre
470 Cleveland St,
Surry Hills. Map 5 A5.
[9699 8663.

Paris Cake Shop
91 Bondi Rd, Bondi.
[9387 2496.

Prasit Thai
415 Crown St, Surry Hills.
Map 5 A3. [9319 0748.

Vaucluse House Tea Rooms
Vaucluse House,
Wentworth Rd, Vaucluse.
[9388 8188.

Sydney Pubs and Bars

CONFUSINGLY for the overseas visitor, Australian pubs and bars are more commonly known as hotels. This is because licensing laws originally required any place serving alcohol to provide accommodation, too. In the cities, at least, hotels have changed radically and what were once the domains of beer-swilling males have now evolved into far more civilized spots.

Pub menus have also undergone a metamorphosis. In place of the former meat pie and sauce, most pubs now offer hearty snacks, such as *nachos*, *focaccia*, pasta, grills and salads, at remarkably low prices. All pubs serve basic mixed spirit-based drinks and often wine by the glass, but cocktails tend to be the preserve of the more up-market venues. Pubs are also often good venues for entertainment ranging from rock to jazz *(see pp214–15)*.

RULES AND CONVENTIONS

IN THEORY, pubs are open from 10am to 10pm every day. This often extends to midnight closing on Fridays and Saturdays, and even to 3am when live entertainment is provided. Some pubs, in areas where there are large numbers of shift workers, will open at 6am and are known as "early openers". Others, particularly in tourist haunts, have a 24-hour licence. You must be at least 18 years of age (and able to provide the proof) to buy or consume any alcohol. However, children under 18 may accompany adults into beer gardens and into hotel restaurants. Dress requirements are purely at the discretion of the publican and the management always has the right to refuse service.

One aspect of traditional pub culture is the custom of "shouting", or buying drinks for your companions. It can be very expensive to become involved in buying "rounds" – when someone buys you a drink, it is considered bad form if you do not return the favour. If you are on a budget and do not want to offend, simply explain that you are only staying for one drink or make some other excuse.

Apart from being very good places to soak up some local atmosphere, pubs are also ideal spots for watching any televised major international or local sporting matches in the company of like-minded people. Many hotels broadcast matches on a big screen and locals gather to watch.

Pubs are also excellent spots for live entertainment – many Australian rock music names first performed in hotels. The daily newspapers are a good source of information on dates, times and venues *(see p221)*.

JOIN THE LOCALS

PUBS PROVIDE the chance to observe Sydney at play. At Circular Quay, the **Customs House Bar** has been serving drinks since 1826. On Friday nights, up to 2,000 people spill out into Macquarie Place to talk shop and gossip under the trees. **Miro Tapas Bar** is an equally trendy destination, with floor-to-ceiling murals and Spanish-style snacks to go with the *sangría* and melon and peach "shooters". The **Dendy Bar & Bistro** is in the Dendy cinema complex *(see p210)*; here office workers mix with film-goers and coffee is served alongside cocktails.

A little further afield in Surry Hills, the **Trinity Bar** offers honest bar food. There are pool tables at the busy **Palace Hotel** in Darlinghurst, but a big drawcard is the new Thai restaurant run by the team from Lime & Lemongrass, formerly in Kings Cross. Also in Darlinghurst, the **Green Park Hotel**, offers tempting and tasty bar food from Fez Cafe across the road.

There are plenty of "locals" in Paddington, most of which serve above-average bar food to their discerning clientele. The **London Tavern**, which opened in 1875, has 5 English beers on tap. The sign outside welcomes all except for dogs, giraffes, elephants and children under 18 for drinks. Five Ways *(see p126)* is dominated by the **Royal Hotel**, an 1880s three-storey corner establishment, where cocktails are served in the upstairs Elephant Bar and the restaurant below extends out onto an iron-lace encrusted veranda. Both the bistro at the **Paddington Inn** and the dining room of the **Bellevue Hotel** offer good Modern Australian cuisine.

UP-MARKET BARS

IF YOU ARE looking for a more elegant atmosphere, head for **Horizon's Bar** at the top of the ANA Hotel *(see p172)*. You can admire views extending from Botany Bay to Manly while you sip a Toblerone (liquid chocolate with a kick). Or drop into **The Cortile** in the glamorous lobby of the Hotel Inter-Continental and sip a cocktail in the comfort of the cane armchairs. There is imported Champagne by the glass at **Wine Banc**, as well as cocktails, an excellent selection of wines and fine food in the stylish bar in the city's central business district.

The **Regent Club Bar** in the Regent Sydney *(see p172)* is another hotel lounge that is ideal either for pre- or post-theatre drinks and nibbles.

For a livelier experience, **Kinsela's Middle Bar** has one of the best-stocked bars in town, as well as modern decor, DJs and a balcony with views over Sydney's most colourful areas.

The **Civic Hotel** has been beautifully renovated, keeping its art deco heritage intact. In addition to a small, elegant cocktail bar, there is a large main bar, which has DJs on Friday and Saturday nights, playing house, lounge and even retro groove until 4am. On these popular club nights, velvet curtains are drawn around the walls of the pub, giving the room an intimate, club-like atmosphere.

Hugo's Lounge, known for its luscious fruit daiquiris, has an outdoor balcony perfect for warm evenings. Inside, its restaurant serves tempting dinners in a well-designed, contemporary setting.

Popular with a younger crowd, **Establishment** is a pioneer in the CBD, bringing glamorous nightlife to an otherwise quiet part of town. The bar, with a huge glass atrium, is always lively and often packed.

HISTORIC PUBS

A WALK ALONG George Street will reveal some of The Rocks' old pubs, but two of the more significant ones are a few streets back. The **Hero of Waterloo**, built in 1843, has a maze of stone cellars underneath which testify to its nefarious past (*see p69*). The **Lord Nelson Brewery Hotel**

was first licensed in 1841 and is now a "pub brewery" with a range of ales brewed on the premises. It also has Nelson's Bistro and, upstairs, 10 guest rooms (*see p172*).

The **Tank Bar** at GPO is located underground in the former GPO building. The design takes advantage of its historical setting, retaining the original sandstone walls, but nothing else about this bar is old-fashioned. Here, cocktails are consumed by some of Sydney's high-flyers, as they also enjoy quality bar nibbles.

ENTERTAINMENT

T HE OLD **Manly Boatshed** has been a top venue for both local and international comedians for years. Every Monday night, comedy is on the menu, as well as a robust pub meal. You can just relax with a drink from the bar or

there's usually dance music after the show. At the **Nag's Head** in Glebe, soloists and duettists perform everything from Neil Diamond to Pearl Jam, Thursday to Saturday nights. There's an a la carte menu and bar food.

In Surry Hills, there are live bands every Saturday night at the **Hopetoun Hotel** and all manner of music is played there. There's jazz, funk and blues, as well as the rock for which it is famous. The **Orient Hotel** in the heart of The Rocks is very popular with both locals and tourists, especially on New Years Eve. There is live music from Wednesday to Sunday, as well as a nightclub on Friday and Saturday nights. There is also a restaurant, two dining rooms, snacks available in the beer garden and a couple of pool tables to keep you busy.

DIRECTORY

THE ROCKS AND CIRCULAR QUAY

Customs House Bar
Sydney Renaissance Hotel, Macquarie Place.
Map 1 B3.
9259 7316.

Establishment
252 George St. **Map** 1 B3.
9240 3000.

Hero of Waterloo
81 Lower Fort St, Millers Point. **Map** 1 A2.
9252 4553.

Horizon's Bar
Level 36, ANA Hotel, 176 Cumberland St, The Rocks. **Map** 1 A3.
9250 6000.

Lord Nelson Brewery Hotel
19 Kent St, Millers Point.
Map 1 A2.
9251 4044.

Orient Hotel
89 George St, The Rocks.
Map 1 B2.
9251 1255.

CITY CENTRE

Civic Hotel
388 Pitt St. **Map** 1 B5.
8267 3183.

Dendy Bar & Bistro
19 Martin Place. **Map** 1 B4.
9221 1243.

Miro Tapas Bar
76 Liverpool St. **Map** 4 E3.
9267 3126.

Stock Exchange Hotel
7 Bridge St. **Map** 1 B3.
9252 6888.

Tank Bar at GPO
1 Martin Place. **Map** 1 B4.
9229 7766.

Wine Banc
53 Martin Place. **Map** 1 B4.
9233 5399.

BOTANIC GARDENS AND THE DOMAIN

The Cortile
Hotel Inter-Continental, 117 Macquarie St.
Map 1 C3. 9253 9000.

KINGS CROSS AND DARLINGHURST

Green Park Hotel
360 Victoria St, Darlinghurst. **Map** 5 B2.
9380 5311.

Hugo's Lounge
33 Bayswater Rd, Potts Point **Map** 5 B1.
9357 4411.

Kinsela's Middle Bar
383 Bourke St, Darlinghurst. **Map** 5 A5.
9331 3100.

Palace Hotel
122 Flinders St, Darlinghurst. **Map** 5 A3.
9361 5170.

PADDINGTON

Bellevue Hotel
159 Hargrave St, Paddington. **Map** 6 E3.
9363 2293.

London Tavern
85 Underwood St, Paddington. **Map** 6 D3.
9331 3200.

Paddington Inn
338 Oxford St, Paddington. **Map** 6 D4.
9380 5277.

Royal Hotel
237 Glenmore Rd, Paddington. **Map** 5 C3.
9331 2604.

FURTHER AFIELD

Bondi Hotel
Corner Campbell Parade and Curlewis St.
9130 3271.

Hopetoun Hotel
416 Bourke St, Surry Hills. **Map** 5 A3.
9361 5257.

Nag's Head Hotel
162 St Johns Rd, Glebe.
Map 3 A5.
9660 1591.

The Old Manly Boatshed
40 The Corso, Manly.
8902 0989.

Trinity Bar
505 Crown St, Surry Hills.
9319 6802.

SHOPS AND MARKETS

FOR MOST TRAVELLERS, shopping can be as much of a voyage of discovery as sightseeing. The variety of shops in Sydney is wide and the quality of merchandise is usually good. The city has many elegant arcades and shopping galleries, with plenty of nooks and crannies to explore. The range of goods on offer is

Souvenir boomerangs

vast – most international labels are imported and local talent in many fields, notably jewellery, fashion and indigenous arts and crafts, is promoted. Nor does the most interesting shopping stop at the city centre; there are several "satellite" alternatives. The best shopping areas are highlighted on pages 200–201.

A typical junk-shop-cum-café in Balmain *(see p131)*

SHOPPING HOURS

MOST SHOPS ARE open from 9am to 5:30pm during the week, and from 9am to 4pm on Saturdays. On Thursdays, many shops stay open until 9pm. Some are open late every evening and most of these also open on Sundays.

HOW TO PAY

MAJOR CREDIT cards are accepted at many shops, but there may be a minimum purchase requirement. You will need identification, such as a valid passport or driver's

licence, when using traveller's cheques. Shops will generally exchange goods or refund your money if you are not satisfied, provided you have some proof of purchase. There is also a Goods and Services Tax (GST) which usually adds about 10 per cent to most items.

SALES

MANY SHOPS conduct sales all year round. The big department stores of **David Jones** and **Grace Bros** have two clearance sales a year. The post-Christmas sales start on 26 December and last into January. Keen bargain-hunters queue from dawn for substantial savings. The other major sale time is during July, after the end of the financial year.

TAX-FREE SALES

DUTY-FREE SHOPS are found in the centre of the city as well as at Kingsford Smith Airport. Some shops also have branches in the larger suburbs.

Overseas visitors can save around 30 per cent on goods such as perfume, jewellery, cameras and alcohol at shops

that offer duty-free shopping. You must show your passport and onward ticket when the goods are collected.

Most duty-free merchandise must be kept in its sealed bag until you leave. Cameras and video cameras are exceptions. Some duty-free shops in the city will deliver your goods to the airport where you can pick them up on your departure.

Chifley Tower, with the Chifley Plaza shopping arcade at its base

ARCADES AND MALLS

ARCADES AND shopping malls in Sydney range from the ornately Victorian to modern marble and glass. The **Queen Victoria Building** *(see p82)* is Sydney's most palatial shopping space. Four levels contain more than 200 shops. The top level, Victoria Walk, is devoted to merchandise such as silver, antiques, designer knitwear and high-quality souvenirs.

The elegant **Strand Arcade** *(see p84)* was originally built in 1892. Jewellery, lingerie, high fashion, fine antiques and gourmet coffee shops and tea rooms are its stock in trade.

Pitt Street Mall is home to several other shopping centres. **Skygarden** is the place for

Interior design shop on William Street in Paddington *(see p124)*

homeware, classy fashion from Australian and international designers, and art galleries of distinction. A spacious food gallery offers everything from antipasto to Thai takeaway. The bustling **Mid City Centre** is home to the huge HMV music store and shops selling clothes, accessories and gifts. **Centrepoint** has more than 140 speciality shops that stock everything from avant-garde jewellery to leather goods.

Nearby in Pitt Street, the marble and glass of **Piccadilly** houses more than 40 stores and flashy boutiques, including very good shoe shops, quality jewellers and cafés.

Both the **MLC Centre** and the nearby **Chifley Plaza** cater to the prestige shopper. Gucci, Cartier, Tiffany & Co, MaxMara, Kenzo and Moschino are just some of the shops found here.

The **Harbourside Shopping Centre** has dozens of shops, plus several waterfront restaurants. The atmosphere is festive and the merchandise includes fine arts, jewellery, duty-free shopping, beachwear and Australiana.

Greengrocer's display of fresh fruit and vegetables

Gowings menswear store logo

floor. The building has seven floors of quality merchandise, including women's clothing, lingerie, baby goods, toys and stationery. The Market Street store nearby specializes in menswear, kitchenware, furniture, china, crystal and silver. The food hall on the lower ground floor is famous for its range of gourmet food and fine wines. **Grace Bros** is a good pit stop for the visitor in need of cosmetics, hats, sunscreen or casual clothing, while the **Argyle Department Store** in The Rocks *(see p68)* is chock-full of fashion boutiques.

Gowings, which has operated continuously since 1868, is a Sydney institution. This unpretentious family-owned and family-run menswear store also sells such things as sunglasses, watches, Swiss army knives, fishing gear, miners' lamps and genuine Australiana such as kangaroo leather wallets and plaited leather belts.

BEST OF THE DEPARTMENT STORES

THE SPRING and Mother's Day floral displays in the **David Jones** Elizabeth Street store are legendary, as is the luxurious perfumery and cosmetics hall on the ground

SHOPPING FURTHER AFIELD

GOOD SHOPPING is also found outside central Sydney. Other areas well worth visiting include Double Bay, with its sophisticated, village-style shopping, to the east, and the Left Bank-style student haunts of Newtown to the south and Glebe to the west. Bargains can be found at the factory outlets at Surry Hills and Redfern to the south, Market City in Chinatown and Birkenhead Point to the west.

Part of the spring floral display, David Jones department store

ARCADES, SHOPPING MALLS AND DEPARTMENT STORES

Argyle Department Store
12–24 Argyle St, The Rocks. **Map** 1 B2. 9251 4800.

Centrepoint
Cnr Pitt, Market & Castlereagh Sts. **Map** 1 B5.

Chifley Plaza
2 Chifley Square. **Map** 1 B4. 9221 4500.

David Jones
Cnr Elizabeth & Castlereagh Sts. **Map** 1 B5. 9266 5544.
Also: Cnr Market & Castlereagh Sts. **Map** 1 B5. 9266 5544.

Harbourside Shopping Centre
Darling Harbour. **Map** 3 C2. 9281 3999.

Gowings
45 Market St. **Map** 1 B5. 9264 6321.

Grace Bros
436 George St. **Map** 1 B5. 9238 9111.

Mid City Centre
197 Pitt Street Mall. **Map** 1 B5. 9221 2422.

MLC Centre
19–29 Martin Place. **Map** 1 B5. 9224 8333.

Piccadilly
210 Pitt St. **Map** 1 B5. 9267 3666.

Queen Victoria Building
455 George St. **Map** 1 B5. 9265 6855.

Skygarden
77 Castlereagh St. **Map** 1 B5. 9231 1811.

Strand Arcade
412–414 George St. **Map** 1 B5. 9232 4199.

Sydney's Best: Shopping Streets and Markets

SYDNEY'S BEST SHOPPING AREAS range from galleries, arcades and department stores selling expensive gifts and jewellery *(see pp198–9)*, to boutiques of extroverted or elegant cutting-edge fashion and its accessories. The range of styles is impressive – both international couture brands and acclaimed local designer labels *(pp204–5)*. The city's hip fringe areas are alive with street fashion and its accoutrements.

Colourful markets are a delight for collectors and bargain-hunters alike *(p203)*, while those who seek out the quirky and one-off items are well catered for, as are those looking to take home quality craft and indigenous art as mementos of their visit. Specialist browsers will find a tempting selection of book and music shops *(pp206–7)* from which to choose.

The Rocks Market
At weekends, the stalls offer affordable arts and crafts and jewellery. (See p203.)

THE ROCKS
AND CIRCULAR
QUAY

Darling Harbour
Quality Australiana, surf and beach wear, souvenir ideas, children's clothes, colourful knits and art and craft shops abound.

Queen Victoria Building
This elegant shopping gallery offers four floors of designer wear, gifts, and speciality stores amid cafés.

CITY
CENTRE

DARLING
HARBOUR

Sydney Fish Market
You can buy fresh seafood daily in the colourful fishmongers' halls or order from the cafés which spill out on to the sunny terrace alongside the marina. (See p202.)

Chinatown
This is the place to find discounts on watches, gold jewellery, opals and even fabrics. There are also Chinese butchers' shops, herbalists and supermarkets.

| 0 metres | 500 |
| 0 yards | 500 |

City Centre
Dazzling shopping arcades and smart malls are dotted throughout the city centre, notably Pitt Street Mall, Strand and Piccadilly Arcades, and Centrepoint.

Castlereagh Street
The city's designer row is home to Chanel, Gucci, Hermés and others. The most exclusive names cluster near the King Street intersection.

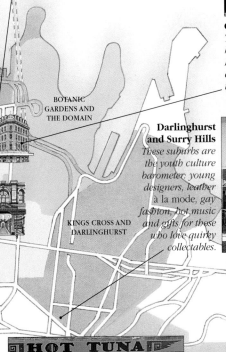

BOTANIC
GARDENS AND
THE DOMAIN

Darlinghurst and Surry Hills
These suburbs are the youth culture barometer: young designers, leather à la mode, gay fashion, hot music and gifts for those who love quirky collectables.

KINGS CROSS AND
DARLINGHURST

PADDINGTON

Paddington Markets
Considered by many to be Sydney's best market and a showcase for the up-and-coming fashions, it is held every Saturday. (See p203.)

Paddington and Woollahra
Up-market clothing, shoes, homeware and jewellery are on show. Bookshops, cafés and galleries add to the allure. Queen Street, Woollahra, is the antique shop strip.

Sydney Fish Market

EACH DAY, 65 tonnes (tons) of fresh fish and other seafood are sold at the Fish Market's Dutch Clock auction. According to this system, prices start high, and gradually descend on a computerized "clock", until a buyer puts in a bid. At this point, no other bids are accepted, and the deal is made. This unusually quiet auction starts at 5:30am every Monday to Friday, and runs for two to three hours until all the seafood is sold. Members of the public can follow the auction proceedings from a viewing area.

Balmain bug

The waterfront cafés offering fine seafood at reasonable prices make dining here a rare treat.

Blue swimmer crabs have a mild flavour and are found all around the Australian coastline.

About 30 wholesalers, many of them family concerns, buy bulk quantities of the day's catch; some also have retail outlets at the market itself.

DE COSTI Seafoods

Local fishermen send their fish to the market anytime between 4pm the previous day and 8am on the day of the auction. Most of the catch is from the far coasts of New South Wales.

SELECTING YOUR FISH

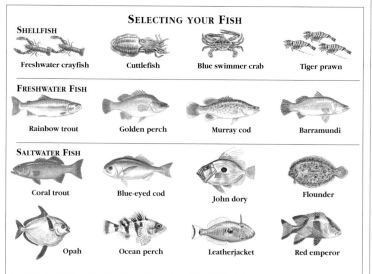

SHELLFISH

Freshwater crayfish   Cuttlefish   Blue swimmer crab   Tiger prawn

FRESHWATER FISH

Rainbow trout   Golden perch   Murray cod   Barramundi

SALTWATER FISH

Coral trout   Blue-eyed cod   John dory   Flounder

Opah   Ocean perch   Leatherjacket   Red emperor

Markets

SCOURING MARKETS FOR THE CHEAP, the cheerful and the chic has become a popular weekend pastime in Sydney. Weekly or monthly markets that suit both the bargain-hunter and the serious shopper have sprung up all over Sydney's suburbs. Caps, souvenir T-shirts, bargain leather jackets, high-class art – there is bound to be something to suit every taste. Just as popular are the Sydney Fish Market and the produce markets, which have turned shopping for staples into a big day out.

Balmain Market

Cnr Darling St and Curtis Rd, Balmain. 🚌 442, 434. 🕐 7:30am–4pm Sat.

Held in the grounds of the Balmain Congregational Church, in the shade of a fig tree said to be more than 150 years old, this compact, high-calibre market attracts both locals and tourists. Fees from stallholders contribute to the ongoing restoration of the church, which was built in 1853. As well as children's wear, second-hand books, contemporary and antique jewellery, arty mirrors, recycled stationery, stained-glass mobiles and Chinese healing balls, there's a food hall where you can find fresh and aromatic Japanese, Thai, Indian and specialist vegetarian dishes in the making.

Bondi Beach Market

Bondi Beach Public School, Campbell Parade, North Bondi. 🚌 380, 382, 389. 🕐 9am–5pm Sun in summer (4pm in winter).

Arrive early (some of the stalls are all set up by 9am) for the best second-hand clothing buys; funky 1970s gear is particularly popular. The best bargain clothes are near the back of the market. Expect to see the odd pop star and stars of Australian television soap operas among the browsers. The market is also noted for its cactus plants, glassware and tourist art – scenes of Bondi Beach are a speciality.

Glebe Market

Glebe Public School, Glebe Point Road, Glebe. **Map** 3 B5. 🚌 431, 433. 🕐 10am–4pm Sat.

A treasure-trove for the junk shop enthusiast and canny scavenger, this market is bright, changeable and popular with the inner-city grunge set. Best buys are bric-a-brac (get there early for bargain porcelain and, if you're lucky, the odd undervalued lithograph) and crafts made from recycled wood, metal and glass. Eccentricities include patchwork velvet jesters' caps, suitcases full of amber and turquoise beads, and handpainted light bulbs. Second-hand clothes are a good buy here, as are leather wallets, silver rings and pendants, amulets and plaited friendship bands, books, CDs and records.

Paddington Markets

(See p126.)

Like Paddington itself, this market reflects the latest trends and fashions in the contents of its stalls. From nouveau to novelties, there is always something tempting here, and it is unlikely you will come away empty-handed. You can preview clothes and fashion trends before they hit the shops. Silver jewellery is abundant, so prices are very competitive; there are also smart children's clothes, leather goods, unusual buckles, belts, stationery, candles, handcrafts and oddities such as babies' baseball caps and rubbery novelty masks.

Paddy's Market

(See p99.)

In the 19th century, Paddy's in the Haymarket was the city's fringe market and also the location of fairgrounds and circuses. Today it has between 500 and 1,000 stalls under one roof. Early birds will get the best flowers, fruit, vegetables and seafood. There are also good buys in caneware, luggage, leather goods, tools, homeware, ornaments, gifts, souvenirs and toys . . . not to mention pet rabbits, puppies, kittens and cockatoos.

The Rocks Market

George St, The Rocks. **Map** 1 B2. 🚌 431, 432, 433, 434. 🕐 10am–5pm Sat & Sun.

At weekends, rain or shine, a sail-like canopy is erected at the top end of George Street, transforming the area into an atmospheric marketplace. Get there early to beat the afternoon crowds. The market was designed with Sydneysiders in mind, but it has now become just as popular with visitors. There are about 140 stalls, whose wares are unique rather than inexpensive. Quality is a priority here. Look out for wind chimes, pewter picture frames, pub poster prints, stained-glass homeware, lace, oils, leather goods, wooden toys, gold-plated bush leaves, and jewellery made from wood, shell, silver or crystal. There are also new paperbacks for sale at half price. Every Friday in November The Rocks Market hosts "Markets by Moonlight", a combination of night markets, live music and outdoor bars.

Sydney Fish Market

(See p131.)

Sydney is famous for its fresh seafood and the Sydney Fish Market is the ideal place to buy it. You can choose from over 100 species, both live and prepared, in the fishmongers' halls. The displays of seafood are arresting, with coral reds, marble pinks, blacks, greys and iridescent yellows to take your mind off the sloshy floors and the smell of the sea. The market also has sushi bars; fish cafés (where you can sit inside or outside on the waterfront); a bakery; a gourmet delicatessen (their chutneys and olives are delicious); a poultry and game specialist; a shop selling fine wines to complement the gourmet meal you are planning; and a fresh fruit and vegetable shop. The Sydney Seafood School operates above the market, offering lessons in preparing and serving seafood.

The Tarpeian Market

Western Boardwalk, Sydney Opera House. **Map** 1 C2. 🚌 438. 🕐 9am–6pm Sun & public hols.

Sir Joseph Banks named what is now the southern rock face and walkway of the Opera House after the Tarpeian Rock in Rome, hence this market's unusual name. Under calico market umbrellas, you will find arts and crafts in a spectacular setting. Some call this a distillation of the best, and certainly you won't find T-shirts and cheap souvenirs, but rather goods that have been either hand-made or hand-finished. It is an eclectic mix: from English porcelain thimbles to welded art (such as miniature motorcycles), ornate wooden smoking pipes, framed prints of Sydney, jewellery, groovy hats and healing crystals. If you are lucky, you can catch performance artists – who are often happy to pose for pictures. The morning may be a more pleasant time to go in summer, but you will miss the afternoon entertainment.

Clothes and Accessories

SMART CASUAL IS A TERM often heard in Sydney, applied to both dress and occasion. Particularly in summer, the style is visibly relaxed with warm weather encouraging dressing down rather than dressing up. Shops do not neglect the formal dresser, however, and stylish Australian labels vie with the international designer names on offer.

WOMEN'S CLOTHES

SMART DAYWEAR and casual clothes in classic, if a little unadventurous, styles are the province of **Country Road**, which has shops throughout Sydney. **Carla Zampatti** is an Australian designer whose speciality is elegant day and evening wear. **David Jones** stocks Australian labels such as Robert Burton, Leonie Levy and Jodie Boffa swimwear, while international labels such as Sonia Rykiel, Donna Karan and Missoni are to be found on the exclusive seventh floor. **Grace Bros** carries impressive Australian designers such as Jane Lamerton, Covers, Anthea Crawford and Trent Nathan.

Emporio Armani can also be found in Sydney, with its trademark quality fabric, cut and design excellence. The **Witchery** stores are great for bright accessories and up-to-the-minute fashions. **Collette Dinnigan** uses Italian and French lace, silk and tulle to make exquisite lingerie that includes teddies, bustiers and romantic, wispy dresses.

MEN'S CLOTHES

THE EXCELLENT menswear department in **David Jones** stocks everything from casual to formal dress. **Polo Ralph Lauren** has sweaters, jackets, shirts and accessories for the designer-orientated.

Stewart's Gentlemen's Outfitters also stocks up-market men's labels, including Bally, Zegna and Gant. **Marcs** has locally-made clothing (for both men and women), and top imports such as Yohji Yamamato and Issey Miyake.

For men who do not enjoy fussy shopping, **Gowing Bros** is the answer. This department store stocks absolutely everything imaginable from socks, shirts and detachable collars to made-to-measure suits, pyjamas, hats and even regulation whites for lawn bowling – all at very competitive prices.

AVANT-GARDE AND STREET FASHION

PADDINGTON, Darlinghurst, Surry Hills and King Street in Newtown are the places to find some of Sydney's best street fashion. **Bracewell** and **Saba** design chic clothes for women and men. **Akira Isogawa** uses luxurious materials in modern and traditional ways. **Lisa Ho** and **Scanlan & Theodore** also cater for the style-conscious woman.

Skin Deep has retro gear for men – Hollywood-style shirts, suits from the 1940s and 1950s, old silk ties and great tie pins. Watch the markets, Glebe and Paddington in particular (*see p203*), for the up-and-coming designers. **Aussie Boys**, popular with the gay crowd, stocks cheeky casual clothes for men and women, as well as trendy gym gear and the latest party wear. **Dangerfield** is another shop filled with funky fashion.

ESSENTIALLY AUSTRALIAN

AUSTRALIAN "outback fashion", from elastic-sided riding boots and Akubra hats to the stylish Driza-bone oilskin coats, are found at **R. M. Williams**. Beach and surf wear labels to look for are Hot Tuna, 100% Mambo, Rip Curl, Speedo and Brian Rochford. Shops carrying these brands include **Hot Tuna**, **Surf Dive 'n Ski** and major department stores. The **Mambo Friendship Store** carries Mambo label surf and street wear and accessories. **General Pants Co.** is another retail outlet for Mambo.

KNITWEAR

CHUNKY HANDKNITS adorned with Australian motifs are sold at **Dorian Scott**, alongside children's wear, hats and an eclectic range of casual wear. You will also find the rainbow-coloured Coogi knits here. Knitwear specialists **Sydneyscope Artwear** has

SIZE CHART

Women's clothes

Australian	6	8	10	12	14	16	18	20
American	4	6	8	10	12	14	16	18
British	6	8	10	12	14	16	18	20
Continental	38	40	42	44	46	48	50	52

Women's shoes

Australian	6–6½	7	7½–8	8½	9–9½	10	10½–11
American	5	6	7	8	9	10	11
British	3	4	5	6	7	8	9
Continental	36	37	38	39	40	41	42

Men's suits

Australian	44	46	48	50	52	54	56	58
American	34	36	38	40	42	44	46	48
British	34	36	38	40	42	44	46	48
Continental	44	46	48	50	52	54	56	58

Men's shirts

Australian	36	38	39	41	42	43	44	45
American	14	15	15½	16	16½	17	17½	18
British	14	15	15½	16	16½	17	17½	18
Continental	36	38	39	41	42	43	44	45

Men's shoes

Australian	7	7½	8	8½	9	10	11	12
American	7	7½	8	8½	9½	10½	11	11½
British	6	7	7½	8	9	10	11	12
Continental	39	40	41	42	43	44	45	46

more than 1,000 Coogi creations in each of its two stores. **Vivian Chan Shaw** specializes in hand-loomed women's knitwear in a variety of fibres.

SHOES

THE SHOE FETISHIST is very well served in Sydney, with shops like **Edward Meller**, **Evelyn Miles** and **Gary Castles** appealing to all tastes. **Bally** has top-notch styles,

while **Platypus Shoes** imports Shelleys and Merrell from the UK and has a permanent discount on R.M. Williams. **Grace Bros** and **David Jones** carry the smart designs of Elle Effe, as well as a good range of men's shoes.

HATS

SYDNEY'S MARKETS (see p203) have hats galore, ranging from raffia to plush velvet.

Helen Kaminski sells her original designs in the historic Argyle Centre (see p68). The **Strand Hatters** stocks styles for men and women, from typical bush hats to wide-brimmed straw creations.

   Jane Lambert Hats designs bespoke hats to order in everything from simple straw to lavish velvet. **Helen Kaminski**'s distinctive rafia and felt hats are sold at David Jones and Dorian Scott.

DIRECTORY

WOMEN'S CLOTHES

Carla Zampatti
143 Elizabeth St. **Map** 1 B5.
(9264 3257.

Collette Dinnigan
33 William St, Paddington.
Map 6 D3.
(9360 6691.

Country Road
142 Pitt St. **Map** 1 B5.
(9394 1818.
One of several branches.

David Jones
See p199.

Emporio Armani
4 Martin Place. **Map** 1 B4.
(9231 3655.

Grace Bros
See p199.

Witchery
Pitt St Mall. **Map** 1 B5.
(9231 1233.
One of several branches.

MEN'S CLOTHES

David Jones
See p199.

Gowing Bros
See p199.

Stewart's Gentlemen's Outfitters
Rydges Wentworth Hotel,
61 Phillip St. **Map** 1 B4.
(9221 2203.

Marcs
Mid City Centre, Pitt Street
Mall. **Map** 1 B5.
(9221 4583.
One of several branches.

Polo Ralph Lauren
Queen Victoria Building.
Map 1 B5.
(9267 1630.

AVANT-GARDE AND STREET FASHION

Akira Isogawa
12a Queen St,
Paddington. **Map** 6 E4.
(9361 5221.

Aussie Boys
102 Oxford St,
Darlinghurst. **Map** 5 A2.
(9360 7011.

Scanlan & Theodore
443 Oxford St,
Paddington. **Map** 6 D4.
(9361 6722.
One of three branches.

Bracewell
274 Oxford St,
Paddington. **Map** 5 C3.
(9331 5844.

Dangerfield
330 Crown St,
Surry Hills.
Map 5 A2.
(9380 6924.

Lisa Ho
2a–6a Queen St,
Woollahra. **Map** 6 E4.
(9360 2345.

Saba for Men
270 Oxford St,
Paddington. **Map** 5 C3.
(9331 2685.

Skin Deep
141 Elizabeth St. **Map** 1 B5.
(9264 1239.

ESSENTIALLY AUSTRALIAN

Bondi Surf Co
178 Campbell Parade,
Bondi Beach.
(9130 3271.

General Pants Co.
391 George St. **Map** 1 B5.
(9299 3565.
One of several branches.

Mambo
17 Oxford St, Paddington.
Map 5 B3. (9331 8034.

R. M. Williams
389 George St. **Map** 1 B5.
(9262 2228.
One of five branches.

Surf Dive 'n Ski
462 George St. **Map** 1 B5.
(9267 3408.
One of several branches.

KNITWEAR

Dorian Scott
Hotel Inter-Continental,
Macquarie St. **Map** 1 C3.
(9247 1818.
One of three branches.

Sydneyscope Artwear
Harbourside Shopping
Centre, Darling Harbour.
Map 3 C2.
(9211 1081.
One of two branches.

Vivian Chan Shaw
Queen Victoria Building.
Map 1 B5. (9264 3019.

SHOES

Bally
Queen Victoria Building.
Map 1 B5.
(9267 3887.

David Jones
See p199.

Edward Meller
St James Centre.
Map 1 B5. (9232 1807.
One of three branches.

Evelyn Miles
MLC Centre. **Map** 1 B4.
(9233 1569.

Gary Castles
Strand Arcade. **Map** 1 B5.
(9232 6544.
One of four branches.

Grace Bros
See p199.

Josephs Shoe Store
Strand Arcade. **Map** 1 B5.
(9233 1879.

Platypus Shoes
385 Oxford St,
Paddington. **Map** 6 D4.
(9360 1218.

Vendor
108 Oxford St,
Paddington. **Map** 5 C3.
(9331 8860.

HATS

David Jones
See p199.

Dorian Scott
See Knitwear.

Strand Hatters
Strand Arcade. **Map** 1 B5.
(9231 6884.

Jane Lambert Hats
15 Paddington St.
Map 6 F1. (9380 5200.

Helen Kaminski
Argyle Department Store,
12–24 Argyle St, The
Rocks. **Map** 1 B2.
(9251 9850.

Specialist Shops and Souvenirs

SYDNEY OFFERS AN EXTENSIVE RANGE of gift and souvenir ideas, from unset opals and jewellery to Aboriginal art and hand-crafted souvenirs. Museum shops, such as at the Museum of Sydney (see p85) and the Art Gallery of NSW (see pp108–11), often have specially commissioned items that make great presents or reminders of your visit.

ONE-OFFS

SPECIALIST SHOPS abound in Sydney – some practical, some eccentric, others simply indulgent. **Ausfurs** sells everything from luxurious sheepskin coats and jackets to pure wool handknits and mohair rugs.

Red Earth sells reasonably priced cosmetics, usually containing natural ingredients.

Wheels & Doll Baby is a powder-room, 1950s chic, a mixture of rock'n'roll heaven and Hollywood glamour. For hip watches with a high-tech look and unusual telephones, explore **Hello Darling**. **The Watch Gallery** stocks more traditional watches. Designer sunglasses such as Armani and Jean Paul Gaultier can be found at **The Looking Glass**.

AUSTRALIANA

AUSTRALIANA has become more than just a souvenir genre; it is now an art form in itself. **Australian Craftworks** sells souvenirs that double as desirable art, including woodwork, pottery and leather goods.

Done Art and Design has distinctive prints by Ken and Judy Done on a wide range of clothes, swimwear and accessories, while at **Weiss Art** you will find tasteful, mainly black and white, minimalist designs on clothes, umbrellas, baseball caps and cups. **Makers Mark** is a showcase for exquisite work by artisans in wood, glass and silver. The Queen Victoria Building's Victoria Walk (see p82) is dominated by shops selling Australiana: souvenirs, silver, antiques, art and crafts.

The **Australian Museum** (see pp88–9) has a small shop on the ground floor. It sells slightly unusual gift items such as native flower presses, bark paintings and Australian animal puppets, puzzles and games.

BOOKS

THE LARGER CHAINS such as **Dymocks** and **Angus & Robertson's Bookworld** have a good range of guide books and maps on Sydney.

For more eclectic browsing, visit **Abbey's Bookshop, Ariel** (open until midnight), and **Gleebooks**. **The Bookshop Darlinghurst** specializes in gay and lesbian fiction and non-fiction. The **State Library of NSW** (see p112) bookshop has a good choice of Australian books, particularly on history.

MUSIC

SEVERAL SPECIALIST music shops of international repute can be found in Sydney. **Red Eye Records** is for the streetwise, with its collectables, rarities, alternative music and concert tickets. At **Good Groove Records** the vinyl comeback is heralded. Classic jukebox-style vinyl 45s are a speciality here, as are reissues on CD from the 1950s, 1960s and 1970s. **Central Station Records and Tapes** has mainstream grooves, plus rap, hip hop and cutting edge dance music. **Birdland** stocks blues, jazz, soul and avant-garde, **Anthem Records** funk, soul and R&B. **Folkways** specializes in world music, **Waterfront** in world and left-of-centre and **Utopia Records** in hard rock and heavy metal. **Michael's Music Room** sells classical music only.

ABORIGINAL ART

TRADITIONAL PAINTINGS, fabric, jewellery, boomerangs, carvings and cards can be bought at the **Aboriginal and Tribal Art Centre**. At **New Guinea Primitive Arts** you will find a range of tribal artifacts from Aboriginal Australia, Papua New Guinea and Oceania.

The **Coo-ee Aboriginal Art Gallery** boasts a large selection of limited edition prints, hand-printed fabrics, books and Aboriginal music. The long-established **Hogarth Galleries Aboriginal Art Centre** has a fine reputation and usually holds work by Papunya Tula and Balgo artists and respected painters such as Clifford Possum Tjapaltjarri (see p111). Works by urban indigenous artists can be found at the **Boomalli Aboriginal Artists' Cooperative**.

OPALS

SYDNEY OFFERS a variety of opals in myriad settings. Both **Flame Opals** and **Opal Fields** sell opals from all the major Australian opal fields. At **The Rocks Opal Mine** you can board a mine shaft elevator for some simulated opal mining – and buy gems into the bargain. **Giulian's** has unset opals, including blacks from Lightning Ridge, whites from Coober Pedy and boulder opals from Quilpie. The **Gemstone Boutique** sells an extensive range of opals, and also stocks coral, pearls, jade and gold nugget jewellery.

JEWELLERY

LONG-ESTABLISHED Sydney jewellers with 24-carat reputations include **Fairfax & Roberts, Hardy Brothers** and **Percy Marks**. World-class pearls are found in the waters off the northwestern coast of Australia. Rare and beautiful examples can be found at **Paspaley Pearls**.

Victoria Spring Designs evokes costume jewellery's glory days, with filigree and glass beading worked into its sumptuous pendants, rings, earrings and Gothic crosses. **Dinosaur Designs** made its name with colourful, chunky resin jewellery, while at **Love & Hatred**, jewelled wrist cuffs, rings and crosses recall lush medieval treasures.

Glitz Bijouterie has lots of affordable hip silver and glitzy gold necklaces in up-to-the-minute styles.

DIRECTORY

ONE-OFFS

Ausfurs
Clocktower Square, Cnr
Harrington and Argyle Sts,
The Rocks. **Map** 1 B2.
☎ 9247 3160.

Hello Darling
Queen Victoria Building.
Map 1 B5.
☎ 9264 8303.

The Looking Glass
Queen Victoria Building.
Map 1 B5.
☎ 9261 4997.

Red Earth
Queen Victoria Building.
Map 1 B5.
☎ 9264 4019.
One of several branches.

The Watch Gallery
142 King St. **Map** 1 B5.
☎ 9221 2288.

Wheels & Doll Baby
259 Crown St,
Darlinghurst.
Map 5 A2.
☎ 9361 3286.

AUSTRALIANA

Australian Craftworks
127 George St, The Rocks.
Map 1 B2.
☎ 9247 7156.
One of two branches.

Australian Museum
6 College St.
Map 4 F3.
☎ 9320 6150.
One of two branches.

Done Art and Design
123 George St, The Rocks.
Map 1 B2.
☎ 9251 6099.
One of several branches.

Makers Mark
72 Castlereagh St. **Map**
1 B5. ☎ 9231 6800.

Weiss Art
85 George St, The Rocks.
Map 1 B2.
☎ 9241 3819.

Also: Harbourside
Shopping Centre, Darling
Harbour. **Map** 3 C2.
☎ 9281 4614.

BOOKS

Abbey's Bookshop
131 York St. **Map** 1 A5.
☎ 9264 3111.

Angus & Robertson Bookworld
Pitt St Mall, Pitt St.
Map 1 B5.
☎ 9235 1188.
One of many branches.

Ariel
42 Oxford St, Paddington.
Map 5 B3.
☎ 9332 4581.

The Bookshop Darlinghurst
207 Oxford St, Darlinghurst.
Map 5 A2. ☎ 9331 1103.

Dymocks
424 George St.
Map 1 B5.
☎ 9235 0155.
One of many branches.

Gleebooks
49 Glebe Point Rd, Glebe.
Map 3 B5.
☎ 9660 2333.

Lesley Mackay's Bookshop
346 New South Head
Road, Double Bay.
☎ 9327 1354.

State Library of NSW
Macquarie St. **Map** 1 C4.
☎ 9273 1611.

MUSIC

Anthem Records
9 Albion Place. **Map** 4 E3.
☎ 9267 7931.

Birdland
3 Barrack St. **Map** 1 A4.
☎ 9299 8527.

Central Station Records and Tapes
46 Oxford St,
Darlinghurst. **Map** 4 F4.
☎ 9361 5222.

Fish Records
350 George St **Map** 1 B3.
☎ 9233 3371.

Folkways
282 Oxford St,
Paddington. **Map** 5 C3.
☎ 9361 3980.

Good Groove Records
336 Crown St, Surry Hills.
Map 2 D5. ☎ 9331 2942.

Michael's Music Room
Shop 17, Town Hall
Square. **Map** 4 E3.
☎ 9267 1351.

Red Eye Records
66 King St, Sydney. **Map**
1 B5. ☎ 9299 4233.

Utopia Records
Hoyts Cinema Complex,
505 George St. **Map** 4 E3.
☎ 9283 2423.

ABORIGINAL ART

Aboriginal and Tribal Art Centre
117 George St, The Rocks.
Map 1 B2. ☎ 9247 9625.
One of several branches.

Boomalli Aboriginal Artists' Cooperative
191 Parramatta Rd,
Annandale. **Map** 3 A5.
☎ 9560 2566.

Coo-ee Aboriginal Art Gallery
98 Oxford St, Paddington.
Map 5 B3. ☎ 9332 1544.

Hogarth Galleries Aboriginal Art Centre
7 Walker Lane, off Brown
St, Paddington. **Map** 5 C3.
☎ 9360 6839.
One of two branches.

New Guinea Primitive Arts
8th Flr, Dymocks Building,
428 George St. **Map** 1 B5.
☎ 9232 4737.
One of two branches.

OPALS

Flame Opals
119 George Street,
The Rocks. **Map** 1 B2.
☎ 9247 3446.

Gemstone Boutique
Shop 1, 388 George St.
Map 1 B5.
☎ 9223 2140.

Giulian's
2 Bridge St. **Map** 1 B3.
☎ 9252 2051.

Opal Fields
190 George St, The Rocks.
Map 1 B2.
☎ 9247 6800.
One of three branches.

Rocks Opal Mine
Clocktower Square,
35 Harrington St,
The Rocks. **Map** 1 B2.
☎ 9247 4974.

JEWELLERY

Dinosaur Designs
Strand Arcade.
Map 1 B5.
☎ 9223 2953.
One of several branches.

Fairfax & Roberts
44 Martin Place.
Map 1 B4.
☎ 9232 8511.

Glitz Bijouterie
Imperial Arcade, Pitt St.
Map 1 B5.
☎ 9231 1383.

Hardy Brothers
77 Castlereagh St.
Map 1 B5.
☎ 9232 2422.

Love & Hatred
Strand Arcade.
Map 1 B5.
☎ 9233 3441.

Paspaley Pearls
142 King St. **Map** 1 A4.
☎ 9232 7633.

Percy Marks
60–70 Elizabeth St.
Map 1 B4.
☎ 9233 1355.

Victoria Spring Designs
110 Oxford St,
Paddington.
Map 5 D3.
☎ 9331 7862.

ENTERTAINMENT IN SYDNEY

SYDNEY HAS THE STANDARD of entertainment and nightlife you would expect from a cosmopolitan city. Everything from opera and ballet at Sydney Opera House to Shakespeare by the sea at the Balmoral Beach amphitheatre is on offer. Venues such as the Capitol, Her Majesty's Theatre and the Theatre Royal play host to the latest musicals, while Sydney's many smaller theatres are home to interesting fringe theatre,

A Wharf Theatre production poster

modern dance and rock and pop concerts. Pub rock thrives in the inner city and beyond; and there are many nightspots for jazz, dance and alternative music. Movie buffs are well catered for with film festivals, art-house films and foreign titles, as well as the latest Hollywood blockbusters. One of the features of harbourside living is the free outdoor entertainment so, for children, a Sydney visit can be especially memorable.

Signs outside the Dendy repertory cinema in Martin Place (see p210)

INFORMATION

FOR DETAILS OF events in the city, you should check the daily newspapers first. They carry cinema, and often arts and theatre, advertisements daily. The most comprehensive listings appear in the *Sydney Morning Herald*'s "Metro" guide every Friday. The *Daily Telegraph* has a gig guide on daily, with opportunities to win free tickets to special events. The *Australian*'s main arts pages appear on Fridays and all the papers review new films in weekend editions. **Tourism NSW** information kiosks have free guides and the quarterly *What's on in Sydney*. Kiosks are located at Town Hall, Circular Quay and Martin Place. *Where Magazine* is available at the airport and the Sydney Visitors' Centre at The Rocks. Hotels are also a good source of free guides.

Music fans are well served by the free weekly guides such as *On the Street* and *Beat Magazine,* found at video and music shops, pubs and clubs.

Many venues have leaflets about forthcoming attractions, while the major centres have information telephone lines.

BUYING TICKETS

SOME OF THE popular operas, shows, plays and ballets in Sydney are sold out months in advance. While it is better to book ahead, many theatres do set aside tickets to be sold at the door on the night.

You can buy tickets from the box office or by telephone. Some orchestral performances do not admit children under seven, so check with the box office before buying. If you make a phone booking using a credit card, the tickets can be mailed to you. Alternatively, tickets can be collected from the box office half an hour before the show. The major agencies will take overseas bookings.

If you are desperate to see a sold-out rock concert, there may be touts selling tickets

A busker at Circular Quay

outside, but often at hugely inflated prices. If all else fails, hotel concierges have a reputation for being able to secure hard-to-get tickets.

BOOKING AGENCIES

SYDNEY HAS two main ticket agencies: **Ticketek** and **Ticketmaster**. Between them, they represent all the major entertainment and sporting events.

Ticketek has more than 60 outlets throughout NSW and the ACT, open from 9am to 5pm weekdays, and Saturdays from 9am to 4pm. Opening hours vary between agencies and call centres, so check with Ticketek to confirm. Call. Phone bookings: 8:30am–10pm, Monday to Saturday, and 8.30am–5pm Sundays. For internet bookings, try www.ticketek.com.au.

The annual Gay and Lesbian Mardi Gras Festival's Dog Show (see p49)

Ticketmaster outlets are open 9am-5pm Monday to Friday. Phone bookings: 9am-9pm Monday to Daturday and 10am-5pm Sundays. The Ticketmaster web site is www.ticketmaster.com.au.

Agencies accept traveller's cheques, bank cheques, cash, Visa, MasterCard (Access) and Amex. Some agencies do not accept Diners Club. A booking fee applies, plus a postage and handling charge if tickets are mailed out. There are generally no refunds (unless a show is cancelled) or exchanges.

If one agency has sold out its allocation for a show, it is worth checking with another.

Halftix selling cut-price tickets in Sussex St, Darling Park

DISCOUNT TICKETS

WHEN A SHOW isn't sold out, **Halftix** offers half-price tickets (plus a small booking fee) for the theatre, concerts, opera and ballet from noon on the day of the performance only (except for matinees and Sunday performances, tickets to which can be bought the day before). Bus tour, theatre restaurant, harbour cruise, art gallery and Sydney Aquarium tickets are also available at half price. There is no limit on the number of tickets you can buy.

You can ring Halftix from 11am for recorded information on which shows are offering discounts. Be there early to beat the queues during the Sydney Festival *(see p49)*. Half-tix is also a Ticketek agency for regular advance sales.

Tuesday is budget-price day at most cinemas. Some independent cinemas have special prices throughout the week.

The **Sydney Symphony Orchestra** *(see p212)* offers a special Student Rush price to full-time students under 28

The Spanish firedancers Els Comediants at the Sydney Festival *(p49)*

only when tickets are available. These can be bought on the day of the performance, from the box office at the venue. A student card must be shown.

CHOOSING SEATS

IF BOOKING IN person at either the venue or the agency, you will be able to look at a seating plan. Be aware that in the State Theatre's stalls, row A is the back row. In Sydney, there is not as much difference in price between stalls and dress circle as in other cities.

If booking by phone with Ticketek, you will only be able to get a rough idea of where your seats are. The computer will select the "best" tickets.

DISABLED VISITORS

MANY OLDER venues were not designed with the disabled visitor in mind, but this has been redressed in most newer buildings. It is best to phone the box office beforehand to request special

seating and other requirements or call **Ideas Incorporated**, who have a list of Sydney's most wheelchair-friendly venues. The **Sydney Opera House** has disabled parking, wheelchair access and a loop system in the Concert Hall for the hearing impaired. A brochure, *Services for the Disabled*, is also available.

The highly respected Australian Chamber Orchestra *(see p212)*

Theatre and Film

Sydney's theatrical venues are notable for both their atmosphere and their quality. There is a stimulating mix of productions, from musicals, classic plays and Shakespeare-by-the-sea (and in the park) to contemporary, fringe and experimental theatre. Comedy is also finding a strong niche as a mainstream performance art. Prominent playwrights include David Williamson, Steve J Spears, Stephen Sewell and Louis Nowra.

Australian film-making has earned an international reputation in recent years and there is a rich variety of both local and international films to see, plus annual film festivals showcasing the best local and overseas offerings.

THEATRE

The larger, mainstream musicals, such as those of Andrew Lloyd Webber, are staged at the **Theatre Royal**, the opulent **State Theatre** (see p82) and the **Capitol Theatre** (p99). The **Star City** casino has a showroom and a lyric theatre for musical productions and stage shows.

The smaller venues offer a range of interesting plays and performances. These include the **Seymour Theatre Centre**, which has three theatres; the **Belvoir Street Theatre**, which has two; the **Ensemble**, a theatre-in-the-round by the water; **NIDA Theatre** and the **Footbridge Theatre**. The **Stables Theatre** specializes in works by new Australian playwrights.

The well-respected **Sydney Theatre Company** (STC) is the city's premier theatre company. Most STC productions are at **The Wharf** at Walsh Bay or in the Drama Theatre of the **Sydney Opera House**. The **Bell Shakespeare Company** gives the Bard an innovative slant without tampering with the original text. Its productions are ideal for young or wary theatregoers. While venues vary, there are two Sydney seasons – one in the autumn and one at the beginning of summer.

Street performance and open-air theatre are popular during the summer months when life in Sydney, in general, moves outdoors. Especially popular is the **Shakespeare by the Sea** production, which is performed at Balmoral Beach (see p55). Visitors can purchase tickets through Ticketek (see p209).

For the more adventurous theatre-goer, **Sydney Fringe Festival** offers a celebration of original Australian theatre, film, dance, music and visual arts. Contrary to its "fringe" tag, the festival is accessible in its approach to performances and all works staged are usually of a high standard. It is held over the second half of January at the Bondi Pavilion (see p144) and satellite venues, among them Bondi Beach.

CHILDREN'S THEATRE

Sydney thrives on spectacles that delight children. You will often find jugglers, mime artists and buskers at Circular Quay. Free entertainment of this sort can also be found in Darling Harbour's Tumbalong Park on most days. Nearby, Harbourside Festival Marketplace often has street theatre and magic shows.

In the suburb of Killara, the **Marian Street Children's Theatre** puts on the occasional theatrical production. If you are lucky, you may be able to see the incredibly athletic **Flying Fruit Fly Circus**. This troupe, aged from eight to eighteen, excels in aerial gymnastics and performs in Sydney every year.

FILM

The city's main commercial cinema complex is in George Street, just one block south of Town Hall. **Village Hoyts** and **Greater Union** show all the latest films. Similar multi-screen complexes can be found in many suburbs.

Film buffs and cinephiles have plenty to choose from at the Paddington end of Oxford Street (the **Academy Twin** and the **Verona**, and the **Chauvel** in Paddington Town Hall).

The **Dendy** cinemas show the latest art-house films – the Martin Place Dendy has a bar and bistro, plus a shop filled with movie memorabilia: soundtracks, videos, books, posters and magazines. The **Cinema Paris** at Fox Studios is another repertory venue.

Most cinemas offer half-price tickets on Tuesdays, although competition has seen budget prices extend to other days of the week.

The **Imax Theatre** in Darling Harbour has a giant, 8-storey screen and shows 2D and 3D films made specifically for the large screen.

The **Movie Room** shows art-house films and mainstream blockbusters. This cinema is situated above a restaurant, food from which is included in the cost of admission. At the **Australia Cinema**, the latest Chinese movies, with English subtitles, are shown regularly.

Night owls will usually find late screenings of films at most of the major cinema complexes and some of the independent cinemas.

FILM FESTIVALS

One of the best events in Sydney's calendar is the **Sydney Film Festival** (see p51). The main venue is the State Theatre, but there are satellite screenings at other venues. Some 200 new

---

FILM CENSORSHIP RATINGS

G For general exhibition
PG Parental guidance recommended for those under 15 years
M 15+ Recommended for mature audiences aged 15 and over
MA 15+ Restricted to people 15 years and over
R 18+ Restricted to adults 18 years and over

features, shorts and documentaries from all over the globe are presented, and there are often tribute sessions and retrospectives.

The **Flickerfest International Short Film Festival** is held at the Bondi Pavilion Amphitheatre at Bondi Beach in early January. It screens films from Australia and around the world in both day and evening sessions.

Sydney's Festival of Jewish Cinema runs every November at the **Chauvel Twin Cinemas**. Highly acclaimed international films with a Jewish theme are shown. Ring the cinema for details.

The **Y2Queer 2000 Mardi Gras Film Festival** runs over two weeks, starting mid-February. Films are shown at various inner-city venues, as part of the **Gay and Lesbian Mardi Gras** (p49).

COMEDY

SYDNEY'S MOST established comedy venue, the **Comedy Store**, based at Fox Studios, Moore Park, is open from Tuesday to Saturday. Tuesday is open night, Wednesday new comics, Thursday cutting edge, Friday and Saturday the best of the best.

Monday is comedy night at **The Old Manly Boatshed**, where you can find both local and visiting comics, including top acts such as Jimoen, Mr Methane and The Regurgitator. Monday is also the night for laughs at the Fringe Bar in the **Unicorn Hotel**. Tuesday is comedy night at Glebe's **Bridge Hotel**, and the long-running comic show *He Died With a Falafel in His Hand* runs every Friday and Saturday night.

DIRECTORY

THEATRE

Bell Shakespeare Company
88 George St, Sydney.
℃ 9241 2722.

Belvoir Street Theatre
25 Belvoir St, Surry Hills.
℃ 9699 3444.

Capitol Theatre
13 Campbell St,
Haymarket. Map 4 E4.
℃ 9320 5000.
Box office ℃ 136100.

Ensemble Theatre
78 McDougall St, Kirribilli.
℃ 9929 0644.

Footbridge Theatre
University of Sydney,
Parramatta Rd, Glebe.
Map 3 A5.
℃ 9266 4800.

NIDA Theatre
215 Anzac Parade,
Kensington.
℃ 9697 7613.

Seymour Theatre Centre
Cnr Cleveland St & City Rd, Chippendale.
℃ 9351 7940.

Shakespeare by the Sea
℃ 9557 1651.

Stables Theatre
10 Nimrod St, Kings
Cross. Map 5 B1.
℃ 9250 7799.

Star City
80 Pyrmont St, Pyrmont.
Map 3 B1.
℃ 9777 9000.
Lyric Theatre Box office
℃ 9657 8500.

State Theatre
49 Market St. Map 1 B5.
℃ 9373 6655.
Box office ℃ 136100.

Sydney Fringe Festival
℃ 8308 1017.

Sydney Opera House Bennelong Point.
Map 1 C2. ℃ 9250 7111.

Theatre Royal
MLC Centre, King St.
Map 1 B5. ℃ 9224 8444.

Wharf Theatre
Pier 4, Hickson Rd,
Millers Point. Map 1 A1.
℃ 9250 1777.

CHILDREN'S THEATRE

Flying Fruit Fly Circus
℃ (02) 6021 7044. [W]
www.fruitflycircus.com.au

Marian Street Children's Theatre
2 Marian Street, Killara.
℃ 9498 3166.

FILM

Academy Twin
3a Oxford St, Paddington.
Map 5 B3. ℃ 9361 4453.

Australia Cinema
61 Goulburn St.
Map 4 E4. ℃ 9281 2883.

Chauvel Twin Cinemas
249 Oxford St, Paddington.
Map 5 C3. ℃ 9361 5398.

Cinema Paris
Fox Studios, Sydney.
℃ 9332 1633.

Dendy Cinema
Martin Place
MLC Centre, 19 Martin
Place. Map 1 B4.
℃ 9233 8166.
Opera Quays
Shop 9/2, East Circular
Quay. ℃ 9247 3800.
Newtown
261-263 King St,
Newtown. ℃ 9550 5699.

Greater Union
525 George St. Map 4 E3.
℃ 9267 8666.

Hoyts Fox Studios
℃ 9332 1300.

Imax Theatre
Southern Promenade,
Darling Harbour. Map 4 D3.
℃ 9281 3300.

Movie Room
112 Darlinghurst Rd,
Darlinghurst.
℃ 9360 7853.

Verona Cinema
17 Oxford St, Paddington.
Map 5 B3.
℃ 9360 6099.

Village Hoyts Centre
505 George St. Map 4 E3.
℃ 9273 7431.

FILM FESTIVALS

Flickerfest
℃ 9365 6877.

Gay and Lesbian Mardi Gras
℃ 9557 4332.

Sydney Film Festival
℃ 9660 3844.

COMEDY

Bridge Hotel
135 Victoria Rd,
Glebe.
℃ 9810 1260.

Comedy Store
Fox Studios, Moore Park.
℃ 9357 1419.

Hopetoun Hotel
416 Bourke St,
Surry Hills. Map 5 A3.
℃ 9361 5257.

The Old Manly Boatshed
40 The Corso, Manly.
℃ 8902 0989.

Unicorn Hotel
106 Oxford St,
Paddington. Map 5 B3.
℃ 9360 3554.

Opera, Classical Music and Dance

MUSIC BUFFS CANNOT POSSIBLY visit Sydney without seeing an opera or hearing the city's premier orchestra perform in the Sydney Opera House. And that is just the start. Since the 1970s, music played in Sydney has considerably broadened its base, opening the door to all manner of influences from Asia, Europe and the Pacific, not to mention local compositions. For the visitor, there is a wealth of orchestral, choral, chamber and contemporary music from which to choose.

OPERA

AUSTRALIA has produced a number of world-class opera singers, including Joan Sutherland, and eminent conductors such as Sir Charles Mackerras, Simone Young and Stuart Challender. The first recorded performance of an opera in Sydney was in 1834. For the next 120 years, most opera came from overseas.

In 1956, the Australian Opera (now called **Opera Australia**) was formed. It presented four Mozart operas in its first year. But it was the opening of the **Sydney Opera House** (see pp74–7) in 1973 that heralded a new interest in opera. The OA's summer season is held from early January to early March; the winter season from June to the end of October. Performances are held in the Opera Theatre of the Sydney Opera House. Crowd-pleasers over the years have included *Turandot* and *La Bohème*. Every year at the hugely popular Opera in The Domain (see p49), members of Opera Australia perform excerpts from classical operas.

ORCHESTRAL MUSIC

SYDNEY'S main provider of orchestral music and recitals is the **Sydney Symphony Orchestra** (SSO). Numerous concerts are given each year, mostly in the Sydney Opera House Concert Hall, the City Recital Hall, Angel Place, or the **Sydney Town Hall** (see p87).

This season is complemented by the Meet the Music series – twilight concerts aimed at adventurous younger classical fans. These feature a new Australian work introduced by the composer or soloist, a masterpiece and a concerto. There's a Tea and Symphony series mid-year, held on Friday mornings at the Sydney Opera House. The Babies' Proms are held in the **Eugene Goossens Hall** for children under five years of age.

The recently renovated **Conservatorium of Music** (see p106), set in the picturesque Royal Botanic Gardens, provides a wonderful atmosphere and location in which to listen to music. The Conservatorium of Music holds a number of free and inexpensive concerts throughout the year at which you can listen to the Conservatorium's symphony, wind or chamber orchestras, or jazz big bands. The **Sydney Youth Orchestra** was formed in 1973 and is highly praised for its talent, enthusiasm and impressive young soloists. It has attracted a loyal following since its inception and stages a number of performances in Sydney's major concert venues throughout the year.

CONTEMPORARY MUSIC

THE VERY FIRST concert held by **Musica Viva** was in December 1945, at the NSW Conservatorium of Music. What began with just a string chamber ensemble today promotes concerts of all kinds. Chamber music was Musica Viva's first love, but it now presents string quartets, jazz, piano groups, percussionists, soloists and international avant-garde artists as well. Concerts are held at the Sydney Opera House and the City Recital Hall, Angel Place, between Pitt and George Streets.

Synergy is one of Sydney's best contemporary music groups and one of Australia's foremost percussion quartets. The group commissions works from all over the world and gives its own concert series at the Sydney Opera House and at Sydney Town Hall. Synergy also collaborates with dance and theatre groups.

CHAMBER MUSIC

UNDER DIRECTOR Richard Tognetti, the **Australian Chamber Orchestra** has considerably raised the profile of large chamber orchestras. This acclaimed orchestra is noted for its creativity and interesting choice of venues, including museums, churches and even wineries. Its main concerts are held at the Sydney Opera House and the City Recital Hall, Angel Place.

The **Australia Ensemble** is the resident chamber music group at the University of New South Wales. It performs six

---

FREE CONCERTS

Lunchtime concerts are a part of Sydney life. There are free concerts every week in the Martin Place performance space (see p84). The Sydney Conservatorium of Music holds a weekly series of free lunchtime concerts at St Andrew's Cathedral (see p87) during the university semester. Staff and students hold classical, contemporary, jazz in ensemble, soloist and chamber-music performances. You will find buskers, jazz bands, string ensembles, guitarists or dancers most weekends and right through school holiday periods at Circular Quay, The Rocks and Darling Harbour. If the weather is fine, the Sydney Opera House provides free entertainment from noon on Sundays and public holidays on the Forecourt or Northern Boardwalk. During the Sydney Festival (see p49), there are free concerts aplenty, the most popular being Opera in the Park, Symphony under the Stars and the Australia Day Concert, all held in The Domain.

times a year at the **Sir John Clancy Auditorium** and also appears for Musica Viva. Many choral groups and ensembles, such as the **Macquarie Trio** of violin, piano and cello, like to book **St James Church** because of its atmosphere and acoustics. The trio also performs at the **Macquarie Theatre**.

CHORAL MUSIC

COMPRISING THE 120-strong Sydney Philharmonia Symphonic Choir and the 40-member Sydney Philharmonia Motet Choir, the **Sydney Philharmonia Choirs** are the city's finest. They perform at the Sydney Opera House, and December is the focal point of Sydney's choral scene, with massed choir performances of Handel's *Messiah* performed regularly.

The **Australian Youth Choir** is booked for many private functions, but if lucky, you may catch one of their major annual performances. One of the city's most impressive vocal groups is the **Café at the Gate of**

Salvation, described as "a feral Aussie blend of *a capella* gospel". Ring the Sydney A Capella Association for details of this and other groups.

DANCE

THERE IS AN eclectic variety of dance on offer in Sydney. The **Australian Ballet** has two seven-week Sydney seasons at the Sydney Opera House: one in March/April, the other in November/December. The company's repertoire spans traditional through to modern, although it is perhaps most noted for classical ballets such as *Swan Lake* and *Giselle*.

Sydney Dance Company is the city's leading modern dance group, often combining its vigorous productions with innovative musical scores. It has performed in Italy, New York, London and China. Productions are mostly staged at the Sydney Opera House, but are, on occasion, held at their studio at **The Wharf**.

The **Performance Space** is very popular for experimental dance and movement theatre. Artists with backgrounds in

everything from dance, mime and circus work to Butoh and performance art are likely to appear here.

Bangarra Dance Theatre uses traditional Aboriginal and Torres Strait Islander dance and music as its inspiration, infused with contemporary elements. It makes international, outback and interstate tours, but is based in Sydney. The **National Aboriginal and Islander Skills Development Association**'s students hold mid- and end of year performances in contemporary dance with a traditional flavour.

The smaller experimental companies rely on year-to-year funding or community-based work. These include Kinetic Energy Theatre Co., which has the **Edge Theatre** as its head-quarters, the collaborative **One Extra Dance Company**, which performs contemporary, exploratory dance and performance in workshops, at the Gay and Lesbian Mardi Gras, in youth theatre, concerts and in communities.

DIRECTORY

OPERA

Opera Australia
☎ 9319 1088.

ORCHESTRAS AND CHOIRS

Australian Chamber Orchestra
☎ 8274 3800.

Australia Ensemble
☎ 9385 4874.

Australian Youth Choir
☎ 9808 5561.

Macquarie Trio
☎ 9850 7309.

Musica Viva
☎ 8394 6666.

Sydney A Capella Association
☎ 9954 7612.

Sydney Philharmonia Orchestra Choirs
☎ 9251 3115.

Sydney Symphony Orchestra
☎ 9334 4600.

Sydney Youth Orchestra
☎ 9251 2422.

DANCE COMPANIES

National Aboriginal and Islander Skills Development Association
☎ 9252 0199.

Australian Ballet
☎ 9252 5500.
W www.australianballet.com.au

Bangarra Dance Theatre
☎ 9251 5333.

One Extra Dance Company
☎ 9351 7948.

Sydney Dance Company
☎ 9221 4811.

CONCERT AND DANCE VENUES

City Recital Hall
Angel Pl. **Map** 1 B4.
☎ 8256 2222.

Conservatorium of Music
Macquarie St. **Map** 1 C3.
☎ 9351 1263.

Edge Theatre
642 King St, Newtown South. ☎ 9516 1954.

Eugene Goossens Hall
Australian Broadcasting Commission, 700 Harris St, Ultimo. **Map** 4 D5.
☎ 9333 1500.

Macquarie Theatre
Macquarie University, Cnr Epping and Balaclava Rds, Nth Ryde. ☎ 9850 7605.

Performance Space
199 Cleveland St, Redfern.
☎ 9698 7235.

St James Church
173 King St. **Map** 1 B5.
☎ 9232 3022.

Seymour Theatre Centre
Cnr Cleveland St & City Rd, Chippendale.
☎ 9351 7940.

Sydney Opera House
Bennelong Point. **Map** 1 C2. ☎ 9250 7111.

Sydney Town Hall
Cnr George and Druitt Sts. **Map** 4 E2. ☎ 9265 9189.

The Wharf
Pier 4, Hickson Rd, Millers Point. **Map** 1 A1.
☎ 9250 1777.

Music Venues and Nightclubs

SYDNEY DRAWS the biggest names in contemporary music all year round. Venues range from the cavernous Sydney Entertainment Centre to small and noisy back rooms in pubs. Most of the venues cater for a variety of music tastes – rock one night, jazz, blues or folk the next. The many weekly gig guides *(see p208)* will tell you what to see and when to see it.

GETTING IN

FOR THE MAJOR shows and outdoor concerts you can buy tickets through booking agencies such as Ticketek and Ticketmaster *(see p208)*. Prices can vary considerably, depending on the act. You may pay from $10 to $35 for something at the Metro, but nearly $100 for the best seats at a Rolling Stones concert.

With smaller venues, you pay at the door on the night. The price often depends on the band's popularity and the takings are usually the band's total earnings for the night.

Dance clubs often have a cover charge, but some venues will admit you free before a certain time in the evening.

ROCK MUSIC

THE ROCK WORLD'S biggest names usually perform at the **Sydney Entertainment Centre**. Alternative venues which are frequently used are sports grounds such as the **Eastern Creek Raceway**, **Sydney Football Stadium**, and the **Sydney Olympic Park** sites.

There are also intimate locations for local and international rock acts, including the **State Theatre**, the **Enmore Theatre** and the musically adventurous **Metro**, opposite the city's cinema strip.

The Australia Day Concert *(see p49)*, a free evening event which takes place on 26 January, brings the best of Australia's rock acts together at **The Domain** *(see p107)*.

Pub rock is a constantly changing scene in Sydney. Weekly listings, appearing on Fridays in the *Sydney Morning Herald* and on Thursdays in *The Daily Telegraph*, have the latest news on when and where to see bands *(p208)*. Hotel venues such as the **Annandale Hotel**, **Bridge Hotel**, **Hopetoun Hotel** and Selina's at **Coogee Bay Hotel** draw big crowds to their everchanging rota of bands and performers.

JAZZ

FOR CONSISTENTLY excellent contemporary jazz **The Basement** is almost an institution. This popular venue has hosted the best of both local and international artists, and the music played includes blues and, at times, even respectable pop.

Soup Plus is another option for those wanting excellent music and good inexpensive food. The **Harbourside Brasserie** and the **Orient Hotel** also host live jazz, funk, dance and blues. **Rhythm Boat Cruises** leaves the Pyrmont Bay Wharf at Darling Harbour for a variety of music and cruising.

The **Side On Café** in Annandale is a jazz club and restaurant offering live jazz music every night of the week. **WineBanc** in Martin Place hosts live jazz every Tuesday, Friday and Saturday. They also offer extensive wines and food.

BLUES

THE BEST SPOTS to hear blues, funk and folk rock in Sydney are the **Bridge Hotel**, the **Cat & Fiddle**, **The Basement** and the Harbourside Brasserie, which also has jazz on some nights.

NIGHTCLUBS

WITHIN SYDNEY's vibrant and ever-changing club scene, dance clubs come and go, as they do in every city, but there is always a quality night to be found to suit every taste. Mainstays in the scene, such as **Q**, **Soho Lounge Bar**, **Club 77** and **Goodbar** are always popular, playing dance music from house to hip hop. The larger clubs, such as **Home**, **Gas** and **Tank**, also play a variety of dance music styles.

Expect something sophisticated from **The Globe** and **The Slip Inn**, where the house and breakbeat keep the small dance floors paced until the early hours.

Sydney is also renowned for its parties. These take place on any night of the week, in venues that change frequently. The free street press, out every Monday, will provide you with an essential guide to the week ahead.

GAY AND LESBIAN VENUES

SUNDAY NIGHT is the big night out for many of Sydney's inner-city gay community, although there is plenty of action all through the week. Popular hotspots include the **Beresford**, **Flinders** and **Oxford** hotels, and the **Midnight Shift**. The Phoenix Bar at the **Exchange** draws big crowds on Thursday and Sunday nights. The **Exchange Hotel** has a gay and lesbian dance space from Wednesday to Saturday, while its mixed-space Lizard Lounge is a popular spot for cocktails, as is the Oxford Cocktail Bar at the **Oxford Hotel**. The **Icebox Nightclub** operates as a nightclub, restaurant and cocktail bar, with a growing gay and lesbian following.

In Newtown, the **Imperial** and **Newtown** hotels are popular venues for the gay and lesbians crowd. Many of these gay venues have regular drag shows.

CABARET

THERE'S ENTERTAINMENT most nights at the **Harbourside Brasserie**, ranging from dinner shows to jazz, rock and late-night dance bands.

DIRECTORY

ROCK MUSIC

Annandale Hotel
17–19 Parramatta Rd,
Annandale.
9550 1078.

Bridge Hotel
135 Victoria Rd,
Rozelle.
9810 1260.

Coogee Bay Hotel
Cnr Coogee Bay Rd and
Arden St, Coogee.
9665 0000.

The Domain
Art Gallery Road.
Map 1 C5.

**Eastern Creek
Raceway**
Horsley Rd, Eastern Creek.
9672 1000.

Enmore Theatre
130 Enmore Rd,
Newtown.
9550 3666.

Golden Sheaf Hotel
429 New South Head
Road, Double Bay.
9327 5877.

**Great Northern
Hotel**
522 Pacific Highway,
Chatswood.
9419 4555.

**Hopetoun
Hotel**
416 Bourke St,
Surry Hills.
9361 5257.

Metro
624 George St.
Map 4 E3.
9264 2666.

State Theatre
49 Market St. Map 1 B5.
9373 6655.

**Sydney Entertain-
ment Centre**
Harbour St, Haymarket.
Map 4 D4.
9320 4200.
1900 957 333.

**Sydney Football
Stadium**
Moore Park Rd and Driver
Ave, Moore Park.
9360 6601.

JAZZ

The Basement
29 Reiby Place.
Map 1 B3.
9251 2797.

**Harbourside
Brasserie**
Pier 1, Hickson Rd, Millers
Point. Map 1 B1.
9252 3000.

Orient Hotel
89 George St, The Rocks.
Map 1 B2.
9251 1255.

**Rhythm Boat
Cruises**
Departs Pyrmont Bay
Wharf, Darling Harbour.
Map 3 C1. 9879 3942.

**Rose of
Australia**
1 Swanson St, Erskineville.
9565 1441.

Side On Café
83 Parramatta Rd,
Annandale
9516 3077.

Soup Plus
383 George St.
Map 1 B5.
9299 7728.

Tilbury Hotel
22 Forbes St,
Woolloomooloo.Map
2 D5. 9368 1955.

Wine Banc
53 Martin Place
Map 1 B4.
9233 5399.

BLUES

The Basement
See Jazz.

Bridge Hotel
See Rock Music.

**Cat & Fiddle
Hotel**
456 Darling St, Balmain.
9810 7931.

**Harbourside
Brasserie**
See Jazz.

NIGHTCLUBS

Cave
Star City, Pirrama Rd,
Pyrmont.
9566 4755.

Club 77
77 William St, East Sydney.
9361 4981.

EP1 Nightclub
1 Earl Pl, Potts Point.
9358 3990.

Gas
477 Pitt St, Haymarket.
9211 3088.

Goodbar
11a Oxford St, Paddington.
Map 5 B3.
9360 6759.

Home
101 Cockle Bay,
Darling Harbour.
9266 0600.

Icebox Nightclub
2 Kellett St, Kings Cross.
Map 5 B1.
9381 0058.

Q
Level 2, 44 Oxford St,
Darlinghurst. Map 4 F4.
9360 1375.

Slipp Inn
111 Sussex St, Sydney.
Map 1 A3.
9299 2199.

Soho Lounge Bar
171 Victoria St, Potts Point.
9358 4221.

Tank Nightclub
252 George St, Sydney.
Map 1 B5.
9240 3094.

The Globe
60 Park St. Map 4 E2.
9264 4844.

GAY AND LESBIAN
VENUES

Beresford Hotel
354 Bourke St,
Darlinghurst. Map 5 A3.
9331 1045.

D.C.M Nightclub
33 Oxford St,
Darlinghurst. Map 4 F4.
9267 7380.

Exchange Hotel
34 Oxford St,
Darlinghurst. Map 4 F4.
9331 1936.

Flinders Hotel
63 Flinders St,
Darlinghurst. Map 5 A3.
9360 4929.

Imperial Hotel
35 Erskineville Rd,
Erskineville.
9519 9899.

Midnight Shift
85 Oxford St,
Darlinghurst. Map 5 A2.
9360 4319.

Newtown Hotel
174 King St, Newtown.
9557 1329.

Oxford Hotel
134 Oxford St,
Darlinghurst. Map 5 A2.
9331 3467.

**Taylor Square
Hotel/Zee Bar**
1–5 Flinders St,
Darlinghurst. Map 5 A2.
9360 6373.

CABARET

**Harbourside
Brasserie**
See Jazz.

**Showroom, Star
City Casino**
80 Pyrmont St, Pyrmont.
Map 3 B4. 9777 9000.

Sydney Hilton
259 Pitt St. Map 1 B5.
9266 2000.

SURVIVAL
GUIDE

PRACTICAL INFORMATION 218-227
TRAVEL INFORMATION 228-237

PRACTICAL INFORMATION

ALTHOUGH SYDNEY has only fairly recently become a major destination for international tourists, facilities are now well established and most services are of a very high standard. Hotels in the city are generally expensive, but clean, comfortable cheaper accommodation is available (see pp168–77). There are cafés and restaurants in all price brackets that offer a wide range of international cuisines (see pp178–97). Public transport is reliable and inexpensive, especially

Lifesavers at Coogee Surf Carnival

if you take advantage of the numerous composite travelcards that offer combined bus, ferry and train travel (see p230). Bureaux de change and cash dispensers are conveniently located throughout the city and major credit cards are accepted by most hotels, restaurants and shops. Visitors will find Sydney a safe, clean and welcoming city. They should encounter few practical problems as long as they follow a few common-sense guidelines about personal security (see pp222–3).

Visitor information kiosk inside Central Railway Station

TOURIST INFORMATION

SYDNEY'S PRINCIPAL tourist information for tours and travel is the **NSW Visitor Information Line**. The **Sydney Visitor Centre** can book tours as well as accommodation at certain listed hotels. Information booths can also be found at Sydney's major attractions and beaches, and at several central Sydney locations. These booths also have free maps, brochures and entertainment listings (see p208).

For visitors arriving by air, there is another branch of the NSW Visitor Information Line at Sydney Airport, open from 5am to midnight, or while flights are operating.

For information and brochures about Sydney and the rest of Australia before you travel, visit the **Australian Tourist Commission**.

MUSEUMS AND GALLERIES

MOST OF SYDNEY'S major museums and galleries are close to the city centre and readily accessible by public transport (see pp230–35).

Although opening hours and admission charges vary, the majority of museums and galleries are open 10am–5pm daily (smaller galleries are usually closed on Mondays). Admission is quite often free or else only a moderate fee is charged. There are concessions available for senior citizens, students and children.

Museums and galleries are often at their busiest on weekends, particularly when special exhibitions are being staged.

Art Gallery of New South Wales

SMOKING

SMOKING is strictly forbidden in shops and department stores and many workplaces; on public transport and outside the designated smoking areas in restaurants, theatres and entertainment venues. It is best to ask about smoking policies when making reservations in hotels and restaurants.

AUSTRALIAN TOURIST COMMISSION OFFICES

UK
Gemini House, 10–18 Putney Hill Rd, London SW15 6AA.
📞 020 8780 8600.
FAX 020 8780 1496.

USA and Canada
2049 Century Park East, Suite 1920, Los Angeles, CA 90067.
📞 1310 229 4870.
FAX 1310 552 1215.

TOURIST INFORMATION

NSW Visitor Information Line
City Centre
📞 132077.
Kingsford Smith Airport
International Arrivals Hall.

Sydney Visitor Centre
106 George St, The Rocks.
Map 1 B2.
📞 9255 1788.
⏱ 9am–6pm daily (may close earlier on public holidays).

Darling Harbour Sydney Visitor Centre
Next to IMAX Theatre, Darling Harbour. **Map** 3 D2.
📞 9281 0788.
⏱ 10am–6pm daily.

Central Railway Station
Sydney Terminal. **Map** 4 E5.
⏱ 6am–10pm daily.

Casual dress at a beachside café

ETIQUETTE AND TIPPING

WHILE SYDNEY customs are generally casual, there are a few rules to follow. Eating and drinking is frowned at on public transport, and also when travelling in taxis.

Dress code is generally smart casual, but is more relaxed in summer – although people do like to go all out for formal occasions. Topless bathing is accepted on many beaches, but not at public swimming pools.

People do not depend on tips for their livelihood so this is generally optional. However, it is the custom to leave a little extra for good service in cafés and restaurants *(see p179)*, to tip hotel porters *(see p169)* and to leave any small change for bartenders and taxi drivers.

GUIDED TOURS AND EXCURSIONS

TOURS AND EXCURSIONS offer the visitor many different ways of exploring the city and its surroundings – from bus tours of the city's night spots, jaunts on the back of a Harley Davidson, guided nature walks, harbour cruises and river runs, to aerial adventures by hot-air balloon, seaplane or helicopter.

As well as being an easy way to take in the sights, a guided tour can help you to get a feel for your new surroundings.

Perhaps the most economical and flexible introductions to Sydney's attractions are the unregimented tours provided by the State Transit Explorer Buses *(see p231)*. The **State Transit Tourist Ferries** also run special sightseeing routes. In addition, commuter ferries *(see pp234–5)* provide a less costly alternative to all-out commercial harbour cruises.

Top-sail schooner

STUDENT TRAVELLERS

STUDENT TRAVELLERS carrying the International Student Identity card are eligible for discounts in museums, theatres and cinemas, as well as a 40 per cent reduction on internal air fares and 15 per cent off interstate coach travel.

Overseas visitors who are full-time students in Australia can purchase an International Student Identity card (with a guidebook included) for $16.50 from Sydney branches of the **Student Travel Association**.

DIRECTORY

COACH AND MOTORCYCLE TOURS

Newmans Coach Tours
1300 300 036.

Bikescape Motorcycle Rentals and Tours
9356 2453.
www.bikescape.com.au

HARBOUR AND RIVER CRUISES

Captain Cook Cruises
Wharf 6, Circular Quay.
Map 1 B3. 9206 1111.

Matilda Cruises
Pier 26, Darling Harbour.
Map 4 D2. 9264 7377.

State Transit Tourist Ferries
Wharves 4 and 5, Circular Quay.
Map 1 B3. 131500.

Bounty Cruises
29 George Street, The Rocks.
Map 1 B2. 9247 1789.

WALKING TOURS

Maureen Fry Sydney Guided Tours
15 Arcadia Rd, Glebe.
9660 7157.
mpfry@aussiemail.com.au

The Rocks Walking Tours
Shop K4, Kendall Lane, The Rocks.
Map 1 B2. 9247 6678. www.rockswalkingtours.com.au

AIR TOURS

Cloud 9 Balloon Flights
9686 7777.

Sydney Harbour Seaplanes
9388 1978.

Sydney Helicopters
9637 4455.

STUDENT INFORMATION

Student Travel Association
855 George St, Sydney.
9212 1255.

Seaplane moored at Rose Bay, available for scenic flight charter

DISABLED TRAVELLERS

SYDNEY HAS RECENTLY made much-needed advances in catering for the disabled. State Transit is phasing in specially designed buses with doors at pavement level and ramps that allow people in wheelchairs to use the bus service. There is also priority seating for those with a disability and bus hand-rails and steps are marked with bright yellow paint to assist visually impaired passengers.

The Circular Quay railway station is completely accessible to wheelchair users. Several other stations have wide entrance gates and most have ramps installed. The Transport Infoline *(see p230)* can give details on disabled access at each station.

Museums, newer hotels and some major sights cater to the less mobile, including those in wheelchairs, as well as people with other disabilities. You are strongly advised to phone all sights in advance to check on facilities, allowing the most effective forward planning.

For detailed information on accessible services and venues, *Accessing Sydney (see p170)* is available from The Australian Quadraplegic Association. A map and directory for those with limited mobility can be obtained from the **Sydney City Council One-Stop Shop**.

Sydney City Council One-Stop Shop

Town Hall House, Sydney Square, George St. **Map** 4 E3. ☎ *9265 9255.*

SYDNEY TIME

Sydney is in the Australian Eastern Standard Time zone (AEST). Daylight saving in New South Wales starts on the last Sunday in October and finishes on the last Sunday in March. The Northern Territory, Queensland and Western Australia do not observe daylight saving, so check time differences when you are there.

City and Country	Hours + or – AEST
Adelaide (Australia)	*–½*
Brisbane (Australia)	*same*
Canberra (Australia)	*same*
Darwin (Australia)	*–½*
Hobart (Australia)	*same*
Melbourne (Australia)	*same*
Perth (Australia)	*–2*
London (UK)	*–9*
Los Angeles (USA)	*–17*
Singapore	*–2*
Toronto (Canada)	*–14*

IMMIGRATION AND CUSTOMS

ALL VISITORS TO Australia, except New Zealand passport holders, must hold a valid passport and visa, an onward ticket and proof they have sufficient funds for their visit. However, visitors should always check requirements before travelling.

The customs allowance per person over 18 entering Australia, is up to the value of A$400, 1.125 litres (about 2 pints) of alcohol and a carton of 250 cigarettes.

Quarantine regulations in Australia are strict because of the debilitating effect that introduced pests and diseases would have on agriculture, and the country's unique flora and fauna. The importation of

Overseas cruise ship in port at Circular Quay passenger terminal

fresh or packaged food, fruit, vegetables, seeds, live plants and plant products is prohibit-ed. It is also illegal to bring in any items or products made from endangered species.

On all international flights to Sydney, the aircraft cabin is sprayed with insecticide just before landing. The customs declaration forms issued on the plane must be filled out and given to customs officers as you enter the country. The penalties for importing illegal drugs of any sort are severe.

DEPARTURE TAX

AS IN MANY other countries, Australia has a departure tax. All passengers aged 12 or over are required to fill out a form and pay a departure tax when leaving the country. This tax is usually included in the cost of your airline ticket.

If you have not already paid departure tax, airport check-in staff will refer you to a post office *(see p227)*. Departure tax can be paid for in advance at most Australia Post offices.

Entrance gates with wheelchair access at Circular Quay railway station

MEDIA

SYDNEY'S CHIEF daily morning newspaper is the *Sydney Morning Herald*. It includes a comprehensive listing of local entertainment on Fridays and Saturdays. The other Sydney daily is the *Daily Telegraph*.

The *Australian* is a daily national paper with the most comprehensive coverage of overseas news, and the *Australian Financial Review* largely reports on international monetary matters. The *Bulletin* and *Time* are Australia's leading international news magazines; the *Bulletin* is also known for its excellent arts and media coverage. Many major foreign newspapers and magazines are widely available for sale at many newsstands.

Sydney is well served with AM and FM radio stations. The state-run ABC (Australian Broadcasting Corporation) stations cater for various tastes from rock to classical, as well as providing a range of services, including news, rural information for farmers, arts commentary and magazine-style programmes. There are also community radio stations that cater to local cultural and social interests. Details of current programming are available in local newspapers.

Sydney has two state-run television stations. The ABC's Channel 2 provides news and current affairs coverage, children's programmes and high quality local and international drama. The multicultural Special Broadcasting Service (SBS) caters to Australia's many cultures with foreign language programmes. In addition, there are three commercial television stations, Channels 7, 9 and 10, offering a variety of entertainment from sport and news to soap operas.

PUBLIC TOILETS

FREE PUBLIC TOILETS are to be found in Sydney's public places, galleries and museums, department stores and all bus and railway stations. They are generally well serviced and clean. Baby changing facilities

Drinking fountain in the city

are also quite common, particularly in department stores and major museums and galleries.

Clean drinking fountains can be found throughout the city. Spring, or distilled, water is also often freely available from dispensers in waiting areas of chemist shops, travel agents and offices.

Standard Australian three-pin plug

ELECTRICAL APPLIANCES

AUSTRALIA'S ELECTRICAL current is 240–250 volts AC. Electrical plugs can have either two or three pins. Most good hotels will provide 110-volt shaver sockets and hair dryers, but a flat, two- or three-pin adaptor will be necessary for other appliances. These can be bought from electrical stores.

CONVERSION TABLE

Imperial to Metric
1 inch = 2.54 centimetres
1 foot = 30 centimetres
1 mile = 1.6 kilometres
1 ounce = 28 grams
1 pound = 454 grams
1 pint = 0.6 litres
1 gallon = 4.6 litres

Metric to Imperial
1 centimetre = 0.4 inches
1 metre = 3 feet, 3 inches
1 kilometre = 0.6 miles
1 gram = 0.04 ounces
1 kilogram = 2.2 pounds
1 litre = 1.8 pints

Personal Security and Health

Sother large cities, but it does exist. You can minimize
your risk of becoming a victim of crime by exercising
reasonable caution. Members of Sydney's police patrol
the city's streets and public transport system in pairs.
Mobile police stations, set up at crowded tourist areas
and at public events, have proved particularly successful
and are popular with the public. Further afield, the surf
beaches and natural bushland can present a few dangers
of their own, and the following information offers some
practical advice for coping with environmental hazards.

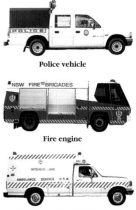

Police vehicle

Fire engine

Intensive care ambulance

LOOKING AFTER YOUR PROPERTY

LEAVE VALUABLES and important
documents in your hotel
safe, and don't carry large sums
of cash with you. Traveller's
cheques are generally regarded
as the safest way to carry large
sums of money. It is also worth
photocopying vital douments
in case of loss or theft.

Be on guard against purse
snatchers and pickpockets in
places where big
crowds gather. Prime
areas for petty theft
are popular tourist
areas, beaches,
markets, sporting
venues and on
public transport.

Never carry your
wallet in an outside pocket
where it is an easy target for a
thief and wear shoulder bags
and cameras with the strap
across your body and the bag
or camera in front with the

clasp fastened. If you have a
car, always try to park in well-
lit, reasonably busy streets.
Remember to lock the vehicle
securely. It is also important
not to leave any valuables or
property visible inside the car
that might attract a thief.

PERSONAL SAFETY

SYDNEY HAS NO definite off-
limit areas during the day,
but it is probably wise to
avoid the more unsavoury
side streets and
lanes of areas such
as Kings Cross. If
you take reason-
able care, you can
go into most areas
at night, although
visitors are advised
to stay clear of deserted, poorly
lit streets and toilets in parks.

When travelling by train at
night, stay close to security
points on platforms and use
those parts of the train in the

Ambulance paramedic

marked "Nightsafe" area of
the platform. Although more
expensive, taxis are probably
the safest, most efficient means
of travel at night, especially
for shorter journeys.

MEDICAL TREATMENT AND INSURANCE

SYDNEY HAS excellent medical
services, with highly trained
doctors and modern hospitals.
However, overseas visitors are
not covered by Australia's
"Medicare" government health
scheme, and medical, dental
and ambulance costs are quite
expensive. Before leaving your
own country, be sure to purchase adequate insurance for
any medical, hospital or dental
costs you may incur during
your stay. Under a reciprocal
arrangement, British passport
holders are entitled to free
basic emergency medical and
hospital treatment.

If you are in need of urgent
medical attention, dial 000 for
an ambulance or go to the
emergency department of the
nearest main public hospital.
For less urgent treatment, look
under "Medical Centres" in the
Yellow Pages of the Sydney
telephone directory.

The **Traveller's Clinic** offers
medical treatment for travel-
related illnesses as well as a
vaccination service. For non-
urgent dental treatment, look
under "Dentists" in the Yellow
Pages of the telephone directory. The **Emergency Dental
Service** has an after-hours
phone line for urgent cases.

Policewoman   Policeman   Fire officer

PHARMACIES

PHARMACIES ARE generally known as "chemist shops" in Sydney and are liberally scattered throughout the city and suburbs. They sell a wide range of unrestricted drugs and other medical supplies over the counter. Pharmacists can be a source of advice on simple ailments such as colds and stomach upsets. You can ring **After-Hours Pharmacy** information if you need to find one that is open outside normal business hours.

Doctor's prescriptions from your own country cannot be filled by an Australian pharmacist unless they are first endorsed by a medical practitioner practising locally.

Chemist shop in The Rocks

ENVIRONMENTAL HAZARDS

TAKE CARE WHEN going out in the sun – the ultraviolet rays are very intense, even on cloudy days. You should wear SPF 30+ sun block at all times and re-apply it regularly.

A hat and sunglasses are also recommended, as is staying out of the sun between 10am and 2pm (11am and 3pm during daylight saving). When swimming at an ocean beach, always check that there are lifesavers on patrol and swim within the "flagged" areas.

In their red and yellow caps, surf lifesavers keep an eye out for changing surf conditions, people in difficulty and surfers coming too close to areas set aside for swimmers only (see p54). If signs on the beach indicate that the surf is dangerous, do not go in under any circumstances. Popular beaches have loudspeakers to warn people of hazards that may suddenly arise. If you plan to bushwalk, do not hike alone.

Lifesaving flag Always tell someone where you are going and when you will be back. It is wise to take a map and a basic first-aid kit, as well as food and fresh water, and warm, waterproof clothing.

When walking through the bush, be aware that you are passing through the habitat of native animals, including some poisonous snakes and spiders. It is very unlikely that you will encounter any, but you should wear substantial footwear, keep a close eye on where you step and check around logs and rocks before sitting on them.

Snake bite victims should be kept calm and, most important, remain still while emergency medical help is sought. Try to identify the snake by size and colour so that the correct anti-venom can be administered.

The funnel-web (see p89) and the redback spider are both poisonous species found in the Sydney region. Anyone bitten by either of these should seek urgent medical attention.

Surf lifesaving sign indicating a dangerous undertow or "rip"

Banking and Local Currency

S YDNEY IS AUSTRALIA'S financial capital. In the central business district are the imposing headquarters of several of the country's leading banks, as well as the Australian head offices of major foreign banks. Visitors will find local, state and national bank branches dotted at convenient intervals throughout the city and suburbs.

There is no limit to the amount of personal funds that visitors can bring into Australia. Most currencies can be exchanged on arrival at the airport (beyond immigration and customs). Although banks generally offer the best exchange rates, money can also be changed at bureaux de change, larger department stores and major hotels.

High street bank logos

BANKING

B ANK TRADING hours are generally from 9:30am to 4pm Monday to Thursday, and 9:30am to 5pm on Fridays. Some are also open to midday on Saturdays. Major city banks open 8:30am to 5pm on weekdays.

A valid passport or another form of photographic ID is usually needed if you are cashing traveller's cheques. The current exchange rates, which can vary considerably from day to day, are displayed in the windows or foyers of many banks.

AUTOMATIC CASH DISPENSERS

A UTOMATIC CASH dispensers can be found in most bank lobbies or on an external wall near the bank's entrance. Ask your own bank which Sydney banks and cash dispensers will accept your card and what the transaction charges will be.

Australian currency (in $20 and $50 denominations) can be withdrawn from your bank

or credit account. Most cash dispensers will accept various Australian bank cards, Visa and MasterCard (Access), as well as certain others. They are not only convenient, but may also provide a better exchange rate than cash transactions.

Automatic cash dispenser

CREDIT CARDS

A LL WELL-KNOWN international credit cards are widely accepted in Australia. Major credit cards such as American Express, MasterCard (Access), Visa and Diners Club can be used to book and pay for hotel rooms, airline tickets, car hire, tours and concert and theatre tickets. Credit cards are accepted in most restaurants and shops, where the logos of all recognized cards are usually shown on doors and counter tops. You can also use credit cards in automatic cash dispensers at most banks to withdraw cash.

Credit cards are a convenient way to make phone bookings and avoid the need to carry large sums of cash. They can be especially useful in emergencies or if you need to fly home at short notice.

CASHING TRAVELLER'S CHEQUES

A USTRALIAN DOLLAR traveller's cheques issued by major names like Thomas Cook and American Express are usually accepted (with a passport) in larger shops in Sydney. You may have problems, however,

in smaller outlets. Foreign currency cheques can be cashed at banks, bureaux de change and established hotels.

Banks are generally the best places to go as their fees are lower. Some banks will cash traveller's cheques in Australian dollars without charge. Other banks have varying transaction charges, so shop around.

BUREAUX DE CHANGE

S YDNEY HAS MANY bureaux de change in the popular shopping districts. Most are open Monday to Saturday from 9am to 5:30pm. Some branches also operate on Sunday.

While their extended hours can make bureaux de change a convenient alternative to a bank, their commissions and fees are generally higher than those charged by major banks.

LOCAL CURRENCY

THE AUSTRALIAN currency is the Australian dollar ($ or A$), which breaks down into 100 cents (c). The decimal currency system now in place has been in operation since 1966.

Single cents may still be used for some prices, but as the Australian 1c and 2c coins are no longer being circulated, the total amount to be paid will be rounded up or down to the nearest five cent amount.

It can be difficult to get $50 and $100 notes changed, so avoid using them in smaller shops and cafés and, more particularly, when paying for taxi fares. If you do not have change, it is always wise to tell the taxi driver before you start your journey to avoid any misunderstandings. Otherwise, when you arrive at your destination, you may have to find change at the nearest shop or automatic cash dispenser.

To improve security, as well as increase their circulation life, all Australian bank notes have now been plasticized.

Bank Notes

Australian bank notes are produced in denominations of $5, $10, $20, $50 and $100. There are two types of bank note in circulation: the older paper notes, which are still legal tender, and plasticized notes in similar colours.

$100 note

$50 note

$20 note

$10 note

$5 note

5 cents (5c)

10 cents (10c)

20 cents (20c)

50 cents (50c)

Coins

Coins currently in use are 5c, 10c, 20c, 50c, $1 and $2 (shown here at actual sizes). There are several 50c coins in circulation; all are the same shape, but have different commemorative images on the face. The 10c and 20c coins are useful for local telephone calls (see p226).

1 dollar ($1)

2 dollars ($2)

Using Sydney's Telephones

Sydney's public payphones are generally maintained in good working order. Their prevalence on streets throughout the city and suburbs – as well as in hotels, cafés, shops and public buildings – means that users seldom have to queue to make calls. To save money, avoid making calls from hotel rooms. Hotels set their own rates and a call from your room will invariably cost more than one made from a payphone in the hotel lobby.

Telstra Corporation logo

Using a mobile phone at Bondi

PUBLIC TELEPHONES

Most payphones accept both coins and phonecards, although some operate solely on phonecards and major credit cards.

Phonecards can be bought from selected newsagents and news kiosks, as well as many other outlets displaying the blue and orange Telstra sign.

Although slightly varied in shape and colour, all public telephones have a hand receiver and 12-button key pad, as well as clear instructions (in English only) and a list of useful phone numbers. The **Telstra Phone Centre** has ten payphones and is open 24 hours a day.

Telstra payphones

PAYPHONE CHARGES

Local calls (those with the 02 area code) are untimed and cost 40 cents. Charges for long-distance calls can be obtained at no cost by calling 012 (for within Australia) and 0102 (for international). Phonecard and credit card phones debit 40-cent units in the same way as other telephones; however, all credit card calls have a $1.20 minimum fee, making them uneconomical for local calls. Long-distance calls are less expensive if you dial without the help of an operator. Most international calls can be dialled direct and there is little need for operator assistance unless you wish to make a reverse-charge call. Savings can be made on both national and international calls

by phoning during off-peak periods. In general, peak and discount calling times fall into three ascending price brackets: economy, 6pm Sat–8am Mon, or 10pm–8am daily; night rate, 6pm–10pm Mon–Fri; day rate, 8am–6pm Mon–Sat. Special rates and times may apply to calls to certain countries.

MOBILE PHONES

Mobile telephones are used extensively in Australia. You can rent one from Vodafone at the airport international arrivals hall. Rates cost $4–10 a day (calls are extra), and you'll need a credit card and your passport.Other rental companies are listed in the Yellow Pages telephone directory under "Mobile Telephones". Ask your service provider about whether your own digital mobile phone will work in Australia.

FAX SERVICES

Most sydney post offices offer a fax service. There are also many copy shops that will send or receive faxes on your behalf. Look under the heading "Facsimile &/or Telex Communication Services" in the Yellow Pages phone directory for an agency near you.

Post offices charge per-page fees to send a fax to another fax machine within Australia. The cost per page is reduced after the first page. A fax can be sent to a postal address for the same charge, in which case the fax is sent to the local post office and delivered with the mail, usually the following day. A same-day fax to a postal

USING A COIN/PHONECARD OPERATED PHONE

1 Lift the receiver and wait for the dialling tone.

2 Insert the coins required or insert a Telstra phonecard in the direction of the arrows shown on the card.

3 Dial the number and wait to be connected.

5 Replace the receiver at the end of the call and withdraw your card or collect any unused coins. Payphones do not give change.

4 The display shows you how much value is left on your phonecard or coins. When your coins or phonecard run out you will hear a warning beep. To continue, insert more coins if using coins. If using a phonecard, remove the old card and insert a new one.

6 When you finish your call, the phonecard is returned to you with a hole punched in it showing the approximate remaining value.

Phonecards
Telstra phonecards are available in $2, $5, $10, $20 and $50 denominations.

address must be dispatched by 1pm, and there is a delivery fee. Delivery within 2 hours is available for a higher charge.

Overseas faxes can also be faxed to another fax machine or sent to a postal address. The cost is on a per-page rate, as with faxes to local numbers.

USEFUL INFORMATION

Telstra Phone Centre
100 King St. **Map** 1 B5.

Time
C 1194.

REACHING THE RIGHT NUMBER

- To ring Sydney from the UK, dial 0061 2, then the local number.
- To ring Sydney from the USA and Canada, dial 011 61 2, then the local number.
- For long-distance direct-dial calls outside your local area code, but within Australia (STD calls), dial the appropriate area code, then the number.
- For international direct-dial calls (IDD calls): dial **0011**, followed by the country code (USA and Canada: 1; UK: 44; New Zealand: 64), then the city or area code (omit initial 0) and then the local number.
- International directory enquiries: dial **1225**.
- Local directory enquiries: dial **12455**.
- STD directory enquiries: dial **12455**.
- International operator assistance: dial **1234**.
- Local operator assistance: dial **1234**.
- Reverse charge calls within Australia: dial **12550**.
- International reverse charge calls: dial **12550** or **1800 801 800** to access operator in home country.
- Numbers beginning with **1800** are toll-free numbers.
- Numbers with the prefix **014**, **015**, **018**, **019** or **041** are mobile or car phones.
- *See also* Emergency Numbers, *p223*.

Postal Services

Australia Post logo

POST OFFICES ARE open 9am–5pm week days. Almost all post offices offer a wide range of services, including poste restante, fax, money orders, electronic post, express delivery, parcel post and telegrams, as well as stamps, envelopes, packaging, stationery and post-cards. Stamps can also be bought from hotels and shops where postcards are sold, and from some newsagents.

Australia Post postman

POSTAL SERVICES

ALL DOMESTIC MAIL is first class and usually arrives within one to five days, depending on distance. Be sure to include postcodes on mailing addresses to avoid delays in delivery.

Express Post, for which you need to buy one of the special yellow and white envelopes sold in post offices, guarantees next-day delivery in designated areas of Australia. International air mail takes from five to ten days to reach most countries.

Labels used for overseas mail

Typical stamps used for local mail

Stamp from a scenic series issue

There are two types of inter-national express mail. EMS International Courier is the fastest service and will reach nearly all overseas destinations within two to three days. Alternatively, Express Post International will reach most destinations throughout the world in four to five days.

Standard and express postboxes

POSTBOXES

SYDNEY HAS BOTH red and yellow postboxes. The red boxes are for normal postal service; yellow boxes are for Express Post within Australia.

POSTE RESTANTE

ADDRESS POSTE RESTANTE letters to Poste Restante, GPO Sydney, NSW 2001, but collect them from 310 George St, Hunter Connection, opposite Wynyard Station. The GPO is purely a retail shop and mail centre. You will need to show your passport or other proof of identity before collecting mail sent to you poste restante.

USEFUL INFORMATION

General Post Office (GPO)
1 Martin Place. **Map** 4 E1.
C 131318 (enquiries). ○ 8:15am–5pm Mon–Fri, 9am–2pm Sat.
Poste restante ○ 8:15am–5pm
Mon–Fri. C 9244 3732.

TRAVEL INFORMATION

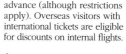

RAVELLING TO SYDNEY can involve a long and tiring flight. Visitors from Europe can take advantage of stopovers in Asia; those from the United States could break their journey in Hawaii or one of the other Pacific Islands. A break can mean the difference between arriving in Sydney jet-lagged or stepping off the plane refreshed and ready to take in the sights. Sydney is linked to Australia's other state capitals

Countrylink and Indian Pacific train logos

by efficient air, rail and coach connections. Long-distance coach travel is comfortable and relatively inexpensive; interstate trains are more expensive, but they are generally a great deal faster. People travelling by coach should consider taking one of the scenic routes with stopovers offered by some coach companies. Car travellers can also plan their journey to Sydney to pass through scenic areas.

ARRIVING BY AIR

INTERNATIONAL FLIGHTS to Sydney can be expensive. They are also often heavily booked, especially between the months of December and February. December is peak season, and therefore the most expensive time to fly. Shoulder season, from 1 January to 12 April, is slightly less costly.

APEX fares are often the cheapest. Some stipulate set arrival and departure dates, or carry penalties if you cancel your flight. Round-the-world fares can be good value and are increasingly popular. **Qantas Airways** and **Virgin Blue**, Australia's international and major domestic carriers, link Sydney with other state capitals and major tourist destinations. Other domestic airlines service shorter routes. Flights within Australia are not cheap, but you can save by booking in

Airport Express bus into the city centre

advance (although restrictions apply). Overseas visitors with international tickets are eligible for discounts on internal flights.

ARRIVING AT SYDNEY AIRPORT

THE MAIN GATEWAY to Australia is Sydney (Kingsford Smith) Airport. As a result of this, congestion, especially at peak periods, can sometimes cause irritating delays. There is a duty-free shop for arriving passengers on the incoming side of the baggage collection and customs area. Just beyond this is Tourism NSW's information kiosk *(see p218)*, as well as gift shops, a bureau de change and car hire desks.

Flight arrivals and departures are displayed on TV monitors and the whereabouts of toilets and other airport facilities are indicated using internationally recognized symbols.

Queueing for taxis at the Sydney Airport domestic terminal

GETTING INTO THE CITY

SYDNEY AIRPORT is about 9 km (5½ miles) from the CBD, 10 minutes on the new rail link or a 30-minute express bus journey. Catch a bus or taxi outside the terminals, or CityRail from underground stations at both terminals.

State Transit has four airport buses: Airport Express 300 to Circular Quay, Airport Express 350 to Kings Cross, Metro route 400 from Burwood to Bondi Junction via the airport, Metro route 100 to Dee Why and route 353 to Bondi Junction.

KST Sydney Airporter leaves for Darling Harbour, the city and Kings Cross every 20-30 minutes from 5am until the last flight. It will drop you off anywhere in these areas, but only picks up from accommodation. Ring to book a seat 24 hours before you depart.

ARRIVING BY SEA

THE MOST delightful way to arrive in Sydney is by ship. Passenger ships berth at the overseas passenger terminals at Circular Quay and Darling

International flight arriving at Sydney Airport

The *QEII* passenger ship berthed at Circular Quay

Harbour. At either terminal, you will find the city on the doorstep. Information booths, tour booking centres, buses, trains, ferries, taxis and water taxis are all close at hand.

ARRIVING BY COACH

Most long-distance bus or coach services arrive at the **Sydney Coach Terminal** at Central Railway Station. The terminal has left-luggage lockers, while shower facilities and food outlets are found in the station above.

Competition between the coach companies is fierce, so it is worth shopping around to get the best price.

ARRIVING BY CAR

The four major routes into Sydney are the Pacific Highway from the north; the Great Western Highway from the west; the Princes Highway, which follows the coast from Melbourne; and the Hume Highway, which runs inland from Melbourne.

As they approach Sydney, these routes feed into freeways or motorways, which in turn lead to priority routes known as "Metroads" (marked by blue and white hexagonal badges). When you reach the city outskirts, look for the Metroad signs and stay in the lanes as marked for the city centre.

ARRIVING BY TRAIN

All interstate and regional trains arrive at Central Railway Station. Australia's nationwide rail network is known by a different name in each state, but it still operates cohesively. The **Countrylink** reservations line will answer queries and take bookings (6:30am–10pm daily) for train services throughout Australia.

CityRail also has slower, but cheaper, services from nearby centres on which seats cannot be booked. The Bus, Train & Ferry Infoline *(see p230)* has information about CityRail's country services.

Country service passenger train waiting at Central Railway Station

DIRECTORY			
SYDNEY AIRPORT	**British Airways** Reservations [8904 8800. Arrivals [131223. Departures [8904 8838.	**United Airlines** Reservations and information [131777.	**McCafferty's Express Coaches** [131499.
Airport Information [9667 9111.		**AIRPORT HOTELS**	**Premier Motor Service** [133410.
	Japan Airlines Reservations and flight information [9272 1111.	**Hilton Sydney Airport** [9518 2000.	**TRAIN INFORMATION**
AIRLINE INFORMATION			
Air New Zealand Reservations [132476. Arrivals and departures [8258 8999.	**Qantas Airways** Reservations [131313. Arrivals and departures [131223.	**Stamford Sydney Airport** [9317 2200.	**Central Railway Station** General inquiries [131 500. Lost property [9379 3341.
		LONG-DISTANCE COACH SERVICES	
Air Canada Reservations [9286 8900. Arrivals and departures [131 223.	**Singapore Airlines** Reservations [131011. Arrivals [131223.	**Sydney Coach Terminal** Cnr of Eddy Ave & Pitt St. **Map** 4 E5. [9281 9366.	**Countrylink** Reservations [132232. Arrivals [132232.
American Airlines Reservations [1300 650 747.	**Thai Airways** Reservations [1300 651 960.	**Greyhound Pioneer Australia** [132030.	**AIRPORT BUS** **KST Sydney Airporter** [9667 0663.

Getting Around Sydney

SydneyPass ticket

IN GENERAL, THE BEST WAY to see Sydney's many sights and attractions is on foot, coupled with use of the public transport system. Buses, trains and the new light railway will take visitors to within easy walking distance of anywhere in the inner city. They also serve the suburbs and outlying areas. Passenger ferries provide a fast and scenic means of travel between the city and harbourside suburbs. The best selection of maps, plus fascinating aerial and satellite views and historical maps, can be found at the excellent **Sydney Map Shop**.

People crossing at pedestrian lights in the centre of the city

WALKING

TAKE CARE when walking around the city. Vehicles are driven on the left and often move quickly. It is wise to use pedestrian crossings. There are two types. Push-button crossings are found at traffic lights. Wait for the green man signal and do not cross at lights if the red warning sign is on or flashing. Zebra crossings are marked by yellow and black signs. Make sure vehicles are stopping before you cross.

COMPOSITE TICKETS

TRAVELLING ON Sydney's trains buses and harbour ferries is not expensive, especially if you use one of the composite tickets or TravelPasses that are readily available.

These can be bought from **State Transit Information and Ticket Kiosks**, railway stations, newsagents and newsstands where the yellow and

black "bus tickets sold here" sign is on display. For some visitors, TravelTen or FerryTen *(see p234)* tickets, which can be used on buses and ferries respectively, may prove useful.

TRAVELTEN TICKETS

TRAVELTEN TICKETS entitle you to make ten journeys on State Transit buses. Bus routes are divided into parts, or "sections". Tickets are colour-coded according to the number of sections for which they can be used on each journey.

These tickets are useful if you need to travel the same route a number of times. Most visitors use a Blue TravelTen, valid for 1–2 sections, a Brown TravelTen valid for 3–5 sections or a Red TravelTen, valid for 6–9 sections.

TravelTen tickets can be transferred from one user to another and can be shared on the same journey.

A Blue Weekly TravelPass, Red TravelTen and Blue TravelTen

TRAVELPASSES

THE MOST ECONOMICAL of the composite tickets are the TravelPasses. These allow you unlimited seven-day travel on Sydney's public buses, trains and ferries as long as you travel within stipulated zones.

They are sold in "bus only" or "bus–ferry" and "bus–ferry–train" combinations. The Red TravelPass, a combined bus–ferry–train ticket, covers all zones included in the usual tourist jaunts. The slightly more expensive Green TravelPass allows for bus, train and ferry travel over a wider area.

SydneyPass

The SydneyPass allows either three or five days' use in any seven-day period, or seven consecutive days of unlimited bus and ferry travel, including trips on the Manly Jetcat, three Sydney Harbour cruises *(see p235)*, the Sydney Explorer and the Bondi Explorer buses and the Airport Express services *(see p228)*.

You can buy a SydneyPass direct from the driver on any Airport Express or Explorer bus, travel agents where you see the SydneyPass sign on display, Circular Quay wharf and State Transit Information and Ticket Kiosks.

All-Day Tickets

If you have only one day for sighseeing, a Daytripper ticket may be useful. Travel on a Daytripper includes unlimited rides on all blue and white STA buses, CityRail suburban area trains and all STA Sydney Ferries. It is not valid on tourism services.

USEFUL INFORMATION

Sydney Map Shop
Land and Property Information, 23 Bridge St. **Map** 1 B3. **(** 9228 6466.

State Transit Information and Ticket Kiosks
Sydney Airport
Outside arrivals halls at international and Qantas domestic terminals.
Circular Quay
Cnr Loftus and Alfred Sts.
Map 1 B3.
Queen Victoria Building
York St. **Map** 1 A5.
Wynyard Park
Carrington St. **Map** 1 A4.

Bus, Train & Ferry Infoline
(131 500.

Sydney Ferries Information Office
Opposite Wharf No. 4, Circular Quay.
Map 1 B3. **(** 9207 3166.

Travelling by Bus

S TATE TRANSIT'S SYDNEY BUSES provides a punctual service that links up conveniently with the city's rail and ferry systems. As well as covering city and suburban areas, there are two Airport Express services *(see p228)* and two excellent sightseeing buses – the Sydney Explorer and the Bondi Explorer. The **Transport Infoline** can advise you on routes, fares and journey times for all Sydney Buses. Armed with the map on the inside back cover of this book and a composite ticket, you can avoid the difficulties and expense of city parking.

Automatic stamping machine for validating composite bus tickets

USING SYDNEY BUSES

R OUTE NUMBERS and journey destinations are displayed on the front, back and left side of all State Transit buses. An "X" in front of the number means that it is an express bus. Only single-journey tickets can be purchased on board regular buses. Single fares are bought from the driver. Try to have coins at hand as drivers are not always able to change large notes. You will be given a ticket valid for that journey only – if you change buses you will have to pay again.

If using a TravelTen ticket or TravelPass, you must insert it in the automatic stamping machine as you board. Ensure the arrow is facing you and pointing downwards. If sharing a TravelTen, insert it into the machine once for each person.

Front seats must be given up to elderly or disabled people. Eating, drinking, smoking or playing music is prohibited on buses. To signal that you wish to alight, press one of the stop buttons – they are mounted on the vertical handrails on each seat – well before the bus reaches your stop. The doors are operated by the drivers.

BUS STOPS

B US STOPS are indicated by yellow and black signs displaying a profile of a bus and a boarding passenger. Sometimes the numbers of the buses travelling along the route are listed below this symbol.

Timetables are usually found on the bus stop sign or nearby shelter. The Sunday timetable also applies to public holidays. While efforts are made to keep bus stop timetables as up-to-date as possible, it is always best to carry a current bus timetable with you. They may be collected from some tourist information facilities and are also available at State Transit Information and Ticket Kiosks in the city, as well as at Bondi Junction and the Manly ferry wharf.

Express bus

SIGHTSEEING BY BUS

T WO SYDNEY BUS services, the distinctive red Sydney Explorer and the blue Bondi Explorer, offer flexible sightseeing with informative commentaries. The Sydney Explorer bus covers a 26-km (16-mile) circuit and stops at 22 of the city's most popular sights and attractions. The Bondi Explorer travels through a number of Sydney's eastern suburbs, taking in much of the area's coastal and harbour scenery along the way.

Red buses run daily every 17 minutes, the blue every 30 minutes. The great advantage of these services is that you can explore at will, getting on and off the buses as often as you wish in the course of a day. The best way to make the most of your journey is to choose the sights you most want to see and plan a basic itinerary. Be sure to note the opening times of museums, art galleries and shops; the bus drivers can advise you about these. Explorer bus stops are clearly marked by the colours of the bus (red or blue).

Tickets can be bought on the buses or from State Transit Information and Ticket Kiosks.

A typical Sydney Bus used for standard services

The Bondi Explorer bus

The Sydney Explorer bus

Travelling by Train and Monorail

CityRail logo

A S WELL AS PROVIDING the key transport link between the city and suburbs, Sydney's railway network also serves a large part of the central business district. The City Circle loop is the main line running through the city centre stopping at Central, Town Hall, Wynyard, Circular Quay, St James and Museum. All suburban lines connect with the City Circle at Central and Town Hall stations. An easy way of exploring the museums and shops of Darling Harbour is to use the Light Rail.

FINDING YOUR WAY AROUND BY RAIL

O PERATING IN the Darling Harbour Area, the new Sydney Light Rail (SLR) links Central Station with Wentworth Park in Wattle Street, Pyrmont. These environmentally friendly trains offer a quicker and quieter way of visiting many places of interest including Chinatown, Paddy's Market, the Convention and Exhibition Centre, Harbourside Shopping Centre, the National Maritime Museum, Star City, John Street Square and the Fish Market.

Buy tickets on board from the conductor. The daily service runs trains every eight to ten minutes during peak times, every 15 minutes between 10pm and midnight, and every 30 minutes until 7am.

Use CityRail to get to outlying suburbs and to the airport. Trains run from 4:30am to about midnight. At night, stand in the "Nightsafe" areas marked on the platform and use carriages near the train guard, signalled by a blue light. After midnight, night-ride buses travel along rail routes, and all routes pick up from George St and Town Hall. Your return rail ticket is valid.

SIGHTSEEING BY MONORAIL AND LIGHT RAIL

M ORE NOVEL THAN practical, the Monorail runs along a 12-minute scenic loop through central Sydney, Chinatown and Darling Harbour. It can be a convenient way to travel and sightsee if you do not feel like walking.

There are seven stops on the Monorail route: City Centre, Darling Park, Harbourside, Convention, Haymarket, World Square and Park Plaza. It runs from 7am–10pm, Mondays to Wednesdays, 7am–midnight Thursday to Saturdays and 8am–10pm on Sundays. A Monorail Day Pass allows unlimited rides all day. It can

Pedestrian concourse outside Central Railway Station

USING THE CITYRAIL ROUTE MAP

The five CityRail lines are colour-coded and route maps are displayed at all CityRail stations and inside train carriages. All five lines travel through Central and Town Hall railway stations. Distances shown on the map are not to scale and the routes that lines are seen to take should not be relied upon for directions.

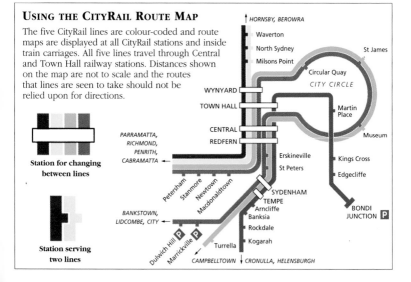

Station for changing between lines

Station serving two lines

HORNSBY, BEROWRA

Waverton
North Sydney
Milsons Point

PARRAMATTA, RICHMOND, PENRITH, CABRAMATTA

WYNYARD
TOWN HALL

CENTRAL
REDFERN

Petersham
Stanmore
Newtown
Macdonaldtown

BANKSTOWN, LIDCOMBE, CITY

Dulwich Hill
Marrickville
Turrella

CAMPBELLTOWN

St James

Circular Quay
CITY CIRCLE

Martin Place

Museum

Erskineville
St Peters

Kings Cross

Edgecliff

SYDENHAM
TEMPE
Arncliffe
Banksia
Rockdale
Kogarah

CRONULLA, HELENSBURGH

BONDI JUNCTION

be bought at any of the monorail information booths.

The Metro Light Rail system, Sydney's newest transport system, runs from the Central Railway Station along the harbourside and through Pyrmont and Glebe to Star City or Lilyfield.

Monorail leaving the city centre, with Sydney Tower in background

COUNTRY AND INTERURBAN TRAINS

STATE RAIL has **Countrylink Travel Centres** throughout the city and suburbs, which provide information about its country rail and coach services and also take bookings. The NSW Discovery Pass, valid for one month, allows unlimited economy travel by rail and coach in New South Wales.

Interurban trains run to the Blue Mountains to Sydney's west, Wollongong in the south and Gosford and Newcastle to the north (see p229).

USEFUL INFORMATION

CityRail Information
Central Railway Station
Map 4 E5. ☎ 131500.
Circular Quay Railway Station
Map 1 B3. ☎ 9224 3553.

Countrylink Travel Centres
Central Railway Station
Sydney Terminal.
Map 4 E5. ☎ 132232.
Circular Quay Railway Station
Map 1 B3. ☎ 9224 3400.
Town Hall Railway Station
Map 4 E3. ☎ 9379 3600.

Metro Light Rail and Monorail ☎ 8584 5288.

MAKING A JOURNEY BY CITYRAIL

1 Study the CityRail route map. Route lines are distinguished by colour, so simply trace the line from where you are to your destination, noting where you need to change and make connections.

2 Buy tickets from ticket dispensing machines or ticket booths at stations (TravelPass tickets can only be bought at stations). To obtain your ticket from a dispensing machine, press the button to indicate destination, then the ticket type (single, return, etc). Insert money into the slot, then collect your ticket and any change.

3 To pass through the ticket barrier, insert your ticket (arrow side up) into the slot at the front of barrier machines (indicated by green arrows). Take your ticket as it comes out of the machine and the barrier gates or turnstile will open.

4 To find the right platform, follow the signs with the same colour code as the line you need and the name of the line's final station.

🚉 **Platform 20** City Circle via Museum
🚉 **Platform 21** City Circle via Museum

5 On the platform, display signs show all the stations the line travels through. Stations at which the next train will stop are lit up and are announced as the train arrives at the station.

indicates train stops at that station

⊕ Town Hall	⊕ Gordon	⊕ Berowra
⊕ Wynyard	⊕ Pymble	⊕ Cowan
⊕ Milson's Point	⊕ Turramurra	Town Hall
⊕ North Sydney	⊕ Warrawee	Wynyard
⊕ Waverton	⊕ Wahroonga	Circular Quay
⊕ Wollstonecraft	⊕ Waitara	St. James
⊕ St. Leonards	⊕ Hornsby	Museum
⊕ Artarmon	Change at	Special
⊕ Chatswood	Hornsby for	Terminates
⊕ Roseville	Asquith	8 Car Train
⊕ Lindfield	Mount Colah	6 Car Train
⊕ Killara	Mt. Kuring-gai	4 Car Train

Tickets
Keep your ticket – you will need it at the end of your journey and possibly to show a ticket inspector on the train. A TravelPass (left) and a single-fare ticket (right) are shown.

Travelling by Ferry and Water Taxi

FOR MORE THAN A CENTURY, harbour ferries have been a picturesque, as well as a practical, feature of the Sydney scene. Today, they are as popular as ever. Travelling by ferry is both a pleasure and an efficient way to travel between Sydney's harbour suburbs. Sightseeing cruises are operated by various private companies as well as by State Transit (see p219). Water taxis can be a convenient, but pricey, alternative to the ferry.

A State Transit harbour ferry

Harbour ferries coming and going at Circular Quay Ferry Terminal

USING SYDNEY'S FERRIES

THERE IS a constant procession of State Transit Sydney Ferries traversing the harbour between 6am and midnight daily. They service most of Sydney Harbour and several stops along the Parramatta River. Frequent services run to and from Manly, Darling Harbour, Balmain, Parramatta, Taronga Zoo, Neutral Bay, Balmain/Woolwich, Mosman and Rose Bay, with numerous stops en route. State Transit's Sydney Buses (see p231) provide convenient connections at most wharves.

Staff at the Sydney Ferries Information Office (see p230), open 7am–7pm daily, will answer passenger queries and provide ferry timetables. You can also phone the Transport Infoline on 131500 (see p230) for advice about connections, destinations and fares between 6am and 10pm daily.

MAKING A JOURNEY BY FERRY

ALL FERRY JOURNEYS start at the Circular Quay Ferry Terminal. Electronic destination boards at the entrance to each wharf indicate the wharf from which your ferry will leave, and also give departure times and all stops made en route.

Tickets can be bought from Sydney Ferries ticket offices located on each wharf at Circular Quay. You can also buy your ticket from the vending machines. At Circular Quay and Manly Wharf there are automatic ticket barrier machines. Put your ticket into the slot with the arrow-side up and the arrow pointing into the slot, to board your ferry.

Manly's large ferry terminal is serviced by ferries, Jetcats and SuperCats. Tickets and information can be obtained from the ticket windows located in the centre of the terminal. No food or drink is permitted on JetCat or SuperCat ferries.

Most, but not all, wharves have wheelchair access. Passengers should check before travelling.

SIGHTSEEING BY FERRY

STATE TRANSIT offers well-priced harbour cruises that take in the history and sights of Sydney Harbour. They are a cheap alternative to the commercial harbour cruises. There are morning, afternoon and evening tours, all with a commentary. Tickets can be purchased from the ferry ticket offices or from local travel agents. Food and drinks are available on board, or you can bring your own.

Morning Harbour Cruise
This 1-hour cruise takes you through the main reach of Sydney's harbour. The cruise goes past Shark and Clarke Islands, travelling close to

A State Transit SuperCat

Manly Ferry Collaroy

A State Transit RiverCat ferry

Electronic destination board for all ferries leaving Circular Quay

Sydney Opera House, the Royal Botanic Gardens and Fort Denison. You will also pass beautiful bays and homes with waterfront gardens. You cruise under Harbour Bridge before returning to Circular Quay.
Departures Wharf 4, Circular Quay. 10am & 11:15am daily.

Afternoon Harbour Cruise
This cruise to Watsons Bay and Middle Harbour takes around 2½ hours. The ferry passes the Opera House and Royal Botanic Gardens, then follows the southern shore past Elizabeth Bay, Double Bay, Rose Bay and Watsons Bay. You can view waterfront gardens and homes and harbour beaches on the way. In the upper reaches of Middle Harbour, the ferry passes between the dense bush covered sandstone hills.
Departures Wharf 4, Circular Quay. 1pm Mon–Fri, 1:30pm Sat, Sun & pub hols.

Evening Harbour Lights
Spectacular night-time views of the city feature on this 1½-hour cruise, which travels as far as Shark Island and Goat Island. This is the best way to see the colourful lights that illuminate the Opera House and Harbour Bridge, and to enjoy the glorious sunsets of summer as they silhouette the city. You will cruise past the Opera House and Fort Denison, beneath the Harbour Bridge, skirting Goat Island and old Balmain and glimpsing the lights of vibrant Darling Harbour before finally returning to Circular Quay.
Departures Wharf 4, Circular Quay. 8pm Mon–Sat.

Other Cruises
There is also an abundance of commercial sightseeing cruises. **Australian Travel Specialists** has information on all river and harbour

cruises from Circular Quay and Darling Harbour. They do not charge a booking fee.

WATER TAXIS

SMALL, FAST TAXI boats will carry passengers to any number of destinations on the harbour. You can flag them down like normal cabs if you spot one cruising for a fare. Circular Quay near the Overseas Passenger Terminal is the place to look. You can also telephone for a water taxi. They will pick up and drop off at any navigable pier. Rates vary, and some charge for the boat (about $40) and a fee per person ($7–8).

A water taxi on Sydney Harbour

USEFUL INFORMATION

Australian Travel Specialists
Wharf 6, Circular Quay; Harbourside Shopping Centre, Darling Harbour.
📞 9555 2700.

Sydney Ferries Lost Property
Wharf 3, Circular Quay. **Map** 1 B3.
📞 9207 3101.

Water Taxi Companies
Harbour Taxi Boats 📞 9555 8888.
Taxis Afloat 📞 9955 3322.

STATE TRANSIT FERRY ROUTES AROUND SYDNEY HARBOUR

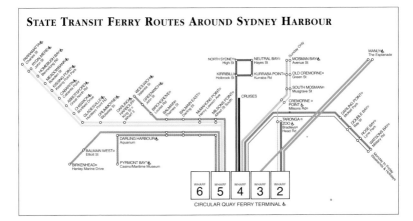

Travelling by Car and Bicycle

DRIVING IS NOT THE IDEAL way to get around central Sydney, although cars can be very convenient for journeys into the suburbs and further afield. The city road network is confusing, traffic is congested and parking can be expensive. If arriving in Sydney by car, make sure that your hotel provides parking. Cycling in the city can also be difficult and dangerous for those unfamiliar with Sydney's traffic and road conditions.

Traffic on the Harbour Bridge

Petrol station with full driveway service (see p131)

DRIVING IN SYDNEY

IF YOU ARE planning to use a car to drive around greater Sydney, you will need a good street directory. It is best to avoid the peak-hour traffic periods (about 7:30–9:30am and 5–7:30pm). Regular traffic update reports are broadcast on many radio stations.

On a positive note, petrol is relatively cheap, being a little more expensive than in North America, but about half the price of petrol in Europe. Dispensed by the litre, it comes in super, regular unleaded, premium unleaded and diesel grades. Most petrol stations are self-service and many of them accept major credit cards.

Kerbside Traffic Signs
Always pay strict attention to Sydney's parking and traffic signs as fines for infringements can be very expensive.

DRIVING REGULATIONS

OVERSEAS VISITORS can use their usual driving licences to drive in New South Wales, but must have proof that they are simply visiting. You must have your licence or an International Driver's Permit with you whenever you are driving.

Australians drive on the left-hand side of the road and overtake on the right. Speed limits and distances are given in metric measurements. The speed limit is 50 km/h (30 mph) in the city and most suburbs, and 100–110 km/h (60–65 mph) on motorways, freeways and highways, unless otherwise indicated. The wearing of seat belts is compulsory for drivers and passengers.

Drivers must give way to all police vehicles, fire engines and ambulances. At some intersections, which are clearly signposted, drivers are allowed to make a left-hand turn at a red light after stopping, but must give way to pedestrians.

The 0.05 per cent maximum blood alcohol level for drivers is enforced by random breath tests. Drivers who are found to be over the legal limit will incur heavy fines, suspension or loss of licence, and even prison sentences. Should you be involved in an accident while over the limit (whether or not you are at fault), your insurance may be invalidated.

The NRMA *(see p223)* has a free 24-hour roadside service for members. Non-members are charged a service fee and joining fee. Most car hire companies provide their own free roadside emergency service.

Beware of kangaroos crossing

PARKING

PARKING IN SYDNEY is strictly regulated with fines for any infringements. In certain areas, particularly along clearways (indicated by signposts), vehicles are towed away if parked illegally. Contact the **Sydney Traffic Control Centre** to find out where your vehicle has been impounded if this happens. There are car parks scattered around the city area. They vary widely, both in how much they charge and their opening hours. Most close after midnight, but many close earlier – check carefully before parking your car for the evening.

Look out for the blue and white "P" signs or seek out one of the metered parking zones. Many metered parking zones apply 7 days a week and as late as 10pm. This varies from council to council.

CAR HIRE

METROPOLITAN RATES offered by the major agencies (**Avis**, **Budget**, **Hertz** and **Thrifty**) range from about $75 a day for a small car to $100 a day for a large car. These rates usually include comprehensive insurance. However, many of the other agencies listed in the Yellow Pages telephone directory offer highly competitive prices, and rentals can be obtained for as little as $35–$40 a day. Be sure to read the fine print on hire agreements as deals may not be as attractive as they first seem – and be aware of the costs you could incur in the event of an accident if you opt for less than full insurance cover.

Generally, rates are lower if you hire for more than three days, or if you take a limited, low-kilometre deal. Charges may apply if you drive over 100 km (60 miles) a day, travel over rough rural roads or for late returns. You must over 21 years old to hire a car from some companies and if you do not have a credit card, you will need to leave a deposit. Make sure you return the car full of fuel, as you will be charged a premium rate for filling it.

TAXIS

TAXIS ARE PLENTIFUL in Sydney and you should have little difficulty in flagging one down in the city and inner suburbs. There are taxi ranks at many city locations and taxis are often found outside the large city hotels. The four main taxi companies provide a reliable telephone service, but you should book your taxi at least 15 minutes before you need it.

Meters indicate the fare plus any extras, such as booking fees and waiting time. Fares, as well as extra charges, are regulated and are more expensive after 10pm. Tips are not normally expected, but it is customary to round the fare up to the next dollar.

Sydney has a new fleet of taxis designed to accommodate disabled passengers, including

Cycling in Centennial Park

those in wheelchairs. These taxis can be booked through any of the major companies. Smoking in taxis is forbidden by law in New South Wales.

SYDNEY BY BICYCLE

WHILE CYCLING IS permitted on all city and suburban roads, visitors would be well advised to restrict their cycling to designated cycling tracks, or to areas where motor traffic is likely to be light. Helmets are compulsory by law.

Keen cyclists who wish to take advantage of Sydney's undulating terrain and pleasant weather can seek advice from **Bicycle New South Wales**. It publishes a handbook, *Bike It, Sydney*, which has a map of good cycling routes.

Centennial Park is one of the most popular spots; on weekends and every evening packs of riders can be seen cycling through the park. You can take your bicycle on CityRail trains *(see p232)*, but you may have to pay an extra child's fare.

Cabcharge is for account customers only, but some taxis also accept American Express and Diners Club.

The orange light, when lit, shows the taxi is available.

Taxi licence number

The taxi company name and phone number are displayed on front driver and passenger doors.

The taxi driver's photo licence must be on clear display within the taxi.

DIRECTORY

CAR HIRE COMPANIES

Avis
(9353 9000 or 136333.

Budget
(132727.

Hertz
(133039.

Thrifty
(1300 367 227.

TAXI COMPANIES

Legion Cabs
(131451.

Premier Cabs
(131017.

RSL Cabs
(132211.

Taxis Combined
(8332 8888.

CYCLE HIRE AND INFORMATION

Bicycle New South Wales
Level 2, 209 Castlereagh St.
Map 4 E3. (9283 5200.

Centennial Park Cycles
50 Clovelly Rd, Randwick.
(Near Centennial Park.)
(9398 5027.

Inner City Cycles
151 Glebe Point Rd, Glebe.
(9660 6605.

Woolys Wheels
82 Oxford St, Paddington.
Map 5 B3. (9331 2671.

USEFUL NUMBERS

Infringement Processing Bureau
130 George St, Parramatta.
(1300 138 118.

Sydney Traffic Control Centre
(132701.
24-hour service.

Taxi Complaints
Department of Transport,
418a Elizabeth St,
Surry Hills. **Map** 4 E3.
(1800 648 478.

SYDNEY STREET FINDER

HE PAGE GRID superimposed on the *Area by Area* map below shows which parts of Sydney are covered in this *Street Finder*. Map references given for all sights, hotels, restaurants, shopping and entertainment venues described in this guide refer to the maps in this section. All the major sights are clearly marked so they are easy to locate. A complete index of the street names and places of interest follows on pages 246–9. The key, set out below, indicates the scale of the maps and shows what other features are marked on them, including railway stations, bus terminals, ferry boarding points, emergency services, post offices and tourist information centres.

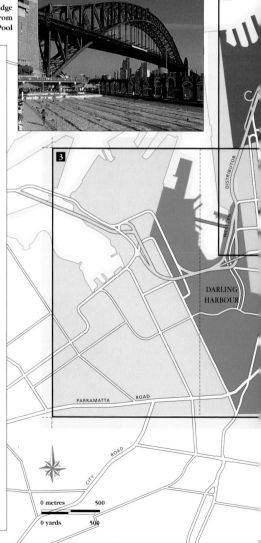

Sydney Harbour Bridge *(see pp 70–71)* viewed from **North Sydney Olympic Pool**

KEY TO STREET FINDER

- Major sight
- Place of interest
- Other building
- CityRail station
- Monorail station
- Sydney Light Rail (SLR) station
- Bus terminus
- Coach station
- Ferry boarding point
- RiverCat/JetCat boarding point
- Taxi rank
- **P** Parking
- Tourist information
- Hospital with casualty unit
- Police station
- Church
- Synagogue
- Mosque
- Post office
- Golf course
- Freeway
- Railway line
- Monorail
- Ferry route
- One-way street
- Pedestrianized street

0 metres	250
0 yards	250

0 metres	500
0 yards	500

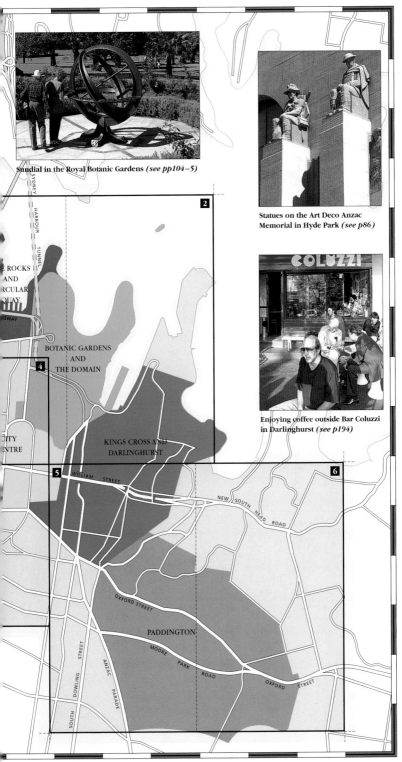

Sundial in the Royal Botanic Gardens *(see pp104–5)*

Statues on the Art Deco Anzac Memorial in Hyde Park *(see p86)*

Enjoying coffee outside Bar Coluzzi in Darlinghurst *(see p194)*

2

HARBOUR TUNNEL

SYDNEY

E ROCKS
AND
RCULAR
QUAY

SSWAY

BOTANIC GARDENS
AND
THE DOMAIN

4

ITY
NTRE

KINGS CROSS AND
DARLINGHURST

5 WILLIAM STREET

NEW SOUTH HEAD ROAD

6

OXFORD STREET

PADDINGTON

MOORE PARK ROAD

OXFORD STREET

SOUTH DOWLING STREET

ANZAC PARADE

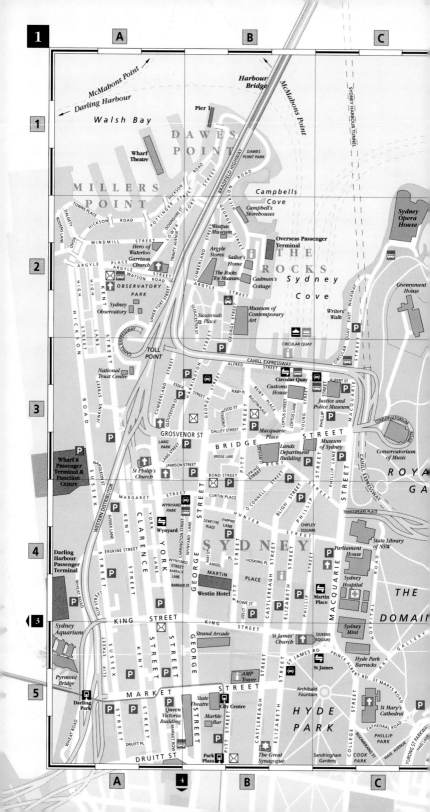

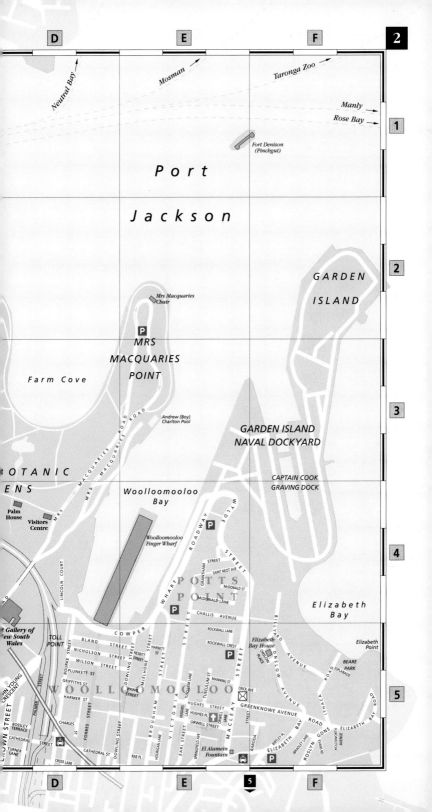

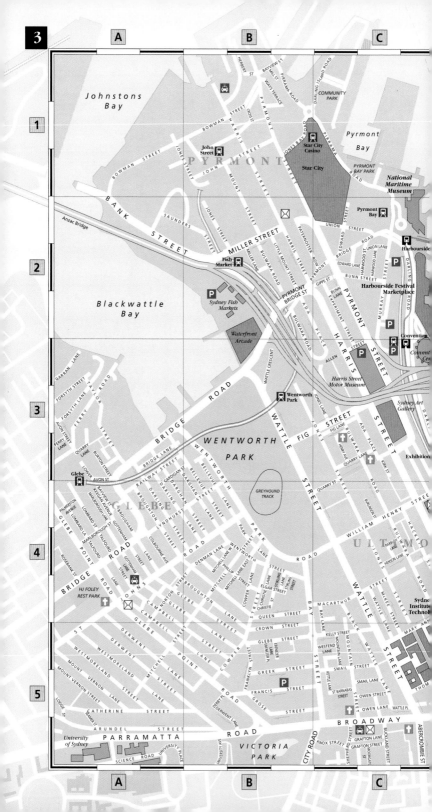

3

A   B   C

1

Johnstons
Bay

HERBERT ST
BAYVIEW ST
PIRRAMA ROAD
WATTS TERRACE

BOWMAN STREET
HARRIS STREET
PYRMONT STREET
PYRMONT CROSS

COMMUNITY
PARK

DARLING ISLAND ROAD

BOWMAN STREET
JONES STREET

John
Street

JOHN STREET
MOUNT STREET

P Y R M O N T

Star City Casino

Star City

Pyrmont
Bay

PYRMONT
BAY PARK

JONES ROAD
PYRMONT BAY ROAD

National
Maritime
Museum

Anzac Bridge

B A N K
STREET

SAUNDERS

JONES STREET

MILLER STREET
BULWARA ROAD

PATERNOSTER ROW
LITTLE MOUNT STREET
HARRIS STREET
PYRMONT STREET

UNION STREET

EDWARD STREET

Pyrmont
Bay

EDWARD LANE

Harbourside

2

Blackwattle
Bay

P

Sydney Fish
Markets

Fish
Market

MILLER STREET

MILLER LANE

BULWARA ROAD

PYRMONT
BRIDGE ST

ADA STREET
BULWARA ROAD

GIPPS ST
BUNN STREET

BUNN LANE
EXPERIMENT STREET

MURRAY STREET
DARLING DRIVE

Harbourside Festival
Marketplace

P

Waterfront
Arcade

WATTLE CRESCENT

HARRIS STREET

ALLEN STREET

P

P

Convention

Convent
Cen

3

GARRAN LANE
TAYLOR ROAD

FORSYTH STREET

FERRY ROAD

AVON LANE

QUARRY STREET
BURTON STREET

Glebe

LOWER AVON ST

B R I D G E
R O A D

BRIDGE LANE

RAILWAY STREET
CARDIGAN
DARLING
OAKMAN LANE
BELLEVUE
WENTWORTH

Wentworth
Park

W E N T W O R T H
P A R K

WATTLE STREET
FIG STREET

Harris Street
Motor Museum

JONES LANE

FIG LANE

FISH LANE

HENRY ROAD

ADA PLACE

QUARRY LANE

Sydney Art
Gallery

DARLING

Exhibition

4

PALMERSTON AVENUE

G L E B E

ROEBANK ST
LOMBARD LA

MARLBOROUGH ST
GOTTENHAM
TALFOURD

BAYSWATER AVENUE
KEELAN AVENUE
MARLBOROUGH ST

COUBOURNE AVE

LYNDHURST STREET

OAKMAN LANE

GLEBE POINT ROAD

GOTTENHAM LANE

JOHNS LANE
JOHNS STREET

HJ FOLEY
REST PARK

P

BROUGHTON STREET
CAMPERDOWN LANE
CAMPBELL LANE
ST JOHNS LANE

GLEBE STREET

DENMAN LANE
MITCHELL LANE
WENTWORTH

PHILLIP STREET

MITCHELL STREET
STIRLING
CHRISTIE

ELGAR STREET

COWPER STREET
WENTWORTH PARK ROAD

QUEEN STREET

WATTLE STREET

BAY LANE

MACARTHUR STREET

WILLIAM HENRY STREET

U L T I M O

PARRIS LANE

HACKE

JONES STREET

MIKEE LANE
WATTLE LANE

HENSON LANE

Sydne
Institute
Technolo

5

LODGE ST
CATHERINE STREET

MOUNT VERNON STREET
MOUNT VERNON LANE

WESTMORELAND STREET
WESTMORELAND LANE

DERWENT STREET
DERWENT LANE

MITCHELL STREET
MITCHELL LANE

GLEBE POINT ROAD

CAMPBELL STREET
COWPER STREET

CROWN STREET

GLEBE STREET

GREEK STREET

FRANCIS STREET
FRANKLIN LANE
EBENEZER LANE
EBENEZER

P

GROSE STREET

KELLY STREET
WESTEND LANE
MOUNTAIN LANE

SMAIL STREET

LITTLE LANE

BLACK MOUNTAIN STREET

ST BARNABAS STREET

SMAIL LANE

OWEN STREET
OWEN LANE

WATTLE LANE

MARY STREET
THOMA

University
of Sydney

P A R R A M A T T A

ARUNDEL STREET

GRIMES ST

SCIENCE ROAD

UNIVERSITY PLACE

VICTORIA
PARK

C I T Y   R O A D

ROAD

B R O A D W A Y

GRAFTON LANE

KNOX STREET
GRAFTON STREET

SHEPHERD STREET
BUCKLAND STREET
BUCKLAND LANE
MOORHEAD ST

ABERCROMBIE ST

A   B   C

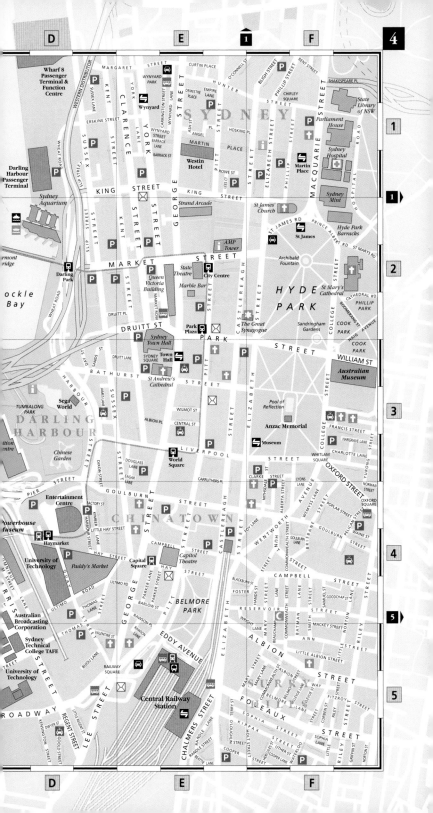

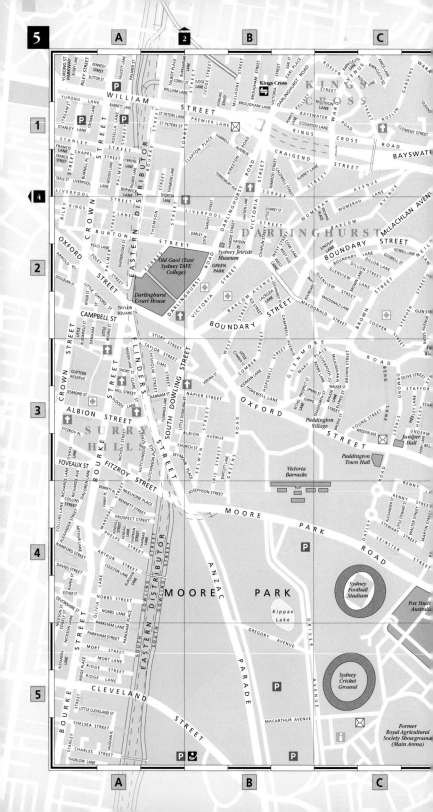

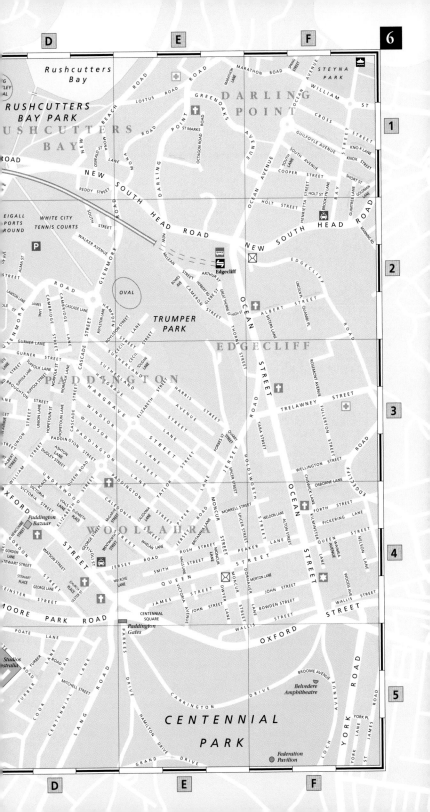

Street Finder Index

A

Abercrombie Street	3 C5
Ada Place	3 B2
Albert Square	6 D3
Albert Street (Edgecliff)	6 F2
Albert Street (Paddington)	6 D3
Albert Street (Sydney)	1 C3
Alberta Street	4 F4
Albion Avenue	5 A3
Albion Place	4 E3
Albion Street	4 F5
continues	5 A3
Albion Way	4 F5
Alexander Street (Paddington)	5 C4
Alexander Street (Surry Hills)	5 A4
Alexandra Lane	5 A5
Alfred Street	1 B3
Allen Street	3 C3
Alma Street	6 D2
Alton Street	6 F4
Amos Lane	5 C1
Angel Place	1 B4, 4 E1
Ann Street	4 F5
Anzac Parade	5 B4
Argyle Centre	1 B2
Argyle Place	1 A2
Argyle Street	1 A2
Arnold Place	5 A2
Art Gallery of New South Wales	2 D5
Art Gallery Road	1 C5
Arthur Lane	5 A4
Arthur Street (Edgecliff)	6 E2
Arthur Street (Surry Hills)	5 A4
Arundel Street	3 A5
Ash Street	1 B4, 4 E1
Ashton Lane	6 D3
Australian Broadcasting Corporation	4 D4
Australian Museum	4 F3
Avon Street	3 A3

B

Bank Street	3 A1
Barcom Avenue	5 B2
Barlow Street	4 E4
Barncleuth Lane	5 C1
Barncleuth Square	5 C1
Barnett Lane	5 A1
Baroda Street	2 F5
Barrack Lane	1 A4
continues	4 E1
Barrack Street	1 A4
continues	4 E1
Bartlett Lane	5 B3
Bates Avenue	5 C3
Bathurst Street	4 D3
Batman Lane	4 F5
Bay Lane	3 C4
Bay Street (Double Bay)	6 F2
Bay Street (Glebe)	3 B4
Bayswater Road	5 B1
Bayview Street (Glebe)	3 A4

Bayview Street (Pyrmont)	3 B1
Beare Park	2 F5
Beattie Lane	4 E5
Beauchamp Lane	4 F5
Begg Lane	5 C3
Bellevue Lane (Glebe)	3 B3
Bellevue Lane (Surry Hills)	4 F5
Bellevue Street (Glebe)	3 B3
Bellevue Street (Surry Hills)	4 F5
Belmore Lane	4 F5
Belmore Park	4 E4
Belmore Place	5 C3
Belmore Street	4 F5
Bennett Place	5 A4
Bennett Street	5 A4
Bennetts Grove Avenue	6 D3
Bent Street (Paddington)	6 D4
Bent Street (Sydney)	1 B3
continues	4 F1
Berwick Lane	5 A1
Bethel Lane	5 B3
Bijou Lane	4 D5
Billyard Avenue	2 F4
Birtley Place	2 F5
Blackburn Street	4 E4
Blackwattle Lane	3 C4
Bland Street	2 D5
Bligh Street	1 B4
continues	4 F1
Bond Street	1 B3
Boomerang Street	1 C5
continues	4 F2
Bossley Terrace	2 D5
Boundary Lane	5 B2
	& 5 C2
Boundary Street	5 B2
Bourke Street	5 A5
Bowden Street	6 F4
Bowes Avenue	6 E2
Bowman Street	3 A1
Bradfield Highway	1 B1
Bradley Lane	2 F5
Bridge Lane (Glebe)	3 A3
Bridge Lane (Sydney)	1 B3
Bridge Road (Glebe)	3 A4
Bridge Street	1 B3
Brisbane Street	4 F4
Britannia Lane	6 E4
Broadway	3 C5
Brodie Street	5 C3
Brooklyn Lane	6 F2
Broome Avenue	6 F5
Brougham Lane (Glebe)	3 A4
Brougham Lane (Potts Point)	5 B1
Brougham Street	2 E5
continues	5 B1
Broughton Lane	3 B4
Broughton Street (Glebe)	3 A4
Broughton Street (Paddington)	6 D3
Brown Lane	5 C2
Brown Street	5 C3
Browns Place	5 C2
Buckland Street	3 C5

Bulletin Place	1 B3
Bulwara Road	3 B2
Bunn Lane	3 C2
Bunn Street	3 C2
Burdekin Lane	5 A4
Burlinson Street	3 C4
Burnell Place	5 A1
Burrahore Lane	5 A1
Burton Street (Darlinghurst)	5 A2
Burton Street (Glebe)	3 A3
Busby Lane	5 A1

C

Cadman's Cottage	1 B2
Cahill Expressway	1 B3
Caldwell Street	5 B1
Caledonia Lane	6 E4
Caledonia Street	6 D4
Cambridge Lane	6 D2
Cambridge Street	6 D2
Cameron Street	6 E2
Campbell Avenue	5 B2
Campbell Lane	3 A4
Campbell Street (Glebe)	3 A4
Campbell Street (Haymarket)	4 E4
Campbell Street (Surry Hills)	5 A2
Campbell's Storehouses	1 B2
Capitol Theatre	4 E4
Cardigan Street	3 A4
Carrington Drive	6 E5
Carrington Street	1 A4
continues	4 E1
Cascade Lane	6 D2
Cascade Street	6 D3
Castlereagh Street	1 B5
continues	4 E5
Cathedral Road	1 C5
Cathedral Street	2 D5
continues	4 F2
Catherine Street	3 A5
Cecil Lane	6 E3
Cecil Street	6 E3
Centennial Lane	6 D5
Centennial Park	6 E5
Centennial Square	6 E4
Central Railway Station	4 E5
Central Street	4 E3
Centre for Contemporary Craft	1 B2
Challis Avenue	2 F4
Chalmers Street	4 E5
Chapel Street	5 A1
Chaplin Street	5 B2
Chapman Lane	5 A4
Chapman Street	5 A4
Charles Street (Surry Hills)	5 A5
Charles Street (Woolloomooloo)	2 D5
Charlotte Lane	4 F3
Chelsea Street	5 A5
Chifley Square	1 B4
continues	4 F1
Chinatown	4 D4
Chinese Garden	4 D3
Chisholm Street	5 A3
Chiswick Lane	6 F3
Christie Lane	3 B4

Christie Street	3 B4
Church Place	6 D4
Church Street	5 A3
Circular Quay East	1 C3
City Road	3 B5
Clapton Place	5 B1
Clare Street	5 A3
Clarence Street	1 A4
continues	4 E1
Clarke Street	4 F3
Clement Street	5 C1
Cleveland Street	5 A5
Clifton Reserve	5 A3
Colbourne Avenue	3 A4
College Street	1 C5
continues	4 F3
Collins Lane	5 A4
Collins Street	5 A4
Comber Street	5 B3
Commonwealth Street	4 F5
Community Park	3 C1
Conservatorium of Music	1 C3
Conservatorium Road	1 C3
Convention and Exhibition Centre	3 C3
Cook Park	1 C5
continues	4 F2
Cook Road	6 D5
Cooper Lane	4 F5
Cooper Street (Double Bay)	6 F1
Cooper Street (Paddington)	5 C2
Cooper Street (Surry Hills)	4 E5
Corben Street	4 F5
Corfu Street	5 A1
Coulton Lane	5 A4
Cow Lane	5 B2
Cowper Lane	3 B4
Cowper Street	3 B5
Cowper Wharf Roadway	2 D5
Craigend Street	5 B1
Crane Place	1 B3
Crick Avenue	2 E5
Cross Lane	2 D5
Cross Street (Pyrmont)	3 B1
Cross Street (Double Bay)	6 F1
Crown Lane	5 A1
Crown Street (Glebe)	3 B5
Crown Street (Woolloomooloo)	2 D5
continues (Surry Hills)	5 A3
Cumberland Street	1 A3
Curtin Place	1 B4
continues	4 E1
Customs House	1 B3

D

Dalgety Road	1 A2
Dalley Street	1 B3
Dargan Lane	3 B3
Darghan Street	3 A3
Darley Place	5 B2
Darley Street	5 B2
Darling Drive	3 C2

Darling Harbour
Passenger
Terminal 1 A4
& 4D1
Darling Island Road 3 C1
Darling Lane 3 A4
Darling Point Road 6 E1
Darling Street 3 A4
Darlinghurst Court
House 5 A2
Darlinghurst Road 5 A2
Davies Street 5 A4
Davoren Lane 5 A4
Dawes Point Park 1 B1
Day Street 4 D3
Demestre Place 1 B4
continues 4 E1
Denham Street 5 A3
Denman Lane 3 B4
Derby Place 3 B5
Derwent Lane 3 A5
Derwent Street 3 A5
Devonshire Street 5 A4
Dillon Lane 5 C2
Dillon Street 5 C2
Dixon Street 4 D3
Domain, The 1 C4
Dorhauer Lane 6 E4
Douglass Lane 4 E3
Dowling Street 2 D5
continues 5 B1
Downshire Street 1 A2
Driver Avenue 5 B4
Druitt Lane 4 D3
Druitt Place 1 A5
continues 4 D2
Druitt Street 1 A5
continues 5 E2
Dudley Street 6 D3
Duxford Street 6 D3
Dwyer Lane 6 E4
Dwyer Street 4 D5

E

Eagar Lane 4 E3
Earl Place 5 B1
Earl Street 2 E5
continues 5 B1
Eastern Distributor 5 A2
Ebenezer Lane 3 B5
Ebenezer Place 3 B5
Eddy Avenue 4 E5
Edgecliff Road 6 F2
Edgely Street 5 A5
Edward Lane 3 C2
Edward Street 3 C2
Egan Place 5 A1
El Alamein Fountain 2 E5
Elfred Street 5 C3
Elger Street 3 B4
Elizabeth Bay House 2 F5
Elizabeth Bay Road 2 F5
Elizabeth Place 6 D4
Elizabeth Street
(Paddington) 6 D4
Elizabeth Street
(Sydney) 1 B5
continues 4 E5
Empire Lane 1 B4
continues 4 E1
Entertainment Centre 4 D4
Erskine Street 1 A4
continues 4 D1
Esplanade 2 F5
Essex Street 1 A3
Esther Street 5 A4
Evans Road 2 F5
Experiment Street 3 C2

F

Factory Street 4 D4
Fanny Place 5 A4
Farrell Avenue 5 B1
Faucett Lane 5 A1
Ferry Lane 3 A3
Ferry Road 3 A3
Fig Street 3 B3
Fitzroy Place 5 A3
Fitzroy Street 4 F5
continues 5 A3
Five Ways 5 C3
Flemings Lane 5 A3
Flinders Street 5 A3
Floods Lane 5 A3
Foley Street 5 A2
Forbes Street
(Darlinghurst) 5 A2
Forbes Street
(Paddington) 6 E3
Foreshore Road 3 B1
Forsyth Lane 3 A3
Forsyth Street 3 A3
Fort Denison 2 E1
Forth Street 6 F4
Foster Street 4 E4
Foveaux Street 4 E5,
continues 5 A3
Fox Studios 6 D5
Francis Lane 5 A1
Francis Street
(Darlinghurst) 4 F3
Francis Street
(Glebe) 3 B5
continues 5 A1
Franklyn Street 3 B5
Fullerton Street 6 F3
Furber Lane 6 D5
Furber Road 6 D5

G

Garran Lane 3 A3
Garrison Church 1 A2
George Lane 6 D4
George Street
(Paddington) 6 D4
George Street
(Sydney) 1 B5
continues 4 E4
Gipps Street
(Paddington) 5 B3
Gipps Street
(Pyrmont) 3 B2
Glebe Island Bridge 3 A2
Glebe Lane 3 A4
Glebe Point Road 3 A4
Glebe Street
(Edgecliff) 6 E2
Glebe Street
(Glebe) 3 A4
Glen Street 5 C2
Glenmore Road 5 B3
Glenview Lane 5 C2
Glenview Street 5 C2
Gloucester Street 1 B2
Goderich Lane 5 B1
Goldman Lane 6 F1
Goodchap Street 4 F4
Goold Street 4 D5
Gordon Lane 6 D4
Gordon Street 6 D4
Gosbell Lane 5 C2
Gosbell Street 5 C2
Gottenham Lane 3 A4
Gottenham Street 3 A4
Goulburn Lane 4 F4

Goulburn Street 4 D4
continues 5 A2
Government House 1 C2
Grafton Lane 3 C5
Grafton Street 3 C5
Grand Drive 6 E5
Grantham Street 2 E4
Great Synagogue 1 B5
Great Thorne Street 6 E2
Greek Street 3 B5
Green Park 5 B2
Greenknowe Avenue 2 E5
Greenoaks Avenue 6 E1
Greens Road 5 B3
Gregory Avenue 5 B5
Gresham Street 1 B3
Griffin Street 4 F5
Griffiths Street 2 D5
Grose Street 3 B5
Grosvenor Street 1 A3
Guilfoyle Avenue 6 F1
Gumtree Lane 6 F2
Gurner Lane 6 D2
Gurner Street 6 D3

H

Hackett Street 3 C4
Haig Avenue 1 C5
continues 4 F2
Haig Lane 1 C5
Halls Lane 6 E4
Hamilton Drive 6 E5
Hampden Street 6 D2
Hands Lane 4 F4
Hannam Street 5 A3
Harbour Street 4 D3
Harbourside Festival
Marketplace 1 C2
Hardie Street 5 B2
Hargrave Lane
(Darlinghurst) 4 F3
Hargrave Lane
(Paddington) 6 D3
Hargrave Street 6 D3
Harmer Street 2 D5
Harnett Street 2 E5
Harrington Street 1 B3
Harris Street
(Paddington) 6 E3
Harris Street
(Pyrmont) 3 B1
Harris Street Motor
Museum 3 C3
Harwood Lane 3 C2
Harwood Street 3 C2
Hay Street 4 D4
Hayden Lane 5 B2
Hayden Place 5 B2
Heeley Lane 5 C3
Heeley Street 5 C3
Henrietta Street 6 F2
Henry Avenue 3 C3
Henson Lane 3 C4
Herbert Road 6 E2
Herbert Street 3 B1
Hercules Street 4 F5
Hero of Waterloo 1 A2
Hickson Road 1 A2
High Lane 1 A2
High Street
(Edgecliff) 6 E2
High Street
(Millers Point) 1 A2
Hill Street 5 A3
HJ Foley Rest Park 3 A4
Hoddle Street 6 D2
Holdsworth Avenue 2 F5

Holdsworth Street 6 E3
Holt Street
(Double Bay) 6 F2
Holt Street
(Surry Hills) 4 F5
Hopetoun Lane 6 D3
Hopetoun Street 6 D3
Hopewell Lane 5 B3
Hopewell Street 5 B3
Hoskin Place 1 B4
continues 4 E1
Hospital Road 1 C5
continues 4 F2
Hourigan Lane 2 E5
Hughes Lane 2 E5
Hughes Place 2 E5
Hughes Street 2 E5
Hunt Street 4 F4
Hunter Street 1 B4
continues 4 E1
Hutchinson Lane 5 A3
Hutchinson Street 5 A3
Hyde Park 4 F2
Hyde Park Barracks 1 C5

I

Ice Street 5 B2
Iris Street 5 B4
Ithaca Road 2 F5

J

James Lane
(Darling Harbour) 4 D3
James Lane
(Paddington) 6 D2
James Street
(Darling Harbour) 4 D3
James Street
(Woollahra) 6 E4
Jamison Street 1 A3
Jenkins Street 1 A3
Jersey Road 6 D4
Jesmond Street 5 A3
John Street
(Pyrmont) 3 B1
John Street
(Woollahra) 6 E4
Jones Bay Road 3 B1
Jones Lane 3 C3
Jones Street 3 A1
Josephson Street 5 B4
Judge Lane 5 B1
Judge Street 5 B1
Junction Lane 2 D5
Juniper Hall 5 C3
Justice and Police
Museum 1 C3

K

Keegan Avenue 3 A4
Kellett Street 5 B1
Kells Lane 5 A2
Kelly Street 3 C5
Kendall Lane 5 A4
Kendall Street 5 A4
Kennedy Street 5 A1
Kensington Street 4 D5
Kent Street 1 A2
continues 4 D1
Kettle Lane 3 C5
Kidman Lane 5 B3
Kilminster Lane 6 F4
Kimber Lane 4 D4
King Street 1 A4
continues 4 D1

Kings Cross Road 5 B1
Kings Lane 5 A2
Kippax Street 4 E5
Kirk Street 3 C3
Kirketon Road 5 B1
Knox Lane 6 F1
Knox Street
 (Chippendale) 3 C5
Knox Street
 (Double Bay) 6 F1

L

Lacrozia Lane 5 B2
Lands Department
 Building 1 B3
Lang Park 1 A3
Lang Road 6 D5
Lang Street 1 A3
Lawson Lane 6 D2
Lawson Street 5 C2
Lee Street 4 D5
Lees Court 1 B4
 continues 4 E1
Leichhardt Street 5 B2
Leinster Street 5 C4
Lincoln Court 2 D4
Lincoln Place 6 F2
Lindsay Lane 5 C2
Little Albion Street 4 F5
Little Bloomfield
 Street 5 A2
Little Bourke Street 5 A2
Little Cleveland
 Street 5 A5
Little Comber Street 5 B3
Little Dowling Street 5 A3
Little Hay Street 4 D4
Little Mount Street 3 B2
Little Oxford Street 5 A2
Little Regent Street 4 D5
Little Riley Street 4 F5
Little Stewart Street 5 C4
Little Surrey Street 5 A1
Liverpool Lane 5 A1
Liverpool Street 4 E3
 continues
 (Darlinghurst) 5 A1
Liverpool Street
 (Paddington) 5 C3
Loch Avenue 6 F5
Lodge Street 3 A5
Loftus Lane 1 B3
Loftus Road 6 E1
Loftus Street 1 B3
Lombard Lane 3 A4
Lombard Street 3 A4
Lower Avon Street 3 A3
Lower Fort Street 1 A2
Lyndhurst Street 3 A4
Lyons Lane 4 F3

M

Macarthur Avenue 5 B5
Macarthur Street 3 C4
Macdonald Lane
 (Paddington) 5 C2
McDonald Lane
 (Potts Point) 2 E4
Macdonald Street
 (Paddington) 5 B2
McDonald Street
 (Potts Point) 2 E4
McElhone Place 5 A4
McElhone Street 2 E5
 continues 5 B1

McGarvie Street 6 D4
McKee Street 3 C4
Mackey Street 4 F5
McLachlan Avenue 5 C2
McLaughlan Place 5 C3
Macleay Street 2 E5
Macquarie Place 1 B3
Macquarie Street 1 C4
 continues 4 F1
Maiden Lane 5 A3
Manning Road 6 F2
Manning Street 2 E5
Mansion Lane 5 C1
Marathon Lane 6 E1
Marathon Road 6 E1
Marble Bar 1 B5
Margaret Street 1 A4
 continues 4 D1
Market Row 1 A5
 continues 4 E2
Market Street 1 A5
 continues 4 D2
Marlborough Lane 3 A4
Marlborough Street 3 A4
Marshall Street 5 A4
Martin Place 1 B4
 continues 4 E1
Martin Street 5 C4
Mary Ann Street 3 C5
Mary Lane 4 F5
Mary Place 5 B3
Mary Street 4 E5
Melrose Lane 6 D4
Merchants' House 1 B2
Mill Street 3 B1
Miller Lane 3 B2
Miller Street 3 B2
Mitchell Lane East 3 B4
Mitchell Lane West 3 B4
Mitchell Street
 (Centennial Park) 6 D5
Mitchell Street
 (Glebe) 3 A5
Mona Lane 6 D1
Mona Road 6 E1
Moncur Lane 6 E4
Moncur Street 6 E4
Moore Park 5 A4
Moore Park Road 5 B4
Moorgate Street 3 C5
Morrell Street 6 E4
Mort Lane 5 A5
Mort Street 5 A5
Morton Lane 6 F4
Mount Street 3 B1
Mount Vernon Lane 3 A5
Mount Vernon Street 3 A5
Mountain Lane 3 C5
Mountain Street 3 C5
Mrs Macquaries
 Chair 2 E2
Mrs Macquaries
 Road 2 D4
Murray Street 3 C2
Museum of
 Contemporary Art 1 B2
Museum of Sydney 1 B3

N

Napier Street 5 B3
Napoleon Street 1 A3
National Maritime
 Museum 3 C2
National Trust
 Centre 1 A3
Neild Avenue 5 C2
Nelson Lane 6 F4

Nesbitt Street 2 E5
New Beach Road 6 D1
New McLean Street 6 E2
New South Head
 Road 6 D1
Newcombe Street 6 D4
Nichols Street 5 A3
Nicholson Street 2 D5
Nickson Lane 5 A5
Nickson Street 5 A5
Nimrod Street 5 B1
Nithsdale Street 4 F4
Nobbs Lane 5 A4
Nobbs Street 5 A4
Norfolk Lane 6 D3
Norfolk Street 6 D3
Norman Street 4 F4
Norton Street
 (Glebe) 3 A4
Norton Street
 (Surry Hills) 4 F5

O

O'Briens Lane 5 A1
O'Connell Street 1 B4
 continues 4 E1
O'Loughlin Street 4 E5
O'Sheas Lane 5 A3
Oatley Road 5 C4
Observatory Park 1 A2
Ocean Avenue 6 F2
Ocean Street 6 E2
Octagon Road 6 E1
Olive Street 5 C3
Olivia Lane 5 A4
Omnibus Lane 4 D4
Old Gaol,
 Darlinghurst 5 A2
Onslow Avenue 2 F5
Onslow Place 2 F5
Ormond Street 5 C3
Orwell Lane 2 E5
Orwell Street 2 E5
Osborne Lane 6 F4
Oswald Street 6 D1
Overseas Passenger
 Terminal 1 B2
Owen Lane 3 C5
Owen Street 3 C5
Oxford Square 4 F4
Oxford Street 4 F3
 continues 5 A2

P

Paddington Bazaar 3 C5
Paddington Lane 6 D3
Paddington Street 6 D3
Paddington Town
 Hall 5 C3
Paddington Village 5 C3
Paddy's Market 4 D4
Palmer Lane 5 A1
Palmer Street 2 D5
 continues 5 A2
Palmerston Avenue 3 A4
Parbury Lane 3 C4
Park Lane 3 B4
Park Street 4 E2
Parker Lane 4 E4
Parker Street 4 E4
Parkes Drive 6 E5
Parkham Lane 5 A4
Parkham Place 5 A5
Parkham Street 5 A5
Parliament House 1 C4

Parramatta Road 3 A5
Paternoster Row 3 B2
Peaker Lane 6 E4
Pelican Street 4 F4
Pennys Lane 5 B1
Perry Lane 5 C3
Phelps Street 5 A4
Phillip Lane 1 C4
Phillip Park 1 C5
 continues 4 F2
Phillip Street (Glebe) 3 B4
Phillip Street
 (Sydney) 1 B4
 continues 4 F1
Pickering Lane 6 F4
Pier Street 4 D4
Pitt Street 1 B5
 continues 4 E4
Plunkett Street 2 D5
Poate Lane 6 D5
Poate Road 6 D5
Point Piper Lane 6 E4
Poplar Street 4 F4
Pottinger Street 1 A2
Powerhouse
 Museum 4 D4
Premier Lane 5 B1
Prince Albert Road 1 C5
 continues 4 F2
Pring Street 2 E5
Prospect Street
 (Paddington) 5 B3
Prospect Street
 (Surry Hills) 5 A4
Pyrmont Bay Park 3 C1
Pyrmont Bridge 1 A5
 continues 4 D2
Pyrmont Bridge
 Road 3 B2
Pyrmont Street 3 B1

Q

Quambi Place 6 F2
Quarry Lane (Glebe) 3 A3
Quarry Lane
 (Ultimo) 3 C3
Quarry Street
 (Paddington) 6 E3
Quarry Street
 (Ultimo) 3 C4
Quay Street 4 D4
Queen Road 6 D4
Queen Street
 (Glebe) 3 B4
Queen Street
 (Woollahra) 6 E4
Queen Victoria
 Building 1 B5
Queens Avenue 5 C1
Queens Square 1 C5

R

Rae Place 2 E5
Railway Square 4 D5
Railway Street 3 A4
Rainford Street 5 A4
Randle Lane 4 E5
Randle Street 4 E5
Raper Street 5 A4
Rawson Lane 4 E5
Rawson Place 4 E4
Reddy Street 6 D1
Regent Street
 (Chippendale) 4 D5
Regent Street
 (Paddington) 5 C4

Reiby Place	1 B3	Slip Street	1 A5, 4 D2	Tara Street	6 F3	Wattle Crescent	3 B3
Renny Lane	5 C4	Smail Lane	3 C5	Taylor Square	5 A2	Wattle Lane	3 C4
Renny Street	5 C4	Smail Street	3 C5	Taylor Street (Glebe)	3 A3	Wattle Place	3 C5
Reservoir Street	4 E4	Smith Street		Taylor Street		Wattle Street	3 B3
Richards Avenue	5 A4	(Surry Hills)	4 F5	(Paddington)	6 E4	Ways Terrace	3 B1
Richards Lane	5 A4	Smith Street		Taylor Street		Weedon Avenue	5 C3
Ridge Lane	5 A5	(Woollahra)	6 E4	(Surry Hills)	5 A3	Weldon Lane	6 F4
Ridge Place	5 A5	Sophia Lane	4 F5	Terry Street	4 E5	Wellington Street	6 F3
Ridge Street	5 A5	Sophia Street	4 E5	Tewkesbury Avenue	5 B1	Wemyss Lane	4 F4
Riley Street	1 C5	Soudan Lane	6 E3	Thomas Lane	4 D4	Wentworth Avenue	4 F4
continues	5 A2	South Avenue	6 F1	Thomas Street	3 C5	Wentworth Park	3 B3
Rockwall Crescent	2 E5	South Dowling Street	5 A5	Thomson Lane	5 A1	Wentworth Park	
Rockwall Lane	2 E5	South Lane	6 F1	Thomson Street	5 A2	Road	3 B3
Rodens Lane	1 A2	South Street	6 D2	Thorne Street	6 E2	Wentworth Street	
Rosebank Street	3 A4	Spence Lane	5 A1	Thurlow Lane	5 A5	(Glebe)	3 B4
Rosella Lane	5 A1	Spicer Street	6 E3	Tivoli Street	6 D4	Wentworth Street	
Rosemont Avenue	6 F3	Spring Street		Towns Place	1 A2	(Paddington)	6 D4
Roslyn Gardens	2 F5	(Double Bay)	6 F1	Trelawney Street	6 F3	West Avenue	5 B2
continues	5 C1	Spring Street		Trinity Avenue	1 A2	West Lane	5 B2
Roslyn Lane	5 C1	(Paddington)	5 B3	Trumper Park	6 E2	West Street	5 B3
Roslyn Street	5 C1	Springfield Avenue	2 E5	Tumbalong Park	4 D3	Westend Lane	3 C5
Rowe Lane	5 C3	Stafford Lane	5 C3	Turner Lane	2 D5	Western Distributor	1 A4
Rowe Street	1 B4	Stafford Street	5 C3	Tusculum Lane	2 E5	continues	4 D1
continues	4 E1	Stanley Lane	5 A1	Tusculum Street	2E5	Westin Hotel	1 B4
Royal Agricultural		Stanley Street				Westmoreland Lane	3 A5
Society (RAS)		(Darlinghurst)	5 A1			Westmoreland Street	3 A5
Showground	5 C5	Stanley Street		**U**		Westpac Museum	1 B2
Royal Botanic		(Redfern)	5 A5	Ulster Street	6 D4	Wharf Theatre	1 A1
Gardens	1 C3	State Library of NSW	1 C4	Ultimo Road	4 D4	Wheat Road	1 A5
Roylston Lane	6 D2	State Theatre	1 B5	Underwood Street		continues	4 D2
Rush Street	6 E4	Stephen Lane	5 C2	(Paddington)	5 C3	Whelan Lane	6 E4
Rushcutters Bay Park	6 D1	Stephen Street	5 C2	Underwood Street		White Lane	6 D3
Ryder Street	5 A2	Stewart Place	6 D4	(Sydney)	1 B3	Whitlam Square	4 F3
		Stewart Street	5 C4	Union Lane		William Henry Street	3 C4
		Steyna Park	6 F1	(Paddington)	6 D3	William Lane	5 A1
S		Stirling Lane	3 B4	Union Lane		William Street	
Sailors' Home	1 B2	Stirling Street	3 B4	(Pyrmont)	3 C2	(Darlinghurst)	4 F3
St Andrew's		Strand Arcade	1 B5	Union Street		continues	5 A1
Cathedral	4 E3	Stream Street	5 A1	(Paddington)	6 D3	William Street	
St Barnabas Street	3 C5	Sturt Street	5 A2	Union Street		(Double Bay)	6 F1
St James' Church	1 B5	Suffolk Street	6 D3	(Pyrmont)	3 B2	William Street	
St James Road	1 B5	Surrey Lane	5 B1	University Avenue	3 B5	(Paddington)	6 D3
continues	4 F2	Surrey Street	5 B1	University Place	3 A5	Wilmot Street	4 E3
St James Road	6 F5	Susannah Place	1 B2	University of Sydney	3 A5	Wilson Street	2 D5
St Johns Road	3 A5	Sussex Lane	1 A4, 4 D1	Upper Fig Street	3 C3	Windmill Street	1 A2
St Marks Road	6 E1	Sussex Street	1 A3, 4 D1	Upper Fort Street	1 A2	Windsor Lane	6 D3
St Mary's Cathedral	1 C5	Sutherland Avenue	6 D3	Uther Street	4 F5	Windsor Street	6 D3
St Marys Road	1 C5	Sutherland Street	6 D3			Wisdom Lane	5 A1
continues	4 F2	Suttor Street	5 A1			Womerah Avenue	5 B2
St Neot Avenue	2 E4	Sydney Aquarium	1 A5	**V**		Womerah Lane	5 C2
St Peters Lane	5 A1		& 4 D1	Valentine Street	4 D5	Woods Avenue	6 F4
St Peters Street	5 A1	Sydney Art Gallery	3 C3	Vaughan Place	5 A5	Woods Lane	5 A1
St Philip's Church	1 A3	Sydney Cricket		Verona Street	5 B3	Woolloomooloo	
Samuel Street	4 F4	Ground	5 C5	Vialoux Avenue	6 D2	Finger Wharf	2 D4
Sandringham		Sydney Dance and Theatre		Vials Lane	6 D4	Wright Lane	4 E4
Gardens	1 C5, 4 F2	Company	1 A1	Victoria Avenue	6 E4	Writers' Walk	1 C2
Sands Street	4 D3	Sydney Fish Market	3 B2	Victoria Barracks	5 B4	Wylde Street	2 E4
Saunders Street	3 A2	Sydney Football		Victoria Park	3 B5	Wynyard Lane	1 B4, 4 E1
Science Road	3 A5	Stadium	5 C4	Victoria Place	6 D4	Wynyard Park	1 A4
Seale Street	5 A1	Sydney Harbour		Victoria Street		continues	4 E1
Seamer Street	3 A5	Bridge	1 B1	(Paddington)	6 D4	Wynyard Street	1 A4
Sega World	4 D3	Sydney Harbour		Victoria Street		continues	4 E1
Selwyn Street	5 B3	Tunnel	1 C2	(Potts Point)	2 E5		
Seymour Place	5 A3	Sydney Hospital	1 C4	continues	5 B2		
Shadforth Street	5 C3	Sydney Jewish				**Y**	
Shakespeare Place	1 C4	Museum	5 B2	**W**		York Lane	1 A4
continues	4 F1	Sydney Mint Museum	1 C4	Waimea Avenue	6 F4	continues	4 E1
Shepherd Street	3 C5	Sydney Observatory	1 A2	Waine Street	4 F4	York Lane	
Sherbrooke Street	5 A2	Sydney Opera House	1 C2	Walker Avenue	6 D2	(Bondi Junction)	6 F5
Short Street		Sydney Tower	1 B5	Walker Lane	5 C3	York Place	6 F5
(Darling Point)	6 F1	Sydney Town Hall	4 E2	Walker Street	5 C3	York Road	6 F5
Short Street		Systrum Street	4 D4	Wallis Street	6 E5	York Street	1 A4
(Paddington)	5 A3			Walter Street	5 C4	continues	4 E1
Shorter Lane	5 A1			Waratah Street	5 C1	Young Street	1 B3
Sims Street	5 A3	**T**		Ward Avenue	5 C1	Young Street	
Sir John Young		Talbot Place	5 A1	Waterloo Street	4 F5	(Paddington)	5 C3
Crescent	2 D5	Talfourd Lane	3 A4	Watson Road	1 A2	Yurong Lane	5 A1
Sisters Lane	6 F2	Talfourd Street	3 A4	Watson Street	6 D4	Yurong Street	4 F3

General Index

Page numbers in **bold** type
refer to main entries.

A

Aaron's (hotel) 174
Abbey's Bookshop 206, 207
Aboriginal and Tribal Art
  Centre 206, 207
Aboriginal peoples
  art 111, 154, 206, 207
  community 41, 42
  culture 34
  land rights 29
  rock art 18–19, 154
Academy Twin 210, 211
Across the black soil plains
  (Lambert) 110
Admiralty House 132
Air New Zealand 229
Air travel 228–9
Airport hotels 229
Akira Isogawa 204, 205
Alhambra 185, 193
Alishan International
  Guesthouse 177
All Seasons Premier Menzies
  Hotel 173
Allan, Percy 98
Aloha Surf 54
Ambulance 223
American (United States)
  Consulate General 221
American Express 224
AMP Building 63
AMP Tower (see Sydney Tower)
ANA Hotel Sydney 172
Andrew (Boy) Charlton Pool 57,
  105
Anglican Church 221
Angus and Robertson's
  Bookworld 206, 207
Annandale Hotel 214, 215
Ansett Australia 228, 229
Anthem Records 206, 207
Anzac Day 50, 84
Anzac Memorial **86**
  history 26
  Sydney's Best 36, 39
AQA 169, 170
Aqua Dining 185, 186
Aqua Luna 184, 191
Archibald Fountain 78, 86
Archibald Prize 26
Archibald, Wynne, Sulman and
  Dobell Exhibitions 50
Architecture **36–9**
  Elizabeth Bay House 22–3
  Sydney Opera House 77
Argyle Stores 38, **68**
Argyle Cut 64
Ariel (bookshop) 206, 207

Armistice 26
Armstrong's Manly 185, 188
The Arrest of Bligh 21
Art Gallery Brasserie 194, 195
Art Gallery of New South Wales
  15, **108–111**
  area map 103
  Asian art 111
  Australian art 110
  contemporary art 111
  European art 110
  photography 110
  prints and drawings 111
  Sydney's Best 33, 34
  Yiribana Gallery 111
Ausfurs 206, 207
Aussie Boys (shop) 204, 205
Australia Cinema 210, 211
Australia Day 51
Australia Day Concert 49
Australia Ensemble 212, 213
Australia Square 39
Australian Accommodation
  Services 168, 170
Australian Ballet, The 213
Australian Beach Pattern
  (Meere) 33
Australian Book Fair 51
Australian Chamber Orchestra
  212, 213
Australian Craftworks 206, 207
Australian Museum **88–9**
  shop 206, 207
  Sydney's Best 33, 34–5
Australian rules football 52
Australian Sailing Academy 54
Australian Tourist Commission
  Offices 218
Australian Women's Weekly 27
Australian Youth Choir 213
Australiana 206, 207
Automatic cash dispensers 224
Autumn Racing Carnival 50
Autumn in Sydney 50
Avalon 55
Avillion Hotel 173
Avis 236, 237
AWA Radiolette 27

B

Baby changing facilities 221
Bacon, Francis
  Study for Self Portrait 110
The Balcony (2) (Whiteley) 110
Bally 205
Balmain **131**
  market 131, **203**
  Birchgrove 143
  court house 143
  Darling Street 142–3
  East Balmain 142

Balmain (cont)
  fire station 143
  guided walk 142–3
  post office 143
  town hall 143
Balmoral 54, 55
Balmoral Sailboard School 54
Banc (restaurant) 178, 184, 186
Bangarra Dance Theatre 42, 213
Bank of New South Wales 22
Bank notes 225
Banking 224
Banks, Sir Joseph 17, 138
Baptist church 221
Bar Coluzzi 194, 195
Barnaby's Riverside 185, 186
Barnet, James 72
  Australian Museum 88
  Lands Department
    Building 84
Barney, Lieutenant Colonel
  George 127
Barrington 20
Barton, Edmond 26
Bars *see* Pubs and bars
Basement, The 214, 215
The Basin 55, 155
Basketball 52
Bass, George 21
The Bathers Pavilion
  (restaurant) 185, 186
Bayswater Brasserie 185, 188
  Sydney's Best 185
BBQ King 184, 189
Beaches 54–5
  map 55
  Sydney's Top 30 Beaches 55
Beare Park **120**, 121
Beccafumi, Domenico
  *Madonna and Child with
  Infant St John the Baptist* 108
Beckmann, Max
  Old Woman in Ermine 110
Bed and Breakfast Sydneyside
  170
Bel Mondo 184, 191
Bell Shakespeare Company, The
  210, 211
Bellevue Hotel 196, 197
Belvoir Street Theatre 210, 211
Bennelong 20
Beppi's 184, 191
Beresford Hotel 214, 215
Betty's Soup Kitchen 194, 195
Beyond Sydney 151–65
  area map 152–3
  Blue Mountains 160–61
  Hawkesbury 156–7
  Hunter Valley 158–9
  Pittwater and Ku-ring-gai
    Chase 154–5
  Royal National Park 164–5

Beyond Sydney (cont)
Southern Highlands 162–3
Bibb, John 66
Bicentenary 28
Bicentennial Park 44
Bicycles 52, **237**
Biennale of Sydney 50
Bikescape Motorcycle Rentals
and Tours 219
Bilgola 55, 155
Bill's (café) 194, 195
Billy Kwong 185, 189
Birchgrove
Balmain Walk 143
park 143
Birdland (records) 206–7
Birtley Towers 119
Bistro CBD 184, 192
Bistro Lulu 185, 188
Bistro Moncur 185, 192
Blacket, Edmund 87
Garrison Church 69
Justice and Police Museum 72
St Philip's Church 73
University of Sydney 130
Blacket Hotel 173
Bligh, Governor William 20
Bligh House 38
Blue Mountains National Park
160–61
camping 170, 171
Cathedral of Ferns 161
Govett's Leap 160
Grose River 160
history 18
Jamison Valley 161
Jenolan Caves 160
King's Tableland 161
Leura 161
map 160–61
Mount Tomah Botanic
Gardens 161
Mount Wilson 161
The Three Sisters 160
Wentworth Falls 161
Yester Grange 161
Zig Zag Railway 160
Boathouse on Blackwattle Bat,
The 185, 189
Boats
The Borrowdale 20
The Bounty 219
Carpentaria 92, 95
Dunbar 24, 136, 148
Endeavour (replica), 95
ferries **234–5**
ferry sightseeing cruises 235
harbour and river cruises 219
HMB *Endeavour* 32
HMS *Beagle* 23
HMS *Sirius* 72
Lady Juliana 20

Boats (cont)
Matilda Cruises 219
National Maritime Museum 93,
94–5
Orcades 94
Pittwater and Ku-ring-gai
Chase **154–5**
Royal National Park **164–5**
sailing 54, 56
Vampire 93, 95
water taxis 235
The Waverly 25
Bodhi in the Park 184, 190
Boer War 24
Bondi Baths
Bondi Beach **137**
Aboriginal art 19
baths 144
beaches 54–5
Campbell Parade 144
guided walk 144–5
Hotel Bondi 144
map 129
market **203**
Pavilion 144
Surf Bathers' Life Saving Club
137, 144
Bondi Beach Coke Classic 49
Bondi North 144
Bondi Pavilion
Bondi Beach to Clovelly Walk
144
Bondi Surf Bathers' Life Saving
Club 137, 144
Bondi Surf Co. 54, 205
Bookshop Darlinghurst, The
206, 207
Bookshops 206, 207
Boomalli Aboriginal Artists'
Cooperative 206, 207
Boomerangs 19
Botanic Gardens and The
Domain **102–15**
area map 103
hotels 175
restaurants 184, 186
spring festival 48
Street-by-Street map 104–5
Botanic Gardens Restaurant 184,
186
Bounty Cruises 219
Boy in Township (Nolan) 110
Boyd, Arthur 110
Bracewell 204, 205
Bradfield, Dr John 71
Bradleys Head 45
Bradman, Donald 27
Breakout Tours 170
Brett Whiteley Studio 34, **130**
The Bridge in Curve
(Cossington-Smith) 71
Bridge Hotel 211, 214, 215

BridgeClimb 71
British Airways 229
British community 42
Bronte
beaches 54–5
Bronte Gully 145
Bronte House 145
Bronte Park 145
Bondi Beach to Clovelly Walk
144–5
Bubonic plague 59
Bungaree 23
Budget (car hire) 236, 237
The Bulletin 25
Bunny, Rupert
A Summer Morning 110
Summer Time 110
Buon Ricardo 185, 191
Bureaux de change 224
Burke (Nolan) 110
Buses **231**
sightseeing by bus 231
tickets 230–1
Busby's Bore 87
Busby, John 87
Buzo 185, 193

C

Cabaret venues 214, 215
Cabramatta 18, 40, 43
Cadman, John 68
Street-by-Street map 65
Cadman, Elizabeth
Street-by-Street map 65
Cadman's Cottage 68
museums and galleries 35
Sydney's Best 36, 38
Cadmus 184, 193
Café at the Gate of Salvation 213
Café Dendu 194, 195
Café Hernandez 194, 195
Cafés **178–85**, **194–5**
coffee and tea 194, 195
galleries and garden 194, 195
snacks and light meals 194, 195
takeaway food 195
Camp Cove
beaches 54–5
Watsons Bay and Vaucluse
Walk 148
Campbell Parade
Campbell, Robert 66, 139
Campbell's Storehouses **66**
Camping 170, 171
Canadian Airlines 229
Canadian Consulate General 221
Capitol Square Hotel 173
Capitol Theatre **99**, 210, 211
Captain Cook Cruises 219
Captain Cook's Landing Place
138

Car hire companies 237
Carla Zampatti 204, 205
Carlton Crest 174
Carnivale 48
Carols in the Domain 49
Carrington Hotel 177
Cars **236–7**
  car hire 236, 237
  driving in Sydney 236–7
  driving to Sydney 229
  driving regulations 236
  Infringement Processing
    Bureau 237
  parking 236
  Sydney Traffic Control Centre
    237
Casa Asturiana 184, 193
Castlereagh Inn 173
Castlereagh Street
  Sydney's Best 201
Cat and Fiddle 214, 215
Catalina Rose Bay 185, 186
Catholic church 221
Cave (nightclub) 214, 215
Ccino's 194, 195
Celsius (restaurant) 184, 186
Cenotaph 84
  Street-by-Street map 81
Centennial Park 15, **127**
  cycling 52
  Sydney's Best 45
Centennial Park Café and
  Restaurant 194, 195
Centennial Park Cycles 53, 237
Central Park Hotel 173
Central Railway Station 218,
  229
Central Station Records and
  Tapes 206, 207
Centrepoint 199
Centre for Contemporary Craft
  72
Certo Ristorante 184, 191
Chamber music 212
Charlton, Andrew "Boy" 27, 57
*Chaucer at the Court of Edward
  III* (Madox Brown) 110
Chauvel (cinema) 210, 211
Chifley Plaza 199
Children's theatre 210, 211
Chinatown **99**
  Sydney's Best 200
Chinese community 41, 42
Chinese Garden 92, **98**
Chinese New Year 49
Chisholm, Caroline 23, 25
Christmas at Bondi Beach 49
Churches
  Anglican church 221
  Baptist church 221
  Catholic church 221
  Garrison Church **68–9**

Churches (cont)
  Presbyterian church 221
  St Andrew's Cathedral **87**
  St Andrew's Church 143
  St James Church 36, 38, **115**
  St Mary's Cathedral 25, 38, **86**
  St Philip's Church **73**
  Uniting Church 221
Cinema Paris 210, 211
Circular Quay, The Rocks and
  city shoreline 59
City Centre **79–89**
  area map 79
  hotels 173–4
  restaurants 184
  Street-by-Street map 80–81
  Sydney's Best 201
City Circle Railway 87
City Extra 194, 195
City Mutual Life Assurance
  Building 39
City Recital Hall, The 212, 213
City shoreline
  Garden Island to Farm Cove
    56–7
  Sydney Cove to Walsh Bay
    58–9
City to Surf Race 51
CityRail 232–3
CityRail Information 233
Civic Hotel 196, 197
Claude's (restaurant) 185, 192
Clifton Gardens 55
Climate 48–51
Clontarf
  Balmain Walk 142
Clothes and accessories
  204–5
Cloud 9 Balloon Flights 219
Clovelly
  beaches 55
  Bondi Beach to Clovelly Walk
    145
Club 77 214, 215
Coach services 229
Coast (restaurant) 184, 186
Coburn, John
  Curtain of the Moon 75
Cockatoo Island 106
Cockle Bay 91, 93
  Street-by-Street map 92–3
Coins 225
Collins Beach 147
Colonial history 35
Collette Dinnigan (shop) 204, 205
Comedy Store 211
Comedy venues 211
Commonwealth Savings Bank 39
Concourse Café 194, 195
Conder, Charles
  *Departure of the Orient –
    Circular Quay* 110

Conservatorium of Music **106**
  concerts 212, 213
Convention and Exhibition
  Centre (Darling Harbour) **98**
  Street-by-Street map 92
Conversion table 221
Coo-ee Aboriginal Art Gallery
  206, 207
Coogee 19
  beaches 54–5
Coogee Bay Hotel 214, 215
Coogee Surf Carnival 49
Cook, Captain James
  history 17, 138
Cook and Phillip Centre 79
Cook's Obelisk 138
Cooper, Robert 126
The Corso 146
The Cortile 196, 197
Cossington-Smith, Grace
  The Bridge in Curve 71
  Interior with Wardrobe Mirror
    110
Country Road 204, 205
Countrylink Travel Centres 170,
  233
Courtney's Brasserie 185, 188
Cox, Philip 39
Cranbrook International 177
Credit cards 224
Crescent on Bayswater (hotel)
  175
Cricket 52
  Donald Bradman 27
  test matches 49, 52
  World Series 29
Criterion 184, 193
Cultures
  Aboriginal Peoples 18–19
  Sydney's Many Cultures
    40–43
Culwalla Chambers 26
Curl Curl 55
Currency 225
The Currency Lass (Geoghegan)
  23
Curtain of the Moon (Coburn) 75
Customs House **72**
Customs House Bar 196, 197
  Sydney's Best 184
Cycling *see* Bicycles

D

Dame Mary Gilmore (Dobell) 29
Dance **213**
Dangerfield (shop) 204, 205
Darling Harbour **91–101**
  area map 91
  Circus and Street Theatre
    Festival 50

Darling Harbour (cont)
  hotels 174–5
  Jazz Festival 51
  restaurants 184
  Street-by-Street map 93
  visitors centre 218
Darling Mills 185, 186
No. 10 Darling Street
  Balmain Walk 142
Darling Street Wharf
  Balmain Walk 142
  ferry routes map 235
Darlinghurst Court House
  121
  Sydney's Best 37, 38
Darlinghurst and Surry Hills
  Sydney's Best 201
Darwin, Charles 23
David Jones 198, 199
  history 23
  men's clothes 204
  shoes 205
  women's clothes 204
David Jones Spring Flower
  Show 48
Dawn (Louisa Lawson) 25
Dawson, Alexander 72
Dayes, Edward
  A View of Sydney Cove 20
D.C.M Nightclub 214, 215
Dee Why 55
Delfin House 39
Deli on Market 195
Dellit, Bruce 36, 39
Del Rio 117, 119
Dendy (cinemas) 210, 211
Dendy Bar & Bistro 196, 197
Dentists 222, 223
*Departure of the Orient –
  Circular Quay* (Conder) 110
Departure tax 220
*Desmond, a New South Wales
  Chief* (Earle) 17
Destination Downunder 170
Dhanyula Nyoka, Tony
  Mud Crabs 32
Dinosaur Designs 206, 207
Diprotodon 18, 33
Disabled travellers 169, 170,
  209, 220
Discount agencies 170, 209
Dive Centre Manly 54
Dixon Street 99
Dobell, William 110
  Dame Mary Gilmore 29
Dobell Memorial Sculpture
  (Flugelman) 84
The Domain 45, **107**, 212
  area map 103
  rock concerts 214, 215
Done Art and Design 206, 207
Dorian Scott (shop) 204, 205

Doyle's Seafood Restaurant 136,
  148, 185, 189
Dragon Boat Race Festival 50
Drinking fountains 221
Driving regulations 236
Drysdale, Russell 110
  Sofala 108
Dugong Hunt
  (Wurrabadalumba) 34
  Dunbar 24
  Watsons Bay 136, 148
Dupain, Max
  Sunbaker 108
Duxford Street
  Street-by-Street map 124
Dymocks 206, 207

E

Earle, Augustus
  *Desmond, a New South Wales
    Chief* 17
  View from the Summit 22
The Early Colony 20–21
East Sail 54
Eastern Creek Raceway
  rock concerts 214, 215
Eastern Suburbs Railway 29
ECQ 184, 188
Edge Theatre 213
Edge of the Trees (Laurence and
  Foley) 85
Edna's Table 184, 186
dward Meller 205
Edward, Prince of Wales 26
El Alamein Fountain **120**
Electrical appliances 221
Eleni's 185, 193
Elio 185, 192
Elizabeth II, Queen 28
Elizabeth Bay 15, 119
Elizabeth Bay House **22–3**, **120**
  history 22–23
  Street-by-Street map 119
  Sydney's Best: Architecture 37,
    38
  Sydney's Best: Museums and
    Galleries 33, 35
Elizabeth Farm **138**
  colonial history 21, 35
Elston, Hocking and Woods 210,
  211
Embassies and consulates 221
  Canada 221
  New Zealand 221
  Republic of Ireland 221
  United Kingdom 221
  USA 221
Emden gun 87
Emergency services 223
Emporio Armani 204, 205
Endeavour, HMS 138

Enmore Theatre 214, 215
Ensemble Theatre 210, 211
Entertainment in Sydney **208–15**
  buying tickets 208
  children's theatre 210
  comedy 211
  disabled visitors 209
  discount tickets 209
  gay and lesbian venues 214,
    215
  information 208, 209
  music venues and nightclubs
    214–15
  opera, orchestras and dance
    212–13
  theatre and film 210–11
Environmental hazards 223
EP1 Nightclub 214, 215
SH Ervin Gallery 73
Establishment (bar) 196, 197
Establishment Hotel 173
Eternity, Mr (Arthur Stace) 29
Etiquette 219
Eugene Goossens Hall 212, 213
Euro-Asia Rex Hotel 175
Evelyn Miles 205
Ewenton
  Balmain Walk 142
Exchange Hotel 214, 215
Experiment Farm Cottage **139**
  colonial history 21, 35

F

Fairfax and Roberts 206, 207
Fairy Bower 55, 146
Farm Cove 57
Fat Duck 194, 195
Fax services 226
Federation 26
Federation architecture 26
  Sydney's Best 38, 39
Female Factory 23
Ferries 230, **234–5**
  Bundeena 165
  Circular Quay Ferry Terminal
    234
  ferry tickets 234
  Hawkesbury River 153
  JetCat 234
  Portland 157
  RiverCat 234
  Sackville 156
  sightseeing by ferry 235
  Sydney Ferries Information
    Office 234
  Webbs Creek 157
  Wisemans 157
Ferrython 49
Festival of the Winds 48
Fez Café 184, 193
Film 210, 211

Film censorship ratings 210
Film festivals 210–11
  Academy Twin 211
  Festival of Jewish Cinema 211
  Flickerfest International Short
    Film Festival 211
  Gay and Lesbian Film Festival
    211
  Sydney Film Festival 210
The First Fleet 16, 20
First Fleet Ship (Holman) 20
Fishermans Beach 55
Fish Records 207
Fishface 184, 188
Five Ways 126
  Street-by-Street map 124
Flame Opals 206, 207
Flinders Hotel 214, 215
Flinders, Matthew 21, 22, 23
  cat statue (Trim) 112
Flugelman, Bert
  Dobell Memorial Sculpture 84
Flying Fruit Fly Circus 210, 211
Folkways 206, 207
Food and drink
  beers and spirits 179
  pubs and bars 196–7
  what to drink 182–3
  what to eat 180–1
  see also Cafés; Restaurants
Footbridge Theatre 210, 211
Forbes Terrace 170
Foreign currency exchange
    224
Fort Denison 107
Forty One (restaurant) 184, 187
The Founding of Australia
    (Talmage) 73
Foukes, Francis
  Sketch and Description of the
    Settlement of Sydney Cove 17
Four Points Sheraton 174
Fox Studios 123, 126
Franklin, Miles
  My Brilliant Career 26
Frattini 185, 192
Freshwater 55
Fruit Bats (Onus) 111
Fuel Bistro 194, 195
Fu Manchu (restaurant) 184, 189
Funnel-web spider 46, 89, 223
  Australian Museum 89
Furama Hotel Darling Harbour
    174

G
Gallipoli 26
The Gap
  Watsons Bay 136
  Watsons Bay and Vaucluse
    Walk 148, 149

Garden Island 56
Garie Beach 153
Garigal National Park 44
Garrison Church 68–9
  Street-by-Street map 64
Gary Castles 205
Gas (nightclub) 214, 215
Gay and lesbian
  accommodation 170
  Film Festival 211
  Mardi Gras Festival 28, 49
Gemstone Boutique 206, 207
General Pants Co. 204, 205
General Post Office (GPO) 38,
    84, 227
Geoghegan, Edward
  The Currency Lass 23
George Street 66
The Georgian Era 22–3
Gibbs, May 35, 132
  Snugglepot and Cuddlepie 67,
    132
Ginger Meggs 67
Ginn, Henry 69
Giulian's 206, 207
Glasser, Neil 82
Glebe 131
  market 131, 203
Gleebooks 206, 207
Glenbrook Crossing 18
Glitz Bijouterie 206, 207
Globe Nightclub 214, 215
Glover, John
  Natives on the Ouse River, Van
    Diemen's Land 110
Golden Century (restaurant)
    184, 190
The Golden Fleece – Shearing at
    Newstead (Roberts) 109, 110
Golden Harbour (restaurant)
    184, 190
Gold rush 24
Golf 52
Goodbar (nightclub) 214, 215
Good Groove Records 206, 207
Gordons Bay 54, 55
Government House 58, 106
Governor Phillip Tower 36,
    39, 85
Gowing Bros 199, 204–5
Grace Bros 198, 199
  shoes 204
  women's clothes 204
Grace Hotel, The 173
Grand National (hotel) 176
Grappa 185, 192
Great Synagogue 38, 86
Greater Union (cinemas) 210,
    211
Greek community 41, 42
Green Bans 29, 120
Green Park Hotel 196, 197

Greenway, Francis 114
  Conservatorium of Music 106
  Hyde Park Barracks 114
  Macquarie Lighthouse 22, 137
  Macquarie Place obelisk 72
  St James Church 36
Greyhound Pioneer Australia 229
La Grillade 185, 193
de Groot, Francis 70
Grotto Point 45
Ground Zero (nightclub) 214,
    215
GST 198
Guide to Sydney for Travellers
    with Disabilities 169
Guided tours and excursions 219
  air tours 219
  coach and motorcycle tours
    219
  ferry sightseeing cruises 235
  harbour and river cruises 219
  walking tours 219
Guillaume at Bennelong 184,
    193
Gumbooya Reserve 19
Gumnut Café 194, 195

H
Halftix 209
Hampton Villa
  Balmain Walk 142
Harbour cruises 58
  Captain Cook Cruises 219
  Quayside Booking Centre 235
Harbour Kitchen and Bar 184,
    187
Harbourside Apartments 177
Harbourside Brasserie 214, 215
Harbourside Shopping Centre
    199
  Street-by-Street map 92
Hardy Brothers 206, 207
Hambledon Cottage 35, 139
Hard Rock Café 194, 195
Harry's Café de Wheels 57, 195
Hawkesbury 156–7
  Hawkesbury Heritage Village
    152, 156
Hawkesbury River ferry 153
Haymarket 99
Hellen Kaminski 205
Hello Darling 206, 207
Helplines 223
Hero of Waterloo 69, 197
  Street-by-Street map 64
Hertz 236, 237
Hilton Sydney 168, 174
  cabaret 214, 215
History 16–29
  Early Colony 20–21
  Georgian Era 22–3

History (cont)
Postwar Sydney 28–9
Sydney Between the Wars 26–7
Sydney's Original Inhabitants 18–19
timeline 18–29
Victorian Sydney 24–5
HMB *Endeavour* 32
HMS *Beagle* 23
HMS *Sirius* 72
Hoff, Raynor 36
Hogarth Galleries Aboriginal Art Centre 206, 207
Holey dollar 22
Holman, Francis
First Fleet Ship 20
Home (nightclub) 214, 215
Home Computer Show 51
Homestay Network 170
Hoopla Circus and Street Theatre Festival 50
Hopetoun Hotel 197, 214, 215
Horderns Stairs
Street-by-Street map 118
Horizons Bar 196, 197
Hornby Lighthouse
Watsons Bay and Vaucluse Walk 149
Hospital casualty departments 223
Hostels 170
Hot Gossip Deli 194, 195
Hotel Altamont 175
Hotel Bondi
Bondi Beach to Clovelly Walk 144
Hotel Inter-Continental Sydney 175
Hotels **168–77**
airport hotels 229
booking addresses 170
Botanic Gardens and The Domain **175**
budget accommodation 170
children 169
chooser chart 216–17
City Centre **173–4**
Darling Harbour **174–5**
disabled assistance 170
disabled travellers 169
discount rates 169
further afield **177**
gay and lesbian accommodation 170, 171
halls of residence 170, 171
hidden extras 169
how to book 168
Kings Cross and Darlinghurst **175**
Paddington **176**

Hotels (cont)
private homes 170
The Rocks and Circular Quay **172–3**
self-catering apartments 169
where to look 168
Hoyts (cinemas) 210, 211
Hughenden Boutique Hotel 176
Hugo's (restaurant) 185, 187
Hugo's Lounge 197
Hume and Hovell 22
Hunter Valley **158–9**
Convent at Pepper Tree 159
Golden Grape Estate 158
Lake's Folly 159
Lindemans 158
Rothbury Estate 152, 159
Wyndham Estate 159
Hyde Park 44, 86
Hyde Park Barracks **114**
Sydney's Best: Architecture 37, 38
Sydney's Best: Museums and Galleries 33, 35
Hyde Park Barracks Café 194, 195
Hyde Park Plaza Suites 173

I
Icebox Nightclub 214, 215
Ideas Incorporated 169, 170, 209
IGLTA (International Gay and Lesbian Travel Association) 170
Il Porcellino 113
Immigration and customs 220
Imperial Hotel 214, 215
Implement blue (Preston) 110
Infrigement Processing Bureau 237
Inner City Cycles 287
Insurance
cars 236–7
medical 222
Interdenominational church 221
Interforex 224
Interior with Wardrobe Mirror (Cossington-Smith) 110
International Student Identity Card 219
Interpreting services 223
Irish community 41, 43
Islamic
community 40
religious services 221
Islay 82
Italian community 41, 43

J
Jacob's Ladder
Watsons Bay and Vaucluse Walk 148, 149
Jane Lambert Hats 205
Japan Airlines 229
JetCat ferry 234
Jewellery 206, 207
Jewish
community 41
Great Synagogue **86–7**
religious services 221
Sydney Jewish Museum 35, **121**
synagogue 221
Johnson, Richard 131
Jordon's International Seafood Restaurant 184, 189
Josephs Shoe Store 205
Juniper Hall **126**
Justice and Police Museum 35, **72**

K
Kame Kngwarreye, Emily 111
Kamogawa 184, 190
Keba
Balmain Walk 143
Kings Cross
Bed Race 50
Carnival 48
Kings Cross and Darlinghurst **110–21**
area map 117
hotels 175–6
restaurants 184–5
Street-by-Street map 118–19
Kingsford Smith (Sydney) Airport 228, 229
Kingsford Smith, Charles 27
Kinsela's Middle Bar 196, 197
Kirchner, Ernst
Three Balloons 110
Kirketon Hotel 175
Kirklands Coach Service 229
Kirribilli House 132
Kirribilli Point 132
Ku-ring-gai Chase National Park **154–5**
Aboriginal carvings 19
camping 170, 171

L
Lady Bay Beach
Watsons Bay and Vaucluse Walk 148
Lady Juliana 20

Lake Mungo, New South Wales
history 18
Lambert, George
Across the black soil plains 110
Lamrock Hostel 170
Lands Department Building 38,
84
Land Titles Office 115
Landmark Hotel 119
Lane Cove National Park 44
La Passion du Fruit 194, 195
Laurence, Janet and Foley, Fiona
Edge of the Trees 32, 85
Lawson, Henry 24
Lawson, Louisa
Dawn 25
Lebanese community 43
Legion Cabs 237
Le Kiosk 185, 187
Leslie Mackay's bookshop 206,
207
Leura Garden Festival 48
Lewin, John
Waratah 21
Lewis, Mortimer 88, 121
Lilianfels Blue Mountains 177
Lindsay, Norman
The Magic Pudding 67
Lisa Ho (shop) 204, 205
Little Shark (Nolan) 76
London Hotel
Balmain Walk 143
London Tavern 196, 197
Street-by-Street map 124
Longrain (restaurant) 185, 190
Long Reef 54, 55
Long-Distance Coach Services
229
The Looking Glass 206, 207
Lord Nelson Brewery Hotel 172
historic pub 14, 197
Lost property
State Rail 223
Sydney Buses 223
Sydney Ferries 223, 235
Lótel 175
Love and Hatred 206, 207
Lower Fort Street 38
Lucio's 185, 192
Luna Park 27, **132**

M

Macarthur, John and Elizabeth
138
McCafferty's Coach Service 229
McElhone Stairs
Street-by-Street map 118
Mackennal, Bertram 84, 86
Mackenzies Point
Bondi Beach to Clovelly Walk
144, 145

Macleay, Alexander 22
Macleay Serviced Apartments
175
Macleay Street Bistro 184, 189
Macquarie, Governor Lachlan
22, 72
Elizabeth 22, 106
Macquarie Chair, The 22
Macquarie Lighthouse **137**
history 22
Watson Bay and Vaucluse
Walk 148
Macquarie Place **72**
Macquarie Street 112–15
Macquarie Theatre 213
Macquarie Trio 213
McRae, George 82
*Madonna and Child with Infant
St John the Baptist*
(Beccafumi) 108
Madox Brown, Ford
*Chaucer at the Court of
Edward III* 110
The Magic Pudding (Lindsay) 67
Maitland House
Balmain Walk 142
Maker's Mark 206, 207
Malaya (restaurant) 184, 190
Mambo Friendship Store 204,
205
Manly **133**
Collins Beach 46, 147
The Corso 133, 146
Fairy Bower 146
food and wine festival 51
guided walk 146–7
Jazz Festival 48
Little Manly Cove 147
Manly Beach 54, 55, 146
Manly Wharf 146
New Brighton Hotel 146
North Head 133, 147
Oceanworld 133
Parkhill Sandstone Arch 147
St Patrick's Seminary 38, 146
Shelly Beach 54, 55, 146
viewing platforms 146
Manly Pacific Parkroyal 177
Man O'War Steps 58
Maps
Australia 10–11
beaches 55
Blue Mountains 160–61
Botanic Gardens and The
Domain 103
Central Sydney 14–15
Central Sydney and suburbs
12–13, 129
City Centre 79, 80–81
CityRail route map 323
city shoreline 56–9
Darling Harbour 91, 92–3

Maps (cont)
Early Colony 20
Exploring Beyond Sydney
152–3
ferry routes 235
Georgian Era 22
Greater Sydney and Environs
11
guided walks 141
Hawkesbury River 156–7
Hunter Valley 158–9
Kings Cross and Darlinghurst
117
19th-century Sydney 17
Paddington 123, 124–5
Pittwater and Ku-ring-gai
Chase 154–5
Postwar Sydney 28
Potts Point 118–19
The Rocks 64–5
The Rocks and Circular Quay
63
Royal Botanic Gardens 104–5
Royal National Park 164–5
Southeast Asia and Pacific Rim
10
Southern Highlands 162–3
Street Finder 238–5
Sydney Between the Wars 26
Sydney's Original Inhabitants
18–19
Taronga Zoo 134–5
Victorian Sydney 24
Walk Around Balmain 142–3
Walk Around Manly 146–7
Walk from Bondi Beach to
Clovelly 144–5
Walk in Watsons Bay and
Vaucluse 148–9
Marble Bar **82**
Street-by-Street map 80
Marcs 204, 205
Marigold (restaurant) 184, 190
Mariners Court Hotel 175
Marion Street Children's Theatre
210, 211
Markets **203**
Paddington Markets 201, **126**,
203
Paddy's Market **99**, 203
The Rocks Market 65, 203
Sydney Fish Market **131**, 200,
202, 203
Maroubra 19, 54, 55
Marsden, Samuel 115, 139
Martin Place **84**
Street-by-Street map 81
Matilda Cruises 219
Maureen Fry Sydney Guided
Tours 219
Maya Indian Sweets Centre 195
MC Garage 185, 187

MCA Café 184, 193, 194, 195
Media 221
Medical treatment 222
Medina Executive Apartments 177
Medina 170
Medusa (hotel) 176
Meere, Charles
  Australian Beach Pattern 33
Melbourne Cup Day 48
Mercantile Hotel 172
Metro (music venue) 214, 215
Mezzaluna 185, 192
Michael's Music Room 206, 207
Mid City Centre 199
Middle Head and Obelisk Bay 45
Midnight Shift (nightclub) 214, 215
Miro Tapas Bar 196, 197
Mitchell, Dr James 69
Mitchell Library 112
Mitchell, Sir Thomas 22
MLC Centre 39, 199
Mobile phones 226
Mohr Fish 185, 189
Monorail 29, 232–3
Moonlight, Captain 25
Moore, Henry
  Reclining Figure: Angles 110
Moore Park 45, 52
  golf club 52
  tennis courts 52
Moreton Bay fig *(Ficus macrophylla)* 47
Morgan's Hotel 176
Mort Bay Reserve
  Balmain Walk 142
Mrs Macquaries Chair 105, **106**
  city shoreline 56
  Victorian Sydney 24
Motor World Museum and Gallery 34, **98**
Movie Room 210, 211
Mowarljarlai, David
  Rock Painting 88
Mud Crabs (Dhanyula Nyoka) 32
Mundey, Jack 67
Museum of Contemporary Art **73**
  Street-by-Street map 64
  Sydney's Best 32, 34
Museums and galleries (general)
  Sydney's Best 32–5
  tourist information 218
Museums and galleries (individual)
  Art Gallery of New South Wales 33, 34, **108–11**
  Australian Museum 33, 34, **88–9**

Museums and galleries (cont)
  Brett Whiteley Studio 34, **130**
  Cadman's Cottage 21, 35, **68**
  Elizabeth Bay House 22–3, 33, 35, 119, **120**
  Elizabeth Farm 21, 35, **138–9**
  Experiment Farm Cottage 21, 35, **139**
  Hambledon Cottage 35, **139**
  Hyde Park Barracks 33, 35, **114–15**
  Justice and Police Museum 35, **72**
  Macleay Museum, University of Sydney 130
  Motor World Museum and Gallery 34, **98**
Museums and galleries (cont)
  Museum of Contemporary Art 32, 34, 64, **73**
  Museum of Sydney 32, 35, **85**
  National Maritime Museum 32, 34–5, 93, **94–5**
  Nicholson Museum, University of Sydney 130
  Nutcote 35, **132–3**
  Old Government House 23, 35, **139**
  Powerhouse Museum 32, 34, **100–101**
  The Rocks Toy Museum 63, 65, **66**
  Sailors' Home 35, **67**
  SH Ervin Gallery 35, 73
  Sherman Gallery 125
  Sotheby's Gallery 125
  Susannah Place 25, 35, **67**
  Sydney Jewish Museum 33, 35, **121**
  Vaucluse House 35, **136**
  Victoria Barracks **127**
  War Memorial Art Gallery, University of Sydney 130
  Westpac Museum 35, **68**
Music 212–15
  blues 214, 215
  cabaret venues 214, 215
  chamber **212**
  choral **213**
  free concerts **212**
  jazz **214**, 215
  music venues 214
  opera, orchestras and dance **212–13**
  rock music 214, 215
Musica Viva 212, 213
Music shops 206, 207
Myall Creek massacre 23
My Brilliant Career (Franklin) 26

N

Nag's Head (hotel) 197
Narrabeen 54, 55
National Aboriginal and Islander Skills Development Association 42, 213
National Herbarium of New South Wales 105
National Maritime Museum **94–5**
  Street-by-Street map 93
  Sydney's Best: Architecture 36, 39
  Sydney's Best: Museums and Galleries 32, 34–5
National Mutual Building 38
National parks
  Blue Mountains National Park **160–61**
National parks (cont)
  camping 170, 171
  Garigal National Park 44
  Ku-ring-gai Chase National Park **154–5**
  Lane Cove National Park 44
  Royal National Park **164–5**
National Trust Centre **73**
National Trust Heritage Week 50
Natives on the Ouse River, Van Diemen's Land (Glover) 110
Naval Memorial Chapel
  Watsons Bay and Vaucluse Walk 148
Nelson, Michael Tjakamarra
  The Possum Dreaming 74
Nepean River
  history 18
New Guinea Primitive Arts 206, 207
New South Wales Corps (Rum Corps) 20
New South Wales National Parks and Wildlife Service 68
New Theatre 210, 211
New Year's Eve 49
New Zealand Consulate General 221
Newmans Coach Tours 219
Newport 54, 55
Newspapers 221
Newtown Hotel 214, 215
NIDA Theatre 210, 211
Nielsen, Juanita 120
Nielsen Park 45, **136**
  Greycliffe House 136
Nightclubs 214, 215
Nolan, Sydney
  Boy in Township 110
  Burke 110
  Little Shark 76
No Names (restaurant) 184, 192
North Arm Walk 44

North Head **133**
   reserve 147
   Quarantine Station 133
   Sydney's Best 45, 46
Novotel Century 175
Novotel Sydney on Darling
   Harbour 175
Nowra, Louis 210
NRMA (National Roads and
   Motorists Association) 168, 170
NSW Visitor Information Line
   218
   entertainment information
   208, 209
   hotel bookings 168, 170
Nude in a Rocking Chair
   (Picasso) 109, 110
Nutcote 35, **132**

O
Obelisk 87
Obelisk Bay 55
Observatory Hotel, The 172
Oh! Calcutta! 184, 191
O'Keefe, Johnny 28
Old Gaol, Darlinghurst **121**
Old Government House
   (Parramatta) 23, 35, **139**
Old Manly Boatshed, The 197,
   211
Old Sydney Holiday Inn 172
Old Woman in Ermine
   (Beckmann) 110
Olsen, John
   Salute to Five Bells 76
Olympic Games 29, 48, **53**, **138**
One Extra Dance Company 213
Onkaparinga
   Balmain Walk 142
Onus, Lin
   Fruit Bats 111
Opals 206, 207
Opal Fields (shop) 206, 207
Opera Australia 212
Opera in the Domain 49
Orchestral music **212**
Orient Hotel 197, 214, 215
Otto 185, 187
Overseas Passenger Terminal
   Street-by-Street map 65
Oxford Hotel 214, 215
Oz magazine 29

P
Pacific International Suites 170
Paddington 37, **123–7**
   area map 123
   hotels 176
   restaurants 185
   Street-by-Street map 124–5
   Sydney's Best 201

Paddington Markets **126**, 203
   Sydney's Best 201
Paddington Inn 196, 197
Paddington Street 38, **126**
   Street-by-Street map 124–5
Paddington Town Hall 123, **127**
Paddington Village **127**
Paddington and Woollahra
   Sydney's Best 201
Paddy's Market **99**, 203
Palace Hotel 196, 197
Palm Beach 54, 55, 155
Paradiso Brolga Terrace 194, 195
Paralympic Games 48
Paris Cake Shop 194, 195
Park Hyatt Sydney 172
Park, Ruth
   Poor Man's Orange 130
   The Harp in the South 130
Parkes, Henry 24
Parking 236
Parkroyal at Darling Harbour
   175
Parks and reserves (individual)
   Beare Park **120**
   Bicentennial Park 44, 47
   Birchgrove Park 143
   Blue Mountains National Park
   53, **160–61**, 170, 171
   Bradleys Head 45, 46
   Bronte Park 145
   Captain Cook's Landing Place
   138
   Centennial Park 45, 47, 53,
   127
   Chinese Garden **98–9**
   The Domain 45, 47, **107**
   Fitzroy Falls 162
   Garigal National Park 44, 46
   Grotto Point 45, 46
   Gumbooya Reserve 19
   Hyde Park 44, 47, **86–7**
   Ku-ring-gai Chase National
   Park 19, 53, **154–5**, 170, 171
   Lane Cove National Park 44,
   46–7
   Macquarie Place **72**
   Middle Head 45, 46
   Moore Park 45, 52
   Mort Bay Reserve 142
   Mount Tomah Botanic
   Gardens 161
   North Arm 44, 46
   Nielsen Park 45, **136**, 149
   North Head 45, 46, **132**, 147
   Obelisk Bay 45, 55
   Royal Botanic Gardens **104–5**
   Royal National Park 19,
   164–5, 170, 171
   Seven Mile Beach 163
   South Head 45, 46, 148–9
   Sydney's Best 44–7

Parks and reserves (cont)
   Taronga Zoo **134–5**
   Yurulbin Point Reserve 143
Parks and reserves (geographic)
   city parks 47
   coastal hinterland 46
   open eucalypt forest 46
   rainforest and moist forest 46
   wetlands 47
Parliament House **112**
Parramatta 18, 35
   Experiment Farm Cottage 35,
   139
   Hambledon Cottage 35, **139**
   Elizabeth Farm 35, **138**
   James Ruse 139
   Old Government House 23,
   35, **139**
   St John's Cemetery **139**
   Samuel Marsden 139
Parsley Bay
   beaches 55
   Watsons Bay and Vaucluse
   Walk 149
Paspaley Pearls 206, 207
Pemulwy 21
Percy Marks (jewellers) 206, 207
Performance Space 213
Periwinkle Manly Cove 177
Personal security and health
   222–3
Perspecta 49
Pharmacies 223
   After-Hours Pharmacy
   Information 223
Phillip, Captain Arthur 17, 64,
   73
Phonecards 226
Picasso, Pablo
   Nude in a Rocking Chair 109,
   110
Piccadilly (arcade) 199
The Pier (restaurant) 185, 189
Pilot boats
   Watsons Bay and Vaucluse
   Walk 149
Pinchgut (Fort Denison) 107
Pittwater and Ku-ring-gai Chase
   154–5
   Aboriginal rock art 154
   Akuna Bay 154
   Barrenjoey Lighthouse 154
   Bilgola Beach 55, 155
   camping 170, 171
   Coal and Candle Creek 154
   history 19
   horse riding 53
   Palm Beach Wharf 155
   Pittwater 155
   Whale Beach 55, 155
Platypus Shoes (shop) 205
Poisons Information 223

Police 222, 223
Polo Ralph Lauren 204, 205
The Possum Dreaming
  (Tjakamarra) 74
Poster for the Vienna Secession
  (Schiele) 111
Postal services 227
Poste restante 227
Post Office, General (GPO) 227
Postwar Sydney 28–9
Potts Point
  Street-by-Street map 118–19
Powerhouse Museum **100–101**
  Sydney's Best 32, 34
  Victorian Sydney 25
Poyntes, Edward
  *The Visit of the Queen of
  Sheba to King Solomon* 110
Prasit Thai 194, 195
Premier Cabs 237
Premier Motor Service 229
Presbyterian church 221
Preston, Margaret
  Implement blue 110
  *Western Australian Gum
  Blossom* 110
Prime (restaurant) 184, 187
Prince Alfred Hospital 24
Pro Dive Coogee 54
Pruniers 185, 187
Public holidays 51
Public telephones 226
Public Transport Info Line **230**,
  231, 234
Pubs and bars **196–7**
  blues 214, 215
  cabaret venues 214, 215
  entertainment 197
  gay and lesbian venues 214,
  215
  historic pubs 197
  jazz 214, 215
  rock music 214, 215
  rules and conventions 196
  up-market bars 196
Pukumani Grave Posts 109, 111
Pyrmont Bridge **98**
  Street-by-Street map 93

Q
Q (nightclub) 214, 215
Qantas Airways 228, 229
  history 28
Quarantine regulations 220
Quay (restaurant) 184, 187
Quay Grand 172
Quayside Booking Centre 235
Queen Victoria Building (QVB)
  14, **82**
  arcades and malls 198, 199
  Street-by-Street map 80

Queen Victoria Building (cont)
  Sydney's Best: Architecture 36,
  38
  Sydney's Best: Shopping
  Streets and Markets 200
Queen Victoria Statue
  Street-by-Street map 80
Quintus Servinton 22

R
Radio 221
Radisson Plaza Hotel 174
Rainfall 50
Ravesi's on Bondi Beach (hotel)
  177
Ravesi's on Bondi Beach
  (restaurant) 185, 189
Reclining Figure: Angles
  (Moore) 110
Red Earth 206, 207
Red Eye Records 206, 207
Regal (restaurant) 184, 190
Regent Sydney (hotel) 172
Regents Court (hotel) 176
Religious services 221
Republic of Ireland Embassy
  221
Renaissance Sydney 172
Restaurants **178–97**
  Asian 190–91
  bistros and brasseries
  188–9
  Botanic Gardens and The
  Domain 184
  Chinese 189–90
  chooser chart 184–5
  City Centre 184
  contemporary 186–8
  Darling Harbour 184
  dress codes 179
  eating with children 179
  French 192–3
  further afield 185
  how much to pay 178
  Italian 191–2
  Kings Cross and Darlinghurst
  184–5
  licensing laws 179
  Mediterranean and Middle
  Eastern 193
  opening times 178
  Paddington 185
  reservations 178–9
  The Rocks and Circular Quay
  185
  seafood 189
  tax and tipping 179
  what to drink in Sydney 182–3
  what to eat in Sydney
  180–81
  where to eat 178

Restaurant VII 184, 191
The Revenge 20
Rhythm Boat Cruises 214,
  215
Riberries 187, 188
Riche, The (nightclub) 214,
  215
Riley, Edward and Mary 67
Ristorante Riva 185, 192
RiverCat ferry 234
RM Williams (shop) 204, 205
Roberts, Tom
  *The Golden Fleece – Shearing
  at Newstead* 109, 110
Rock Painting (Mowarljarlai)
  88
Rockpool (restaurant) 184,
  189
The Rocks and Circular Quay
  63–77
  area map 63
  city shoreline 59
  history 21
  hotels 172–3
  market 203
  restaurants 184
  The Rocks Opal Mine 206,
  207
  Street-by-Street map 64–5
  Sydney's Best 200
  walking tour 219
The Rocks Toy Museum 63, 65,
  66
Rockwall 119
Roma Caffè Ristorante 194,
  195
Rose of Australia 214, 215
Rossini Restaurant 194, 195
Rowe, Thomas 86
Royal Botanic Gardens 57,
  104–5
  Spring Festival 48
Royal Clock 82
Royal Easter Show 50
Royal Hotel 126, 196, 197
  Sydney's Best 185
Royal National Park **164–5**
  Aboriginal carving 19
  Audley 164
  Bundeena 165
  camping 170, 171
  Cronulla 165
  Curracurrang 165
  Deer Pool 165
  Figure Eight Pool 165
  Forest Path 164
  Garie Beach 153, 164
  Hacking River 164
  Heathcote 164
  Jibbon Head 165
  Jibbon Head Lagoon 165
  Lady Carrington Drive 164

Royal National Park (cont)
  Little Marley Beach 165
  Wattamolla Lagoon 165
  Werrong 164
Roy's Famous 194, 195
RSL Cabs 237
Rugby league 52
  grand final 51
Rugby union 52
  grand final 51
Rum
  Corps (New South Wales
    Corps) 20, 21
  Hospital 113, **114**
  Rebellion 21, 138
Ruse, James 139
Rushcutters Harbourside Sydney
  177
Russell (hotel) 172

S

Saba 204, 205
Sailing 54, 56
Sailors' Home 35, **67**
Sailor's Thai 184, 191
Salt (restaurant) 185, 188
St Andrew's Cathedral **87,** 212
St Andrew's Church
  Balmain Walk 143
St James Church **115**
  concerts 213
  Sydney's Best 36, 38
St John's Cemetery **139**
St Mary's Cathedral 25, 38, **86**
St Michael's Golf Club 53
St Patrick's Day Parade 50
St Patrick's Seminary 38, 146
St Philip's Church **73**
Salute to Five Bells (Olsen) 76
Sandringham Garden 86
Savoy Double Bay 177
Scanlan & Theodore 204, 205
Schiele, Egon
  *Poster for the Vienna
    Secession* 111
Scuba diving 54
Sculpture
  Art Gallery of New South
    Wales 110
Sean's Panaroma 185, 187
Sebel Pier One Sydney, The
  172
Seidler, Harry 39
Self-catering agencies 170
Seven Shillings Beach 55
Sewell, Stephen 210
Seymour Theatre Centre
  theatre 210, 211
  music 212, 213
SH Ervin Gallery 34
Shakespeare by the Sea 210, 211

Shark Bay
  beaches 54, 55
  Watsons Bay and Vaucluse
    Walk 148
Sharp, Ronald 76
Shelly Beach
  beaches 54, 55
  Manly Walk 146
Sheraton on the Park 174
Sherman Gallery
  Street-by-Street map 125
Ships *see* Boats
Shops and markets **198–207**
  arcades and malls 198
  department stores 199
  further afield 199
  how to pay 198
  markets 202–3
  sales 198
  shopping hours 198
  Sydney's Best: Shopping
    Streets and Markets 200–201
  tax-free sales 198
Sicard, François 86
Side On Café 214, 215
Signal Station
  Watsons Bay and Vaucluse
    Walk 148
Silver Spring (restaurant) 184,
  190
Simpsons of Potts Point 169,
  176
Singapore Airlines 229
Sir Stamford Double Bay 177
Sir Stamford Circular Quay
  175
Sir Stamford Plaza 177
*Sketch and Description of the
  Settlement of Sydney Cove*
  (Fowkes) 17
Skin Deep 204, 205
Skygarden 198–9
  Street-by-Street map 81
Slipp Inn 214, 215
Sloane's Café 194, 195
Smith, Richard 25
Smoking 218
Snugglepot and Cuddlepie
  (Gibbs) 132
Sodersten, Emil 39
Sofala (Drysdale) 108
Soho Lounge Bar (nightclub)
  214, 215
Solander, Daniel 138
Sorriso 185, 192
Soup Plus 214, 215
South Head 45, 148–9
Southern Highlands **162–3**
  Berrima 162
  Berrima Gaol
  Berry 163
  Bowral 162

Southern Highlands (cont)
  Bundanoon 162
  Fitzroy Falls 162
  Kangaroo Valley 162
  Kiama 152, 163
  Seven Mile Beach 163
Specialist shops and souvenirs
  206–7
Spencer, John 84
Spirit of Australia 34
Sporting Sydney **52–5**
Spring in Sydney 48
Spring Racing Carnival 48
Stables Theatre 210, 211
Stafford Quest Apartments 172
Star City 175, 210, 211, 214, 215
State Library of NSW **112**
  Bookshop 206, 207
State Theatre **82**, 214, 215
  rock music 214, 215
  Street-by-Street map 80
  theatres 210, 211
State Transit Information and
  Ticket Kiosks 230
State Transit Tourist Ferries 219
Statues
  Flinders, Matthew 112
  Mort, Thomas 72
  Prince Albert 115
  Queen Victoria Statue 80, 82
Stewart's Gentlemen's Outfitters
  204, 205
Stock Exchange Hotel 196, 197
Strand Arcade **84**
  arcades and malls 198, 199
  architecture 38
  Street-by-Street map 81
Strand Hatters 205
The "Strasburg" Clock 25
Streeton, Arthur 25
Student Travel Association 219
Study for Self Portrait (Bacon)
  110
Suez Canal (The Rocks) 64
Suites on Sussex 170
Sullivans Hotel 176
Summer in Sydney 49
A Summer Morning (Bunny)
  110
Summer Time (Bunny) 110
The Summit (restaurant) 184,
  188
Sunbaker (Dupain) 108
Sunshine 49
Surfing 54
Surf Dive 'n Ski 204, 205
Surf Life Saving NSW 54
Surry Hills **130**
Susannah Place 35, 38, **67**
Sushi-E 184, 191
Swimming 54, 223
Swimming pools 55, 105, 144

Sydney
  Between the Wars 26–7
  coat of arms 17
  getting around Sydney 230–37
Sydney A Capella Association
  213
Sydney (Kingsford Smith)
  airport 228
  airport information 229
Sydney Airport Hilton 229
Sydney Airport Stamford 229
Sydney Aquarium 96–7
  Street-by-Street map 93
Sydney Centre YHA 170
Sydney City Council One-Stop-
  Shop 220
Sydney Cricket Ground 52
Sydney Dance Company 213
Sydney Entertainment Centre
  52, 214, 215
Sydney Ferries Information
  Office 230, 234
Sydney Festival 209
Sydney Film Festival 51, 210, 211
Sydney Fish Market 131, 202, 203
  Sydney's Best 200
Sydney Football Stadium 39,
  52
  rock concerts 214, 215
Sydney Fringe Festival 49, 210,
  211
Sydney Gazette 21
Sydney to the Gong Bicycle
  Ride 48
Sydney Harbour Bridge 31,
  70–71
  BridgeClimb 71
  city shoreline 58
  history 26–7
Sydney Harbour Oceanarium 97
Sydney Harbour Seaplanes 219
Sydney Harbour Tunnel 29
Sydney Helicopters 219
Sydney to Hobart Yacht Race
  28, 49
Sydney Hospital 113
Sydney International Boat Show
  51
Sydney Jewish Museum 33, 35,
  121
Sydney Marriot 174
Sydney Mint 23, 35, 114
Sydney Morning Herald
  Half Marathon 50
Sydney Observatory 69
  Street-by-Street map 64
Sydney Olympic Park 138
Sydney Opera House 74–7
  Bennelong Restaurant 75
  city shoreline 58
  Concert Hall 75, 76, 212
  design 77

Sydney Opera House (cont)
  disabled visitors 209
  Drama Theatre 76, 210
  history 28
  Information and booking 209
  Northern Foyers 74
  opera, orchestras and dance
  212
  Opera Theatre 74, 76
  The Playhouse 75, 76
  roofs 75
  Sydney's Best 37, 39
Sydney Philharmonia Orchestra
  Choirs 213
Sydney Swans 52
Sydney Symphony Orchestra
  209, 212, 213
Sydney Theatre Company 69,
  210, 211
Sydney Tower 83
  Street-by-Street map 81
Sydney Town Hall 87
  concerts 212, 213
  Sydney's Best 36, 38
Sydney Traffic Control Centre
  237
Sydney Tropical Centre 104
Sydney University 129, 130, 170
Sydney Visitor Centre 168, 170,
  218
Sydney Youth Orchestra 212,
  213
Sydneyscope Artwear 204, 205
Symphony Under the Stars 49
Synergy 212, 213

T

Tabou (restaurant) 185, 193
Takeaway food 195
Talmage, Algernon
  The Founding of Australia 73
Tamarama
  beach 54, 55
  Bondi Beach to Clovelly Walk
  145
Tank (nightclub) 214, 215
Tank Bar 197
Tank Stream 59, 72
Taronga Zoo 134–5
Tarpeian Market 203
Tasman Map 112
Taxis 237
  water taxis 235
Taxis Combined 237
Taylor Square Hotel/Zee Bar 215
Te Aroha Festival 43
Telephones 226–7
Television 221
Telstra Phone Centre 226, 227
Temperature 51
Tennis 52

Tetsuya's 185, 188
Thai community 40
Theatres 210, 211
Theatre Royal 210, 211
  Street-by-Street map 81
Thomas Cook 224
Three Bathers (Kirchner) 110
Three Mimis Dancing (Wagbara)
  111
Thrifty 236, 237
Thunderbolt, Captain 106
Ticketek 52, 208, 209
Ticketmaster 208, 209
Ticket-of-leave 20
Tickets
  booking agencies 208–9
  CityRail tickets 233
  composite tickets 230
  discount 209
  ferry ticket machines 234
  monorail 232–3
  public transport 230, 231
  Quayside Booking Centre 235
Tidal Cascades Fountain
  Street-by-Street map 92
Tilbury Hotel 214, 215
Time zones 220
Tipping 219
  hotels 169
  restaurants 179
Tivoli Theatre 25
Tjapaltjarri, Clifford Possum and
  Tim Leura Tjapaltjarri
  Warlugulong 111
Toilets 221
Tourist information 218
  Central Railway Station 218
  Darling Harbour 218
  NSW Travel Centres 218
  The Sydney Visitor Centre 218
Traffic signs 236
Train
  arriving by train 229
  CityRail 232–3
  Country and interurban 233
  Countrylink Travel Centres
  229, 233
  tickets 230, 233
  train information 229
Travel information 228–37
  air 228
  bicycle 237
  bus 228, 230, 231
  car 229, 236–7
  coach 229
  departure tax 220
  disabled travellers 220
  ferry 230, 234–5
  getting around Sydney 230
  guided tours and excursions
  219
  immigration and customs 220

Travel information (cont)
  monorail **232–3**
  public transport 230–35
  sea 228–9
  State Transit Information and
    Ticket Kiosks 230
  student travel 219
  taxis 237
  trains 229, **232–3**
  Transport Infoline 220, 230–31
  water taxis **235**
Travelex 224
Traveller's cheques 224
Travellers' Clinic 222, 223
Travellers' Info Service 169, 170
Trinity Bar 196, 197
Tropfest 49
Tropicana Coffee Lounge 194, 195
Turkish community 40
Tusculum Villa 38, 118

U

Uchi Lounge 185, 191
Ulm 27
Una's Coffee Lounge 194, 195
Unicorn Hotel 211
United Airlines 229
United Kingdom Consulate 221
Uniting Church 221
University of Sydney 129, **130**,
  170
Unkai (restaurant) 184, 191
Utopia Records 206, 207
Utzon, Jørn 37, 77

V

Vampire 93, 95
Vaucluse 148, 149
Vaucluse House 35, **136**
  history 23
  Tea Rooms 195
  Watsons Bay and Vaucluse
    Walk 149
Vegemite 26
Vendor (shoes) 205
Verge, John 37, 120
Vernon, WL 108
Verona (cinema) 210, 211
Victoria Barracks 37, 38, **127**
  CityRail tickets 233
Victoria Court Hotel 176
Victoria Spring Designs 206, 207
Victoria Street (Potts Point) **120**
  Street-by-street map 118–19
Victorian Sydney 24–5

Victorian terrace houses 25
  Paddington Street 126
  Street-by-Street maps 118–19,
    124–5
  Sydney's Best 37
Vidette
  Balmain Walk 143
Vietnamese community 40, 43
Vietnam War 28
View from the Summit (Earle) 22
A View of Sydney Cove (Dayes)
  20
Viewing platforms
  Manly Walk 146
Village (cinemas) 210, 211
*The Visit of the Queen of Sheba
    to King Solomon* (Poynter)110
Vivian Chan Shaw (shop) 205

W

W Sydney 176
Wagbara, Samuel
  Three Mimis Dancing 111
Waldorf Apartment Hotel 174
Walks 141–9
  Balmain 142–3
  Bondi Beach to Clovelly 144–5
  Manly 146–7
  Watsons Bay and Vaucluse
    148–9
Walking in Sydney **230**
Waratah (Lewin) 21
Wardell, William 86
Warlugulong (Tjapaltjarri) 111
Warwick
  Street-by-Street map 125
Watch Gallery, The 206, 207
Watch House, The
  Balmain Walk 143
Water taxis **235**
Waterman's Cottage, The
  Balmain Walk 142
Watermark (restaurant) 185, 188
Watsons Bay **136**
  beaches 55
  guided walk 148–9
  pilot boats 149
Wattle House Travellers'
  Accommodation 170
Waverley Cemetery
  Bondi Beach to Clovelly
    Walk 145
The Waverly 25
Weather 48–51
Weiss Art 206, 207
Wentworth, D'Arcy 139

Wentworth, WC 136
Werrington 118
*Western Australian Gum
    Blossom* (Preston) 110
The Westin Hotel 174
Westpac Museum 35, **68**
Whale Beach 55, 155
The Wharf Restaurant 184, 189
Wharf Theatre **69**
  city shoreline 59
  theatres 210, 211
Wheels and Dolly Baby 206, 207
White, Patrick 28
Whiteley, Brett 29, 130
  The Balcony (2) 110
Whitlam, Gough 29
Williams, Fred 110
Williamson, David 210
Williamson, JC 120
William Street (Darlinghurst) 116
Windsor Street (Paddington)
  Street-by-Street map 125
Windsurfing 54
Wine Banc 196, 197, 214, 215
Winter in Sydney 51
Wisemans Ferry 157
Witchery 204, 205
Woodward, Robert 92
Woolloomooloo Finger Wharf
  57, **107**
Woolloomooloo Waters
  Apartment Hotel 176
Wooly's Wheels 237
World Series Cricket 29
World War II 27
World Youth Hostel 170
Writers' Walk 72
Wurrabadalumba, Jabarrgwa
  Dugong Hunt 34

X

Xo (restaurant) 185, 191

Y

YHA 170
Ying's 185, 190
Yiribana Gallery 34, 111
York, The (hotel) 174
Yulefest 51
Yurulbin Point
  Balmain Walk 143
  ferry route map 235

Z

Zofrea, Salvatore 76
Zoo *see* Taronga Zoo

Acknowledgments

DORLING KINDERSLEY would like to thank the following people whose help and assistance contributed to the preparation of this book.

MAIN CONTRIBUTORS
Ken Brass grew up on Sydney's Bondi Beach. He began his career in journalism with the *Sydney Morning Herald* and later worked as a London correspondent before becoming a staff writer on national daily newspapers in the United Kingdom. Returning home, he worked on the *Australian Women's Weekly*, *Weekend Australian* newspaper and *Australian Geographic* magazine. His photographs appear regularly in Australian magazines.

Kirsty McKenzie grew up on a sheep station in outback Queensland. She entered journalism after completing an arts degree. After making Sydney her home in 1980, she worked on a number of lifestyle and travel publications. Since becoming a freelance writer in 1987, she has regularly contributed to food, interior design and travel magazines.

ADDITIONAL TEXT AND RESEARCH
Angus Cameron, Leith Hillard, Kim Kitson, Sherry Collins, Siobhán O'Connor, Rupert Dean.

ADDITIONAL PHOTOGRAPHY
Claire Edwards, Leanne Hogbin, Siobhán O'Connor.

ADDITIONAL ILLUSTRATIONS
Leslye Cole, Stephen Conlin, Jon Gittoes, Steve Graham, Ray Grinaway, Helen Halliday, David Kirshner, Alex Lavroff, Iain McKellar, Chris Orr, Oliver Rennert.

ADDITIONAL CARTOGRAPHY
Land Information Centre, Sydney.
Dorling Kindersley Cartography, Sydway.

EDITORIAL AND DESIGN
DEPUTY EDITORIAL DIRECTOR Douglas Amrine
DEPUTY ART DIRECTORS Gillian Allan, Gaye Allen
MAP CO-ORDINATORS Michael Ellis, David Pugh
PRODUCTION David Proffit
PICTURE RESEARCH Wendy Canning
DTP DESIGNER Leanne Hogbin
MAPS Gary Bowes, Fiona Casey, Anna Nilsson, Christine Purcell, Richard Toomey (Era-Maptec Ltd)
EDITORIAL AND DESIGN ASSISTANCE Charis Atlas, Jenny Cattell, Stephanie Driver, Joy Fitzsimmons, Clare Forte, Emily Green, Gail Jones, Lisa Kosky, Jim Marks, Rebecca Milner, Kylie Mulquin, Louise Parsons, Helen Partington, Clare Pierotti, Tracey Timpson.

INDEX
Jenny Cattell.

SPECIAL ASSISTANCE
Art Gallery of New South Wales, in particular Sherrie Joseph; Australian Museum, in particular Liz Wilson; Ann-Marie Bulat; the staff of Elizabeth Bay House; Historic Houses Trust; Lara Hookham; Info Direct, in particular Frank Tortora; Professor Max Kelly; Lou MacDonald; Adam Moore;

Museum of Sydney, in particular Michelle Andringa; National Maritime Museum, in particular Jeffrey Mellefont and Bill Richards; National Trust of Australia (NSW), in particular Stewart Watters; Bridget O'Regan; Royal Botanic Gardens, in particular Anna Hallett and Ed Wilson; State Transit Authority; Sydney Opera House, in particular David Brown and Valerie Tring; Diane Wallis.

PHOTOGRAPHY PERMISSIONS
DORLING KINDERSLEY would like to thank all those who gave permission to photograph at various cathedrals, churches, museums, restaurants, hotels, shops, galleries and other sights too numerous to thank individually.

PICTURE CREDITS
t = top; tl = top left; tlc = top left centre; tc = top centre; trc = top right centre; tr = top right; cla = centre left above; ca = centre above; cra = centre right above; cl = centre left; c = centre; cr = centre right; clb = centre left below; cb = centre below; crb = centre right below; bl = bottom left; b = bottom; bc = bottom centre; bcl = bottom centre left; br = bottom right; brb = bottom right below; d = detail.

Every effort has been made to trace the copyright holders. Dorling Kindersley apologizes for any unintentional omissions and would be pleased, in such cases, to add an acknowledgment in future editions.

Works of art have been reproduced with the permission of the following copyright holders:
© MUSEUM OF SYDNEY 1996: *Edge of the Trees* Janet Laurence and Fiona Foley: on the site of First Government House: 32tr, 85b; © LIN ONUS 1996 – Lin Onus (1948–) *Fruit Bats* 1991, 95 fibreglass polychrome fruit bats, Hills Hoist, polychrome wooden disks, Art Gallery of New South Wales: 111cr.

The publisher would like to thank the following individuals, companies and picture libraries for their kind permission to reproduce their photographs:

ACP: 27cb, 28bc; ANTHONY CRICKMAY: 76cla; EMANUEL ANGELICAS: 42br; ART GALLERY OF NEW SOUTH WALES: 25cb; © Sir William Dobell Art Foundation 1996 *Dame Mary Gilmore* 1957 William Dobell (1899–1970), oil on hardboard 90.2 x 73.7 cm, gift of Dame Mary Gilmore 1960: 29ca; © Bundanon Trust 1996 *The Expulsion* 1947–48 Arthur Boyd (1920–), oil on hardboard 99.5 x 119.6 cm: 31c; © Ms Stephenson-Meere 1996 *Australian Beach Pattern* 1940 Charles Meere (1890–1961) oil on canvas 91.5 x 122 cm: 33tl; 34b; © The Cazneaux family 1996 *Bridge Pattern* Harold Cazneaux (1878–1953), gelatin silver photograph 29.6 x 21.4 cm, gift of the Cazneaux family 1975: 58bc(d); © Lady Drysdale 1996 *Sofala* 1947 Russell Drysdale (1912–81), oil on canvas on hardboard 71.7 x 93.1 cm: 108cla;

108ca; 108clb; © Tiwi Design Executive 1996 *Pukumani Grave Posts, Melville Island* 1958 various artists, natural pigments on wood 165.1 x 29.2 cm, gift of Dr Stuart Scougall 1959: 109tc; © DACS 1996 *Nude in a Rocking Chair* 1956 Pablo Picasso (1881–1973), oil on canvas 195 x 130 cm: 109ca; 109crb; 109bc; © Estate of Francis Bacon *Study for Self Portrait* 1976 Francis Bacon (1901–92), oil and pastel on canvas 198 x 147.5 cm: 110tr; 110cla; © Wendy and Arkie Whiteley 1996 *The Balcony 2* 1975 Brett Whiteley (1939–92), oil on canvas 203.5 x 364.5 cm: 110bl; *Warlugulong* 1976 Clifford Possum Tjapaltjarri (1932–) and Tim Leura Tjapaltjarri (1939–84), synthetic polymer paint on canvas 168.5 x 170.5 cm: 111tr; AUSCAPE INTERNATIONAL: Kevin Deacon 96bl; AUSTRALIAN INFORMATION SERVICE: 29tl(d); AUSTRALIAN MUSEUM: C. Bento 18tl, 18clb, 18cb, 19tl, 19c, 19crb; Carl Bento/Nature Focus 32cla; AUSTRALIAN PICTURE LIBRARY: John Carnemolla 28clb.

BANC: 178c; BANGARRA DANCE THEATRE: Greg Barrett 42cla; GREG BARRETT: 209bc; BARTEL PHOTO LIBRARY: 160bc; MERVYN G BISHOP: 20crb; BRUCE COLEMAN: John Cancalosi 45bc; Francisco Futil 44tr; BRIDGECLIMB SYDNEY: 71tl; BULA'BULA ARTS: Tony Dhanyula *Nyoka* (Mud Crabs), circa 1984, ochres and synthetic polymer on bark, J.W. Power Bequest, purchased 1984 by the Museum of Contemporary Art, Sydney: 32clb.

CENTREPOINT MANAGEMENT: 83br; CIRCUS SOLARUS: 48cr; COO-EE HISTORICAL PICTURE LIBRARY: 9ca, 61ca, 151ca, 167ca, 217ca; CORBIS: E. O. Hoppé 65cra.

DAVID JONES (AUSTRALIA) P/L: 23crb(d); RUPERT DEAN: 182cl, 182crb; DIXSON GALLERIES, STATE LIBRARY OF NEW SOUTH WALES: 8–9, 18tr, 20blb(d), 24cla, 70tr, 138br; MAX DUPAIN: 77br.

FAIRFAX PHOTO LIBRARY: 26bl; 52ca; 71bra; 114cl(d); 77tc; ASCUI 51br; Dallen 29cra; Gerrit Fokkema 28br; Ken James 209tr; McNeil 120bl; White 41bl.

GOVERNMENT PRINTING OFFICE COLLECTION, STATE LIBRARY OF NEW SOUTH WALES: 24clb, 26clb, 76blb.

HAPPY MEDIUM PHOTOS: 41tc; C MOORE HARDY: 208br; HOOD COLLECTION, STATE LIBRARY OF NEW SOUTH WALES: 71bl, 137br(d). THE IRISH-AUSTRALIAN: 43cla.

LAKE'S FOLLY VINEYARDS: 159cr; LIBERTY WINES: 158cla; LUNA PARK TRUST: 128tc; MAZZ IMAGES: 28–9; MEDUSA HOTEL: 171t; MITCHELL LIBRARY, STATE LIBRARY OF NEW SOUTH WALES: 19br, 19bcb, 20br(d), 20-21, 21tl, 21ca(d), 21cb, 22clb(d), 22cb(d), 22bl, 23tl, 23ca(d), 23bl(d), 24cr, 24bc, 24br, 25tl, 25br, 27ca(d), 27blb, 29cb, 44tl, 71cra, 112tl; DAVID MOORE: 28cla.

NATIONAL LIBRARY OF AUSTRALIA, CANBERRA: 22tl, 22cla, 23brb(d), 25bc; NATIONAL MARITIME MUSEUM: 20cl, 34tl, 42tl, 95 cra; NATURE FOCUS: Carl Bento 32 cla; Kevin Diletti 47br(d); John Fields 44bl; Pavel German 47tr.

OLYMPIC CO-ORDINATION AUTHORITY: 139t/b.

PARLIAMENT HOUSE: The Hon Max Willis, RFD, ED, LLB, MLC, President, Legislative Council, Parliament of New South Wales. The Hon J Murray, MP, Speaker, Legislative Assembly, Parliament of New South Wales. Artist's original sketch of the historical painting in oils by Algernon Talmage, RA, *The Founding of Australia*. Kindly loaned to the Parliament of New South Wales by Mr Arthur Chard of Adelaide: 73bl; PARRAMATTA CITY COUNCIL: S. Thomas 40tr, 43tr; POWERHOUSE MUSEUM: 20tl, 21br, 22bcb, 24tl, 26tl, 26cla, 26cb, 26bc, 27crb, 27bc, 32t, 32br; Sue Stafford 100tl; Tyrrell Collection 106tc.

ROYAL BOTANIC GARDENS: Jaime Plaza 48bl.

SOUTHCORP WINES EUROPE: 183tr; STATE LIBRARY OF TASMANIA: 20clb; STOPMOTION: 160tr; SUZIE THOMAS PUBLISHING: Thomas O'Flynn 74bc, 76clb; SYDNEY AQUARIUM: 97cra, 97bl; SYDNEY FILM FESTIVAL: 51clb, SYDNEY FREELANCE: J Boland 49cl; SYDNEY JEWISH MUSEUM: 33br; SYDNEY OPERA HOUSE TRUST: 74tr, 74cla, 75tc, 75br, 75blb, 76br, 77cla, 77ca, 77cra, 77c; Willi Ulmer Collection 77bc.

VINTAGE ESTATES: 159cl; WESTPAC BANKING CORPORATION: 68br.

YALUMBA WINES CO: 182cra.

JACKET
Front - DK PICTURE LIBRARY: Rob Reichenfeld bc, clb, Alan Williams crb; GETTY IMAGES: Chris Rawlings main image. Back - DK PICTURE LIBRARY: Max Alexander b, Alan Williams t. Spine - GETTY IMAGES: Chris Rawlings.

All other images © Dorling Kindersley.
For further information see: www.dkimages.com

DORLING KINDERSLEY SPECIAL EDITIONS

DORLING KINDERSLEY books can be purchased in bulk quantities at discounted prices for use in promotions or as premiums. We are also able to offer special editions and personalized jackets, corporate imprints, and excerpts from all of our books, tailored specifically to meet your own needs.

To find out more, please contact: (in the United Kingdom) – Sarah.Burgess@dk. com or SPECIAL SALES, DORLING KINDERSLEY LIMITED, 80 STRAND, LONDON WC2R 0RL.

(in the United States) – SPECIAL MARKETS DEPARTMENT, DK PUBLISHING, INC., 375 HUDSON STREET, NEW YORK, NY 10014.

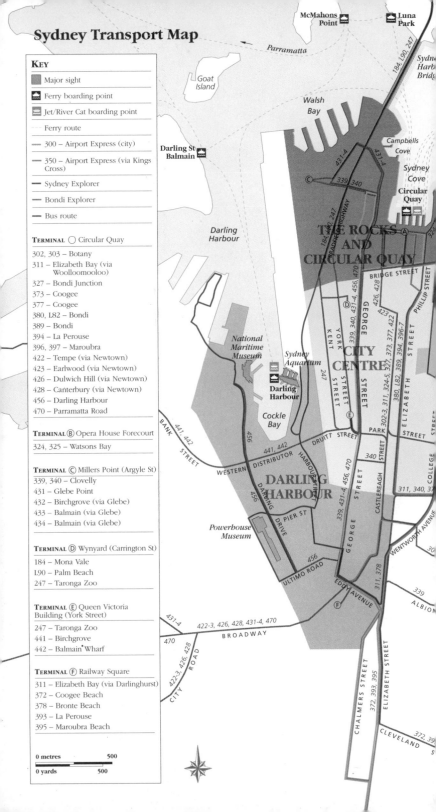